NEW ENGLAND IN THE REPUBLIC
1776-1850

THE PROVIDENTIAL DETECTION

A FEDERALIST CONCEPTION OF THE THWARTING OF JEFFERSON

From an original engraving in the American Antiquarian Society

NEW ENGLAND IN THE REPUBLIC 1776-1850

BY

JAMES TRUSLOW ADAMS, LL. D., LITT. D.

Author of "The Founding of New England" and
"Revolutionary New England, 1691-1776"

With Illustrations

Gloucester, Mass.
PETER SMITH
1960

PREFACE

THE first volume of this series dealt with the earliest explorations and settlements and the life of the New England colonies from the beginning until 1691. It was, as its title indicated, the story of *The Founding of New England*. In the second volume, *Revolutionary New England, 1691–1776*, the narrative was continued to cover the period between the dates named. An attempt was made to trace the origin of grievances on the part of the people at large, the rise of a radical party, and the slow growth of revolutionary sentiment for many decades before what is generally considered the revolutionary period proper, that is, the decade of agitation from 1763 onward. Apart from the imperial relations and quarrels of the time, we tried to show how discontent steadily grew, how there came to be an increasing self-consciousness on the part of the lower classes, and how they gradually demanded more and more of a share in the political power of their small commonwealths.

In what may be considered as more distinctively the period of revolution in the sense of a crisis in the relations with England, the leaders of that movement found it both desirable and necessary to influence popular sentiment by a propaganda which stressed the rights of man and the sovereignty of the people. It was a heady draught to hold to the lips of classes who, owing to the frontier conditions under which to a great extent they lived, had already advanced generations ahead of their time in a fervent devotion to a philosophy of personal independence and individualism.

In the present volume we try to follow the working-out of the situation which resulted, during the remainder of the period in which New England may be considered as having been a distinct section. Our story closes with the year 1850, for from that mid-point of the century the current of nationalism swept the New England states into the swift movement of what had by then become a genuinely national life. In a sense, indeed, the United States is still made up of sections, and New England, the South, the Middle West, and the Far West retain certain sectional characteristics and interests, but not in the same way that they possessed them in the earlier half of the nineteenth century, when one and another were urging secession on almost every pretext, and the national bonds still rested but lightly upon them.

From the beginning of the present volume we have to deal with a situation which is entirely different from that with which we were concerned in the earlier two. During the colonial period the New England colonies were to a great extent independent states, in spite of their colonial status within the empire. Their political relations to the mother country and their own local political movements had an interest and importance which after the Revolution attaches rather to those of the new nation than to those of its component states. The latter, although still considering themselves "sovereign" in many respects, become rather administrative units, and their local politics sink to a more provincial level. In a single volume covering the period of this one it would be impossible to give a continuous and intelligible account of the local political life of six states, and it has not been considered essential to attempt it. On the other hand, purely national political events have been ruled out by the fact that this is the history of a section and not of the nation.

We are, therefore, to a greater extent than in the preceding volumes, concerned with the life of the people as expressed in forms other than political. The main theme of the book may be considered to be the continued struggle of the common man to realize the doctrines of the Revolution in the life of the community. We discuss politics in so far as he attempted to realize his ideals in his political life, but the movement broadened steadily to embrace many other spheres of life as well. Moreover, although our period includes two wars, we have little to do with purely military events, as these not only belong rather to national history but also took place — for the most part — outside of the borders of our section.

In the first three chapters we consider the life of the people during the Revolution and the economic and moral effects of the war upon them. The structure of the governments under which they lived is briefly traced, and we then proceed to consider the unrest that grew out of the war conditions, culminating in the armed rebellion in Massachusetts. The formation of the Union and the adoption of the Federal Constitution are touched upon only in their local aspects, and we are more concerned with the struggle which took place between the forces of reaction and those which tended to maintain and extend the doctrines which had been preached in 1776. The leaders of the earlier period, having achieved their object in securing independence from England, endeavored to stop the revolutionary movement from proceeding further and altering the relations of classes and the structure of society in America. Such an alteration in their favor, however, was just what had been preached to the common people in the war propaganda, and for many decades after 1783 this struggle between these two groups constitutes the main interest of our history. We attempt to touch upon it briefly in all its various aspects — in business, politics, religion, education, the relations between capital and labor, and finally in the great question of slavery. In dealing with such matters from decade to decade a certain amount of repetition as to topics becomes inevitable. In spite of this, it has been thought better to describe each period as it passes rather than to treat each topic separately and continuously. Society was changing rapidly, and we cannot understand each period unless, as far as possible in a brief review, we consider all its factors simultaneously. We try, therefore, to picture the life of each successive period down to the great outburst of humanitarianism and reform between 1830 and 1850. A secondary topic throughout is the gradual growth of sectionalism, culminating at the time of the War of 1812, and its subsequent decline until New England became genuinely merged in the Union in the slavery struggle of the Civil War.

In writing this volume, as the other two, I owe a very sincere debt of gratitude to Dr. Herbert Putnam and other

members of the staff of the Library of Congress for innumerable courtesies accorded me during work there in the
winters. Without the facilities there offered it would have
been impossible to complete the work without far more labor
and time than have been spent upon it in the past six years,
while the cordial hospitality extended to scholars makes all
work there a pleasure. I also wish to express my appreciation of assistance given by Mr. Clarence S. Brigham of the
American Antiquarian Society, and by Miss Louisa Blake,
who searched some of the newspaper files in that library on
certain topics. The Widener Library at Harvard permitted
me to have a copy made of the manuscript thesis of the
late Joseph P. Warren on Shays's Rebellion, which proved of
great value, and which I used with the kind permission of
Mr. Warren's widow, Mrs. Maud Radford Warren. Through
the courtesy of the Yale University Press and Dr. A. B.
Darling I was enabled to examine the proof sheets of
Dr. Darling's forthcoming volume on *Political Changes in
Massachusetts*. To Dr. W. E. Ladd of Boston I am indebted
for permission to publish a copy of the portrait of William
Ladd that is in his possession. The Hampton Library of
this village and the State Library at Albany have, as always,
been very kind in coöperating to afford me the use of certain
volumes, and many others have assisted me in one way and
another. To all I offer most cordial thanks.

JAMES TRUSLOW ADAMS

BRIDGEHAMPTON, NEW YORK
    October 8, 1925

CONTENTS

ILLUSTRATIONS

NEW ENGLAND IN THE REPUBLIC

1776-1850

NEW ENGLAND
IN THE REPUBLIC

1776–1850

CHAPTER I

THE WAR

Divergence of American and English Political Ideas — Geographical Isolation of New England — Erroneous Forecasts as to the War — Military Events — Privateering — Administration of the Army

"IF you want war, nourish a doctrine" was one of the sayings of the late William Graham Sumner.[1] Doctrines had been nourished in plenty on both sides of the Atlantic during the dozen years that had elapsed since the conquest of Canada and the Peace of Paris in 1763. The power of Parliament "to bind the colonies and people of America . . . in all cases whatsoever," "no taxation without representation," "natural rights," "consent of the governed" — these and other rhetorical phantasms impenetrable to analysis had kindled passion instead of arousing reason. Such questions as those relating to the laws of trade or of taxation to meet the needs of the new imperialism which was beginning to replace the old mercantilism might, indeed, have yielded to reason had the two parties understood one another or been in a mood for compromise. But, as we have tried to show in the preceding two volumes,[2] there had been, almost from the beginning, a steady

---

[1] *War and Other Essays,* (Yale University Press, 1919), p. 36.
[2] J. T. Adams, *Founding of New England,* (Boston, 1921); *Revolutionary New England, 1691–1776,* (Boston, 1923).

divergence in political concepts between the two portions of the English race divided by the ocean and subject to different influences of environment.[1]   In England, insular, conservative, and governed since the revolution of 1688 by a middle class which was singularly inert mentally, a certain complex of political ideas was held tenaciously and seemed flawless to its possessors.   In America a wholly different complex of ideas, developed from the frontier and colonial conditions, was held equally tenaciously and seemed equally flawless there.   Both sides had made a show of appealing to reason and precedent, but this was merely attempting to validate, by rationalizing, positions already assumed.   The extremists on either side had failed to understand one another, had found no common ground, and then by a series of acts and counter-acts had precipitated the crisis.   At the point which our story had reached at the end of the last volume, that crisis had developed into civil war.   It is now necessary to consider the profound effects of that war upon the people whose destiny we have been following.

Throughout all the varying phases of the economic and political life of New England one of the marked influences has been the geographical isolation of the section, which lies wholly to the south of the St. Lawrence and to the east of the Hudson — the two great northern highways to the interior of the country.   New Englanders, therefore, for most of their history, have looked eastward rather than westward, and their interest has been maritime rather than continental.   The products of the Northwest tended to be diverted in two streams passing through Montreal and New York, following the rivers flowing to the sea past those two cities.   Before the Revolution and for many years afterward American manufactures were negligible as a basis for commerce.   New England possessed no great hinterland from which to draw and had but an ungenerous soil within her borders.   Her carrying trade, therefore, was mainly made up from the export of a moderate agricultural surplus, of horses, lumber, and fish, and from the exchange of

[1] Cf. C. M. Andrews, The Colonial Background of the American Revolution, (Yale University Press, 1924), chap. II, and pp. 181 ff.

commodities between ports of the other colonies and Europe in a circuitous trade. Even before the Revolution, Boston, by far the most important commercial centre in New England, had begun to decline rapidly as compared with her growing rivals, New York and Philadelphia. For forty years the population of the Massachusetts capital had remained almost stationary at about fifteen thousand, whereas that of New York had passed twenty thousand and Philadelphia numbered almost thirty-five thousand.

The geographical situation at once became a factor in determining the military movements of the war. Lord Howe had evacuated Boston with the British army by the nineteenth of March, 1776, and Washington left for New York with all but five of the American regiments a fortnight later. Throughout the remainder of the struggle, lasting for seven years, although New England did not wholly escape the presence and ravages of hostile troops, particularly on her seaboard, all the more important military events occurred outside her borders. The clashes which did take place within them possess only an interest which is almost wholly local and antiquarian, and the scope of the present work does not permit of a detailed narrative of the entire contest in its wider aspects.[1]

The political leaders who had been instrumental in stirring the agitation which precipitated the conflict had quite erroneous ideas as to the nature of the struggle upon which they had urged their fellow citizens to embark. Even by the middle of 1777, when the nature of the contest should have been evident, Samuel Adams was still writing that he hoped the war would " be of short duration." [2] Of necessity, most of the colonists had been limited to a provincial outlook upon the affairs of the world. Those who did take an imperial point of view or who feared, not without reason, that the power of Great Britain

[1] Few subjects have a more voluminous literature than the military history of the Revolution. In spite of the author's well-known and strong anti-American bias, the best short account of the operations is probably that contained in vol. III of the Hon. J. W. Fortescue's *History of the British Army*, (London, 1911). F. V. Green's *The Revolutionary War*, (New York, 1911), is mainly valuable for the series of maps, taken from Avery's *History of the United States*. Captain A. T. Mahan's *The Influence of Sea Power upon History*, (Boston, 1898), is of the first importance.

[2] *Writings of Samuel Adams*, (New York, 1907), vol. III, p. 394.

would prove overwhelming when fully exerted, were naturally found, for the most part, in the Tory ranks, and their opinions were eliminated from the councils of the patriots. Moreover, as we have pointed out in the preceding volume, England had led the colonists to believe, by a long series of concessions, that she would always yield if only pressed hard enough. From a military point of view, whenever the colonists had come into close coöperation with the British troops and navy, as in the Canadian and Jamaican expeditions of the first decade of the century, the Cartagena expedition of 1740, and the joint operations of the Seven Years' War, England had been too apt to show herself at her lowest point of efficiency and military ability, and this led many to underrate her strength.[1]

On the other hand, in spite of much loose talk by the public and some of the politicians in England, the leading military and naval authorities of that country saw the magnitude of the problem more clearly than did the colonial patriots. Although the saving of the empire by force was held to be not only necessary but feasible, the difficulties were not underrated there as were those of defense in the colonies. Indeed, in some respects the English rather over- than under-estimated them. General Conway reckoned that, granted a colonial population of three millions, the colonists could raise an army of a hundred and fifty thousand men — about six times as many as the colonists were ever able to put in the field at one time.

The first plans suggested were abandoned from the impossibility of executing them. Although all of the thirteen colonies had declared themselves in rebellion, it was assumed that New England was the real seat of the trouble, and it was proposed to isolate that section and subdue it separately. A force operating northward from New York and another southward from Canada, along the lines of the Hudson and Lake Champlain, would cut her off from the other colonies, while a third expedition, entering from Boston, could overrun her territory. This, however, it was estimated, would take from thirty to fifty thousand men. The difficulties of transport were such that General Harvey, the Adjutant-General, said that, "taking

[1] Adams, *Revolutionary New England, 1691–1776*, pp. 67 *f.*, 76 *ff.*, 164 *ff.*, 246.

America as it now stands, it is impossible to conquer it with our British Army. . . . To attempt to conquer it by our land force is as wild an idea as ever controverted common sense." [1] While Gage was in Boston, Harvey, growing impatient, wrote that "America is an ugly job" and that "unless a settled plan of operations be agreed upon for next spring our army will be destroyed by damned driblets." [2]

Towns situated on the coast could, indeed, be destroyed and the seaboard ravaged by landing expeditions here and there, but there was no vital centre to be pierced, and to attempt to control a population of three millions scattered along a thousand miles of shore with unlimited back-country to which to retire, by military forces three thousand miles from their home base, was, as the emphatic general perspicuously remarked, "a damned affair indeed."

England did possess one weapon of overwhelming force — her navy; and the Secretary of War and some of the other leaders maintained that she should place her whole reliance upon that arm of the service. It was proposed to occupy and hold the chief colonial ports as naval bases and to cut off the whole external and coasting trade of the colonists. Had England not frittered away her energies but pursued this course energetically and consistently, it is not unlikely that she would have been successful and the colonists been forced to accept some compromise plan of imperial union before France came into the struggle. Had, however, the war been brought to a comparatively early conclusion by this method, it would have been a conclusion wholly different from that counted upon by the patriot leaders.

The deciding factor in the struggle proved eventually to be the naval forces of the Bourbon Powers, when they entered the contest on the side of the colonies in 1778. Certain elements in France may have been swayed by sentimental considerations, such as the desire for revenge upon England and — to a smaller extent — sympathy upon the part of a few with the aspirations of the colonists, but the measures of the Government were

[1] Quoted by Fortescue, *Hist. of Brit. Army*, vol. III, p. 169.
[2] Quoted *ibid.*, p. 171.

taken with more practical points in view. The reconquest of any American continental possession was acknowledged to be out of the question. What France wished was to acquire some of the English West Indies, to possess herself again of her former holdings in India, which had passed to the English, and to lessen the power of England by securing the independence of the colonies or in any other way. She had, however, no intention of entering the struggle unless assured of probable success, and she watched carefully for three years before doing so, to determine whether the colonies would be able to make a sufficient diversion to drain heavily the strength of England. To a great extent, if not wholly, the colonists were able to do this, and to secure the services of their later allies, because of the blunders of British policy. This statement is not intended to lessen in any way the credit which is due to Washington and other officers and to the sacrifice and suffering of the men under them. Had it not been for these, in spite of British blunders the revolt would have collapsed early, and instead of a successful revolution it would have been merely one more suppressed uprising in the long history of the empire.

The blundering military policy was partially due to the same cause which had been at the bottom of some of the political mistakes in the earlier stages of the dispute — the reliance placed upon Tory statements of conditions, and upon the supposed strength of the Tory party. As we have noted, the Loyalist party was numerically a strong one, probably comprising one third of all the colonists and forming a majority in such colonies as New York, Pennsylvania, and South Carolina.[1] The Loyalists, however, lacked both the aggressiveness and the organization of the Revolutionists, and suffered from the violence and intimidation of the methods employed by the latter. From representations made by prominent Tories and by some of the royal governors, the English Government felt that the presence of British troops would serve to strengthen the loyal element, and military operations were planned with a view to securing such support. Tories in great numbers did flock to the royal colors. Indeed, it has been stated, although

[1] Adams, *Revolutionary New England, 1691–1776*, p. 446.

not wholly proved, that more colonials served in the imperial than in the revolutionary army. They served, however, merely as recruits, and nowhere outside the British lines did they organize sufficiently to secure control of any of the governmental organizations or to interfere seriously with the working of the revolutionary governments. As the historian of the British army has pointed out, of all foundations on which to plan a campaign the most treacherous is reliance upon loyal elements in the population. Yet this has always been a favorite policy with England. In the Revolution in America it unquestionably distracted the British counsels and hampered operations.

Long before Washington forced Lord Howe to evacuate Boston that move had been agreed upon by the British officers, both Howe and Clinton having written home in the preceding year that New York and Newport offered better harbors and were strategically more important. When the evacuation occurred Howe sailed first to Nova Scotia, and while there a part of his force had to be diverted to Canada on account of the attack on that province by Montgomery and Arnold.[1] This diversion was perhaps the most important aspect of that ill-fated enterprise, and delayed Howe from proceeding to New York until July.

Meanwhile, with the idea of conquering the colonies south of Virginia by the aid of the Tories, a British fleet had made an unsuccessful attack upon Charleston under Sir Henry Clinton. This expedition was a characteristic blunder. It was persisted in by the Ministry against the advice of the Secretary of War and the military advisers, and was delayed five months beyond the time when the conditions might have given it a certain measure of success. On its failure, Clinton sailed to join Howe at New York. Washington had already arrived there before any of the enemy's forces, but the patriots were forced to retreat across New Jersey and into Pennsylvania. By the end of the year the British were in occupation of New York and the immediately surrounding country, of New Jersey as far south as Trenton and Bordentown, of the island of Rhode Island and the town of Newport, the last named having been captured as

[1] Adams, *Revolutionary New England, 1691–1776*, pp. 430 f.

a result of an attack in November under Lord Percy. Congress had taken refuge in Baltimore, and Washington's army had shrunk to five thousand men. His brilliant dash across the Delaware on Christmas Day and successful surprise of the Hessians at Trenton saved the situation at the last moment; the British were cleared from almost the whole of New Jersey, and Washington took up his winter quarters at Morristown.

The main events of 1777 were the defeat of Washington at the Brandywine; the consequent occupation of Philadelphia by the British; and the unsuccessful attempt by General Burgoyne to invade New York by way of the well-worn route of Lake Champlain and the Hudson. This latter effort had been undertaken for the purpose of isolating New England, and in its far-reaching political effects Burgoyne's disastrous defeat and the surrender of his entire force at Saratoga on October 17 was one of the turning-points of the war.

In New England there were no military movements which rose above the grade of mere raiding or minor engagements. An expedition planned in Massachusetts during the summer to attack Nova Scotia and to protect certain friendly people along the Bay of Fundy was practically abandoned even before it started, and a single company of Maine militia went alone, capturing a small fort and bringing in several families. In August, Burgoyne had detached a mixed force of about five hundred men to attack a store of munitions which had been gathered at Bennington, Vermont, with the expectation that the Loyalists would assist him in the operation.[1] They failed to do so, and in spite of reënforcements of five hundred more men, the force was defeated on the fifteenth by about two thousand recruits from the countryside, hastily raised by the gallant John Stark. The suddenness with which the force appeared and the dash with which they acted opened Burgoyne's eyes to the peril of his position. "The great bulk of the country is undoubtedly with the Congress," he wrote, and "wherever the King's forces point, militia to the amount of three or four thousand assemble in twenty-four hours. They

---

[1] The number of men engaged varies by three hundred per cent in different accounts. Fortescue states that he took the number of 500 from Burgoyne's own list.

bring with them their subsistence; the alarm over, they return to their farms. The Hampshire Grants in particular, a country unpeopled and almost unknown in the last war, now abounds in the most active and most rebellious race of the continent, and hangs like a gathering storm on my left." [1] A month after the battle of Bennington, the results of which elated the patriots as much as they depressed the British commander, a secret expedition was planned by the Massachusetts legislature for an attack upon the British forces on Rhode Island. About three thousand men were raised and marched as far as Tiverton, but the expedition failed and was without any effect upon the British occupation.

In spite of the capture of Burgoyne, the year 1778 opened gloomily for the American cause. The British were in possession of Newport, New York, and Philadelphia. For a battle of Bennington several thousand militia might swarm from their homes to return to them next day, but at Valley Forge the main body of the Continental troops had dwindled to less than three thousand who were ill fed, almost naked, and partly mutinous. In Congress and the army powerful influences were at work to undermine the position of the commander in chief. Even in spite of British blundering, the collapse of the Revolution seemed imminent unless allies could be found who would bolster the falling cause.

From the beginning of the revolt within the empire, England's enemies in Europe had watched events with the most intense interest, for the purpose of obtaining what benefits they could for themselves from the weakening of the greatest of commercial rivals and the mistress of the seas. Spain was hostile to the thought of American independence, as offering a bad example to her own colonies, and the attitude of France has already been noted. For the purpose of exhausting their European rival, both Bourbon states had granted or allowed assistance in money and stores to be sent to the colonists, but the American diplomatic representatives had been playing for an active alliance, and the surrender of Burgoyne gave them

---

[1] Quoted from a dispatch from Burgoyne by R. E. Robinson, *Vermont*, (Boston, 1892), p. 177.

their opportunity. On February 6, 1778 a treaty of alliance was signed with France; and although Spain never became the ally of the United States, she entered the war some months later as the ally of France. With these two events the war passed into a wholly new phase. Howe was succeeded by Sir Henry Clinton in Philadelphia, with orders to evacuate that city, attack the French in the West Indies, harry the New England coast towns, and centre his operations at New York. From this time to the close of the contest there were no major operations in any of the northern states. The effect of the new situation was seen in the sending by England of Commissioners to the United States with terms of peace, which, however, were not acceptable.

The real importance of the war now shifts to the naval struggle between the almost evenly matched powers of England and the two Bourbon kingdoms, far afield from the scene of our local narrative. In New England the year 1778 was marked only by raiding by British troops in the neighborhood of Newport and by the most determined effort that the colonials made during the war to rid Rhode Island of the enemy. As a result of the French alliance, Comte d'Estaing appeared off the Delaware River in July with a powerful fleet, passing thence by way of New York to Newport. A Colonial force of ten thousand men under General Sullivan, with Greene and Lafayette, was raised to coöperate with the French commander in a combined attack upon General Pigott and his five thousand British troops on Rhode Island. Howe, who had received naval reënforcements, sailed from New York to fight d'Estaing, but while both were manœuvring for position a terrific storm arose. The Frenchman, after his vessels had been considerably damaged, put to sea without attacking the inferior British fleet and departed for Boston. The American land forces had already crossed to Rhode Island, and it was only by the exertion of much skill that they were enabled to make good their retreat, after being abandoned by the French ships whose assistance had been an integral part of the plan of attack. By October of the following year (1779) the situation had altered so far by the shifting of interest to the Southern colonies and the West Indies, that Clinton voluntarily withdrew his forces from Newport and evacuated Rhode Island on the twenty-eighth of that month.

Some months earlier, in July, Connecticut had suffered from a raiding expedition by the English fleet under Tryon. On the fourth, New Haven was attacked and plundered; Fairfield was burned on the eighth; the village of Green's Farms the following morning. On the eleventh Tryon destroyed Norwalk; but by that time the people were mustering in strength, and having lost nearly three hundred men in the operations, the British withdrew. The property loss to the colonists was extremely heavy and the people of the ruined villages and towns suffered severely, but the episode was without effect upon the general conduct of the war. In Massachusetts the only incident of the year was an expedition undertaken in June to dislodge about a thousand British troops from the Penobscot. It was planned to raise fifteen hundred men, but only nine hundred could be mustered after drafting had been resorted to. The land force was to act in concert with a small naval flotilla of nineteen vessels, and on July 28 a landing was effected before a newly erected British fortress. The losses of the attacking party were extraordinarily heavy, amounting to one quarter of the number engaged. The fleet did not coöperate properly, and as reënforcements arrived for the British by sea, the undertaking was hastily abandoned with complete failure.

The next year was devoid of even minor military local interest in New England, and the only event which subsequently occurred there before the close of the war was the attack upon New London by the traitor General Arnold on the sixth of September, 1781. The town, although it had been warned of the presence of the hostile fleet, was utterly unprepared for defense, and about nine hundred or a thousand men landed on the New London side of the harbor and burned a considerable part of the town with hardly any opposition. The harbor was full of colonial shipping, and in order to facilitate the destruction of the vessels the enemy landed about eight hundred men on the Groton shore to silence Fort Griswold. Colonel William Ledyard, however, gave this party an unexpected check, and, with a garrison scarcely sufficient to man the posts, made a most heroic defense. Finally forced to surrender, a considerable part of the defenders were massacred by the British, Colonel Ledyard himself being run through the heart with his own sword by the officer to whom he had just surrendered it with a word of courtesy. The whole affair is a blot upon the honor of the British army which is beyond condonation. The property damage in New London included a large part of the shipping, almost all the wharves, sixty-five dwelling houses, thirty-one stores filled with merchandise, and many other buildings. Like almost all the operations in New England, however, the affair was a mere raid and without other result than severe local loss.

The fate of the colonies was not being decided upon the continent of America but upon the sea, in the contest between the English and the allied navies. In April Washington was in despair. "We are at the end of our tether," he wrote to Laurens in Paris. The army could not be provisioned because there was no money; the troops were almost naked and mutinous; the hospitals were without medicines. Without a foreign loan, he added, the troops could not be kept together for that campaign, much less assembled for another year. "If France delays a timely and powerful aid in this critical posture of our affairs," he wrote, "it will avail us nothing should she attempt it hereafter." [1] The end, however, was approaching. The two contestants were so evenly matched at sea that errors were fatal, and England's policy was faulty. Without an ounce of strength to spare, she failed to make the best available use of her resources, and by one blunder — the lengthening of her lines of communication in America by the diversion of a part of her arms to the southern colonies — she gave the American forces their opportunity. When Cornwallis, after his retreat, found himself shut up within the peninsula of Yorktown in Virginia, the arrival of a French fleet under de Grasse with large military forces enabled Washington with the main body of the Continental army to force the surrender of the British

---

[1] *The Writings of George Washington*, ed. by W. C. Ford, (New York, 1891), vol. IX, pp. 212 f.

general with his seven thousand troops on the nineteenth of October, 1781.

From this time onward there was no further attempt on the part of England to continue active hostilities in America, although Clinton remained with his forces in New York. The Americans also settled down in apathy, and disorganization appeared everywhere. The question of the American colonial revolt had been absorbed into a far wider struggle, which continued in the West Indies, on the ocean, in the Mediterranean, and in India. It was two years more before England, struggling against the world, finally acknowledged herself beaten and agreed to a peace. On September 3, 1783, in the Treaty of Versailles, the independence of the American colonies was at last acknowledged, although there had been a provisional treaty arranged eleven months earlier.

The decision of the contest depended in the last analysis upon naval power, but at no time had the navy of the united colonies been a factor of prime importance, in spite of certain brilliant individual exploits. However, in harassing and destroying British commerce, even on the coasts of England herself, in capturing and threatening transports, and in securing much-needed supplies, both Continental ships and privateers had rendered valuable service, and, from the beginning, New England took a leading part in this form of warfare.[1] As early as August 1775 the Rhode Island Assembly had memorialized Congress in favor of the immediate creation of a Continental navy,[2] so that it was not inappropriate that, when formed, a Rhode Island man, Esek Hopkins, should have been appointed its first commander.[3]

It was indeed natural that the naval problems of the war should appeal particularly to the maritime colonies, and John Adams, for Massachusetts, took an important part in the establishment of the revolutionary naval forces. These, however,

[1] For the naval aspects of the struggle as a whole, Mahan, *The Influence of Sea Power upon History*, remains the leading authority. Useful summaries of American participation are found in Gardner W. Allen's *Naval History of the American Revolution*, (Boston, 1913), 2 vols., and Edgar S. Maclay's *History of American Privateers*, (New York, 1899).

[2] *Records of the Colony of Rhode Island and Providence Plantations*, vol. VII, p. 369.

[3] Edward Field, *Esek Hopkins*, (Providence, 1898), chap. III.

so far failed to develop as had been expected, that at no time were there more than three thousand men in the personnel. In addition to the Continental navy, however, eleven of the states, including the four New England ones, had small fleets of their own in commission. Rhode Island put two small sloops in service as early as June 1775; Connecticut followed the next month by providing two vessels, subsequently extending her local force to twelve; Massachusetts, during the course of the war, had as many as fifteen sea-going vessels; and New Hampshire had one or two. The enemy's ships were continually harassing colonial commerce along the coast, Long Island Sound being infested with them, and these little state navies did service of some value, both in protecting colonial shipping near shore and in destroying or capturing small vessels of the enemy.

Of more importance, particularly in the life of the people, were the swarms of privateers which put out from almost every port in America, although it is impossible to reach exact estimates as to their numbers. Commissions were issued both by the Continental Congress and by many of the states. Changes in the name, rig, and ownership of the vessel occur with great frequency, and so tend to duplication in the records, whereas on the other hand, the lack of imagination in finding names counts on the other side of the score. From Beverly alone there were fourteen vessels by the name of Fortune and twenty-four by that of Dolphin.[1] It is probable that the total number of privateers for all the colonies during the war was not far from two thousand, and also that of these nearly one half were owned in Massachusetts. A very conservative estimate of the number of men engaged would place them at not less than ten times those in the regular navy, or over thirty thousand. Of the spirit of speculation which was fostered by this mode of warfare and of its other economic results we shall speak in a later chapter, merely noting here that its military aspects, although not unimportant, were not of the first magnitude. As with the ships of the regular navy, the work of the

[1] O. T. Thorndike, "Beverly Privateers in the American Revolution," Col. Soc. Mass., *Publications*, vol. XXIV, p. 323.

privateers was that of commerce-destroyers. They brought in money, goods, and occasionally military stores of value, and although they undoubtedly did much to hamper British trade, that trade was of too vast extent to be more than wounded by such methods, so that nothing was accomplished against what was, after all, the main element in the situation — the British navy. Stories of success were hailed in the colonial press and probably did much to help the morale of the colonists. For example, in June 1777, after a chronicle of the capture of six prizes by one of the Massachusetts state naval vessels and four by the Continental ship Rising States, we read that "the success of the American cruizers has given a prodigious wound to the British Trade. It is computed in England that £1,500,000 sterling has been taken in the West Indies trade alone. The consequence has been several capital houses in England have failed for large sums and more are expected to share the same fate."[1] Nevertheless, American privateers were frequently captured, the risks were enormous, and the losses inflicted in retaliation by British and Tory privateers on colonial shipping were also very heavy.

At the beginning of the war there was no standing colonial army in any of the colonies, for in all of them there was strong prejudice against such a force, which, like a strong executive, was believed to savor of tyranny. New England, like the rest of America, had militia regiments which mustered certain days in the year, but these had become a farce, and muster-days were merely uproarious picnics on a large scale. Including both the "active" and "alarm" lists, the militia supposedly took in all men between the ages of sixteen and sixty-five, and each company elected its own officers. The difficulties which Washington experienced with his motley collection, both officers and men, at Boston have already been touched upon.[2] He roundly denounced the folly of attempting to carry on war with short-term enlistments of such militia levies, and in September 1776 Congress voted to raise eighty-eight battalions, amounting in all to sixty-three thousand men, for three years

[1] *Massachusetts Gazette*, June 2, 1777.
[2] Adams, *Revolutionary New England, 1691–1776*, pp. 435 ff.

or the duration of the war, but the men actually raised never formed more than a small fraction of that number. Congress also offered a bounty of twenty pounds and a hundred acres of land, to which the individual colonies added further, Massachusetts, for example, beginning with an additional twenty pounds.[1] After the patriotic fervor of the first few months had worn off, the greatest difficulty was experienced throughout the struggle in securing men for the army. New England did her part nobly and none of the colonies exceeded Massachusetts in her efforts, yet even she at no time had her full complement in the field, and at the end of the war had only four thousand three hundred and seventy men in the Continental line as against her quota of eight thousand three hundred and fifty, or about one half.[2]

As large numbers in all New England engaged from time to time in special expeditions such as those already mentioned, or in short-term service locally in the militia, as well as in the Continental army and navy, the state navies, and privateering, a large proportion of the men of military age in New England saw service in some branch of the armed forces during the eight years of war. The Marquis de Chastellux, traveling in that section toward the end of the struggle, noted that "among the men I have met with, above twenty years of age, of whatsoever condition, I have not found two who have not bore arms, heard the whistling of balls, and even received wounds."[3] "I have been endeavoring to add to my help but could not," wrote John Bradford, the Continental agent in Massachusetts, from Boston in 1777, "the young people all having Engag'd in the Army."[4] "More than forty men are now drafted from this town," wrote Mrs. John Adams from Braintree a few months earlier. "More than one half, from sixteen to fifty are now

---

[1] The two most useful works on the administration of the army are: *The Administration of the American Revolutionary Army*, by L. C. Hatch, Harvard Historical Studies, 1904, and *The Private Soldier under Washington*, by C. K. Bolton, (New York, 1902). On raising troops in Massachusetts, *vide* J. Smith, "How Massachusetts Raised her Troops in the Revolution," Mass. Hist. Soc., *Proceedings*, 1922, pp. 345 *ff.*

[2] Smith, *op. cit.*, p. 355.

[3] *Travels in North America in the Years 1780, 1781, 1782*, (Dublin, 1787), vol. I, p. 19.

[4] Letter Book of John Bradford, (manuscript), in Library of Congress, April 9, 1777.

in the service . . . I hardly think you can be sensible how much we are thinned in this province. . . . If it is necessary to make any more drafts upon us, the women must reap the harvests." [1] "I am sorry, however," she continued, "to see a spirit so venal prevailing everywhere . . . no one will go without a large bounty, though only for two months, and each town seems to think its honor engaged in outbidding the others."

The number of men requisitioned for the Continental army from each of the New England states was apportioned among the several towns, which were made responsible for furnishing their quotas under pain of fines. As the difficulty of securing men became steadily greater, owing to their disinclination to enter the service, these fines were increased, as were also the bounties offered by the towns to secure recruits. [2] Drafting was early resorted to as ever-increasing bounties failed to bring results. In most cases the man drafted was required either to serve personally or to provide a substitute within twenty-four hours under pain of a considerable fine, at Northampton, for example, by 1780, this fine being made £150 in the then depreciated currency. [3] Drafting was unpopular, and some towns voted to raise money by taxation to hire men, this being done as early as 1777 in Weston, where it was voted that: "Whereas it is difficult in Coming at Justice in Drafting men to go into the Servise of the United States by a Common Draft," it would be more equitable to levy a town tax as usual and hire men if they could be found. By 1780 this same town was petitioning the legislature for permission to go outside the town limits and hire men wherever they could be found in other towns which might have met their quota. [4] Towns were thus bidding against each other, and the high bounties paid brought about frauds similar to those of the "bounty jumpers" of the Civil War. Men would enlist, receive their bounty money, desert,

---

[1] *Letters of Mrs. Adams*, (Boston, 1840), vol. I, p. 106.
[2] Smith, *op. cit.*, gives the records as to bounties for a number of Massachusetts towns, pp. 361 *ff.* Local histories and town records all repeat the same story, varying only in details. The bounties offered by the state legislatures may be found in the colonial records for each.
[3] J. R. Trumbull, *History of Northampton*, (Northampton, 1902), vol. II, p. 431.
[4] *Records of the Town of Weston*, (Boston, 1893), pp. 231, 233, 289.

and then reënlist elsewhere, sometimes repeating this process a number of times. Sometimes they did not even enlist themselves, but still more meanly hired others to do so for a share in the money, as in the case of one Fostwick, who hired boys at £60 each to enlist and desert, disappearing himself when the lads were caught and disciplined.[1]

Many drafted men at once hired substitutes or merely paid their fines and remained at home. The cry was early raised that the rich and well-to-do were escaping military service, whereas the burden fell upon the poor. "Of the militia that lately went to New York," wrote a complainant from a Connecticut town in 1776, "there was about one hundred and forty, and much the greater part of them were men of little property. Of those other gentlemen that stayed at home, more than one hundred under fifty years of age, all [were] men of interest, and pray what have they done to defend it? Why they paid their rates, and may be have given forty shillings to encourage men to enlist: But what is this compared with his poor neighbor who is called forth when in the midst of his business, has no money, receives but twenty shillings, and that advance pay not as a bounty, obliged to go and leave his affairs running to ruin? I ask are these things equal and just?"[2]

In New England both the colonial and town governments made desperate efforts to meet the demands made upon them, in men, money, and supplies, and in caring for the impoverished families of men serving at the front. The records of the little town of Plymouth, for example, are pathetic and give us a vivid picture of conditions. The town evidently had done everything possible to meet the requisitions of the colonial government. In October 1778, at a town meeting, taxes were laid for "a Sum not Exceeding Sixteen hundred pounds, Chiefly to Support the Famelys of those Soldiers that went into the Continental Armey," and the care of these was farmed out to one Captain Jesse Harlow for one year at seven and a half per cent of his disbursements. The following month it was voted to set to work all those persons who "are Dayly beging from house

---

[1] *Mass. Gazette*, (Springfield), July 2, 1782.
[2] *Connecticut Courant*, Oct. 14, 1776.

Commonwealth of }
MASSACHUSETTS. }

The H O N O R A B L E

HENRY GARDNER, Esq;

Treasurer and Receiver-General of said Commonwealth.

To the Selectmen or Assessors of the Town of Raymondstown *Greeting, &c.*

IN Obedience to a Resolution of the Commonwealth aforesaid, of the Eighth of *March*, 1781, these are in the Name of said Commonwealth, to will and require you forthwith to assess the Sum of

£74.1.8

7 Mar

Seventy Four Pounds 1/8

on the deficient Class or Classes in your Town or Plantations, being the average Price of the Cost of raising the Men to supply the Deficiency of the *Massachusetts* Line of the Army, agreeable to a Notification of his Excellency the Governor and Council of said Commonwealth, transmitted to the Treasurer of said Commonwealth, bearing Date *July* 31, 1782, in Pursuance of the Resolve aforesaid, together with *Twenty per Cent.* added thereto : You are likewise required to levy on each Class deficient as aforesaid, *Two per Cent.* on said Sum, as a Fee for the Constable or Collector to defrey the Expence of collecting the same; which List or Lists, when compleated according to Law, you are to deliver to the Collector or Collectors, Constable or Constables of your Town or Plantation; and make Return to me of the Name or Names of the said Constable or Constables, Collector or Collectors, together with the Sum or Sums to them respectively committed to collect, within Five Days from the Date hereof. Hereof you are not to fail, as you will answer your Neglect at the Peril of the Law.

GIVEN *under my Hand and Seal at* Boston, *the* Thirty-first *Day of* July, *in the Year of our* LORD *One Thousand Seven Hundred and* Eighty-two, *and in the Seventh Year of American Independence.*

H Gardner

DEFICIENCY LEVY ON TOWN, 1782
Library of Congress

to house." The following August it was voted to petition the General Court for an abatement of colonial and Continental taxes, "by reason of the Great losses this town hath met with at sea, & being almost totally Deprived of the fishery since the Present war." On January 1, 1781, in order to meet the requisition for beef, they sold the town shipyard and town lands. By July they had to "remenstrate" to the General Court that it had become "out of our power to pay the Taxes and procure the Clouthing, Provisions and Soldiers, requested by the said Court," and prayed for an abatement or remission.[1] Indeed, by 1779 or 1780 New England was nearly bankrupt and her men were heartily tired of the struggle.

Almost from the beginning, as we have said, it had been difficult to get them to serve, not merely as volunteers but also as paid soldiers or when drafted, and we may now examine a little more closely the conditions which brought this about even in that section of the country which more than any other had insistently precipitated the conflict.

Uneasiness, discontent, and even open mutiny are apt to result if the privates are not provided with officers whom they can respect as officers, apart from any qualities that might make them popular in civil life. Men who from their position or occupation are accustomed to lead, or those from the lower ranks who may develop that ability, are naturally in the minority. Consequently, in a country which has no standing army and trained officers, there is bound to be a dearth of such when occasion suddenly arises for them. In this respect New England was particularly deficient, although it provided some good officers among the higher ranks. The vain, popularity-hunting John Hancock bitterly resented the fact that he was not chosen commander-in-chief, but it was well for the cause that that office was conferred upon the Virginian Washington, though John Adams and some other New England leaders never forgave the choice and remained opposed to Washington throughout the war.

In the beginning, the election of company officers by the men

---

[1] *Records of the Town of Plymouth*, (Plymouth, 1903), vol. III, pp. 356 *f.*, 383, 403, 429.

undoubtedly kept the quality low. Under that condition it was almost impossible to maintain effective discipline, and a man of spirit was not likely to be willing to hold his commission at the whim of his own privates. Few New Englanders — except sea captains, who naturally remained in naval service of some sort — were accustomed to handling men. The farms were mostly one-man affairs, run with the assistance of half-grown sons or of one or two "hired help." There were no industrial plants employing more than a few hands. The New Englanders of the lower classes had no experience in commanding others or in submitting to discipline themselves. The occupations of most of the better classes, such as merchants, ministers, and lawyers in small communities, did not develop as good material for the making of military officers as did the life of the larger plantation-owners of the South, who were accustomed to looking after numerous slaves and dependents in the patriarchal existence of large isolated estates. As to the inferior quality of New England officers at the beginning of the war there would seem to be little doubt. We have already seen Washington making "a pretty good slam among such officers as the Massachusetts Government abound in," when he took command at Cambridge.[1] Charles Lee, although praising the New England privates highly in 1775, spoke of that section as being defective in materials for good officers.[2] Other observers noted the same fact, and Alexander Graydon, a captain in the service, tried to analyze the reasons for it in the early stages of the war, noting that later the New England officers were as good as any from elsewhere. "Was it," he asks, "that the cause was popular only among the yeomanry? Was it, that men of fortune and condition there, as in other parts of the continent . . . were willing to devolve the fighting business on the poorer and humbler classes? Was it, in short, that they held the language of the world and said,

> "Let the gull'd fools the toils of war subdue,
> Where bleed the many to enrich the few?"[3]

[1] Adams, *Revolutionary New England, 1691-1776*, p. 435.
[2] Quoted by Bolton, *Private Soldier*, pp. 133 f.
[3] *Memoirs*, (Edinburgh, 1822), 2d edit., pp. 154 f.

This was a note frequently sounded, and the poor felt that an undue share of the burden, both in taxation and personal service and suffering, was being laid on their shoulders. It was one of the many elements entering into that resentful popular consciousness which formed the psychological background of Shays's Rebellion a few years later.

Throughout the struggle, indeed, the lack of good officers was felt in the entire army and such officers as came from Europe, mostly from France, did not greatly improve the situation. For one Lafayette or Steuben there were dozens of foreigners who, as Washington wrote, "have nothing more than a little plausibility, unbounded pride and ambition, and a perseverance in application not to be resisted but by uncommon firmness, to support their pretensions; men who, in the first instance, tell you they wish for nothing more than the honor of serving so glorious a cause as volunteers, the next day solicit rank without pay, the day following want money advanced to them, and in the course of a week want further promotion, and are not satisfied with anything you can do for them." [1] As the years went on, the material was sifted and conditions became better, but in the earlier stages a good deal of discontent, insubordination, and desertion may be traced to the officers.

There were, however, other causes which afforded ample reason for the disinclination to serve long terms in the Continental line. During the first year of the war, when the army was in Massachusetts, its food supply was fairly abundant. Later the conditions became deplorable, and during the winter of 1777–78 there was no quartermaster-general for nearly six months, the soldiers suffering severely from the inexcusable confusion which resulted. At Valley Forge there was once no bread for a week, and all provisions were so scanty that on several occasions the troops almost mutinied. [2] In February 1777 the speaker of the Massachusetts Senate, writing to Elbridge Gerry of the great difficulty of recruiting, said that "the men do not complain of the fatigues to which they have been exposed, (which we know were very great), but the want of

[1] *Writings*, (Ford), vol. VII, p. 117.
[2] Hatch, *Administration of the Revolutionary Army*, p. 96.

things necessary to make them comfortable in clothing and sustenance. As to the latter, except flour and beef, they could receive little of anything, not even in sickness more than in health, save what they purchased of the sutler, who would strip the poor soldier of his whole month's wages of forty shillings for what he could have bought at home for 3s 4d. . . . The scoundrel, who is too lazy to do the duty of a soldier himself, and never was worth 20s in all his life before, made $3000 at Ticonderoga in one summer! This also I can prove." [1] A year later another correspondent wrote: "In plain terms, 't is probable that the army will disperse if the commissary department is so damnably managed." [2] When Congress, without money and without the means of raising any, tried the plan of apportioning quotas of provisions to be supplied by the several states, the plan failed utterly. In March 1780 there was one of the frequent lapses of supplies and the army almost dissolved. In May the men were on one-quarter to one-eighth rations, and some of the officers lived on bread and water, giving their supplies to the men. [3]

The situation as to clothing was, if anything, even worse. In the beginning the troops had no distinctive dress, and Washington provided them as far as possible with hunting-shirts, long breeches, and gaiters. Although uniforms were adopted later, the soldiers were frequently not clad in them, and the buff-and-blue of popular pictures was never worn by any of the New England troops. [4] In December 1776 Washington stated that many of his men were entirely naked and others so thinly clad as to be unfit for service. The condition of a Rhode Island regiment at Peekskill in the following summer was so scandalous that the village people called it "the Ragged, Lousy, Naked regiment." [5] At Valley Forge in the winter of 1777-78 there were nearly three thousand men unfit for duty at Christmas, and the number increased by another thousand in a month

[1] J. T. Austin, *Life of Elbridge Gerry*, (Boston, 1828), vol. I, pp. 257 *f.*
[2] *Ibid.*, p. 247.
[3] Hatch, *op. cit.*, pp. 106 *f.*
[4] Bolton, *op. cit.*, p. 91; J. C. Fitzpatrick, *The Spirit of the Revolution*, (Boston, 1924), chap. VIII.
[5] Bolton, *op. cit.*, p. 99.

more. Washington complained bitterly that his men had "been left to perish by inches with cold and nakedness." For lack of proper clothing they had to sit by their fires all night, afraid to sleep lest they might freeze — as many did, and lost legs or arms by amputation in consequence. Congress counted upon the individual states to clothe their own men, and in this respect Connecticut did notably well, her men being usually well cared for. At Yorktown many of our troops were so nearly naked that our French allies made jokes at the expense of their nudity. The sufferings of the men were intense, especially in the winter when they had to face freezing cold without clothes and march over frozen ground without shoes.

The main trouble lay in the lack of organization and of any central authority of real power. There was always ample food in the country, could it have been obtained and transported. Clothes, to some extent, had to be imported, but with them, again, the question was of administration. In 1780 Washington wrote that "the situation of the Army in respect to cloathing is really distressing, — By collecting all our remnants, and those of a thousand colors & kinds, we shall scarcely make them comfortable. Uniformity, one of the essentials of discipline, everything in the appearance of a Soldier, must be dispensed with; — and what makes the matter more mortifying is, that we have, I am positively assured Ten thousand compleat suits ready in France & laying there because our public agents cannot agree whose business it is to ship them. . . . You tell me there is cloathing enough lately arrived in private bottoms to supply the army. — This my dear Sir is only tantalizing the Naked — such is the miserable state of the Continental credit that we cannot command a yard of it." [1]

Nakedness, hunger, and the necessary hardships of camp life and campaigning caused an immense amount of sickness and mortality, but the hospital service was as inadequate as the rest. Medical stores were frequently wholly lacking, and the doctors had nothing to do but to watch the sufferings and death of the men. Sanitation was but little understood and

[1] *Writings*, (Ford), vol. IX, p. 51.

anæsthetics and antiseptics were unknown. Hospitals were unpopular in the communities where they were established, and the civilian populace frequently protested at the arrival of sick soldiers.[1] If a soldier had the misfortune to fall into the hands of the enemy, although there were notable exceptions, it was not seldom to suffer further privation or the tortures of the prison ships, the horrible condition of which has been vividly described.[2]

But it was not merely these hardships which wrung the soldiers' hearts. They were not paid, and they felt with increasingly profound bitterness that, while they were suffering, the people at home were not supporting them. Owing to the depreciation in the paper money, prices advanced by leaps, as we shall note in the next chapter, and even when the soldier did receive a part of his promised pay it would purchase almost nothing. "The soldier asks me," wrote the speaker of the Massachusetts Assembly quoted above, "when the state makes the addition of a bounty of twenty pounds to the encouragement of congress, and individuals in the several towns add one hundred to all this, (for I don't know of more than two men of the twelve companies in and about Andover that have been procured under) what security he has, that he shall come home a whit better at the end of the three years than he did at the close of the last year, without a garment to his back or a farthing in his pocket?"[3]

The resentment of the soldiers rose as they compared their condition and prospects with those of many of the civilians at home, who were growing rich and suffering none of the hardships and dangers of military service. As in the last Great War through which we have recently passed, the contrast was most unjust between the man who went into service to suffer, to be mutilated for life, or to die, for a mere pittance, and his fellows at home who were getting high wages in comfort. "Day labourers at home ought, in justice," wrote the *Connecticut Journal* in 1778, "to labour at the old price, since their

[1] Bolton, *op. cit.*, p. 182.
[2] Contemporary conditions in England are described by Francis Abell, *Prisoners of War in Britain, 1756 to 1815*, (Oxford University Press, 1914).
[3] Austin, *Gerry*, vol. I, p. 258.

brethren in the army who are risquing their lives for the common defence are paid at the old price. If labour at home rises, the wages of the soldiers ought to rise, in justice; and must be raised, in policy; or we can never get the army filled up." [1]

The taxes were heavy but, as we shall note later, so devised as to fall heaviest upon the poor. Much larger sums could have been raised had the rich and well-to-do been willing to bear their burden. "Everybody, go where I will," wrote Colonel Timothy Pickering of Massachusetts, "is complaining of heavy taxes; yet those paid the United States are to the last degree insignificant. . . . These brave and deserving soldiers, many of whom have fought for six years, exposed their lives to save their country, who are unhappy enough to have fallen sick, have for a month past been destitute of every comfort of life . . . while the citizens of the United States indulge a luxury to which before the war, they were strangers! . . . Would to God that, in a land blessed with the best food in abundance, the army were not served with the worst! that the sick were not left to perish for want of wholesome diet, or with the cold for want of proper clothing." [2]

In the minds of the soldiers, their own want of pay was closely bound up with the sufferings of their families at home. The bulk of the army was made up, as always, of those who could least afford to lose their means of livelihood, and the want to which their wives and children were exposed preyed constantly on their minds and was one of the main causes of desertion. The terrific uprush of prices for all the necessities of life, while the wage-earners or farmers were serving in the army with little or no pay, rendered the condition of their families desperate in many cases. A correspondent signing himself "A Continental" wrote in 1777: "I ask the question, will your army continue to defend you in the field, while their wives and their children are famishing and crying for bread at home, through your intolerable oppression? or will they turn their arms against you and do themselves justice?" [3]   "Almost two years have

---

[1] Issue of Jan. 28, 1778.
[2] O. Pickering, *Life of Timothy Pickering*, (Boston, 1867), vol. I, p. 376.
[3] *Conn. Courant*, Nov. 25, 1777.

passed," wrote Ebenezer Huntington from the army to his father in Connecticut in 1778, "where we have been buoyed up with Promises at Loose Ends by the people in General . . . we doubt the Willingness of our Countrymen to Assist us. You cannot blame us. Our money is gone, our friends are few, or none who will lend us money. . . . You resolved in your Last Session, that the Soldiers family should be supported, whether they sent Money or not, but it is not done, nor will it be done. Not a Day Passes my head, but some Soldier with Tears in his Eyes hands me a letter to read from his Wife Painting forth the Distresses of his Family in such strains as these 'I am without bread & Cannot get any, the Committee will not Supply me, my Children will Starve, or if they do not, they must freeze, we have no wood, neither can we get any — *Pray Come Home.*'" Again, in 1780, he wrote: "I despise My Countrymen. I wish I could say I was not born in America. I once gloried in it but am now ashamed of it." After describing his own sufferings for lack of clothes and food, he said: "And all this for my Cowardly Countrymen who flinch at the very time when their Exertions are wanted, & hold their Purse Strings as tho they would damn the World rather than part with a Dollar to their Army." The following year he again wrote that the soldiers "have served you from the 1st of Jany '77 & have received but just their wages for '77, the rest is due. . . . If we meet with such Treatment from you when our Services are so much wanted, what can we expect at the Close of the Campaign (should it be Glorious). . . . Cloath feed & Pay us & you may have any Services you wish . . . the State at large don't deserve freedom, nor no other People on Earth, who are neither willing to Contend for Freedom Personally or for those who will defend their Cowardly Souls." [1]

That the morale of the army was maintained at all under such conditions is extraordinary, and must be attributed to the patriotism of the private soldier and the marvelous influence of Washington's character. There were occasional mutinies, as well as much muttering, but these are not to be wondered

---

[1] *Letters Written by Ebenezer Huntington during the American Revolution*, (New York, 1914), pp. 77 *f.*, 87 *f.*, 93 *f.*

at in so long a strain and with so much justified bitterness against the inefficiency of legislators and the civilian population. On the whole, the morals of the men, as well as their morale, seem to have been maintained at a high point. Comments upon the soldiers' relations with women and other matters are by no means lacking, but are far fewer than one would expect.

When the war was finally won and the independence of the colonies acknowledged, it was after a struggle of such desolating force as had been foreseen by none of the promoters of the rebellion. They had hoped that, at the most, two or three campaigns and perhaps the intervention of friendly allies, combined with the usual back-down by Great Britain, would end the matter. The old leaders in business, politics, and society who were on the patriot side expected still to remain in the saddle, and anticipated no change in the status of the poorer and unenfranchised part of the population. Life was to go on as before, only freer and more prosperous. The flames of war, however, left no portion of that life untouched, and against the lurid background of those years we see the dark figures of misery and greed and discontent as well as the nobler ones of patriotism and pure endeavor. It is well to dwell for inspiration upon these latter; but we cannot understand the period nor the events that followed solely from the fervid outpourings of the orators or the high deeds of the chosen few. We must turn to yet other aspects of the lives of the silent millions who were forced by the struggle to face new hardships, new temptations, new problems, new conditions in every phase of daily life. For it is, to a great extent, the dumb tongues of the multitude that will one day speak the living words of history.

CHAPTER II

ECONOMIC EFFECTS OF THE WAR

Scarcity of Food — High Prices — Depreciation of the Currency — Attempts to Regulate Prices — State Currencies — Taxation — Changes in Social Structure — Difficulties of Business — Beginning of Manufactures — Rise of New Men — Agriculture — Laboring Classes — Extravagance

In the last chapter we touched upon some of the changes and hardships which were suffered by the men in the service, and noted that before the years of conflict were over a large part of the male population capable of bearing arms had been in service for longer or shorter periods. In the army almost everyone, officers as well as privates, suffered in one way or another. This is always less true of the civilian population, in which there is ever at such times of social upheaval certain elements which are so situated and of such capacities as to be able to take advantage of the general conditions and distress to their own profit. In every war the two great classes to suffer most are the poor and those who derive moderate fixed incomes either from invested property yielding settled returns or from salaries.

Except for certain manufactured goods, many luxuries, and a few of the articles used for food, such as tea and sugar, the colonies were to a great extent self-sustaining before the war broke, and during its continuance there was little general distress caused by the lack of any of the essential articles of consumption. The need for certain supplies for military use made them scarce from the beginning, and many of them were placed under the charge of the Board of War. One of these was lead for bullets, and in Massachusetts requests were issued to the

people to take the weights from their windows and turn them
in.[1]   The close supervision of the Board of War comes out now
and then in town records, such as those of Groton in 1779,
when we find the town applying to the Massachusetts Council
for a box of glass to replace the broken windows in the school-
and meeting-houses, saying that the request had been passed
by the Board but that the glass could not be had without an
order of Council.[2]   But such matters caused no real hardship.
Most of the clothing, for example, worn by the poorer classes
and small farmers was homespun and of durable quality, and
a very large proportion of articles in use in the households being
of domestic manufacture saved the smaller folk from much of
the suffering which high prices would have caused in a more
complex industrial society.

In certain sections and at certain times food was scarce, but
this was exceptional.   Such difficulties came mainly from dislocation of trade and trouble in distribution.   In the seaboard
towns of Massachusetts, such as Beverly, the people felt
severely the almost complete destruction of the cod-fishery,
which at once took away their means of livelihood and a portion of their food.   Early in 1777 George Williams wrote to
Colonel Pickering that "food is getting scarce and money
scarcer"; and two years later he again wrote that "in this
State on the sea-coast the inhabitants will soon have nothing
to eat," and quoted some of the prevailing prices.[3]

In Rhode Island there had been a severe disturbance of the
population, owing to the British occupation of Newport, and
between two and three thousand people had removed from the
area of occupation to other sections of the small state or across
the borders of its neighbors.[4]   The difficulties of trade through
its ports and the fact that the colony had never been agricul-
turally self-sustaining made special hardships for its inhabitants, who were dependent largely upon Connecticut.   From
time to time embargoes were laid upon the export of food from

[1] Alden Bradford, *History of Massachusetts*, (Boston, 1825), vol. II, p. 135.
[2] S. A. Green, *Groton during the Revolution*, (Groton, 1900), p. 233.
[3] Thorndike, "Beverly Privateers," pp. 341, 355.
[4] *Commerce of Rhode Island*, vol. II; Mass. Hist. Soc., *Coll.*, Ser. VII, vol. X, p. 51;
W. R. Staples, *Rhode Island in the Continental Congress*, (Providence, 1870), p. 76.

By his EXCELLENCY

JONATHAN TRUMBULL, Esquire,

Governor of the State of Connecticut in America.

A PROCLAMATION.

WHEREAS the General Assembly of this State, at their Session at Hartford, in May last, Resolved, That an Embargo be forthwith laid upon the Exportation out of this State, by Land or Water, of the following Articles, viz. Wheat, Rye, Indian-Corn, Peas, Beans, Oats, Bread, Flour, and every Kind of Meal, Pork, Beef, Live Cattle, Sheep, Swine, Rum, Sugar, Molasses, Salt, Bar Iron, Wool, Flax, woollen and linen Cloth, tanned Leather and Shoes, (except necessary Sea Stores for Vessels outward-bound, and except Cattle, Provisions or Cloathing purchased or to be purchased, or procured and sent for the Use of the Army or for the Navy belonging to this State, and not to hinder any particular Person or Persons from carrying or sending to such Soldiers in the Army as may be under the Care and special Relation of such Person, any necessary Cloathing or Provision they may want for their own Use and Consumption), and said Embargo to continue in Force until otherwise ordered : and said Assembly have requested me to issue a Proclamation prohibiting such Exportation accordingly.

I DO therefore, in pursuance of the Request of said General Assembly, issue this Proclamation, hereby notifying all Persons, that such Embargo is laid, and requiring them to comply therewith. And I do hereby strictly prohibit all Persons (without special Licence from the Governor and Council of Safety) from transporting or exporting from this State, by Land or Water, and from shipping for Transportation, driving or carrying any of said Articles, (excepting only as in said Resolve is excepted) under the Pains and Penalty of the Law, in such Case provided. And I do hereby require and enjoin all proper Officers and other Persons to exert themselves, that said Resolve be effectually carried into Execution.

GIVEN under my Hand at Lebanon, in said State, this 19th Day of June, Anno Domini, One Thousand Seven Hundred and Seventy Eight.

JONᵗʰ TRUMBULL.

NEW-LONDON: Printed by T. Green, Printer to the Governor and Company.

the several states, and in 1779 Governor Greene wrote to Congress that it was totally out of the power of the Rhode Island government to provide the people with bread, owing to scarcity of wheat. "Nearly one-quarter of the best plow land is now in possession of the enemy," he wrote, "and other considerable tracts are so exposed, that the occupiers have not dared, nor been able, to plant them for two years past." He complained of the strict embargo from the "southern and western states," and said that the only outside supply came in small quantities from Massachusetts, Connecticut having repeatedly declined to allow any.[1] In the larger towns, such as Boston, which always depended upon the surrounding country, there was also difficulty at times; but for the great mass of the people the main suffering came from the greatly enhanced prices of all the necessaries of life.

At first a real scarcity in some lines, and throughout the war the increased cost of doing business, accounted in part for the advance. High insurance rates, the risks of capture by the enemy, and the necessarily increased rate of profit on such goods as did get through from Europe and the West Indies raised the prices of all imported articles. In the North, because agriculture was practised mainly on small farms tilled by the owner and his family and because many of the articles used by the common people were made at home, the absence of the men of the family in the services naturally tended to decrease production, increase wages, and enhance prices. Speculation also played its part. In any case, the factors always present in the abnormal economic situation of war time would have raised the whole cost of living.

But as the war progressed, the main factor in carrying prices to the fantastic heights which they reached was the depreciation of the Continental and State currencies. The trouble started almost at once. As early as January 1776 a writer who signed himself "Farmer" wrote that "tis rendered impossible

---

[1] *R. I. Records*, vol. VIII, p. 498. In other letters he stated that one third of the land was in possession of the British. *Ibid.*, p. 499. In response to the appeal, Connecticut allowed 7000 bushels of grain to be exported, and contributions were sent both of money and of food.

for some, and extremely difficult for others to pay their debts."
Should payment be enforced by the usual legal process, he
added, it would be injurious to many, ruin some, and might be
productive of great disorders in the state.[1]

The following month, in Massachusetts, a committee was
appointed of representatives in the General Court to consider
the question of high prices and recommend action. For some
months after, petitions flowed in complaining of extortionate
charges and praying for legislation.[2] In December, William
Ellery, then one of Rhode Island's representatives in the Continental Congress at Philadelphia, wrote to the Governor that
prices there had risen between one and two hundred per cent
in less than two years, owing to depreciation in the currency,
the limitation of commerce, and the speculation in the necessaries of life by wealthy men.[3] He expressed the hope that the
situation had not become so critical in his home state. Although — if his estimate of the rise in Philadelphia was correct
— the conditions in New England were not quite so bad, they
had become sufficiently so to warrant the call by Massachusetts for a convention of delegates from the several states of
that section to meet at Providence in the same month in which
Ellery wrote. The original instructions from Massachusetts
to its delegates comprehended only the regulation of the currencies of the several states admitted to Congress, but were
enlarged before the meeting so as to include the placing of
embargoes on exports from each state, the prevention of monopolies, the fixing of prices, and other matters. Massachusetts
itself had prohibited exports of food and lumber from its borders
earlier in the year.[4] The convention, with representatives
from all four New England states, met at Providence the 25th
of December, and on the 31st reported a list of prices which
they recommended should go into effect throughout all New

---

[1] *Conn. Courant*, Jan. 29, 1776.

[2] The situation in Massachusetts can be conveniently followed in the article by
A. McF. Davis, "The Limitation of Prices in Massachusetts, 1776–1779," Col. Soc.
Mass., *Publications*, vol. X, pp. 119–134.

[3] *Rhode Island in the Continental Congress, op. cit.*, p. 105.

[4] "Limitation of Prices," *op. cit.*, p. 120.   The text of the report is in *R. I. Records*,
vol. VIII, pp. 85 ff.

England, and which included almost everything except real estate. The recommendations were adopted by the state legislatures the following year.

As might have been expected, the attempt to regulate prices by law met with but little success. "The complaint of *oppression* and *extortion* has been made, not only from your press but almost every press on the continent, and scarcely a tongue has been silent on the subject," wrote a correspondent in Connecticut.[1] Rufus King wrote from Cambridge in March that the price-fixing Acts had reduced many Massachusetts towns to great distress.   Of the town from which he wrote he said : "No Provisions brought to market. No Wood. In Boston three days past I saw numbers of Families removing into the Country — was told by a Gentleman acquainted with the Town's Situation that he imagined more than an hundred Families in the town were that day entirely destitute of Fuel, except such as they rummaged from the stores in Town.   Those who were in Boston thro' the siege, say they never at any time were in a worse situation for Fuel and Provisions. The clamours of the populace are loud and must be attended to. By information from Connecticut I learn they are in much the same Situation."[2] The *Connecticut Courant*, indeed, was filled with complaints, and in April, in accordance with the new scale of prices then in effect, the subscription of that journal was raised fifty per cent.[3]

In spite of laws intended to prevent "engrossing and forestalling," prices rose steadily. The "engrosser," as he was then called, was the speculator who attempted to control the market by the purchase of the available supply, whereas the "forestaller" attempted to do the same thing by buying the goods before they reached the market. Throughout the war, speculation for the rise in all sorts of goods and commodities was rampant. On the first of January, 1777, gold commanded a premium of only five per cent over the Continental bills, but by October it required two hundred and seventy-five dollars in bills to buy one hundred in gold ; by the first of January, 1778,

---

[1] *Conn. Courant*, March 17, 1777.
[2] C. R. King, *Life and Correspondence of Rufus King*, (New York, 1894), vol. I, p. 25.
[3] *Conn. Courant*, April 28, 1777.

the figure had risen to three hundred and twenty-five; a year later to seven hundred and forty-two; by the first of January, 1780, it had reached two thousand and thirty-four; and three months later it had climbed to four thousand. Under such conditions it is little wonder that prices rose with startling rapidity, and that it was impossible to make merchants and others adhere to the schedules fixed by the legislatures.

Now and then the people took matters into their own hands, and in Boston, in the summer of 1777, "there had been much rout and noise in the town for several weeks." Apparently the merchants had on hand great quantities of coffee and sugar which they were holding for an advance. The high prices and the artificial scarcity aroused the public, and the men seemingly having been impotent in the crisis, one hundred women marched on the store of one of the leading merchants and demanded his keys. On his refusal he was unceremoniously tossed into a cart, and when he capitulated the store was entered and the triumphant housewives went off with their coffee.[1] A similar incident occurred a few months later in Beverly, in which the women were again the aggressors and victors, and by attacking a warehouse and carrying off two hogsheads of sugar forced the merchants to sell at the fixed prices.[2]

Just at the time that the housewives of Boston were securing their coffee by their own simple but effective methods, another convention of delegates from the four colonies and their neighbor New York were preparing to meet at Springfield. Beginning their sittings on the 30th of July, they considered the cognate questions of currency, taxes, and prices. Roger Sherman, of Connecticut, who was in favor of carrying on the war as much as possible by means of taxation and providing the balance by foreign loans, stated that the crops were plentiful and that the people could pay larger taxes than theretofore.[3] In some respects this convention seems to have been the most conservative and the soundest in economic doctrine of the several held in the war years. Although its members advocated

[1] *Letters of Mrs. Adams, op. cit.*, vol. I, p. 109.
[2] Thorndike, "Beverly Privateers," *op. cit.*, pp. 371 *f.*
[3] L. H. Boutell, *The Life of Roger Sherman*, (Chicago, 1896), p. 104.

laws for the prohibition of speculative dealings in commodities, they did not believe in the possibility or advisability of fixing prices by law, and suggested the repeal of all such legislation. On every side the failure of the effort to hold down prices had brought disappointment and disgust, and the Massachusetts legislature not only repealed all price-regulating laws but those against forestalling and engrossing as well.

The agitation against high prices, however, continued. There seems to have been plenty of food in the country districts, as Sherman said, but the towns suffered. In March of the following year (1778), at a Boston town-meeting, it was resolved that: "One Great Reason of the present Excessive Price of Provisions in this Town arises from the Avarice, Injustice and Inhumanity of certain Persons within Twenty Miles of it, who purchase great Part of the same of Farmers living at a greater Distance and put an exhorbitant Advance upon it." [1] The "meatless days" of our own recent experience in the Great War were forecast in the suggestion that the richer citizens should not only subscribe for the relief of the poor, but "on no Occasion whatever have more than *Two Dishes* of Meat on the same Day on their Table," and that they should avoid the use of poultry and have two fish dinners a week.

Meanwhile Congress had taken the matter into its own hands and had divided the states into three groups, of which the northern included the New England ones and those as far south as Delaware. It was recommended that each group hold a convention for the purpose of regulating prices of labor and commodities, and of providing for the seizure of goods in the hands of the speculators. The northern convention was held at New Haven in January 1778, all the states being represented but Delaware. Although specific prices were set on certain goods, the convention ruled that, in general, prices for labor and commodities should both be set at an advance of seventy-five per cent over those prevailing in 1774. [2]

The scale was adopted by several of the states, including Con-

---

[1] Quoted in "Limitation of Prices," *op. cit.*, p. 125.
[2] S. E. Baldwin, "The New Haven Convention of 1778," New Haven Colony Hist. Soc., *Coll.*, vol. III, pp. 32–62.

necticut, but not by Massachusetts.   To some extent the regulating Acts which were passed in accordance with the suggestions of the convention seem to have been effective.   In March,
for example, it was reported from Hartford that the innkeepers
and many of the retailers, "together with a number of respectable merchants" in that and other towns, had entered into the
spirit of the Act and were "now disposing of their dear bought
goods at the stated prices."   "A patriotic example! and as
deserving of *praise*," adds the writer, "as the opposite is
infamy." [1]   On the other hand, there is ample evidence that
many merchants, and the people at large, paid scant attention
to the legislative prices.   "The operation of the State Bill,"
wrote David Lopez, Jr., the Rhode Island merchant, "renders
Business still extremely dull and perplexing, tho' with us it has
the appearance of a very short duration, our markets being
badly provided, and scarce any attention paid to the regulations by those who expose their articles for sale.   At Boston
its dictates seem to be but little better regarded.   On application for the Velvetts which I advised you were offer'd me at
£6 per yard, I was told they were sent to that market and readily sold for £9.   Dry goods instead of descending 20 per Ct.
keep daily rising, and have become very scarce." [2]

Governor Trumbull and many of the leading men were opposed to such interference with the natural laws of trade.   "If
we affix a low price to provisions, and articles of importation,"
wrote the Governor, "we shall find that the Farmer will cease
to till the Ground for more than is necessary for his subsistence,
and the Merchant to resign his Fortune on a small and precarious prospect of gain." [3]

Complaints of the high prices continued and constant demands were made in Massachusetts for the passage of laws
against the speculators.   "If a *market-man* is allow'd to ask
any price he thinks fit, having nothing but his own rapacity
and our necessity to govern him," wrote one Boston complainant, "the whole property of this town may in a little time be

---

[1] *Boston Gazette*, March 30, 1778.
[2] Letter of Sept. 16, 1779, *Rhode Island Commerce*, vol. II, p. 69.
[3] I. W. Stuart, *Life of Jonathan Trumbull, Sr.*, (Boston, 1859), p. 418.

drawn away by purchasing a few *potatoes*, and a few other necessaries of life." [1] Meanwhile, Congress had again recommended the states to take action against the speculators, and in February Massachusetts passed an Act directed against them. Its terms, however, when compared with the far more drastic legislation regulating the amount of food which might be purchased or in the possession of individuals in the recent Great War, would indicate that there was no real scarcity. Bakers, for example, were permitted to buy a three months' supply of flour, and a private family was allowed to have on hand a year's supply both of that commodity and of meat. [2]

The real trouble was depreciation. By April 1779, Continental bills had fallen to $121 in bills for $1 in coin and the "flight," as we have come to term it, from the rapidly depreciating currency was in full progress. Private efforts supplemented those of the legislatures. In June the merchants of Boston met and agreed to limit prices after July first to those prevailing in May, provided the other towns would concur. A convention of the eastern towns was held at Concord in June and agreed upon a scale of prices, but there were no means of enforcement. Individual towns adopted their scales and attempted to enforce them by extra-legal means. No bulwarks, however, could stand against the rising flood of paper money. In October a convention of the New England states and New York met at Hartford and decided that the previous failure to regulate prices was due to the currency. As Congress had set a limit of $200,000,000 to the issues, it was thought that the final depreciation might be determined and a new scale inaugurated. A larger convention, including more states, met at Philadelphia in January 1780. In March, however, Congress declared that the Continental money was worth only one fortieth of its face value, and recommended that the several states call in their quotas of it, issuing new money on the basis of one for forty. Following this repudiation of $3900 out of every $4000, the states in general returned to a specie basis, and prices thereafter were left to take care of themselves.

[1] *Boston Gazette*, Sept. 14, 1778.
[2] "Limitation of Prices," *op. cit.*, p. 126.

In all the colonies there was a great mass of legislation dealing with one aspect or another of the cost of living. It would
be as impossible as it is unnecessary to specify the Acts in detail.
The town records all tell the same story — that of attempting
to restrain the inevitable upward course of prices, which was
working havoc among all who were not self-sustaining or themselves benefiting from speculation for the rise.[1] Almost every
household felt the strain. "I blush whilst I give you a price
current," wrote Mrs. John Adams to her husband, then in
France. "All butcher's meat from a dollar to eight shillings
per pound; corn twenty-five dollars, rye thirty per bushel,
flour fifty pounds per hundred, potatoes ten dollars a bushel
. . . labor six and eight dollars a day; a common cow, from
sixty to seventy pounds; and all English goods in proportion.
This is our present situation. It is a risk to send anything
across the water, I know; yet, if one in three arrives, I should
be the gainer. I have studied, and do study, every method of
economy in my power; otherwise a mint of money would not
support a family."[2]

The mass of Continental paper was not the only currency
evil with which the colonists had to contend. As we have
noted in the previous volumes, all the New England colonies
had tried experiments in paper money, although at the beginning of the war all of them except Rhode Island had become
settled on a specie basis. The colonists were always averse to
taxation, not merely without representation but on principles
of pure selfishness. In an era when the nature of money and
currency was understood by only a few, it was far easier and
more popular to set the printing press to work than the tax-
gatherer. The war during its continuance was, therefore,
financed mainly by paper money and not by taxes, both by the
Continental Congress, which had no power to levy, and by the
separate states. In New Hampshire the local state money had
sunk to about one third of its nominal value by the beginning

---

[1] Cf., e.g., A. P. Marvin, *History of the Town of Lancaster*, (Lancaster, 1879), p. 307.
"Regulation of Prices in Hingham," Col. Soc. Mass., *Publications*, vol. X, pp. 116 ff.;
The subject may be traced in almost all the better town histories and the records.
[2] *Letters, op. cit.*, vol. I, pp. 135 f.

of 1778 and to one eighth by its close.[1] At that time the state had about £151,000 of its own notes outstanding, and this was increased in the following two years by loans of £370,000 more, which probably found their way into circulation as currency.

At the end of 1774 Massachusetts was out of debt, but in May 1775 the Provincial Congress emitted £130,000 in bills of credit, and other issues followed so rapidly that by the close of the war there were probably about £1,500,000 in circulation.[2] Connecticut tried to be more conservative, but between April 1775 and May 1780 that state issued £455,000 in notes, of which £100,000 may have been redeemed in exchange for subsequent issues within the period.[3] These state bills circulated with the Continental money and fluctuated to a considerable extent with it, depreciating rapidly.

The most serious situation developed in Rhode Island, where it had political and social consequences of importance, which will be mentioned in a later chapter. The paper-money mania in that colony greatly alarmed its neighbors, and as early as April 1777 a correspondent of Elbridge Gerry wrote that "Rhode Island in particular must be watched most narrowly, or she will drown New England in paper." [4] The expenses of the Rhode Island government for the years immediately preceding the Revolution had not much exceeded £2000 a year, but in 1775 and 1776 the increase due to the war and the unwillingness to resort to taxation resulted in issuing £150,000 of paper. In the next three years $1,150,000 was added to this, and beginning with October 1780, $200,000 per month in paper had to be issued to meet the quota of the state as apportioned by Congress for the expenses of the struggle. Owing to the British occupation, the little state, with a population of only

[1] C. J. Bullock, *Essays on the Monetary History of the United States*, (New York, 1900), p. 267.

[2] C. J. Bullock, "Sketch of the Finances and Financial Policy of Massachusetts, 1780–1905," American Economic Association, *Publications*, Ser. III, vol. VIII, No. 2, 1907, p. 6.

[3] H. Bronson, "A Historical Sketch of the Connecticut Currency, Continental Money and the Finances of the Revolution," New Haven Colony Hist. Soc., *Papers*, vol. I, p. 87.

[4] Austin, *Gerry*, vol. I, p. 220.

about fifty-five thousand, had suffered more severely than any other in New England. Her commerce was almost at a stand, and there was no means of absorbing the flood of paper which poured steadily from the press.[1]

It is impossible to determine whether the refusal to pay for at least the larger part of the war-cost by taxation was due to inability or a mere disinclination to pay. The steady decline in the currency was in itself a heavy tax, though this was not realized. As we shall see later, there was much money being made during the conflict by those able to take advantage of the conditions, and the calculating business man or speculator was better able to protect himself against loss through the depreciating circulating medium than were the other classes. In addition to mulcting the public in this way, the states did levy a certain amount of taxes during the war, though probably much less than they might have. Perhaps the taxes that bore most heavily on the people were those of the towns, which both taxed themselves and also ran heavily into debt for the bounties to soldiers, the care of their families, and other charges, as we have noted, for example, in Plymouth.

In any case, aside from what was derived from foreign loans, the people paid the cost of the war, whether in the form of taxes or in the more indirect form of loss on account of the depreciation and partial repudiation of the currency. The question was partly one of psychology, as to *how* the people preferred to pay, and partly one of class interest, as to *who* should pay. The incidence of taxation during this period has not yet received that careful study which it deserves and which would provide us with the key to the problem. There is no question but that great injustice was wrought by such taxation as there was. There is ample evidence to show that this bore most heavily upon the poorer classes. For example, the poll tax in Massachusetts accounted for nearly one third of the total amount of money raised, and this naturally was a much more severe burden upon the poor man than upon the rich. In fact, nearly all the taxes seem to have been arranged so as to

[1] *Vide* E. R. Potter and S. S. Rider, *Some Account of the Bills of Credit or Paper Money of Rhode Island*, (Providence, 1880).

fall upon those least able to bear them, though we cannot tell how far this may have been due to design and how far to ignorance. There was so much discussion of the matter, however, that it cannot have been wholly due to the latter. In 1777, Robert Treat Paine, one of the delegates from Massachusetts to Congress, complained to Gerry that his state had just begun taxation by a levy of £105,000, and that the expenses of the towns had been so great, owing to soldiers' bonuses, that the local taxes would equal the state tax. The main evil, he said, was that the war had completely altered the distribution of property, and the incidence of the taxes was therefore very inequitable. While some people were heaping up wealth, most of them were jogging on in the old way under great difficulties. "Cannot some mode be hit upon," he asked, "to draw money by taxation from those who are really the possessors of it?" [1]

In Connecticut the system of taxation was antiquated and very unequal. "According to our present mode," wrote a complainant to the *Connecticut Journal*, "an house with so many fire-places, and such a quantity of land, whether it be in town or country, good or poor, is equally taxed . . . it is undoubted truth of fact, that thousands of the poorer sort, whose whole estate is not worth more than 3 or 400, pay as large a tax as others, whose estate is worth 4 or 5000 pounds." [2] He pointed out that this would be the ruin of "more than a third part of the families in the state, whose lands must immediately fall into the hands of the richer for money to pay their rates." In Rhode Island, owing to the occupation of Newport and other parts of the state by the British, the taxes had to be borne by only a part of the community, and there, again, the poll tax, which was eight shillings in 1777, must have weighed heavily on the impoverished lower classes. [3]

In all discussion of the question of taxes during the period of the war and the trying years of threatened social upheaval which followed, we may again emphasize that it was a question

[1] Austin, *Gerry*, vol. I, p. 221.
[2] Issue of April 8, 1778.
[3] *R. I. Records*, vol. VIII, pp. 150, 176.

rather of incidence than of amount of taxation. By 1781 and 1782 the newspapers were filled with articles on this question, and it is evident that the situation was becoming serious in all the New England states, though the taxes were lighter in Vermont than elsewhere. Evidences of class feeling in this matter became numerous. In Connecticut it was stated that although the "middling people" were hardest pressed by the new taxes, the complaints did not come from them but from those who had grown rich in the war; and this note is sounded with increasing frequency.[1]

Before the war, in spite of the growing feeling between classes and the increasing discontent which we noted in the preceding volume, the social order had been a comparatively stable one. It was largely agricultural, and the farming element was the backbone of all the New England colonies. In the towns the merchants were the social and not seldom the political leaders. Among the professional classes, the clergy, well intrenched, occupied the most prominent position, but both doctors and lawyers had in recent years been coming to hold a more recognized professional status. Everywhere, both in town and in country, the "old families" and the higher social classes maintained a position of recognized superiority, which was felt throughout the entire life of their communities. Their influence among their neighbors and the narrow basis of the franchise had enabled them, as a rule, to control the political situation for their own interests, and in many respects New England was more aristocratic, perhaps we may say snobbish, than was the South.

To a great extent this structure of society, so comfortable for the elect, was rudely disturbed by the war. In a considerable degree this was due to the changed economic position of the former rich — who had also become subject to pressure from the war profiteers — and the democratic elements among the people. These latter had not only learned to make their grievances heard, but had acquired new ones. All methods of earning a living or accumulating wealth were thrown into confusion at the opening of the conflict. The difficulty of securing

[1] *Conn. Courant*, June 11, 1782.

labor and the rapidly changing prices due to the currency completely upset the stability of agriculture. The fisheries were shut down at once. Foreign commerce had to be wholly altered in character. The people who lived on fixed incomes from investments were in many cases ruined by the rise in prices and the fall in money. On the other hand, new methods of gaining wealth quickly came into vogue, and those who were shrewd or unscrupulous enough to profit by them rose rapidly to the top.

The furnishing of the army with all its necessary supplies immediately opened enormously profitable channels of business and speculation. The size of such contracts and the haste with which they have to be fulfilled under the strain and pressure of war always make the opportunity for excess profits. Speculators, as ever, at once took advantage of the nation's predicament. However patriotic the motives for entering the war may have been, business was business, and fortunes were piled up rapidly by those who served their country in the capacity of contractors. Congress complained in 1777 that in every state persons "instigated by the lust of avarice" were assiduously endeavoring to accumulate enormous gains for themselves at the expense of the rest of the community and to the detriment of the public service. The very magnitude of the field which war opens to private gain stimulates greed on the part of even the more reputable elements in the community, while the irresponsible and unscrupulous do their best to reap their harvest.

Operations were conducted on both large and small scales. We have already noted the case of a common sutler in the army who, not worth twenty shillings when he started, accumulated $3000 in one summer. Andrew Craigie, of Boston, who became Apothecary-General, blossomed out at the close of the war as a wholesale merchant with ample capital in New York and became one of the heavy speculators in Government securities.[1] In November 1777, the firm of Otis & Andrews of Boston were appointed Collectors of Clothing for the army and added contracting in very large amounts to their mercantile

[1] J. S. Davis, *Essays in the Earlier History of American Corporations*, (Harvard University Press, 1917), vol. I, p. 140.

business.   At the beginning of July 1778 the firm wrote to the
quartermaster-general that they had sent on in seven months
between sixteen and eighteen thousand suits of clothes, besides
shirts, hats, shoes, blankets, and other material, and that the
United States had been owing them nearly £200,000 lawful
money.[1]   That such contracts must have been extremely profitable is indicated by a letter from Otis to his brother, himself a
member of the local committee on clothing, in which he advises
him that on "winter goods" he may "as well make 100 per
cent as 5 as they grow exceedingly scarce and will be at 20 for
one in a short time."[2]   "Business is business," and culture
and high social position call for a firm substructure of cash on
hand, but it is worth while, when we have to consider the discontent of the so-called lower classes in 1786, to think of such
men as even the Otises, safe out of harm's way in comfortable
rooms in Boston, figuring whether they should make one or
two hundred per cent out of the soldiers' winter clothes, and
to contrast them with the soldiers themselves, shivering and
naked at Valley Forge, dying of cold and starvation.

The prosperity of the old mercantile firms varied greatly.
Merchants had to adapt themselves quickly to wholly altered
conditions, and some were able to do this, whereas others were
not.   A very large part of the New England trade had been
with England, and more particularly the English West Indies.
This trade was, of course, cut off by the war.   Nevertheless,
large quantities of English and West Indian goods found their
way into the states.   Indeed, the supply of the latter must
have become very plentiful by 1779, for their prices were then
falling "very rapidly" in Rhode Island and Boston, although
the prices of other goods were still rising.[3]   Apparently large
amounts of English goods were smuggled in by way of Nova
Scotia, the export figures for English ports showing such heavy
increases in shipments to that colony as to indicate subsequent
clandestine entry into the United States.[4]

[1] S. E. Morison, *Life and Letters of Harrison Gray Otis*, (Boston, 1913), vol. I, p. 21.
[2] *Ibid.*, p. 22.
[3] *R. I. Commerce*, vol. II, p. 63.
[4] E. R. Johnson *et al.*, *History of Domestic and Foreign Commerce of the United States*,
(Washington, 1915), p. 122.

Scattered references in private letters of the period indicate the difficulties with which any commerce was carried on. Owing to the activities of British privateers, the coasting trade was almost wholly suspended. In 1779 the representatives of Rhode Island in Congress wrote to the Governor that "the whole coast from New York to South Carolina is so infested with privateers as to render commerce exceedingly precarious," [1] and the insurance rates quoted from time to time suggest the risks taken. In the autumn of 1776 John Bradford reported to Robert Morris that he could find no one at either Boston or Salem who would take the chance of insuring any vessel bound to Virginia. [2] Insurance rates in England for American ports, which before the war had been as low as two per cent, rose to thirty per cent for vessels sailing with convoy and fifty for those sailing alone. [3] Early in 1778 Bradford again reported to Morris from Boston that the insurance officers there had decided "not to take any more Risque, which will Induce the Adventurers to lay up their Vessells as they arrive." [4] Later, thirty-five per cent in Massachusetts and Rhode Island was considered moderate, and the merchant Champlin wrote from Newport that if he could not insure his vessel on a trip from Philadelphia to Havana and back to Newport for less than forty per cent he would assume the risk himself. [5]

The merchants also suffered from the scarcity of men to man their vessels, the sailors preferring the greater chances of gain in privateering. Bradford's letters all during the war are filled with complaints of the inability to man vessels and get them off. "Sailors are so very Scarce and Wages so intollerable high," is his constant refrain. [6] "The difficulty of getting Vessels to Sea, from this Port is almost insuperable," he wrote again; and in May 1778 he noted that two fine ships, fitted out at enormous expense, had had to be dismantled and hauled up again because they could not be manned. [7] Interest rates

---

[1] Staples, *Rhode Island in the Continental Congress*, p. 210.
[2] Bradford's Letter Book, (Mss. Library of Congress), Sept. 23, 1776.
[3] Maclay, *Privateers*, p. xiii. *Cf.* Boutell, *Sherman*, p. 100.
[4] Letter Book, *op. cit.*, March 16, 1778.
[5] *R. I. Commerce*, vol. II, p. 160.
[6] Letter Book, *op. cit.*, Aug. 7, 1777.   [7] *Ibid.*, March 4, 1778, April 28, 1778.

were also very high, and a reputable Newport merchant stated that he was paying twenty-four per cent on a loan and expected the rate to be advanced to thirty. Moreover, the prices of goods varied greatly, depending upon the arrivals of vessels, and the failure of expected cargoes caused rapid rises. In June 1778 Bradford reported that "lately scarce any inward bound Vessells have escaped the Enemy," and the following January that there had been hardly any arrivals for two months, so that the price of West India goods had advanced very greatly.[1] When we add to all these difficulties and uncertainties the constant and violent alterations in prices due to the currency depreciation, it is evident that the change in business had become so great as to call for different qualities from those possessed by most of the peace-time merchants of the old type. Commerce had become mere speculation, although the profits were correspondingly large when made.

Many merchants turned frankly to privateering as offering no more risk and some advantages. It was far easier to get men to serve on privateers than on merchant ships, and the possible profits in capturing other people's cargoes were greater than in carrying one's own. The privateers were owned by private individuals and firms, and not seldom by groups of persons known as the "propriety," who were interested in one or more vessels on shares. Such was the case, for example, in the General Sullivan, which was owned by a group of ten New Hampshire men.[2] These contributed between them a little over £10,000 lawful money to the enterprise in 1777, and the following year one prize alone was distributed of a value of £168,400. It was customary for the officers and crews to share in the prize money in definite proportions, and not only these shares, but even small fractions of them, came to be traded in like stock certificates and offered a medium of speculation for the smallest purses.[3] It is uncertain whether wages were paid or not in addition to the prize money.

[1] Letter Book, *op. cit.*, June 24, 1778, Jan. 6, 1779.
[2] "Privateer General Sullivan, 1777–1780," Mss. volume in Library of Congress consisting of Articles of Agreement, accounts, etc.
[3] "Beverly Privateers," *op. cit.*, pp. 353 f.

In the early years the ventures seem to have been largely successful, so that Bradford reported in November 1777 that the price of vessels had risen to high figures and that they were being bought principally by "the successful Adventurers in privateers." [1]   A few months later he made the interesting statement that the cost of ships had then climbed still higher, owing to the unlimited prices paid by the French merchants. "When the Frenchmen here are glutted," he wrote, "we may expect to buy them at par; but they stick at no price, and truly while they sell their Goods at such an exhorbitant advance they may afford to give double the Value of a Vessell, one of that Class of Men the other Day gave £6100 for the Lady Gage formerly employed between London and York." [2]

The *Boston Gazette* and other papers were filled with stories of captures, but occasionally we get glimpses of some of the risks run.   Thus in January 1777 we read that another prize taken by the Alfred had arrived at Boston, "after having been re-taken by a British frigate, and again captured by an American cruizer." [3]   The following month it was reported that "Capt. Dowse's Crew had rose upon him, and ran away with his Vessell," [4] a proceeding which seems to have happened in more cases than this, so nearly akin was privateering to open piracy — as it had been in the earlier Seven Years' War.   In fact, even the Continental vessels were not above capturing American ships for prize money, and in 1779 Aaron Lopez of Newport had three of his ships so taken.   One was adjudged to him promptly by "a reference agreed to by the parties"; one was awarded to him by the court at Providence; but in the case of the third judgment went against him in the Admiralty Court in Connecticut, and appeal had to be carried to Congress itself.   After much delay and expense he finally succeeded in recovering his property "from the hands of those voracious pirates," the naval officers of his own country. [5]

The English, moreover, were quite as active at sea as the Americans, and captures by the enemy ruined many an ad-

[1] Bradford, Letter Book, under date.   [3] *Boston Gazette*, Jan. 6, 1777.
[2] Letter Book, *op. cit.*, March 31, 1778.   [4] *Ibid.*, Feb. 17, 1777.
[5] *R. I. Commerce*, vol. II, pp. 53, 55.

venturer.   By the end of the war, Long Island Sound was swept
clean of everything American, and Connecticut shipping had
to "begin anew at the keel."[1]   The extraordinary risks and
also the possibility of gaining almost unheard-of fortunes is
well illustrated in the case of Nathaniel Tracy of Newburyport.
The Marquis de Chastellux relates that, when traveling in
America at the end of the war, this merchant told him that in
1777 he had lost one hundred and forty vessels, and had nothing left but one small privateer brig of eight guns, of which he
had had no news for a long time.   Absolute ruin was staring
him in the face when this little vessel unexpectedly arrived in
port with a prize worth £25,000.   From that time his luck
turned, and he accumulated a fortune of over £600,000 sterling.[2]   De Chastellux's figures may have been a little exaggerated, but in a memorial presented to Congress in 1806, ten
years after Tracy's death, it was stated that he had been the
owner of a hundred and ten merchant vessels which, with their
cargoes, were valued at $2,733,300 in specie, and that all but
thirteen were captured or lost.   In addition, he was the principal owner of twenty-four cruising ships carrying crews of
twenty-eight hundred men.   These ships captured prizes
which were sold for just under $4,000,000.[3]

Before the war nearly every town in eastern Massachusetts
had begun to be supported in part by manufactures, though
these were on a small scale.   Haverhill, for example, in 1767
had forty-four workshops and nineteen mills.   Shoemaking
at Lynn had already become an important industry, that being
the only town which has retained its characteristic manufacture of pre-Revolutionary days.[4]   In many ways the war
immediately stimulated manufacturing, the capital coming
mainly from the mercantile class.   Powder mills were soon
established at such places as Andover, Stoughton, and Bradford, and the metal manufactures of Springfield and Waterbury
date from the establishment at those interior points — chosen

[1] F. M. Caulkins, *History of New London*, (New London, 1895), p. 542.
[2] *Travels, op. cit.*, vol. II, p. 247.
[3] Quoted by J. J. Currier, *History of Newburyport*, (Newburyport, 1906), p. 624 *n*.
[4] V. S. Clark, *History of Manufactures in the United States, 1607–1860*, (Washington,
1916), pp. 186 *f*.

for safety — of the arms factories of this period.[1] Although
nail-making had been a winter household industry on the farms,
small nails and tacks had been imported, mainly from England,
and the shortage during the war inaugurated a new method of
manufacture in America, thus establishing one of the most
important post-war industries in Rhode Island.[2] Necessity
set ingenuity to work, and the superiority of American mills of
various sorts to the English, as noted in some cases by contemporary travelers, dates from these years of rapidly changing
business.

It is impossible to specify all the minor ways in which money
was being quickly accumulated by those shrewd or unscrupulous enough to make use of the opportunities offered. It was
said that considerable fortunes were made even in buying up
the notes of the soldiers at low prices and thus taking advantage
of their ignorance or necessities.[3] By many varied means,
reputable as well as disreputable, new men came rapidly to the
surface. "The war," wrote one observer, "has thrown property into channels where before it never was and has increased
little streams to overflowing rivers: and what is worse, in
some respects by a method that has drained the sources of
some as much as it has replenished others. Rich and numerous
prizes, and the putting six or seven hundred per cent on goods
bought in peace time, are the grand engines. Money in large
sums, thrown into their hands by these means, enables them to
roll the snow ball of monopoly and forestalling." [4] "The old
substantial Merchants" of Boston — wrote Samuel Adams —
"have generally laid aside trade and left it to Strangers or
those who from nothing have raised fortunes by privateering." [5]

On every hand were heard complaints of hawkers and ped-
dlers and persons no one had ever heard of, who had suddenly
risen to affluence and were usurping the places of the old families. These men were of a wholly different type from the conservatives whom they displaced. Most of the ultra-conserva-

[1] J. L. Bishop, *History of American Manufactures from 1609 to 1860*, (Philadelphia,
1861), vol. I, pp. 495, 516.
[2] Clark, *op. cit.*, p. 222.
[3] *Conn. Courant*, June 24, 1783.
[4] Austin, *Gerry*, vol. I, p. 220.
[5] *Writings*, vol. IV, p. 19.

tive element had taken the Tory side at the beginning of the struggle, and had long disappeared from the colonies before its end. So rapid had been the economic changes that even the less conservative men, who had chosen the revolutionary side, had also been pushed out to make room for newcomers, most of whom had had but little or no experience in mercantile or public affairs before the war. It is true that in each of the New England colonies certain staunch leaders remained, but these had now to contend with radical and untrained forces both in politics and in business.

In the former field, partly from the economic failure of the old families, partly from the rise of new moneyed men, and partly from uneasy democratic movements among the people generally, the type which was coming to the front by the end of the war was also changing rapidly. In 1783 Mrs. John Adams wrote that there had been an overturn in the Massachusetts House of Representatives and that at the last election over one hundred new men had been elected.[1] When, five years later, her husband returned from his long foreign mission, he noted that the people had discarded almost all "the old, stanch, firm patriots, who conducted the revolution in all the civil departments, and has called to the helm pilots much more selfish and much less skillful."[2] "When you come," wrote James Bowdoin to ex-Governor Pownall in 1783, "you will scarcely see any other than new faces. . . . The change which in that respect has happened within the few years since the revolution is as remarkable as the revolution itself. It seems to have anticipated the time when 'all old things shall be done away with and all things become new.'"[3]

All along the seacoast the life of the people was completely altered by the war. From the military standpoint there were the constant fears of raids by the enemy and the permanent occupation of Newport. But from the economic point of view there was probably not a family, of however humble circumstances, living on the coast whose life did not feel the

[1] *Letters*, vol. I, p. 183.
[2] John Adams, *Works*, (Boston, 1856), vol. IX, p. 557.
[3] Mass. Hist. Soc., *Coll.*, Ser. VII, vol. VI, p. 22.

strain of war. The thousands of sailors who had manned the merchant ships of the New England carrying trade, working for wages, became speculators in the risks of the privateers upon which they sailed. To pay their own debts or support their families during their absence, they frequently sold part of their possible share in the prize money, before they sailed, to specu-lators who sprang up in this line of business in the privateering ports. But it was not only the merchant sailors who were drawn away from a legitimate occupation to the hazards of a life in which recklessness and lawlessness ruled supreme. The fisheries, upon which was based a large part of the wealth of Massachusetts, were ruined by 1777, and not only were the capital and ships tied up by the complete stoppage of that industry forced to find other employment, which was not always possible, but so also were the thousands of persons who were normally engaged in it. It is impossible to estimate with accuracy the number of men who were so diverted, but some idea may be gained from the fact that although Marblehead was the largest fishing port, the smaller ports of Salem and Beverly dispatched fifty-two privateers in a single season, manned by over four thousand sailors.[1] It has been stated that Newburyport sent out a single fleet of twenty-two vessels with over a thousand men, which was never heard from again. When peace was declared, the small village of Gloucester had lost over three hundred in killed and missing, or one third of her able-bodied men. Between 1772 and 1780 the number of polls in Marblehead dropped from twelve hundred and three to five hundred and forty-four, and the tonnage of its shipping from twelve thousand to fifteen hundred. In this single town at the end of the war there were four hundred and fifty-eight widows and nine hundred and sixty-six fatherless children.[2]

The agricultural towns of the back-country suffered less, and it is rather difficult, in the absence as yet of careful studies of the subject, properly to appraise the economic change which came over the small farms. As we have already noted, the

[1] R. McFarland, *A History of the New England Fisheries*, (Univ. of Penn., 1911), p. 123.
[2] *Ibid.*, pp. 123 *f.*

scarcity of farm labor, together with decreased crops and increased cost, naturally brought high prices to the farmer who had a surplus product for sale. There were constant complaints, both from the army and from civilians, of the extortionate gains of the farmers and of the prices charged by them. But such complaints were heard with respect to all commodities, as prices jumped higher and higher to offset the depreciation in the currency. It would seem doubtful whether the prices of farm produce did more than keep pace with this decline if, indeed, they did that. For example, we may examine two complaints from the state of Connecticut, which was more nearly self-sustaining than any of the others. At the end of 1777 a writer in the *Courant* stated that English hay had risen from forty shillings to £4 and sometimes even to £6. In other words, it had advanced from two to three hundred per cent.[1] At that time, however, the paper money had fallen to the point where it took three hundred and twenty-five dollars to buy one hundred in specie, so that in spite of the apparent great advance in the price of hay, the farmer was really getting less for it than at the beginning of the war. If we take the average of the two prices complained of as £5, we find he was receiving two and a half times his old price, but in paper of which it took three and a quarter times as much to have the same purchasing power. This also holds good of complaints made at the end of the next year. It was stated, for example, that grass-fed beef which had cost from sixteen to twenty shillings a hundred in 1775 then cost £5 to £6, or an advance of from five to six times.[2] But we find that in the steady depreciation of paper money the exchange between paper and specie then stood at about seven hundred and forty-two, so that even with farm prices at five or six hundred, the farmer was falling behind, without, moreover, allowing for increased cost of production.

The great bulk of the farming population tilled small farms which barely supported them in moderate comfort by hard toil.[3] With such small surplus as they could sell they bought

---

[1] *Conn. Courant*, Dec. 2, 1777. [2] *Ibid.*, Dec. 15, 1778.
[3] *Cf.* Adams, *Founding of New England*, p. 8.

those commodities and articles which could not be raised on their own acres or manufactured by themselves and their families. Luxury had always been absent from the small farm, but now the purchase of what had been necessities must have decreased except in the case of such farmers' families as could not withstand the temptation of the extravagance about them and went into debt to meet a rising scale of living. There is evidence that such was not seldom the case. Bradford, for example, from whose manuscript letters we have quoted so frequently, was complaining in 1778 that "the illiberal Spirit of the Farmers is beyond Belief, loosing even first principles" in the prices they were extorting, and yet in the same letter he said, in another connection, that such is "the Parsimony of our Farmers that those French Adventurers now find it difficult to vend their Goods." [1] It would seem as if the fact was that although the farmers might in many cases be infected by the growing taste for extravagance and luxury they were by no means so well-off as prices might indicate to the thoughtless. In the beginning of the war, when prices were rising on account of other causes than depreciation and when the farmer still had a stock of goods on hand, it may have been, as a Boston merchant wrote, that the "farmer and the bulk of the people gain by the war"; [2] but this was probably not true of the average small farmer as the struggle continued. The larger farmer may have worked into a somewhat different position, and it has been claimed that he prospered during the years up to 1780, when his condition rapidly altered for the worse.[3] In Connecticut it was said in 1777 that "these high prices are an advantage to the able, wealthy farmer, who raises much produce for the market; but if I mistake not, are a disadvantage to every other class of men. Now such wealthy farmers are but a small part of the community: yea, they are but a small part even of the farmers." [4] This is a distinction that should not be

[1] Letter Book, March 31, 1778.
[2] April 4, 1777. Quoted by W. B. Weeden, *Economic and Social History of New England*, (Boston, 1890), vol. II, p. 779.
[3] R. V. Harlow, "Economic Conditions in Massachusetts, 1775–1783," Col. Soc. Mass., *Publications*, vol. XX, pp. 177 *f.*, 190.
[4] *Conn. Courant*, Jan. 13, 1777.

lost to sight, and the uneasiness of the small farmers, if the above analysis is correct, would provide much of the basis for the agitation which came after the close of the war. Even before the end the farmers were apparently becoming restive and endeavoring to make themselves felt to a greater extent politically, for it was stated in Connecticut that although the Assemblies had always had a large element in them of agriculturists, the great majority of the representatives were then becoming of that class, and that the farmers were more active politically than at "any period within the memory of man." [1] There is no doubt that the old antagonism between the "court" — or town — and the "country" parties was much accentuated by the existing economic conditions. Samuel Adams might lament in 1777 that "the Country and the Town . . . mutually complain of each other," and that the war was no time for angry disputes, but the recrimination between the two classes in society was maintained with increasing bitterness.[2]

In contrast to the amount of time which has been spent on the topics of slavery and indented servants, there has as yet been no careful study made of the conditions and history of free white labor in any of the colonies during the colonial period. We know less of the numbers, wages, and conditions of free labor than of any other class in colonial society. During the war years there is ample evidence, though much of it is of general character, to indicate that there was a great scarcity of labor of all sorts in the larger centres. We have already noted Bradford's constant complaints on that score in connection with shipping in Boston. The wave of extravagance, of which we shall speak later, also created a demand for labor in new lines, and the number of men employed in the military services naturally reduced the supply.

In fixing the prices of commodities at the various conventions which we have mentioned, regulations were also made covering the wages of laboring men, but it is impossible to tell to what extent these may have been complied with between employer and employed. We know that the prices ordered to be charged

[1] *Conn. Courant*, May 4, 1779.
[2] *Works*, vol. III, p. 365. *Cf*. Harlow, *op. cit.*, pp. 169 f.

for goods were not observed, and it is probable that labor also charged and received more than the legal rates. Bradford stated at the end of 1778 that "money is hourly depreciating in its value and the necessaries of life and labour rising more than the proportion of the declension of the currency."[1] The wages of ordinary labor, however, would not appear to have kept pace with the falling value of the currency in which they were paid. Before the war the wages of a farm hand in Massachusetts were three shillings a day in summer, and an effort was made in that state to keep them at that by statute when the war broke out, and other wages also at their former figures.[2] If we count twenty-six working days to a month, the farm hands would have earned just £4 a month; but in May 1778 Mrs. Adams complained that farm labor was asking £12 a month and none could be obtained for less.[3] We find, however, that farm produce was selling for from five to six times the former rate, and that paper money was at about five hundred, rising to over seven hundred by the end of the year. If labor was receiving only three times the pre-war rate, it was thus falling behind even faster than the small farmer, and accumulating grievances of its own.

The economic dislocation brought about by the war as regards the comparative poverty of the former wealthy and the extravagance of the new rich comes out in innumerable letters of the period. "Your brother Williams," wrote the able physician, Dr. Orne of Salem, to Colonel Pickering, "has lost a great deal of his estate, and it frets him not a little. I don't much wonder at it, when people have been raised by the war from the lowest indigence to affluence." Again he commented, in 1782, "I am weary to death of this dreadful war. It is attended with such irregular distribution of property, such invasion of order, such decay of morals, so much public distress and private extravagance."[4] The extravagance of those who were making money rapidly was condemned on every side and

---

[1] Letter Book, Dec. 3, 1778.
[2] *Acts and Resolves, Province of Mass. Bay*, vol. V, p. 584.
[3] *Letters*, vol. I, p. 121.
[4] Pickering, *Timothy Pickering*, vol. I, pp. 365 f.

freely commented upon. "You can scarcely form an Idea of the increase and growth of the extravagance of the People in their demands for Labour and every Article for sale," wrote William Vernon of the Navy Board at Boston to John Adams in 1778. "Dissipation has no bounds at present; when or where it will stop, or if a reform will take place, I dare not predict." [1]   Henry Marchant of Newport wrote in alarm of "the inordinate extravagance of the times, a lawless thirst for riches, and a spirit of monopolizing and speculation, big with more evils than all the armies of Europe could afford." [2]   Mrs. Adams, on reaching London in 1784, noted with surprise that both men and women were much more plainly dressed than in Boston, and that ladies wore muslin instead of silk, as at home.[3] In the latter years of the war merchants' advertisements in the newspapers offered quantities of all sorts of luxuries for sale and they evidently found a ready market. Samuel Adams complained in vain that people were promoting all kinds of "Superfluity of Dress and Ornament, when it is as much as they can bear to support the Expense of cloathing a naked Army." [4]   At Hartford, East Windsor, and other small towns in Connecticut, merchants offered ivory combs, silver buckles for shoes and stocks, laces, silks, and velvets for the gay war-society of the "Land of steady habits." [5]   The old type of New England Puritan society had been disintegrating for some decades, and, as usual, war not only brought new tendencies into play but emphasized the effects of those already come into operation.

[1] Allen, *Naval Hist. of American Revolution*, vol. I, p. 49.
[2] Staples, *Rhode Island in the Continental Congress*, p. 193.
[3] *Letters*, vol. II, p. 27.
[4] *Works*, vol. IV, p. 236.
[5] *Conn. Courant*, March 12 and Aug. 27, 1782.

CHAPTER III

MORAL EFFECTS OF THE WAR

Propaganda — Treatment of Loyalists — Half Pay of American Officers — Post-War Psychology — The Cincinnati — Effect of the War Intellectually — The Arts — Education — Religion — Morals

IF we accept the estimate that at the beginning of the war one third of the people were in favor of independence, one third opposed to it, and one third indifferent, it is evident that two thirds could not have been counted upon to sustain the patriot side with any ardor. Of the remainder, many drew the line in their patriotism at making any personal sacrifice, and in the last years of the war their weariness of the struggle became pronounced. There were noble examples of disinterested love of country, and on the whole the people bore their sufferings well, but it is difficult to sustain the mass of a population at a high pitch of pure patriotic endeavor or moral fervor for years at a time. In this respect, as the difficulties of enlistment and the orgy of profiteering and self-seeking indicate, the War of the Revolution offered no marked contrast to any other.

Propaganda was necessary from the beginning to stir the popular emotions, and in character that propaganda did not differ greatly from that employed in the great struggle of recent years. Efforts are always made to rouse the herd instinct in a nation at such crises, and the righteousness of the cause need not blind us to the methods employed. The people must be made to feel that there can be no two sides to the question, that they themselves are solely in the right in everything, that all virtue lies with them and all infamy with the enemy, whose

traits and acts are painted in the blackest dye.[1] The lowest
appeals to fear and revenge are stimulated by stories of atrocities, real or imaginary, perpetrated by the enemy, whereas
the propagandist paints his own party in the brightest colors
of virtue and courage. A despot fighting with a standing army
independent of his people's support may be chivalrous in his
opinion of the foe. Apparently a democracy waging war has
to drug itself with lies. Nor is this due to having to secure
the support of the lowest elements in the community; for few
are so independent in judgment as wholly to escape the conta-
gion of mob thinking at such times. It has sometimes been said
that propaganda was a discovery of the last war, but a careful
study — which has not yet been made — of propaganda in
the Revolution would result in matching all the efforts made
between 1914 and 1918, in spite of the wealth of psychology
poured out by experts in the later struggle.

No one was more astute in its use than Samuel Adams, and
it was not many weeks after Bunker Hill before he was urging
the importance of covering some of the shortcomings of the
patriot army. "Some of our military gentlemen have, I fear,
disgraced us," he wrote to Gerry. "It is important that every
anecdote that concerns a man of real merit among them be
improved as far as decency will admit of." [2] This was quite
legitimate, but not so were some of the efforts made to spread
stories of the inhumanity of the British. It was stated, for
example, without any foundation, that they were taking "in-
human pains to propagate" the smallpox among the colonists—
a type of story which has a familiar ring from recent years.[3]
There had been some cases of wanton outrage on the part of
the Hessians on their march through New Jersey, and, although not all the soldiers in the patriot army were above reproach as to property or women, much was made of the enemy
cases for the purpose of arousing the anger of the people. Two
young girls, said to have been ravished, figured prominently
in the newspapers, and handbills were posted telling the

---

[1] *Cf.* W. Trotter, *Instincts of the Herd in Peace and War*, (London, 1921), pp. 216 *ff.*,
et passim.

[2] Austin, *Gerry*, vol. I, p. 114.   [3] *Conn. Courant*, Aug. 12, 1776.

story.[1]   Eventually the usual official report as to the brutality
of the enemy made its appearance, and the results of this Congressional investigation sustaining the stories were spread broad-
cast.[2]   It was falsely reported in Rhode Island that the British
had amused themselves there by digging up dead bodies in the
cemeteries, stripping them of their grave clothes, and leaving
them exposed naked to the public.[3]

On the other hand, the conspicuous humanity of certain
British officers was carefully concealed by the authorities for
fear of its effects.   In October 1776, Sir Guy Carleton took a
number of American prisoners and treated them with such
kindness and courtesy as, in the words of Major Trumbull,
son of the governor of Connecticut, "might have exposed to
great hazard the success of America." [4]   The prisoners, when
released, were warm in their appreciation of the kind treatment
they had received.   Trumbull, fearing that it had made a
"very dangerous impression," hastened to make his report to
General Gates, suggesting "the danger of permitting these
men to have any intercourse with our troops," and accordingly
they were not permitted to land from the boats on Lake George,
but were sent direct to their homes at Skenesborough.   It may
not have been entirely unconnected with the fear expressed
by the Connecticut commander that ten days later a letter
appeared in the *Connecticut Courant*, asking whether Americans "who are millions strong and own near one half the world"
could think of consigning themselves and their posterity "to
the tyranny of such incarnate Demons." [5]   As the people
became more war-weary, the propaganda increased in violence
of appeal.   That by 1781 the people were very weary indeed is
indicated by ample evidence, and there were innumerable
articles and proclamations urging them to one last effort.[6]

All of this propaganda naturally did much to embitter relations between the patriot colonists and the British, as well as

[1] Reprinted in *Conn. Courant*, Dec. 30, 1776.
[2] *E.g., Boston Gazette*, May 26, June 2, 9, 1777.
[3] *Conn. Journal*, Jan. 28, 1778.
[4] *Autobiography of John Trumbull*, (New York, 1841), p. 34.
[5] Issue of Oct. 21, 1776.
[6] *Cf., e.g., Conn. Courant*, July 3, 17, 31, 1781.

to foster many a legend of later times. It also served to give some color of justification in the eyes of many to the atrocious treatment meted out to the Loyalist element in the population — a treatment that, as time went on, had no little of its foundation in a mere desire to plunder the estates of the Tories. The issuing of the Declaration of Independence had drawn the line distinctly between the parties. Thereafter a man had to choose between loyalty to the established and legal government and adherence to the revolution. As we pointed out in the preceding volume, there was much in the Loyalist point of view to appeal to honest and conservative men.[1] Justified on high grounds as the revolution was, we should not lose sight of the fact, in dealing with the period from the contemporary standpoint and before revolt had achieved the sanction of success, that the movement was a revolutionary one, and was carried out at first by a minority, and to a considerable extent by intimidating the unorganized conservative and Loyalist elements.

As soon as the conflict was well under way, voices were raised for even more violent action against all who would not openly declare themselves on the side of revolution. Even before the Declaration was signed, Connecticut had prohibited freedom of speech. The legislature passed a law that any person who, not only by overt act but even in writing or speaking, defamed Congress or the General Assembly of the colony should be tried and, if convicted, fined, disfranchised, or imprisoned, and this law was vigorously enforced.[2] The Committees of Safety took action for disarming the Tories or suspected Tories. In Petersham, for example, Loyalists were required to deliver all their arms to the selectmen; were not allowed to leave town without a pass signed by a majority of the Committee of Correspondence; nor were more than two allowed to meet together for any purpose other than town meeting, public worship, or funerals.[3] In July 1776 it was reported to the Earl of Dartmouth that "the madness of the people . . . is inexpressible";

[1] *Revolutionary New England, 1691–1776*, pp. 447 *ff.*
[2] C. H. Van Tyne, *The Loyalists in the American Revolution*, (New York, 1902), p. 199.
[3] *Conn. Courant*, Sept. 20, 1776.

that many Tories had been obliged to fly for their lives, and those who remained had to conceal their true sentiments.[1]

Letters began to appear in the press calling for the extermination of all Loyalists. "The application of the Halter and Gibbet, I conceive, is the only Remedy that can with safety be relied on" against "this stinking Race," wrote one Connecticut man.[2] Nor was such talk heard only among irresponsible hot-heads. John Adams wrote in 1780 that from the first he had strenuously recommended that "all inimical to the cause" should be fined, imprisoned, or hanged, and that he would have hanged his own brother if he had taken the English side.[3]

Law after law was passed in New England against the Loyalists, and in Massachusetts, in 1776, freedom of speech was drastically suppressed, the legislature enacting that every person who either in public or private discourse should discourage anyone from supporting the Declaration of Independence or even attempt to justify the English position should be fined £50 or go to jail.[4] At the same session it was also enacted that anyone owing allegiance to the state who should give aid or comfort to the enemy by open deed should suffer death.[5]

Efficient machinery was promptly devised for weeding out the Tory element. In Massachusetts it was provided that a meeting of the inhabitants of each town might be called, at which a strong patriot should be chosen as chairman. Any citizen present at the meeting might give in the name of anyone suspected of Tory sympathies and, if a majority present voted affirmatively, the person named was arrested and tried at the next session of court. If convicted, he was shipped as soon as possible, at his own expense, to Europe or the West Indies.[6] Early in 1778 the state passed a law banishing all who refused to take the oath of allegiance to the Revolutionary government. Those refusing were to be put in jail and forty days later deported to some port within British dominions at their own

[1] Ambrose Searle to the Earl, July 25, 1776, Stevens Facsimiles, 2040: 4.
[2] *Conn. Courant*, Sept. 16, 1776.
[3] Quoted by E. Ryerson, *The Loyalists of America*, (Toronto, 1880), vol. II, p. 127.
[4] *Acts and Resolves*, vol. V, p. 612.
[5] *Ibid.*, p. 615.
[6] Van Tyne, *Loyalists*, p. 238.

expense, death without benefit of clergy being the penalty of returning to their homes.[1]   In the earlier stages of the conflict, in all the New England colonies, suspected Tories had been seized and forcibly quartered in new neighborhoods or remote sections.[2]   In September, Massachusetts banished about two hundred and sixty, among whom were many of her most prominent and wealthy citizens, including fifty-three merchants, sixty "esquires," and a good many other "gentlemen," as well as many in lower walks of life.   In the same year New Hampshire also passed a similar act, banishing thirty "gentlemen," eight merchants, four doctors, and others.[3]   Rhode Island took action in 1780 and banished thirty-seven, of whom eighteen were prominent Newport merchants.[4]

The laws regarding the property of the Loyalists show a progressive tendency toward confiscation as the war went on.[5] It had early been recommended by Thomas Paine, the author of *Common Sense*, that the war be financed by the simple method of appropriating the property of all Loyalists, and in 1777 Congress advised the states to confiscate the real and personal property of those who had forfeited "the right to protection."   In time every state did so.   There were protests here and there, citizens in a town meeting at Portsmouth, for example, sending in a remonstrance to the legislature against such an act.   They stated that it was unjust to condemn unheard those who were absent, and that confiscation of property without a trial was "contrary to the principles of civil liberty" for which the colonists were contending.[6]   The rancor against the Loyalists, however, was too strong and the desire to secure their property too great to prevent the acts being passed.   The Massachusetts act made a travesty of justice, in that notification to those proceeded against could be made by publication

[1] Van Tyne, *Loyalists*, p. 239.

[2] *Cf. The Diary of Thomas Vernon*, (Providence, 1881), *passim; Letters and Diaries of John Rowe*, (Boston, 1903), p. 315.

[3] O. G. Hammond, *Tories of New Hampshire in the War of the Revolution*, (Concord, 1917), p. 21.

[4] *R. I. Records*, vol. IX, p. 139.

[5] The best account is that by A. McF. Davis, "The Confiscation Laws of Massachusetts," Col. Soc. Mass., *Publications*, vol. VIII, pp. 50 *ff.*

[6] N. Adams, *Annals of Portsmouth*, (Portsmouth, 1825), p. 269.

in a local newspaper and, when the suit was not contested, trial by jury was done away with. In the cases of all who had been banished or had perforce fled from their homes, their property could thus be taken over without their knowledge and with no opportunity for defense.[1]

That in many cases hostile Tories in some communities had been dangerous to the patriot cause is beyond question, but these were comparatively few as contrasted with the large number of those who could not agree with the revolutionary doctrine and wished merely to live at peace with their neighbors. When Tories were convicted, a large part of the fine went to the informer. Cupidity and frequently personal spite conspired to bring actions against many who were in no wise dangerous and who were at heart no more opposed to the patriot side than many who had given it lip service from fear or policy. When confiscation had become the order of the day, large amounts of money passed to the credit of the states and gave added impetus to denouncing men as Tories. The sales of confiscated estates also afforded opportunity for many to secure coveted lands or pick up bargains. Massachusetts received over £98,000 from the sale of ex-Governor Hutchinson's property alone, and considering that the properties were taken over from enemies and sold to friends, there was probably much undervaluation.[2] Not only were some of the finest estates in all New England thus thrown on the market but, as the Loyalists were in all walks of life, there was no limit to the smallness of the properties which might be seized by the state and which passed into new hands.[3] The total amount of property thus taken over will never be known. The aggregate amount claimed by those who were in a position to appeal to the Commission set up by the British Parliament, which did its work honestly and painstakingly, was over £10,000,000

---

[1] Davis, op. cit., p. 65.

[2] J. H. Stark, The Loyalists of Massachusetts, (Boston, 1910), p. 174. Undervaluation seems clear in the case which has received the most exhaustive examination of any. A. McF. Davis, The Confiscation of John Chandler's Estate, (Boston, 1903), p. 69.

[3] There is wealth of information as to Loyalists of all ranks given by Alex. Fraser in the two volumes of the 2d Report of the Bureau of Archives for the Province of Ontario, (Toronto, 1905).

sterling, of which the Commission disallowed less than £1,000,000.[1] The British Government actually paid compensation to the extent of over £2,000,000, in addition to large sums spent for the benefit of Loyalists who had taken refuge in Nova Scotia and Canada.

In the treaty of peace, the most that the British Government could secure for the benefit of the losers, in what had really been a civil war in the colonies, was a clause that Congress should recommend to the several states a conciliatory policy with reference to them. Unquestionably the fear that newly acquired property rights might be disturbed if the exiled Tories were allowed to return accounts for much of the extreme violence with which any suggestion of lenient treatment was received. "Do not your spirits rise with indignation, your very blood curdle in your veins," wrote one anonymous author in the *Boston Evening Post*, "at the idea of these wretches, whose hands are still smoking with the blood of your slaughtered countrymen, brothers, and fathers, returning to live among you? . . . Can you detach the idea of a robber, and incendiary, or a murderer from one of them?" No method is left, he continues, to prevent the calamity but to unite voluntarily to render their situation such, if they should return, as to make them prefer banishment. "Let it be a crime abhorrent to nature, to have the least intercourse with them. . . . Let them be avoided as persons contaminated with the most deadly plague." He feared that, if this were not done, time might soften the feeling against them and they might be received with humanity.[2]

Town meetings adopted resolutions against permitting their return. Worcester declared with the utmost violence of vituperation that it was inconsistent with "the principles of a free and independent state to admit them ourselves, or to have them forced upon us."[3] So unreasoning was the feeling that

---

[1] Statement of the Claims and Losses, etc., *Parl. Register*, 1790, pp. 623 *f.* *Cf.* J. Eardley-Wilmot, *Historical View of the Commission for Enquiring into the Losses, Services and Claims of the American Loyalists*, (London, 1815) ; and H. E. Egerton, ed., *The Royal Commission on the Losses and Services of American Loyalists*, (Roxburghe Club, 1915).

[2] Issue of April 1, 1783. *Cf.* April 19.

[3] *Worcester Town Records*, (Worcester, 1882), vol. III, p. 443.

Colonel Pickering wrote to Mrs. Higginson that "some there are, indeed, whom the country can never forgive; and, unfortunately, their crimes are imputed to the whole body without distinction. I find it worth a man's popularity to say a word in favor of the most deserving, of characters truly innocent, of men who, instead of injuring, have, during the war, been rendering benefits to this country! For speaking in favor of such, I perceive many good men have this year lost their election in Massachusetts. Dispositions still more violent appear in other states." [1]

It was not only against Tories that public feeling ran high in the first year of peace, and the almost hysterical state of the public mind is indicated also by the violence of expression against the officers of the American army in connection with the "half pay" and "commutation" question. The psychology of the crowd after great wars has certain characteristics, and the year 1783 ran true to type in most unedifying fashion. The pay of the officers, both in itself and as compared with that of the privates, had been notoriously inadequate, even when they received any. As early as 1776 they had asked for an increase, and during the next four years the subject was frequently before Congress in various forms. Great Britain gave her officers half pay for life, and the American officers felt they were entitled to as much. Congress was opposed to such a measure, particularly the representatives of the New England states, the question being largely, as the votes show, a sectional one. As the years went on, the officers became more and more anxious about their financial position and about their future when they should leave the army and have to make a place for themselves once more in civil life. In the earlier months of 1780 there were one hundred and sixty resignations of those who decided they could no longer stand the financial strain. Finally Congress voted half pay to those officers who had served throughout the war, a bonus of a year's pay having earlier been voted to the privates.[2]

---

[1] Pickering, *Timothy Pickering*, vol. I, p. 467.
[2] Hatch, *Administration of the Revolutionary Army*, pp. 71 f. *Cf.* also *A Collection of Papers relative to Half-Pay*, (Boston, 1783).

Congress, however, had made no provision for payment, and in 1782, when it looked as though the army might be disbanded, the officers became yet more uneasy. Congress could pass no appropriation without the consent of nine states, and New England was so parsimoniously opposed to the expense that it seemed doubtful if any such measure could be passed. The pay was much in arrears, the accounts of the officers were not settled, and it appeared as though they would return to civil life, in many cases, with no ready money and without means to support their families. The Massachusetts officers applied to their own legislature for assistance but, although the Council was in favor of granting their plea, the Assembly voted four to one against it.[1] The threatened mutiny of the officers and the "Newburgh Address" belong to the general history of the war rather than to our local account. Congress, whose faith had already been pledged, became alarmed. Finally that body voted to grant the officers five years' full pay in cash or six-percent securities in lieu of the promised half pay for life, and this offer was accepted. Although the representatives of New Hampshire and Rhode Island voted against any grant, enough states voted affirmatively to carry it.

Connecticut and Massachusetts were numbered among these latter, but the measure was intensely unpopular in them. It was claimed that Congress had exceeded its powers and that the grant should be repudiated. The Massachusetts legislature declared that it could not consent to giving Congress the power to levy a tariff because of its action in regard to half pay and commutation. The press teemed for months with scurrilous attacks upon the patriotism and motives of the officers. All the arguments, both for and against allowing them any grant, appeared in much the same terms as in the recent agitation over our own bonus, only in much more violent fashion. In spite of the fortunes made in civil life while the officers had been spending eight years in the harassing service of their country with almost no recompense, it was stated that they were seeking to make themselves into a privileged, aristocratic class at the expense of impoverished widows and orphans. It

[1] Hatch, *op. cit.*, p. 145.

was said that the officers had taken advantage of Congress by threatening that body at a critical moment; that there was "not an officer but what has doubled his interest by the war"; that for every speculator in private life there had been two in the army; that the six-per-cent certificates ought never to be included in any refunding and thus become "of a value exactly proportioned to the services for which they were given." [1]

To perpetuate the associations of the war, the officers had formed an hereditary society, of which Washington was the first president, known as the Cincinnati. Even this came in for a degree of fear and denunciation which it is hard to-day to understand. Nor was the fear confined to the lower classes. Samuel Adams wrote that by such an order the officers "exalted themselves and their Family upon the Ruins of the Common Liberty." [2] It was "an odious hereditary distinction." John Adams considered it "the deepest piece of cunning yet attempted," and wrote that it was "sowing the seeds of all that European courts wished to grow up among us." The wearing of the ribbon which indicated that the wearer or his direct ancestor had fought for the country was "an effectual subversion of our equality," and the formation of the association "an act of sovereignty disposing and creating public rewards presumptuously enterprized by private gentlemen." [3] It was said to be but the first step in the erection of a military despotism. There are aspects of the psychology of the Revolutionary period that seem to belong to the sphere of pathology, so abnormal is the state of mind indicated. Calm and dispassionate observers at the time frequently used the word "phrenzy" to describe the actions of the people, and it appears as though their mental balance, for the time being, had indeed been upset.

Connecticut, in particular, was in a ferment for a year. Town meetings denounced the officers with extraordinary violence. Farmington, for example, after passing a series of denunciatory resolutions as to their services and claims,

[1] Cf., e.g., Conn. Courant, June 17, 24, Aug. 12, Sept. 2, Oct. 14, 1783.
[2] Works, vol. IV, p. 299.
[3] Austin, Gerry, vol. I, pp. 427 f.

threatened open and armed opposition if Congress insisted upon the Commutation Act, and a mob threatened William Judd, who had attempted to collect the bonus for himself and some of his fellow officers. Other towns followed suit and representatives from twenty-eight met in convention at Middletown.

At length the agitation died down, but in no other controversy of the period was more bitterness engendered. In none other were the arguments used on so low a plane or more calculated to appeal to the most sordid passions of the populace. Technically, 1783 was the year of peace, but in no year of the war was the passion of the people so aroused against both their enemies and their defenders. In the press, the town meetings, and the state legislatures, the dominant note was passionate prejudice, not reason, and both controversies left abiding marks. That concerning the Tories affected the social relations of every town and village, and that concerning the officers affected the people's attitude toward the powers of a central government. Peace had come, but it had come to a people embittered by suffering. Society had been shaken to its foundations, and to a great extent had lost the conservatives who had served as a balance wheel. There had been an overturn of the old ruling elements, and intense bitterness had been engendered between the new groups and classes which had emerged.

In some respects the stress of war and its experiences undoubtedly broadened the minds of many. On the other hand, both reading and education appear to have declined. At first the booksellers' advertisements continued, but for the years 1780 to 1784 there was not a single offering of books in the *Boston Evening Post*, with the exception of one colonial library which was offered for sale at auction.[1] In 1782 a Hartford bookseller advertised *Tom Jones*, *Roderick Random*, *Humphrey Clinker*, Pope's *Essay on Man*, *Paradise Lost*, Watts' *Psalms*, Chesterfield's *Letters*, the *Rambler*, and a volume of plays among other items. Politics rather than belles-lettres, however, occupied the thoughts of the reading public, though that they occasionally roamed in other fields is indicated by an amusing

[1] *Boston Evening Post, passim*, and July 19, 1783.

juxtaposition in the above lists of *Thoughts on Liberty*, *Ditto*, *on Adultery*.[1] Some hardy spirit, nevertheless, conceiving that it was time someone came forward to retrieve the situation, advertised in the same year that he intended, were sufficient encouragement shown, to start a new weekly magazine to relieve "the emaciated visage of the true science — the pallid gloom with which the face of literature is overcast, and the rapid advances of a fatal consumption on the vitals of substantial virtue."[2] Unfortunately there is no evidence that he succeeded. Practically all of the reading matter, beyond sermons and political pamphlets, had been imported from England before the war, and with the opening of hostilities importations naturally ceased on any commercial scale. All sorts of goods were indeed smuggled in, but books evidently were not, either because they did not lend themselves easily to this form of import or because there was no market. The new war-rich are rarely cultivated persons and the professional and middle classes were suffering too severely to warrant much expenditure for literature.

Now and then we get a glimpse of the arts. The general New England opinion was probably voiced by "A Member of the General Court" when he classes "painters, (particularly inside house, miniature, and portrait painters)," hairdressers, tavernkeepers, musicians, stage players, buffoons, and exhibitors of birds and puppets as among the unprofitable laborers in the state, because the labors of most of them "exist no longer than the sound which they make is heard, or the sight of them is present."[3]

Of all the arts, music apparently made the most popular appeal in New England, and even in the midst of the war we find advertisements at Hartford of violins, flutes, hautboys, French horns, clarinets, bassoons, psalteries, pipes and tabors, and other instruments, as well as music for them. There was also the advertisement of a gentleman who gave lessons in

[1] *Conn. Courant*, Feb. 5, 1782.
[2] *Boston Evening Post*, March 16, 1782.
[3] *National Arithmetick or Observations on the Finances of the Commonwealth of Massachusetts*, (Boston), [1786], p. 21.

"the composition of music." [1] In Boston, in 1782, William Selby, whose activities on behalf of music in New England would seem to deserve more investigation than has been accorded to them, proposed to "the friends of music and the fine arts" to publish monthly the *New Minstrel*. Each number was to have at least one composition for the harpsichord, piano, or spinet, one for the guitar, one for the flute, one song in French, two in English, and an essay on musical expression. Selby hopefully believed that "with a nation," as he somewhat enigmatically expressed it, "far gone in politeness and the fine arts, even the stern patriot and lover of his country's glory, might be addressed on the present subject with not less propriety than the man of elegance and taste." [2] However, the patriots did not seem to be keenly interested in their country's artistic glory. The centre of culture by this time had shifted from Massachusetts to Connecticut, but as Governor Trumbull remarked in final conclusion, when trying to dissuade his son from becoming an artist, "Connecticut is not Athens." "With this pithy remark," wrote the unconverted son, "he bowed and withdrew and never more opened his lips upon the subject." [3] The arts had been valued only by a cultivated minority, and that minority lost a large part of its numbers and many of its most cultivated members in Boston, Newport, and elsewhere when the Tories fled the country.

In the matter of schools and public education there were conflicting tendencies. The poverty and taxation incident to the war resulted, in many rural sections, in the abandonment of schools or the curtailment of school terms. The first school-law passed in Massachusetts during or subsequent to the Revolution — that of 1789 — was a step backward in educational ideals, and indicates how far short the older laws had come from being complied with. Under the new law, towns of at least fifty families were required to support an English school for only six months in the year instead of the entire twelve; and only towns of two hundred families, instead of one hundred

[1] *Conn. Courant*, Feb. 3, 1777.
[2] *Boston Evening Post*, Feb. 2, 1782.
[3] *Autobiography of John Trumbull*, op. cit., p. 89.

as under the old law, were required to support a grammar
school at any time.   This did away with the obligation on the
part of one hundred and twenty towns out of a total of two
hundred and thirty.[1] This same period, nevertheless, marks
the second beginning of the important "academy" movement,
and from it date the two Phillips Academies, those at Andover,
Massachusetts (1778) and at Exeter, New Hampshire (1781).
Four members of the Phillips family contributed $85,000 to
the two institutions, which became the model for many other
later ones in the Northern states.[2]

Although Harvard was able to continue at Cambridge, the
students of Yale were forced to scatter, "Tutor Dwight"
taking some of them to Wethersfield and Professor Story others
to Glastonbury, with the arrangement that President Daggett
should "visit the different classes as often as he could with
convenience."   On the other hand, a medical department
was added to Harvard in 1782, and the first law school in
America was established at Litchfield, Connecticut, in 1784,
by Judge Tappan Reeve.   A new era was also beginning in
American textbooks; for in 1783 Noah Webster published his
spelling book, and Jedediah Morse his geography in the year
after.   Of the former, fifty million copies were to be sold, in
time, establishing many American spellings and pronunciations.
In one important respect the Revolutionary period marked a
great advance, and after the war a distinct forward movement
took place in the education of girls.   In no place in New
England had there been schools for them above the very lowest
grades, with the one exception of Portsmouth, but after peace
a number were founded and several private schools for boys
were made coeducational.

In many places, during the struggle, churches as well as
schools had had to be closed for lack of funds.   The Episcopalians, perhaps, emerged from the war in the most forlorn
condition of all the sects.   Owing to the close connection of the
Church with England and the fact that a number of the clergy

---

[1] E. G. Dexter, *History of Education in the United States*, (New York, 1922),
pp. 80 ff.; E. E. Brown, *The Making of Our Middle Schools*, (New York, 1921), p. 216.
[2] Brown, *op. cit.*, pp. 192 ff.

were Loyalists, the Church suffered greatly. At the end there were only two parishes left in Maine, two in New Hampshire; and of the fourteen churches in Massachusetts apparently only five had clergymen in 1787. Of the four churches in Rhode Island, one was burned and one was abandoned by the rector. Of the twenty clergy in Connecticut, only fourteen remained.[1]

The established Congregational churches, in spite of their privileged position, also felt the strain greatly. In Hampshire and Berkshire Counties of western Massachusetts, for example, whereas thirty-three towns had ministers throughout the Revolution, thirty-nine had none. In 1779 a motion was laid before the General Association in Connecticut regarding the "dark aspect upon our churches in the discouragement lying upon the candidates entering into the ministry, and the present distress and difficulties of them that are already in office, from whence we fear that these churches may be left without lights in the candlestick," and asking that an address might be made to the government and people to save the churches from ruin.[2]

Besides the purely financial difficulties from which the clergy suffered with others, — such as decrease in income, the depreciation of paper money, and payment in kind, — infidelity and indifference were making rapid inroads among their congregations. As we pointed out in the earlier volume, their position of absolute and acknowledged authority had been undermined steadily for several decades. War, as usual, had brought a complete overturn in the minds of many. Deistic ideas had been introduced by contacts with English officers and soldiers in the Seven Years' War, and now the French were supposed to have played the same part in unbalancing orthodox beliefs. In 1784 Ethan Allan published his deistic work, *Reason the only Oracle of Man*,[3] a crude, coarsely written book, which was more a sign of the times than any great influence in itself. He attacked the clergy, denied the existence of the

[1] *The Religious History of New England*, (Harvard University Press, 1917), pp. 228 ff.
[2] Quoted by E. F. Humphrey, *Nationalism and Religion in America, 1774–1789*, (Boston, 1924), p. 352.
[3] *Reason the only Oracle of Man, or a compendious System of Natural Religion*, (Bennington, 1784).

Devil and the imputation of sin from Adam's fall, and claimed, on the other hand, that "to construe or spiritualize the Bible is the same as to inspire it over again, by the judgment, fancy, or enthusiasm of men." [1]

Apart from the inroads of freethinking, however, there was a distinct weakening of the old bigotry and narrow-mindedness on the part of multitudes, although the Revolutionary period did little, in the way of legal enactments, for the cause of toleration. From the very beginning of the struggle with England, the Baptists under the lead of Isaac Backus had seen an opportunity of securing religious as well as political freedom for the people. As early as 1774 they made an effort — without success — to obtain action from the Continental Congress, and they continued the contest in Massachusetts without a halt. Although they did not succeed in even getting materially better terms written into the constitution of 1780, the publicity they gave to the cause of toleration was not without effect. That a more tolerant attitude was becoming general among the clergy of the established church in that state is indicated clearly by the fact that, in the convention for the discussion of the Federal Constitution in 1787, of a number of clergymen who were delegates, all defended the absence of any religious test, as against the complaints of some of the lay members.[2]

In Connecticut more progress was made than in Massachusetts. In 1777 an act was passed exempting "Separates" from paying taxes for the support of ministers of the established order provided they could prove that they supported their own form of worship. Isaac Holly, who petitioned and wrote against this as insufficient, enlarged on the inconsistency between fighting for civil liberty from England and refusing spiritual liberty to fellow citizens.[3] Even within the established church there was a demand for broader views, and in the "Act for

---

[1] *Reason the only Oracle of Man, or a compendius System of Natural Religion*, pp. 469, 378, 385, 446.

[2] J. Elliott, *Debates in the State Conventions*, (Philadelphia, n. d.), vol. II, pp. 118, 120, 148.

[3] M. L. Greene, *Development of Religious Liberty in Connecticut*, (Boston, 1905), p. 335.

securing the Rights of Conscience in Matters of Religion to Christians of every Denomination," in 1784, the Saybrook Platform was abandoned; all Christians were permitted to attend their own form of worship; were exempted from contribution to the state church; and their congregations were given the same privileges with respect to supporting their ministers and their houses of worship as were those of the Congregational church. Those persons who attended and supported no church were still taxed for the established one.[1] This, indeed, was far from complete toleration, and the fight was to continue for several generations before that was achieved, but the Revolution, with its ferment of thought and insistence upon liberty and freedom, undoubtedly did much to advance the cause. The controversy had ceased to be so much theological as moral and political. The prevailing opinion, outside of Rhode Island, was that the state could not live without the aid of religion, and that if the question of support were left without obligation by the state, it would prove inadequate.

The decline in morals was, indeed, alarming to the older generation, although we need note only two changes which called at the time for much comment and condemnation. Intemperance had always been common in Puritan New England as well as in the South, and even the clergy drank heavily at religious meetings. The hardships, uncertainties, and rapid pace of living during the war seem to have increased this vice, and in the last year of hostilities Massachusetts, while trying to "win the war," had no less than sixty distilleries in operation, exceeding all the other states combined.[2] Both the Bay State and Rhode Island passed laws in 1777 against distilling from grains, but it is noteworthy that the reason given was not the possible harm from liquors but the danger of making grain too scarce for food.[3]

That sensitive barometer, the manners of the young people, which has given rise to so much discussion since the recent

---

[1] V. Stauffer, *New England and the Bavarian Illuminati*, (Col. Univ. Studies, 1918), p. 60.
[2] Bishop, *Manufactures*, vol. II, p. 30.
[3] *Acts and Resolves*, vol. V, p. 731; *R. I. Records*, vol. VIII, p. 357.

Great War, fell rapidly. Indeed, such a condition may be considered as one of the characteristics of post-war periods. The absence of the heads of many families, resulting in lessened control, the excitement attending the military struggle, the changed standards introduced by the war-rich with neither manners nor traditions, and other factors all combine to bring about such a decline. During the Revolution these influences were accentuated, perhaps, by the closing of many of the schools and churches. The Reverend Joseph Strong of Norwich, who preached at New London just after the war, often spoke afterward of the conduct of the young people there at that time. Before the beginning of service there was loud talking between the pews; during it there was so much whispering and moving about that he could scarcely continue; and as soon as the blessing was pronounced the place was in an uproar. Boys and girls called to each other across the church, joked and laughed, and stampeded from the building. Before he had reached his lodging the boys were already playing ball and pitching quoits.[1]

The lack of manners and the loss of control by the elder generation in 1783 are evident when we compare that scene with the staid churchgoing before the war. A few years later in Salem, the Reverend Mr. Bentley, speaking of the young women of that town in the class from which he was considering taking a wife, remarked that the "circles in which the young ladies drank tea were not friendly to the suitable decorum required of the sex, from the want of a guard upon their youthful spirits, and that a wantoness had ensued, which discovered itself in the street by such language as curse you &c." To his horror, he discovered — or thought he had — that the maiden of his choice "in company of her sex did behave disorderly, and use prophane and obscene language . . . common only to sailors."[2]

A new social order and a new outlook upon life were coming into being. In the previous volume I attempted to show, in tracing the history of the preceding half-century, that it is a mistake to consider the Revolution as merely a military struggle to

[1] Caulkins, *New London*, p. 573.
[2] *Diary of William Bentley*, (Essex Institute, 1905), vol. I, p. 118.

decide the political question of the relation of the colonies to the mother country administratively. It is also a mistake to think of the patriots as having simply left their shops and farms for military service and returning to them unchanged when the fight was won. The old order was gone for good by the time they came back to their families and firesides, and a new order, intellectual, social, and political, had begun to form.

CHAPTER IV

THE REVOLUTIONARY GOVERNMENTS

Character of State Governments — New Constitutions — Conflict of Ideas between Classes — Quarrel between Vermont and New York — Vermont Becomes an Independent State — Intrigues with the British

EVERY ordered society of necessity operates within a framework of established law and government, and before continuing our story we must pause to investigate what this framework was during the stormy years of war in New England. As we have already seen, the patriot party had secured control of the established government by peaceable or forcible means in all four colonies by the summer of 1775.[1] In the two corporate colonies of Rhode Island and Connecticut the problem was a simple one on account of the nature of the charter governments which they had always enjoyed. In Massachusetts and New Hampshire, however, where the governors had hitherto been royal appointees, there were complications, and during the travail of war a fifth New England state, Vermont, was born and had to erect the foundations of a wholly new government. In all five the people faced the problem of how to pass from a colonial status within an empire to that of free and independent states. It was as such that they considered themselves during the war, and the formation of a Federal government was still far in the future and out of most men's thoughts. The Continental Congress was not in any sense a federal bond of union, but rather a working committee for the coördination of military effort, and was considered as being composed of representatives of sovereign commonwealths.

[1] Adams, *Revolutionary New England, 1691-1776*, p. 433.

The Declaration of Independence and the casting off of the yoke of the imperial government had left the peoples of the colonies free to determine on any new form of government which they might wish. The crisis of the beginning of hostilities, however, left little time for constitution-making, and for the first few years government was necessarily carried on in somewhat makeshift fashion. In Connecticut and Rhode Island the legislatures and all the officials — with a few minor exceptions such as judges of vice-admiralty, king's attorney, and so on — had been elected by the people under the old charters. So far as the machinery of government was concerned, both colonies had long been virtually independent. In Rhode Island the governor happened to be a Loyalist, but with his prompt deposition no further change was needful. At the May session of the legislature in 1776 it was enacted that thereafter "the Governor and Company of the English Colony of Rhode Island and Providence Plantations" should be substituted for the name and authority of the king in all writs, commissions, and other public papers; and by this simple change the entire transformation of the constitution was effected.[1] In the autumn of the following year a committee was appointed to "form a plan of government," but nothing more is heard of its work.[2]

In Connecticut the transition was equally simple, but gave rise later to discussion as to whether in reality the state possessed a legal constitution or not. In October 1776, the legislature, with no special mandate from the people for that purpose, passed an act that the charter should "be and remain the civil Constitution of this State," and that "the Republic is, and shall forever be and remain, a free, sovereign, and independent State." [3] Even before the end of the war, however, the point was raised as to whether the charter had not been abrogated by the fact that the colony had made war against England, and whether, therefore, the declaration by the legislature reëstablishing it was not extra-legal, however useful it

[1] R. I. Records, vol. VII, pp. 522 f.
[2] Ibid., vol. VIII, p. 304.
[3] Conn. State Records, vol. I, pp. 3 f.

might have been as a temporary expedient. Both this questioning of the legality of the constitutional basis of the state
and the demand for a constitution which should be submitted
to the people for ratification belong to a later period. They
arose not from an overniceness as to legal technicalities, but
from a desire for changes in the constitution itself. As a
matter of fact, in spite of the loud-trumpeted revolutionary
doctrine that all power resided in the people and that government could derive its sanction only from them, none of the
state constitutions made during the war received that sanction.

In the two most independent commonwealths, as we have
just seen, the existing legislatures themselves decreed what the
constitutions should be. That of Connecticut throws considerable light on what was the real political faith of those who
were dealing in the glittering generalities of the doctrines of
natural rights and the sovereignty of the people. The governor
had no power to adjourn or prorogue the legislature, no veto
on their acts, no pardoning power over criminals, and his
patronage was of the slightest. Practically all real power lay
in the legislature, composed of the Council and the lower
house or Assembly. The only check on its will had been the
royal disallowance of laws, and this was removed by the Revolution. The Assembly consisted of two hundred representatives,
which was nearly three times the number in New York, although the population of the two states was practically the
same. The Council — not counting the governor and lieutenant-governor, who sat ex-officio — consisted of only twelve
men, elected from the state at large. It represented the ruling
class and was the entrenched bulwark of wealth, conservatism,
and the established Congregational church. Long in possession
of the supreme power in the colony, the peculiar method of its
election made it almost a self-perpetuating body. In the
September town meetings every freeman might write down a
list of twenty nominees — the freemen, of course, being but a
fraction of the adult males. These nominations were sent to
the legislature, and the twenty receiving the highest number of
votes were listed as candidates. It was always arranged,
however, so that the existing members or ex-members of the

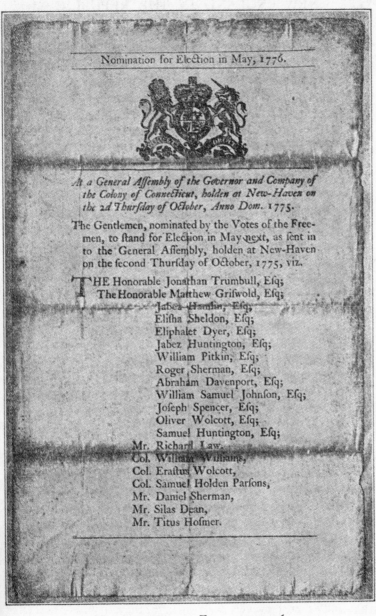

At a General Affembly of the Governor and Company of the Colony of Connecticut, holden at New-Haven on the 2d Thurfday of October, Anno Dom. 1775.

The Gentlemen, nominated by the Votes of the Freemen, to ftand for Election in May next, as fent in to the General Affembly, holden at New-Haven on the fecond Thurfday of October, 1775, viz.

THE Honorable Jonathan Trumbull, Efq;
    The Honorable Matthew Grifwold, Efq;
        Jabez Hamlin, Efq;
        Elifha Sheldon, Efq;
        Eliphalet Dyer, Efq;
        Jabez Huntington, Efq;
        William Pitkin, Efq;
        Roger Sherman, Efq;
        Abraham Davenport, Efq;
        William Samuel Johnfon, Efq;
        Jofeph Spencer, Efq;
        Oliver Wolcott, Efq;
        Samuel Huntington, Efq;
    Mr. Richard Law,
    Col. William Williams,
    Col. Erastus Wolcott,
    Col. Samuel Holden Parfons,
    Mr. Daniel Sherman,
    Mr. Silas Dean,
    Mr. Titus Hofmer.

NOMINATIONS FOR ELECTION, 1776
Library of Congress

Council stood first on the list, regardless of the number of votes cast for them by the "people." At the election the freeman was given twelve slips of paper only. The names of all the candidates were read, and the voter dropped his paper in the ballot box for the candidates in order. Should he wish to vote for a new man, therefore, he had to retain one of his slips until after the first twelve had been voted for; and to do so under the eyes of the minister and those men of wealth and prominence in his community who wanted the first twelve elected and to whose good opinion the voter's welfare might be much beholden.[1]

It would take a very determined innovator indeed, under the conditions of the time, thus publicly to flout the social, moneyed, and ecclesiastical magnates of his community. As the controlling majority within the Council itself consisted of only seven men, and as that body, in turn, controlled the appointment of every judge and justice of the peace, the real grip held by wealth, social position, and the church on the life of the state can readily be seen. The revolt against England had a just basis, but for the leaders to stir the people to that revolt by instilling the doctrines of the equality of all men and the sovereignty of "the people," when they themselves controlled that same people by such an adroitly handled piece of political machinery as the above, seems a little less than candid.

New Hampshire was the first of the thirteen colonies to draft and adopt a wholly new constitution during the war. In answer to the suggestion of Congress to "call a full and free representation of the people" to establish such government as might be necessary, the Provincial Convention, then in session at Exeter, voted that electors for that purpose must possess real estate of the value of £20, and candidates must have holdings of a value of £300.[2] They prepared a constitution providing for a government by one legislative chamber only, and without an executive. When the newly elected members of that body met, however, early in 1776, they themselves elected

---

[1] *Cf.* R. J. Purcell, *Connecticut in Transition*, (Washington, 1918), chap. v.
[2] J. Belknap, *History of New Hampshire*, (Dover, 1812), vol. II, p. 305.

an upper house or Council composed of twelve members. The jealousy of executive power was still in evidence, and no provision was made for a governor in the brief constitution which they drew up. The two houses performed all executive functions when in session, and during adjournment the affairs of the state were carried on by a Committee of Safety, the president of the Council, Meshech Weare, being also president of the Committee. In 1778 the legislature called a special convention for the sole purpose of drawing up a constitution, thus establishing a precedent even earlier than Massachusetts, which has often claimed the honor. The constitution, however, was badly drawn and was promptly rejected by the towns. A second effort was made in 1781, but the proposed instrument was again voted down, as being too conservative. A third attempt, the following year, was no more successful.[1] In June 1784 a fourth convention met and adopted a form which included a governor and a legislature of two houses, the judiciary to be appointed by the executive. The judges, however, were removable for misconduct, by the Governor and Council, on application by both legislative houses. A notable advance was the provision that gave the franchise to all males of twenty-one years and upward who paid a poll tax and had resided two years in their towns. This constitution went into effect in June 1784.

Although New Hampshire had been the first state to adopt a constitution, however imperfect, its neighbor Massachusetts, oddly enough, was the last. Throughout almost all the war, government in that state was carried on by the General Court (without a governor), Committees of Safety, and the town meetings. As in Connecticut and Rhode Island, the colonial charter was considered as still being in effect, but as both governor and lieutenant-governor under that instrument had been royal appointees, there were difficulties in the way which did not obtain in the corporate colonies. The executive powers belonging to those officials were taken over by the Council. Various changes had to be introduced into procedure from time

[1] Allan Nevins, *The American States during and after the Revolution, 1775–1789,* (New York, 1924), p. 183.

to time, but with true English instinct these were made to appear as little revolutionary as possible.

For five years the state was governed as nearly as might be under the forms of the old charter, but the steady trend of public opinion was in favor of organizing the government upon a more permanent basis. As early as 1776 demands had been heard for ignoring the charter and forming an entirely new constitution. The simplest expression of the situation, perhaps, is to be found in the memorial presented to the General Court by the town of Pittsfield in that year. This stated that, owing to the dissolution of the power of Great Britain, America was in a "state of nature," and that "the people are the fountain of power." [1] Indeed, as was the case in the questions raised as to the legality of the government under the Connecticut charter, there can be no doubt that, though as far as possible the form of legality was adhered to, in reality the government was a revolutionary one, to which the people tacitly submitted in part but which derived no direct sanction from them.

The assumption of power by the General Court in 1775 had been generally acquiesced in, but not entirely so. The Council, in lieu of a governor as executive, had reorganized the courts and appointed judges, but these were not always recognized by the people, particularly in the western counties. This was notably the case in Berkshire, where no state courts were allowed to sit, and where government was largely resolved into town meetings. The freemen at the Pittsfield meeting appointed five judges themselves. The Lee meeting voted that they would "obey the laws of this state" and support the civil authority "for the term of one year" — a curious annual grant! [2] On the other hand, Great Barrington voted that, "not having a new constitution and other reasons," the laws of the state should not operate in that town, which thus, in part, seceded from the commonwealth. Ashfield considered that "each town is invested with a native authority to chuse"

---

[1] H. A. Cushing, *History of the Transition from Provincial to Commonwealth Government in Massachusetts*, (Col. Univ. Studies, 1896), p. 198.

[2] L. A. Frothingham, *Brief History of the Constitution and Government of Massachusetts*, (Harvard Univ. Press, 1916), p. 19.

its own judges, except for murder cases! Why "native authority" should have stopped at that precise point is not made
clear, but apparently natural law provided that in such cases
eleven men from eleven towns should be chosen annually to
"jug [sic] and condemn such murderers," the era of judging and
acquitting being reserved for our own more enlightened times![1]
These men of the back-country and small villages applied the
generalities and theories uttered so glibly by radical revolutionaries, such as Samuel Adams, with a literalness that was
disconcerting. In May 1776, for example, the so-called "Con-
stitutionalist Party" in Berkshire wrote to the General Court
saying, bluntly but quite truly, "we have heard much of government being founded on compact: What compact has been
formed as the foundation of government in this Province?"[2]
Many towns agitated the matter of a new constitution,
although the majority of them either were apathetic or were too
much taken up with prosecuting the war to trouble about the
problem. In 1776 the Assembly recommended to the two
hundred and fifty towns of the state that they should vote on
the question as to whether the General Court should draw up
and enact a constitution, and whether it should be submitted
to the people for examination before ratification by the Assembly. Only ninety-seven towns responded, but of these seventy-
four were in favor of the proposition, Boston being among
those opposed. The work of the Assembly, sitting as a con-
stituent convention, was slow, but at length a constitution
was drafted and ready for submission on the fourth of March,
1778.[3] Copies were forwarded to the selectmen of each town,
who were to submit the document to the voters at town meeting
and transmit the action taken. It was decisive, for the proposed constitution was defeated by a vote of ten thousand
against two thousand.
One of the main objections was the absence of any bill of
rights. The knotty point of representation was a particularly

<hr>

[1] *Ibid.*, pp. 19 *f.*
[2] Cited by S. B. Harding, *The Contest over the Ratification of the Federal Constitution
in Massachusetts*, (New York, 1896), p. 4.
[3] Cushing, *op. cit.*, pp. 207 *ff.*

difficult one, the maritime towns thinking the proposed plan made it too nearly equal, whereas the others thought it would be too unequal. Both in town meetings and in the press the matter was thoroughly canvassed. No examination of the question was more interesting or more influential than the findings of a convention of representatives of the towns of Essex County, who met at Ipswich in April. The extremely adverse opinion reached by them was published in a pamphlet, known as the "Essex Result," and in that form was probably the work of Theophilus Parsons of Newburyport.[1]

Throughout all the public discussions of the times we can detect the growing antagonism between those with property and those without, the beginnings of which we have already traced in the preceding volume. The leaders of the revolutionary movement had preached doctrines of the most radical tendency, but most of them drew back from putting them into practice in the internal affairs of their states. The rights of man might be discharged in a fusillade against the British Parliament, but the ruling classes among the patriots had no intention of allowing them to be discharged against themselves by the "lower classes" of their own communities. That was quite a different matter. The leaders loudly proclaimed to George the Third that the people were the sole source of power, and that all men were created free and equal, but when it came to maintaining the existing order of society at home and protecting property rights they displayed no little circumlocution and casuistry in defining their doctrines so as safely to denature them. The writer of the "Essex Result" assented to the propositions — as indeed it would have taken a bold man not to do during the war — that "all men are born equally free," that each man has certain alienable and inalienable rights, and that all are bound to obey only those laws to which they have given their consent.[2] Theophilus Parsons, John Lowell, and the others who had agreed upon the "Result," however, evidently believed that property required to be protected by property-owners, and that the common man, however "equal"

---

[1] Text in T. Parsons, *Memoir of Theophilus Parsons*, (Boston, 1859), pp. 358–402.
[2] *Ibid.*, pp. 365 f.

he might be with the capitalist as a theoretical source of power when being urged to enlist in the army, could not be trusted to exercise that power in civil life. They said, indeed, that "among the bulk of the people, we shall find the greatest share of political honesty, probity, and a regard for the interest of the whole, of which they compose the majority." Nevertheless, in spite of this sop to the Demos, they added that, for wisdom, firmness, and consistency, it is necessary to look to the "men of education and property," and to them should be entrusted the task of drawing up a constitution and subsequently of enacting under it such laws as related to property.[1]

They thus drew a distinction between laws affecting persons and those affecting property, considering that in the passage of the former a consent of a majority of the members of the commonwealth should be obtained, but, as just stated, that in making the latter only property-owners should participate; otherwise, those who made the laws might "give and grant what is not theirs," and such laws would be but a "second Stamp Act." [2] An elaborate machinery was devised to secure a proper "representation" of "property," and the scheme is interesting as showing how, even during the war waged ostensibly for the rights of the individual, the rights of "property" — that is, of course, of the property-owning class — were still uppermost. There is found, naturally, an utter absence of any thought that all men might have rights in property as a social product, regardless of whether they had been able to secure any for themselves in the unequal struggle.

The decisive defeat of the proposed constitution did not halt the discussion and the demand for some such instrument. In 1779, in response to a favorable vote in town meetings on the questions submitted by the General Court as to whether a new constitution was desired, and if so, whether a convention should be called for the sole purpose of framing one, the Court requested the election of delegates from "the several Towns and Places," the number of delegates to be the same as were sent to the Court. It is noteworthy, however, that the electorate was enlarged for this purpose and every freeman of twenty-one

<hr/>

[1] *Ibid.*, pp. 369 f. [2] *Ibid.*, p. 371.

years or more was allowed to vote. The same resolution called for the submission to the people of the constitution when drafted, and that it must be approved, to be accepted, by "at least two-thirds of those, who are free and twenty-one years of age, belonging to this State, and present in the several town-meetings." [1] The convention thus derived its authority solely from the people and was in no way dependent upon the General Court.

The convention held three sessions at intervals, and finished its work in March 1780. A committee appointed to draft the document delegated the task to a smaller one, which, in turn, entrusted the work almost wholly to John Adams.[2] He sailed for Europe in November, and his work was subsequently amended without his presence by a comparatively small number of convention members, the attendance having been greatly reduced by the severe weather of that winter. His able draft was a compromise, and secured the support of the "Essex Junto" and, in Boston, of men of such varying views as James Bowdoin and Samuel Adams.

A complicated method was adopted for its ratification by the people. It was provided that the proposed constitution be discussed in town meetings, every meeting to vote on it, clause by clause, stating their objections, if any. The "people," understood in the above sense, were then to grant to an adjourned convention power to tabulate the votes, ratify the constitution if two thirds of the town-meeting votes favored it, or to amend it if two thirds of the popular vote were not in favor of any particular part of it. In the existing condition of government in the state, the towns, as Dr. Morison says, "were, in fact, the several sovereigns of Massachusetts Bay; their relation to the General Court closely approximated that of the states to the Congress"; only instead of thirteen there were about three hundred.[3]

The difficulty of judging conditions from contemporary

[1] By far the best account of the adoption of the new constitution is that given by S. E. Morison, "The Struggle over the Adoption of the Constitution of Massachusetts, 1780," Mass. Hist. Soc., *Proceedings*, 1917, pp. 353-411.

[2] John Adams, *Works*, vol. I, p. 288.

[3] Morison, *op. cit.*, p. 360.

printed sources is exemplified in this case.   The text of the
constitution was not published in any of the six newspapers;
there was little controversial matter relating to it in any of
their columns, and but two pamphlets appear to have been
brought out regarding it.   Nevertheless, in spite of this apparent public apathy, the returns from the towns show that there
was a vigorous discussion going on and that keen interest was
taken.   Massachusetts proper had then a population of about
three hundred and seven thousand.   If we assume that one
fifth of these were males over twenty-one, then the actual
number voting at the meetings, sixteen thousand, would represent a little more than one in four of those who were entitled to
vote.   In the province of Maine much less interest was shown,
and out of a total population of over fifty-five thousand less
than five hundred voted.   In Biddeford, with a population of
over a thousand, but half a score cast any ballots — though this
saving remnant appended to their report to the convention the
note that "ten men may save a city." [1]

The discussion and opposition centred mainly about the
third article of the Bill of Rights, which practically made Con-
gregationalism the state religion.   The article was a step backward even from the condition theretofore existing with regard
to that church and entrenched it beyond the reach of ordinary
legislation.   Members of dissenting sects, who had been free
from taxation for religious purposes, were now to be taxed, with
the privilege of paying the taxes to ministers of their own sects.
Those minorities, however, who could not afford a pastor were
obliged to contribute to the Congregational church, and new
denominations which came in after 1780 had to maintain expensive lawsuits to obtain recognition as sects in the meaning of
the constitution.   The attack on this clause, and the fight for
religious liberty, was led by the Baptists under the leadership
of Isaac Backus, the Baptist leader of his state and the historian of the sect.   Those who were thus fighting for freedom
of conscience and the separation of Church and State — which
fight has not even yet been wholly won in Massachusetts
— were described by one of their adversaries in the *Independent*

[1] *Ibid.*, p. 366 and *note.*

Ledger at the time as a "junto, composed of disguised Tories, British emissaries, profane and licentious Deists, avaricious Worldlings, disaffected Sectaries, and furious blind bigots" — an unsavory lot of red herrings, indeed, to be drawn across the trail by the members of the established church, who were either disingenuous or blinder bigots than those they accused. Unfortunately the reformers failed, the Congregational church won, and the reactionary clause was written into the constitution.

The basis of representation was another point that gave much trouble. The convention proposed to allow each town one representative for every two hundred and twenty-five members over the first one hundred and fifty, but this would have made a house of unwieldy size. Various plans were suggested, and the western parts of the state were particularly active in opposition. The favorite remedy of that section was to go back to the old system of allowing every town one member, a few two, and Boston four. The dispute was mainly one between the rival interests of the agricultural west and the mercantile east, this point coming out frankly in the protests of two towns, one of which claimed that "the Landage [*sic*] Intrest have not a Proper Weight," and the other that the inland towns ought to have as great representation as the "Marchantile Towns."[1]

The proposed constitution provided that the property qualification for those voting for state officials should be doubled as compared with that under the old charter, and this brought out much opposition. The convention defended this change in terms which have been called a "gratuitous insult to the unpropertied classes"; but in spite of the fact that all freemen over twenty-one could vote on the question, it was carried by two thirds. There was some fear, as was shown in the "Essex Result," that persons without property might not show a due respect for its protection; but, on the other hand, in the protests of various towns it was brought out that the polls were as much in need of protection as was property. This proved to be the case, for under the new constitution the proportion which the poll tax bore to the total amount levied rose from thirty

[1] Quoted by Morison, *op. cit.*, p. 388.

per cent in 1778 to forty per cent in 1786, the year of Shays's Rebellion.

There is no need to specify all the objections raised by one section or another. The returns were received by the convention in June, and the work of tabulating them began. At the start, such a system was adopted as ensured arbitrarily, from its operation, a two-thirds vote in favor of all the clauses, regardless of the actual vote.[1] The members of the convention then voted that the people had accepted the constitution. Dr. Morison, who has made a more careful examination of the facts than anyone else, states that "it is difficult to avoid the conclusion that there was not a two-thirds majority for at least two articles . . . and that the Convention deliberately juggled the returns in order to make it appear that there was." Every article did, however, receive at least a bare majority, and the need for some constitution was so overwhelming that the convention may have been justified in its disingenuous and illegal action, though it is difficult to see why it could not have altered the two articles which had been voted down by the people.

While the four original New England colonies were thus adjusting themselves to the new conditions created by the war, a quite different situation confronted the inhabitants of the northwestern part of that section, which was known as the "New Hampshire Grants." Large numbers of people had settled to the west of the Connecticut River and north of the Massachusetts line, largely on grants derived from New Hampshire. The title to the territory had long been in dispute between that colony and New York, and the governors of the latter had claimed the right to re-grant land, although censured by the English Government for doing so.[2] By an order in Council, 1764, the country in question as far east as the Connecticut River had been adjudged as part of New York, but without intention of upsetting existing titles already derived from New Hampshire.[3] In no other colony, however, in the colonial period was corruption more rampant than in that at

---

[1] Morison, *op. cit.*, pp. 396 *ff.*, where the reader may find the details of the juggling.
[2] Hiland Hall, *The History of Vermont*, (Albany, 1868), pp. 88 *f.*, 105 *ff.*
[3] B. H. Hall, *History of Eastern Vermont*, (New York, 1858), p. 130.

the mouth of the Hudson, and the wealthy land-speculating clique, in collusion with royal governors, continued to disregard the rights of the inhabitants of the Grants as well as of those squatters who, technically, had no rights, and the unhappy settlers had been constantly embroiled for many years before the Revolution broke.

The great majority of the people seem to have been opposed to New York control on both economic and political grounds. The Grants contained the most typical frontier elements to be found in all New England, with the independent and democratic qualities which we find in such societies. On the other hand, both the government and the social structure of the Hudson River colony were peculiarly aristocratic and monopolistic. In the remote sections on both sides of the Green Mountains the settlers had in the beginning managed their own affairs, and any new control imposed from outside would naturally prove irksome. The efforts of the cliques and land sharks from the west to take away their lands or impose rents greatly strengthened the opposition to the attempted rule of New York, although there was a smaller party in favor of that colony. This was composed of those holding New York titles to their lands or having other economic ties to the west, and of some conservatives who wished a stronger government control. All the colonies were split into parties at this period, Tories and Patriots, seaboard and back-country, rich and poor, mercantile and farming — and it is a mistake to think of the people of any of them as forming a unit. The most that can be said is that strong majorities secured and retained control. In the Grants the two parties for and against New York added a conflict of interest which appeared nowhere else, and which at one time threatened civil war. Always during those years it distracted the counsels of the people.

The conflict appeared at once when the question came up of responding to the call for delegates to the Provincial Congress at New York City. Delegates were elected and sent from some of the towns, notably Guilford, which voted in 1775 to remain under the administration of New York. On the other hand, Ethan Allen and his followers were strongly opposed to any recognition of that colony's rights until such time as "the lives and property" of the inhabitants could be secured under its government.[1] There was no power in New York, under the conditions of the beginning of the war, to enforce its claims, and it was hoped that possibly the new revolutionary government set up there might withdraw pretensions to the settled lands. This proved to be fallacious. The interests claiming the lands were in control both of the convention at New York and of the delegation to Congress. Moreover, since there could be no appeal from the new government to England, even that possible hope was cut off. If the settlers submitted to New York and had their cases tried by New York courts, there was no chance of escape for any save those who held by New York titles.

Meanwhile the settlers were governing themselves by committees and conventions. The Committees of Safety in the first year of the war collected taxes, acted as courts in civil and criminal cases, and were practically all the government that existed. On January 31, 1775, however, a convention of twenty-five towns west of the mountains, including Bennington, was held at Manchester. After reciting the acts of the New York government, including certain acts of outlawry against specified Vermonters, the convention voted that the inhabitants could no "longer subsist in such anarchical Circumstances" nor maintain the political connection with New York without "effectual Measures among Ourselves." They proceeded to depose from office all of the officials appointed from New York. It was distinctly stated that there was no intention of interfering with the sheriff of Albany County, in which the towns were included, save in cases relating to lands and riots, but in those all men were prohibited from assisting him, at their peril. The officers of the "Green Mountain Boys" were ordered to see that the soldiers were provided each with "a good Firelock, and Ball or Buck-Shot answerable, and a good Tomahawk," and be ready to enforce the convention.[2]

[1] Hall, *Eastern Vermont*, p. 244.
[2] *Records of the Governor and Council of the State of Vermont*, (Montpelier, 1874), vol. II, pp. 491 *ff.*

Just a year later, representatives from practically the same towns met again, at Dorset, to consider, among other questions, whether they should "associate with New York, or by themselves, in the cause of America," and whether or not to send an agent to the Continental Congress. The latter action was approved, and agents were appointed to carry a remonstrance and petition to that body.[1] In July the convention met once more to receive the report of its agents. The presentation of the petition had been opposed by the New York delegates but had been acted upon by Congress, which body, however, merely passed a resolution recommending the petitioners to submit to the neighboring state without prejudice to their land claims.[2] Heman Allen, one of the agents, reported, nevertheless, that he had had talks with many of the representatives in Congress, who advised that the people of the Grants should do all possible to repel the British but not to submit to New York.[3] In the convention the first steps were taken to form a separate jurisdiction for the Grants, and on January 15, 1777, at an adjourned meeting, a declaration was adopted with only one dissenting vote, proclaiming that the territory usually known as the New Hampshire Grants should thereafter forever be an independent state under the name of New Connecticut.[4] A few months later the name was changed to Vermont (Green Mountain), as it was found that a settlement on the Susquehanna River had already chosen the first one.

The Vermont Declaration of Independence was at once transmitted to Congress at Philadelphia, where, of course, it was strongly opposed by New York. A number of the representatives, however, including such men as Samuel Adams and Roger Sherman, approved of the reasons for the separation of the new state. Congress, throughout the war, was rather between the devil and the deep sea in the matter, for a decision would have antagonized either the powerful state of New York

---

[1] *Records of the Governor and Council of the State of Vermont*, (Montpelier, 1874), vol. I, pp. 11 f., 16 f.; *Vermont State Papers*, (Middlebury, 1823), pp. 61 ff.

[2] *Records of Governor and Council*, vol. I, p. 20.

[3] *Ibid.*, vol. I, pp. 18 f.

[4] *Ibid.*, vol. I, pp. 38 ff., 463 f.

or the population of the Grants, who formed a buffer against the British on the northern frontier.   This reason, as well as press of more important business, resulted in putting off any decision until after the war.   Meanwhile, the government of Vermont, without recognition from Congress of its authority, had to defend itself against the claims of New York and the insurgent minority of "Yorkers" within its own borders, and fight the common enemy as well.   It is impossible in our limited space to trace the complicated story in all its ramifications.

In the application to Congress the petitioners had noted, among other points, that New York had recently completed a new constitution which, should it be put into execution in Vermont, would force the people there to oppose it by every means in their power.[1]   As showing the difference in feeling between the two states, we may call attention to some of the features of this constitution, made while the people were fighting for the doctrinaire rights of man.   The governor and senators — the latter serving four-year terms — were to be elected by only such freeholders as possessed estates of a value of £100 over and above all debts, thus disfranchising all of the population who did not own real estate of that value, including not only all artisans, laborers, many shopkeepers and petty merchants, but even most of the smaller farmers.   The governor and four senators composed a "Council of Appointment" which appointed practically all the civil and military officials in the state, and these held their offices during the pleasure of the appointing Council.   It is obvious that this was a constitution devised in the sole interest of the large landowners, and that the great majority of the people would have under it no voice in the election of the governor and the upper house or in the selection of officials.   It was as far removed as possible from the democratic ideas of such a frontier community as Vermont.

That state adopted its own constitution in 1777, copying to a great extent that of Pennsylvania, including Benjamin Franklin's idea of a single legislative chamber.   It went beyond the

[1] *Records of Governor and Council*, vol. I, p. 50.

Pennsylvania model, however, in a number of respects, and more than any other state constitution adopted at that time endeavored to make practical application of the generalities which the other states and the Declaration of Independence had left in the air.[1] Beginning as usual with the stock phrases that "all men are born equally free and independent" and have certain inalienable rights, it alone went on logically to prohibit slavery.   Moreover, there was no property qualification whatever provided for the suffrage, the governor and legislators being elected by all males of twenty-one years and upward "of a quiet and peaceable behaviour."   Although some of the features had later to be amended, the constitution worked well and was a model in democratic practice for the other states. Its liberality is noteworthy when compared with the theories or practical politics of Massachusetts, New York, or even Connecticut.

New Hampshire was favorable to the setting up of the new state, and in correspondence the previous year its governor had practically acknowledged Vermont to be a sovereign entity. In most cases those entrusted with its destinies handled the extremely complicated and delicate situation with consummate skill, but a blunder was made in 1778 which threatened serious results.   Sixteen towns on the east side of the Connecticut River, within the limits of New Hampshire, applied for admission to the new state and were accorded it.   Far remote from the seaboard and in sympathy with their neighbors just across the river, their action does not seem strange.   New Hampshire, however, naturally objected to this lopping off of a considerable portion of her territory and population, and her former friendliness turned to hostility.   Complaints were made to Congress and finally, having seen their tactical error, the Vermont authorities cancelled the whole transaction in 1779.[2]   Later, however, not only was part of New Hampshire again incorporated but also some of the towns on the western border, well within New York.   It is difficult to say whether these actions represented the wisdom of the serpent in providing

---

[1] *Records of Governor and Council*, vol. I, pp. 83 *ff.*
[2] *Ibid.*, vol. I, pp. 405 *ff.*

Vermont with pawns in her game with Congress or not.   In any case, after that body in 1782 had guaranteed New Hampshire and New York their territories within certain limits, these were accepted by the Vermonters, and the eastern and western unions were again dissolved.[1]

Much mystery hangs over many of the transactions in connection with the establishment of the fourteenth state, and it is not clear whether the claim which Massachusetts set up to the title of a portion of the southeast section of Vermont — which further complicated matters — was made in good faith or only to offset those of New York and New Hampshire and prevent the absorption of the Green Mountain state by them.[2]   With the temporary hostility of New Hampshire, with Massachusetts making her new claim, with the main quarrel with New York complicated by the strife between independents and "Yorkers" within the state itself, with Congress playing a waiting game, and with the British on the borders, the way of the leaders in Vermont was assuredly beset with difficulty and required wary walking.   Not only did the representatives of New York do all that was possible to prevent Vermont's claim to independence from being recognized in Congress, but occasionally a back-fire was set up in the new state itself.   In 1779, for example, ten towns petitioned Congress to restore to them the rights of which they had been unjustly deprived by the "usurped government" of the Vermonters, stating that a majority in some towns and a respectable minority in others in Cumberland County were in favor of government by New York.[3]

In September a resolution was unanimously passed in Congress which declared that the disputes between the four northern states had "risen so high as to endanger the internal peace of the United States," and that New Hampshire, Massachusetts, and New York should pass laws authorizing Congress to determine the questions of disputed boundaries.[4]   Vermont's

[1] *Ibid.*, vol. II, pp. 277 *ff.*, 379 *f.*
[2] *Ibid.*, vol. II, pp. 193 *ff.*
[3] Hall, *Eastern Vermont*, p. 358.
[4] *Records of Governor and Council*, vol. II, pp. 183 *ff.*

side of the case was brought before the public by Stephen R. Bradley in a pamphlet entitled Vermont's *Appeal to the Candid and Impartial World*, and the following year Ethan Allen and Jonas Fay published their *Concise Refutation* of the claims of the other states.[1] The authorizing laws requested by Congress were not passed, and that body, both from press of other business and the fear of burning its fingers, continued to procrastinate and came to no determination in the matter. The issue had become deeply involved with the larger one of the western lands of some of the states forming the union, which was then one of the main political questions of the day.

The situation of the revolting Vermonters, however, was critical. Some of the leaders, such as Ethan Allen, had been outlawed by New York, and they had large estates to lose should Vermont ever be forced back under the government of that state. The property interests at stake for those who had favored independence were large. The "Onion River Land Company," in which four of the five stockholders were members of the Allen family, held title to over three hundred thousand acres, comprising the greater part of eleven townships, and the Allens had other extensive holdings.[2] Should the United States win the war against England, the new nation would be strong enough to compel the obedience of Vermont to its orders, and the result of all the struggle against both New York and the British might then be that the majority of Vermonters would lose their lands, and the leaders face ruin. The state had done its full share in fighting the common enemy, but the other states would give her no assurance that when the war ended she would not be in a far worse position than when it began.

It was this situation that forced some of the leaders into the intrigues with the British to which we must now turn. The enemy had early seen the possible advantage of fishing in the troubled waters of the New Hampshire Grants, and of using the land controversy as a means of securing the allegiance of the people. It is true that in December 1778 Chief Justice

---

[1] Both are reprinted in *Records of Governor and Council*, vol. II.
[2] J. F. McLaughlin, *Matthew Lyon*, (New York, 1900), p. 81.

William Smith, a New York Tory, wrote to the Earl of Carlisle that since his earlier letter he had come to despair of getting Vermont to go over to the British side, but in that same month Sir Henry Clinton was still hopeful.[1] Describing Ethan Allen as "an infamous character," he thought that he might be "made usefull to Government by giving him and his Adherents the property of all the Lands appropriated to Rebels and making that Country a Separate Government dependent on the Crown and Laws of Great Britain." [2] There is certainly much mystery surrounding the whole question of the confiscations of the Tory estates, and the secret records of the Court of Confiscation have never been allowed to see the light. In 1785 Matthew Lyon, who was one of those in the plot, was impeached by the Vermont legislature in connection with these records, but when it was hinted that their production would not only upset land titles but blast reputations, the prosecution was suddenly and completely dropped.[3]

Throughout the intrigue, Ira Allen seems to have been the leader and the one who would have been willing to go the furthest. Both he and his brothers Levi and Ethan were at times suspected of disloyalty to the American cause. Indeed, when family passions ran high, they did not hesitate to accuse each other. Early in 1779 a quarrel between Ethan and Levi was in full swing, and Ethan attempted to appropriate Levi's property by having him declared an enemy to the state. Levi's loyalty at that time was vouched for in testimonials by such men as Oliver Wolcott, and later Ethan denied that he thought his brother an absolute traitor, though with characteristic emphasis and profanity, he said, "God d—— his luke warm soul." [4] The family seems to have been a hot-tempered, boastful, swashbuckling sort, carving fortunes for themselves out of the frontier.

The position of such men as the Allens, who had their whole stake in the country and for whom the unjust and illegal policy

---

[1] Stevens Facsimiles, 109: 1.
[2] *Ibid.*, 549: 2.
[3] McLaughlin, *Matthew Lyon*, p. 179.
[4] Many documents in this controversy are given in the *Conn. Courant*, April 24, 1779.

of New York spelled ruin, was in truth a difficult one. The action of those who had revolted and thrown off the government of New York was quite as justified as was that of all the colonists in throwing off the government of Great Britain. If there was a large body in the Grants who were opposed to such a revolt, so also was there a large body in all the colonies opposed to the revolt against England. All of the other states considered themselves as sovereign bodies, wholly independent of one another, united only in the loosest of bonds for the temporary and specific purpose of carrying on the war. Vermont naturally considered herself in the same light, and if Congress refused to acknowledge that independence, Vermonters could hardly be considered "traitors" should they protect themselves and secure better terms from the British than from the Americans. The whole problem was how best to preserve independence and property. Everything points to the belief on the part of the small group of intriguers that their negotiations with the enemy would in time bring about recognition by Congress, but if it had not done so, there is no reason to think that they would have hesitated to remain within the empire, had their property and practical independence been safeguarded. This point of view, however, was not shared by the people of the state at large.

Negotiations appear to have been opened first through Colonel Beverly Robinson, a Loyalist in New York and a confidant of Sir Henry Clinton. In March 1780 he wrote to Ethan Allen, stating that he believed a large number in Vermont would be willing to help bring America back to the empire, and that if the people of that state would return to their allegiance, they could probably secure terms which would enable them to set up a separate government, of which Allen and his friends would be given the management.[1]

This letter was not received by Allen until July or August, when he at once communicated the contents to Governor Chittenden and some close friends, who decided it best to return no answer. Correspondence, however, was begun with the British General Haldimand for the exchange of prisoners, and

[1] *Records of Governor and Council*, vol. II, pp. 397 ff.

a temporary truce on the northern frontier of New York as well as Vermont. Ira Allen and Joseph Fay were appointed commissioners from Vermont to meet the British commissioners for this purpose, and did so in October. It seems to be unquestionable that they were also, on both sides, to consider confidentially the further question of the possibility of Vermont's returning to the allegiance of Great Britain, provided the independence of every other colony was acknowledged. Haldimand's instructions to his agents embraced that point and referred to information previously received as to the likelihood of Vermont's accepting the terms.[1] Washington had been informed by Chittenden of the proposed negotiation so far as the prisoners were concerned, but not as to the other matter.

In October, Captain Justice Sherwood, on behalf of Haldimand, had had an interview with Ethan Allen within the American lines at Castleton. His business was ostensibly the exchange of the prisoners, but on a walk before breakfast alone with Allen he opened the real object of his visit. He told Allen that he had a matter of importance to divulge, but that before he did so he must ask him to give his word of honor that no advantage should be taken of him and that the subject should be mentioned to no one else while he remained in the country. Allen replied that he would give the required pledges, provided "it was no damned Arnold Plan, to sell his Country and his own Honour by betraying the Trust reposed in him." [2] Sherwood replied that this was not the case, but that General Haldimand was fully aware of the difficulties between Vermont and Congress, that he believed Congress was merely duping the Vermonters "and waited for a favorable opportunity to crush them and that this was a proper time for them to cast off the Congress Yoke and resume their former allegiance to the King of Great Britain, by doing which they would secure to themselves those Privileges they had so long contended for with New York." Allen answered, according to the English negotiator, that "the Proposals so far as they concerned his Personal

---

[1] *Ibid.*, pp. 402 f.
[2] Sherwood's Journal of an Expedition to Negotiate with Vermont, October 1780. Mss. in Canadian Archives, fol. 44.

Promotion had not the weight of a straw with him, that he was not to be purchased at any rate . . . but that the Proposals seemed naturally to concern the whole Body of Vermont whose Liberties and Properties for a Number of Years past were much dearer to him than his own life, he would take them into very serious consideration." [1]

Later Allen told Sherwood that he would send Colonel Ira Allen and Major Fay, ostensibly on the cartel business, and that he would open the other to them, but that "I must not," wrote Sherwood, "communicate to them the whole of our conversation, must be very cautious not to exhibit the smallest Idea to them, of anything than neutrality, nor even that to take place except Congress forced them to it." [2] Finally the agent summed up the results of his several conferences as follows: "General Allen says he finds himself surrounded with Enemies on every side, the most inveterate in New York — that, he is heartily weary of war, and wishes once more to enjoy the sweets of Peace and devote himself to his philosophical studies, that, he is sincerely attached to the liberties of America, and cannot cherish the remotest thought of bearing Arms against his Country, while intuously [?] contending for liberty; and that nothing (short of the same tyrannical proceedings of Congress towards Vermont, which Congress at first complained of suffering from Great Britain, and the manifest appearance of the total subvention of the Liberties and Properties of many thousands of honest people now inhabitants of Vermont) should ever induce him to Harbour the most distant Idea of deviating from the Cause he has been so long engaged in, and for which he has been so great a sufferer — and was he ever so much inclined to take part with Great Britain it is not in his power to do it at present — for in the first place should he now make a declaration of this nature, his own people would cut off his head, but allowing he could reconcile them to such a plan, they are by no means able to defend themselves, nor is Genl. Haldimand at present able to send a force sufficient to protect

[1] Sherwood's Journal of an Expedition to Negotiate with Vermont, October 1780. Mss. in Canadian Archives, fols. 45 f.
[2] Ibid., fol. 47.

them."[1]   He added, however, that as he was persuaded Congress would never recognize Vermont but was in favor of New York, he would publish shortly, with the assistance of the governor and council, a manifesto stating the tyrannical proceedings of Congress, the necessity Vermont was under of declaring herself a neutral Power, and inviting all peoples to trade with her.

Allen said that he expected, as a result of such a proclamation, that Congress would raise a force against him, in which case he would seize Albany, and that many would rise to join him, particularly from western Massachusetts. Help would then be asked from Canada, and it would be well for Haldimand to have troops ready to march. Allen would expect to command his own forces, Vermont would have to be declared by the British free of any other province in America, entitled to choose all her own civil officers, and all land titles from New Hampshire would have to be freed from any claims of New York. He added that a revolution of this sort would be a work of time before the people could be brought around to it.[2]   The negotiations were to be continued secretly with the understanding that if Congress should recognize the independence of Vermont and grant her a seat in that body, they would come to an end. Although further conferences were planned between Sherwood, Ira Allen, and Fay, they had to be abandoned until spring on account of the weather.

In February of the next year, 1781, Allen received another letter from Robinson on the same subject, and sent both this and the earlier one to the President of Congress. In transmitting them, he said truly that they were the only ones he had ever received from Robinson, but made no mention of the far more serious direct negotiations with the British army, his evident purpose being, by an apparent display of candor, to allay the strong suspicions that had been aroused as to the loyalty of the Vermont leaders.[3]   He did say, however, that in view of her situation Vermont had an indubitable right to make her own terms with Great Britain.

[1] *Ibid.*, fols. 48 *f.*
[2] *Ibid.*, fols. 49–51.
[3] *Records of Governor and Council*, vol. II, pp. 406 *ff.*

In May, Ira Allen again met the British commissioners, at Isle aux Noix, for the ostensible purpose of arranging the cartel for exchange of prisoners. Little that was new came of this conference. Allen told the British that Governor Chittenden and a majority of the leading men were in favor of neutrality but dared not make a separate peace with England until the people had been brought around further.[1] Allen's "dark and intricate manner of proceeding," as the British commissioner termed it, puzzled and offended that gentleman not a little.[2] Allen alleged that the Vermonters "hate Congress like the D——l, and have not yet a very good opinion of Britain," which led Sherwood not much further in the "perplexing and muffling business."[3] He told Allen that it looked very much as though he had come merely for the purpose of frightening Congress on the one hand and negotiating away the proper season for a campaign for the British on the other.[4]

Allen spun the negotiation along, telling Sherwood that nothing could be done until a new Assembly met, and suggesting sending new commissioners in July. He added that the most that could be done would be to have the Vermonters declare neutrality during the war, after which they would have to be subject to the winning power, but that if that power should not give them a free charter, they would "retire to the Mountains, turn Savages, and fight the D—— and hell and Human Nature."[5] Sherwood said that Haldimand had too much sense to treat such talk as that with anything but contempt. The conference lasted a little more than two weeks, and in the course of it Allen agreed to instill the idea of reunion with Britain into the people as far as possible, and stated that "he and his Family have large fortunes which they do not intend to lose, if there is a possibility of saving them. At all

[1] Letter of John Sherwood to Captain Mathews, May 8, 1781. Mss. in Canadian Archives, fol. 18.

[2] Same to same, May 11, *ibid.*, fol. 23.

[3] *Ibid.*, fols. 24 *f.*

[4] Same to same, May 11, (second letter), *ibid.*, fols. 26 *ff.*

[5] Journal of Sherwood, Isle aux Noix, May 1781. Mss. in Canadian Archives, fol. 6. Reprinted for the most part, but not entire, in *Records of Governor and Council*, vol. II, pp. 409 *ff.*

risks, he is determined that Congress shall not have the parceling of his Lands to their avaricious Minions." [1]

Ira Allen was always blunter than the rest of the intriguers, and in this statement we probably have the exact truth of the matter, from his standpoint at least. The Allens and others in the conspiracy had large financial interests at stake. They intended to safeguard these and their own dominant position, and the destinies of the state, so far as they could sway them, were subservient to these ends. On the other hand, it ought to be pointed out that there was as yet no national feeling in America and no loyalty to a Federal Union to be compromised. The attitude of the other thirteen states, moreover, certainly did not call for any loyalty to them. The Union asked everything from Vermont in the way of support, and yet would concede her nothing and promise her nothing. It is impossible now to probe the motives of all the group of Vermont leaders who were in the intrigue. When Ira Allen declared on his honor that he preferred union with Great Britain and implicated Ethan in that statement, he may or may not have been telling the truth. Neither of the brothers paid much attention to that when it served their purpose to ignore it. When Allen said bluntly that what he was after was at all costs to save his property, he was probably nearer the truth than at any other time in the negotiations. The delay in these had by now irritated Haldimand and he wrote to Sherwood, through his secretary, that unless something definite could be had all communication should cease.[2] His attitude throughout had been perfectly open and honorable. He had no authority, he said, to make a Treaty of Neutrality, and Vermont would either have to unite with Great Britain or remain at enmity with her.

Meanwhile the Vermont Assembly was becoming uneasy at the persistent rumors of negotiations with the enemy, for, in spite of the small number of persons in the plot, it was a matter of general suspicion throughout all the colonies. In June an inquiry was resolved upon in the legislature, and both the governor and Ira Allen were interrogated. Allen concealed

---

[1] *Records of Governor and Council*, vol. II, p. 414.
[2] *Ibid.*, vol. II, p. 421.

his dealings, convinced the legislature that there was nothing afoot, and must have blushed, had he been capable of it, when complimented by them "for his open and candid conduct." [1] Negotiations were continued through the summer, and various incidents tended to keep suspicion alive also.

General John Stark, who had been ordered by Washington to assume command of the northern department, wrote to Governor Chittenden that, although the people of Vermont were zealously devoted to the American cause, there were reasonable suppositions that there were lurking traitors. These, he said, should be severely punished as soon as discovered, evidently wholly unaware that the very official to whom he was writing was himself concerned in the intrigue.

Allen continued during the rest of the war to negotiate with Haldimand, and even in July 1782, eight months after the surrender of Cornwallis, he wrote that it would be advisable for Haldimand to send agents into New York and the New England provinces to induce as many Loyalists as possible to settle in Vermont, and to get as many of the principal men in New England as he could to buy tracts of land on the Vermont frontier so as to engage their interest. Finally the news of peace in 1783 brought the negotiation to an end, although Congress had taken no action, and the fate of Vermont as an independent commonwealth still remained unsettled.

[1] *Records of Governor and Council*, vol. II, p. 427.

CHAPTER V

GROWING UNREST

Dispute between Connecticut and Pennsylvania — Western Land Claims — Effect of Peace on Business — Relations with England — West India Trade — State Tariffs — English Competition — Financial Crisis — Federal Impost — Rhode Island Paper Money — Resumption of Specie Payment — Debts and Taxes — Increasing Violence

As early as March 1776 John Adams had written to General Gates that "the success of this war depends on a skilful steerage of the political vessel. The difficulty lies in forming particular constitutions for particular colonies, and a continental constitution for the whole. . . . Thirteen colonies, under such a form as Connecticut, or one not quite so popular, leagued together in a faithful confederacy, might bid defiance against all the potentates of Europe." [1] Adams at this time looked upon the various colonies as separate nations, wholly independent of one another, as, indeed, did practically all the leaders of thought and the people generally.

New England, partly from geographical position and partly from the old Puritan notion of a chosen people, has always been particularistic and sectional in its views. The voice that gave expression to a national outlook was heard from the South. Even there, however, Patrick Henry's impassioned utterance in 1774 met with but little response. "Where are your landmarks, your boundaries of colonies? The distinctions between Virginians, Pennsylvanians, New Yorkers, and New Englanders are no more. I am not a Virginian, but an American," he thundered; but instead of the distinctions between colonies

---

[1] *Works*, vol. I, p. 207.

growing less as the years of war continued, they became, in some respects, more marked and bitter.

In the last chapter we followed in brief outline the contest between the people of the New Hampshire Grants and New York, threatening war between that colony and the nascent state of Vermont, with Massachusetts and New Hampshire participants in the dispute. At the same time Connecticut and Pennsylvania were in armed conflict and war was portended between them also. We have already noted the activities of the Susquehanna Company, which had been organized to exploit certain lands on the river of that name to which they laid claim in Pennsylvania.[1] The dangerous course pursued by this company had split the people of Connecticut into two parties, one insisting that the charter extended to the "South Sea," — that is, three thousand miles westward to the Pacific, — and the other accepting the limits of the New York boundary. The question was purely one of economic exploitation, those interested in the company speculation wishing to have the colonial government enforce their claims to the lands, whereas the other party, foreseeing much trouble, some danger, and certain expense, wished to have the government steer clear of the whole matter.

In 1774 the legislature had reversed its former attitude and come to the support of the company by declaring Connecticut's title valid, and by making the new settlements part of the County of Litchfield. This action followed upon a conference between commissioners sent from Connecticut to Governor Penn, to endeavor to arrange a temporary adjustment of the dispute by agreeing to a provisional boundary line for administration. Penn, denying that the Connecticut claim had any validity, declined to do this and insisted that the Connecticut intruders evacuate the territory entirely until a legal decision could be obtained.[2] It was claimed that there were then nearly two thousand Connecticut emigrants in the Valley. The controversy not only continued between the two governments but resulted in bloody encounters in the disputed territory itself. On

[1] Adams, *Revolutionary New England, 1691–1776*, pp. 204, 217, 260, 282, 413.
[2] O. J. Harvey, *A History of Wilkes-Barre*, (Wilkes-Barre, 1909), vol. II, pp. 779 *f.*

September 28, 1775, some of the Yankees were attacked by a force of "Pennamites," who outnumbered them five to one and who broke up one of the Connecticut settlements.[1] The Pennsylvania Assembly resolved to lay the matter before Congress, asking the aid of the body to prevent further encroachment by the Yankees until the controversy should be settled by the King and Council. Governor Trumbull of Connecticut also wrote to Congress, asking them to find some means to quiet the dispute until the more important matter of the war with England should have been terminated. Congress, however, dodged the issue, as in the case of New York and Vermont, and merely resolved in November that the assemblies of both colonies should be asked to take steps to prevent hostilities between their citizens.

The following month war again broke out in the Wyoming region, and on Christmas Day occurred the Battle of Rampart Rocks, in which the Yankees got the best of the Pennamites.[2] About a year later the Connecticut legislature passed an act erecting the town of Westmoreland in Pennsylvania — which had formerly been made a part of Litchfield County, as just stated — into a separate county by itself. Neither Pennsylvania nor Connecticut, owing partly to the dispute over jurisdiction, was able properly to protect the settlers against the British, and on July 3, 1778 the settlements were wiped out in an attack by British and Indians under Major John Butler.[3] Hundreds of the inhabitants were never heard of again after the "Wyoming Massacre," although some of them straggled back from time to time to retake possession of their ruined homes.

Meanwhile, Congress had made slow progress with the plan for a Confederation. It was not until November 1777, by which time it had lost some of its ablest members and much of the confidence of its constituents, that it was ready to offer a definite plan to be accepted by the several states. The details of the development and nature of the Articles of Confederation belong to the domain of national rather than sectional history,

[1] *Ibid.*, vol. II, p. 843.
[2] *Ibid.*, vol. II, pp. 859 ff.
[3] *Ibid.*, vol. II, pp. 954 ff.; Pickering, *Timothy Pickering*, vol. II, pp. 221 ff.

and we are here interested in their adoption merely with reference to local interests. One of the most difficult points in dispute in drafting the Articles — the question of weight of votes of the large as compared with the small states — was decided, after much discussion, on the basis of equal representation. The long delay in ratification, however, was not due to this but to the question of the claims to western lands, such as those set up by Connecticut and Massachusetts. These two were the only New England colonies involved, the other important claimants being New York and Virginia.

These western lands were deemed of great potential value, and it was thought that the states possessing them could rapidly pay off their share of the cost of the war by disposing of them to settlers, leaving the smaller states which had no such claims, such as Rhode Island, New Jersey, Delaware, and Maryland, heavily burdened with debts and taxes, and thus likely to lose their inhabitants to the larger colonies which held the west. It was felt that those latter colonies would not have been able to make their claim good had it not been for the common efforts of all in winning the war, and that therefore they should relinquish their claims to the states as united in the Confederacy, for the common benefit of all. Rhode Island, it may be noted in view of her later recalcitrancy as to the Federal constitution, agreed to signing the Confederation within a few months, but it was not until after Connecticut, New York, and Virginia had taken steps to cede their claims to the general government that Maryland signed the Articles in March 1781, and that the Confederation went into effect.[1]

One of the articles provided that Congress should have power to appoint courts of arbitration to settle boundary disputes between the states, and Pennsylvania promptly asked for an adjudication of the Susquehanna dispute with Connecticut. The court met at Trenton, and in January 1783 handed down a decision that all the lands claimed by Connecticut in the Susquehanna region belonged to Pennsylvania.[2] This settled

[1] Cf. H. B. Adams, *Maryland's Influence upon Land Cessions to the United States*, (Johns Hopkins Univ. Studies, 1885), *passim.*

[2] *Journals of Continental Congress*, vol. XXIV, pp. 6 ff., 31.

the matter, though James Madison noted that "the delegates from Connecticut were more captious on the occasion than was consistent with a perfect acquiescence." [1] The court did not, however, determine the larger question of the state's claim to western territory, and Madison probably had this in mind when he said that "in a national view it is not perhaps advisable to invalidate the title of this State, however defective it may be, until a more important controversy is terminated." [2] It was evidently felt that it might be well, in case Connecticut could be induced to cede her western lands to the confederated states, that her title to them should not be called in question. She did finally surrender her claims to the Federal government, though not until 1786, and received as compensation, six years later, a tract of about five hundred thousand acres, known as the "Western Reserve of Connecticut," in what is now northeastern Ohio. The year of the cession marked almost the lowest ebb of the power of the Confederation, and it was felt by many that Connecticut had taken advantage of the situation to get a clear title to a definite tract of land in exchange for a highly questionable one to the somewhat absurd strip sixty miles wide and three thousand miles long. Washington wrote that to his mind the compromise was a disadvantageous one for the Union and that might had triumphed over right. In Congress it was said that the advocates of the plan urged its adoption because "the claim of a powerful state, although unsupported by right, was, under the circumstances, a disagreeable thing." [3]

Toward the end of the war, the situation as regarded Vermont had made no advance, and Congress was more hostile than ever to her pretensions of independence. At the session of November 1782, Madison noted that the temper of that body "was less favorable than on any preceding one." [4] The belief was gaining ground rapidly — for reasons given in the last chapter — that leading Vermonters were traitors and should be

---

[1] *Writings*, Gaillard Hunt, ed., (New York, 1900), vol. I, p. 303.
[2] *Ibid.*, pp. 261 *ff.*
[3] Washington, *Writings*, (Ford), vol. XI, p. 44 and *note*.
[4] *Writings*, vol. I, p. 261.

taken into custody.[1] Rhode Island alone stood by the new state, though it was openly hinted in Congress that this was because of interests in certain lands. By February 1783, however, there seems to have been a more conciliatory spirit, and it was said that both Washington and the principal men in New England supported Vermont's pretensions.[2]

The political situation in New England when peace was signed at Paris, September 3, 1783, may be briefly summarized. New Hampshire had a new and untried constitution. That of Massachusetts, adopted three years before, was especially designed to favor the lawyers and merchants and "directed toward something like quarter-deck efficiency in government, and the protection of property against democratic pirates."[3] Rhode Island was acting under its old charter, but was torn by the ravages of war and the British occupation. Connecticut was split into parties, and the legal validity of her constitution had been questioned. Vermont was acting the part of an independent state, but her claims were nowhere recognized. It was under these conditions as to government that the great economic and social forces let loose by the war and the changes following peace had to be guided and controlled.

With the coming of peace, the commercial life of New England had to be built up anew. Army contracts and privateering ceased abruptly. Even before the treaty was signed, the mercantile firm of Thurston & Jenkins of Rhode Island wrote to their correspondents that "the full confidence all Ranks of People puts in this News of Peace has stagnated Business exceedingly."[4] A few months later Samuel A. Otis of Boston, the wealthy merchant whom we have noted as handling large government contracts, was bankrupt. The transition from war to peace is always difficult, but in New England after the Revolution it was peculiarly so, as it necessitated fundamental changes in almost all her commerce. The great empires of that day laid stress upon trade rather than the political relations

---

[1] *Writings*, vol. I, p. 276.
[2] *Ibid.*, pp. 276, 281, 292, 356.
[3] S. E. Morison, *The Maritime History of Massachusetts*, (Boston, 1921), p. 28.
[4] *R. I. Commerce*, vol. II, p. 172.

between colonies and mother country. By the signing of the treaty of peace and the acknowledgment of the independence of the United States, the former colonies ceased to be integral parts of a great trade system and became simply a foreign nation. The "mercantile theory" of empire was not confined to the English, but was the common doctrine of the times, even among the vast majority of the American colonists. It was not strange, therefore, that as soon as the war was over France annulled such decrees as had given us special privileges while serving as her ally, and that Spain closed many of her ports to our ships.

According to contemporary doctrine, the policy adopted by the British Government can only be considered as liberal with reference to the United States, whatever may be thought of its wisdom from her own standpoint. We have had frequent occasion to note in the earlier volumes that our colonial forefathers often showed the natural human inclination to eat their cake and have it too, to retain all the advantages of being integral parts of an empire while acting as though they were independent of it when such action suited their desires or purses. Now that they had seceded they seemed to think that they were still entitled to the trading privileges that membership conferred. Not a single responsible statesman in Europe at that time believed in free trade, though occasional writers advocated it.[1] In America it was not discussed as an economic theory, but merely asserted as a right whenever it appeared to offer profitable employment to American ships. Thus, in 1783, David Howell of Rhode Island wrote of the prohibition of the West Indian trade that "we have a natural right to carry our own trade, and a natural right will create, in the event, an interest in our favor which will secure to us the exercise of this right."[2]

The dogmatic assertion of "natural right" might be made to cover, in America, anything which one wished it to do, but in reality there was no escape from the logic of the situation

---

[1] Cf., e.g., [Thos. Pownall] A Memorial Most Humbly Address'd to the Sovereigns of Europe . . . (London, 1780), pp. 113 ff.

[2] Staples, Rhode Island in the Continental Congress, p. 462.

as expressed by one of the numerous pamphleteers who soon took part in the controversy. "It is in the light of a foreign nation that America must henceforward be viewed," wrote Lord Sheffield. "It is the situation she herself has chosen by asserting her independence, and the whimsical definition of a people *sui generis* is either a figure of rhetoric which conveys no distinct idea, or the effort of cunning to unite at the same time the advantages of two inconsistent characters. By asserting their independence, the Americans have renounced the privileges, as well as the duties, of British subjects. If, in some instances, as in the loss of the carrying trade, they feel the inconvenience of their choice, they can no longer complain; but if they are placed on the footing of the most favored nation, they must surely applaud our liberality and friendship, without expecting that, for their emolument, we should sacrifice the navigation and the naval power of Britain." [1] In his larger work, published the next year, Sheffield much expanded his arguments in favor of retaining the system of the Navigation Act. It had originally prevented the Dutch, he said, from becoming the carriers of British commerce, and the "violation or relaxation of that act in favor of the West-India Islands, or the American States, will give that advantage to the New-Englanders, and encourage to the greatest degree the marine of America, to the ruin of our own."

By a great diplomatic victory scored by John Adams, one of the commissioners to negotiate peace, Americans had been given the right to fish on all the banks and along the shores of British North America as well as within the Gulf of St. Lawrence, with liberty to land, for curing and drying, on any unsettled portions of the coast.[2] But although the fishing grounds were thus left open for the New England fishermen, the markets to which they had been accustomed to carry their product before the war were now largely closed to them. The trade relations between the new nation and the British Empire

---

[1] *Observations on the Commerce of the American States with Europe and the West Indie* . . . by an American, (Philadelphia, 1783). This was by Lord Sheffield, who chos to cloak himself under this anonymity. The same sentence appears, p. 2, in his large work under the same title, (London, 1784).

[2] Adams, *Works*, vol. III, pp. 332 *f.*; McFarland, *New England Fisheries*, p. 127.

were defined by Parliament in an Act for facilitating Trade and Intercourse, which was renewed annually until the end of the century.[1] The first promulgation of this, however, was soon followed by a proclamation, July 3, 1783, which absolutely forbade American vessels from participating in the carrying trade of the West Indies, and denied the privilege to Americans of sending salted meats or fish to the islands, even in British vessels.[2] Whale oil was no longer allowed to be imported into England, and the loss of the only market for that important commodity resulted in a decline of the whaling fleet of Massachusetts from three hundred vessels before the war to one hundred in 1789.[3]

In England the defenders of the Navigation Acts and the closed mercantile system argued very much as did George Chalmers, who claimed that England could supply the islands with all the lumber needed and that Nova Scotia could raise sufficient wheat for their consumption. The proclamation, he said, provided that the West Indians should be cared for in the "most *reasonable* manner," and he scolded them violently because they preferred to "be accommodated in the most *profitable*." "If the West Indians expect protection from Great Britain, they must study to be useful to her." "By the consent of civilized communities," he said, in another place, "it was early established . . . that the sovereignty as well as traffick of every plantation should exclusively belong to the State which had formed it"; and the West Indian policy, as he truly showed, was one which Britain "continued rather than adopted." [4]

From the standpoint of business and not imperial theory, however, it was at once disputed in England that the West India Islands could be provided with necessary supplies within the empire. One writer showed that these could not possibly be provided at any economically profitable cost elsewhere than

[1] 23 Geo. III, chap. ix.
[2] The proclamation has been reprinted many times, *e.g.*, by Brian Edwards, *Thoughts on the late Proceedings of Government* . . . (London, 1784), pp. 7 *ff.*, *note*.
[3] Johnson, *Domestic and Foreign Commerce*, vol. II, p. 10.
[4] *Opinions on Interesting Subjects of Public Law and Commercial Policy Arising from American Independence*, (London, 1784), pp. 58, 75, 78, 120.

from the United States.   Another wrote that the annual supplies received from Canada and Nova Scotia in the British West Indies on an average for the years 1771–73 amounted to only £3750, whereas they derived from the rest of America supplies to the amount of £997,034.[1]   Brian Edwards, one of the leading English authorities on the islands, said that as soon as the proclamation was published in the islands the prices of American supplies had jumped three hundred per cent.[2]   It was also pointed out that the American vessels employed in the trade were small sloops and schooners of from a hundred to a hundred and fifty tons, operated by five or six men and a boy, making several trips a year, and that the English could not compete on account of the higher cost of shipbuilding and longer trips.[3]   The policy of the proclamation was opposed in every way possible by the West Indians themselves,[4] and the whole problem was a continuation of that which we have already discussed at length in its colonial aspects.[5]

England was wholly justified in her attitude as to the exclusion of American vessels from this trade.   It was merely a question of expediency, and it seems probable that by her policy she did succeed in strengthening her merchant marine and naval forces and was thus better prepared for the great struggle with France early in the next century.[6]   Colonials, however, are never very observant of imperial regulations that run counter to their own local interest, and American shipowners had found the West Indian governors, customs officials, and planters on their side when caught smuggling goods into the islands.   It is difficult to say how far this trade may have been revived in the years immediately following the Revolu-

[1] *A Free and Candid Review of a Tract entitled 'Observations on the Commerce of the American States'* . . . (London, 1784), pp. 40 *ff.*   *Cf.* [Richard Champion] *Considerations on the Present Situation of Great Britain and the United States,* (London, 1784), pp. 84 *ff.*

[2] *Thoughts on the late Proceedings, op. cit.,* pp. 4, 6.

[3] *Reflections on the Proclamation of the 3d of July 1783 relative to the Trade between the United States of America and the West India Islands,* (London, 1783), p. 5.   *Cf.* Wm. Bingham, *A Letter from an American,* (Philadelphia, 1784).

[4] *Cf., e.g.,* the resolutions of the Committee of West India Planters and Merchants, April 11, 1783, given in *Thoughts on the late Proceedings,* pp. 45 *f.*

[5] Adams, *Revolutionary New England, 1691–1776, loc. cit.*

[6] *Domestic and Foreign Commerce, op. cit.,* vol. I, p. 130.

tion.[1] Vessels would sail to certain French "free ports," such as Martinique, and thence smuggle goods into the English islands. Others sailed under old certificates of British registry, the Spanish flag, or forged passes.

It would seem, however, that the prohibition was effective to a considerable extent, and that in the years immediately following the war American merchants were severely handicapped by the impossibility of trading directly and openly with their old customers in what had been the most important branch of commerce. It was still thought that the West India trade was absolutely essential, in order to secure the specie or bills of credit necessary to pay for imports from Europe in the absence of sufficient direct exports; and this was true until wholly new channels of trade were opened up some years later. The decrease in the island trade also affected that along the coast, for the New Englanders had been accustomed to using West India goods to pay for the staples bought in the southern colonies. With the decline in commerce, the shipbuilding industry also suffered a severe setback. Before the war, about one hundred and twenty-five vessels had been built annually in Massachusetts. This output had declined to fifteen or twenty by 1785.[2]

For some months, in the riot of extravagance following peace, the accumulations of specie made during the struggle served to meet the needs of exchange with England for the imported goods which flooded the markets. Even before the signing of the treaty, the Boston newspapers had commented bitterly upon the return of British mercantile activity. "With what true pleasure," commented sarcastically the *Evening Post*, "must we see those commercial advantages so warmly expected from a peace, not only flowing in their wonted *channels;* but even monopolized by the factors of such very sincere partizans

---

[1] Edward Channing says that "by 1786, it had become evident that the Order in Council closing the West Indian trade to American shipping was practically a dead letter, except when Nelson with the *Boreas* was in sight." *Hist. of U. S.*, vol. III, p. 421. On the other hand, Johnson denies this, and states that the trade did not revive after the war and that the development of American commerce up to 1789 was due to the reëstablishment of trade with England and the building up of new trade with the Mediterranean and the Far East. *Domestic and Foreign Commerce*, vol. I, p. 130.

[2] Morison, *Maritime History*, p. 34.

of American independence as the *Lanes* and *Dickersons* of London." [1] In similar tone the *Freeman's Journal* said that "all the specie in the country is vanishing; the people cannot pay their debts nor their taxes . . . but the British trade must not be discouraged." [2]

The New England seaboard states, with the exception of Connecticut, which had had no European trade before the war, all adopted tariffs designed not only for revenue but for protection of certain home industries, and which discriminated against goods carried in British bottoms. [3] Rhode Island levied duties on goods imported in British vessels which were three times those on goods brought in under other flags, and later excluded British ships wholly from her ports. Massachusetts, however, passed the most numerous tariff laws of any of the states. The Confederation had no power to enact trade legislation or impose duties, and the situation soon became confused by the multiplicity of state statutes. Moreover, British goods continued to pour in, the return of peace having led to an era of unwarranted hopefulness, extravagance, and extended credit. The position was well realized in England. "The Americans are relapsing into their former luxury and enjoyments," wrote one observer. "The war precluded them for a time, but a spirit of indulgence now breaks forth, with increased force, and the orders for goods which have been lately transmitted, are filled with as many superfluities as necessaries. Whether this is a wise conduct in such states, must be the consideration of their own government; but it will not be a wise conduct in us, if we neglect the means of drawing them into that dependence which their trade will produce." [4]

In 1785 the *Massachusetts Centinel* had numerous articles dealing with the imports and activities of the British merchants. The tone of these articles strongly resembles that of many during the years of early agitation, and some of them, signed "Joyce, Junior," recall the days of the Stamp Act riots.

[1] *Boston Evening Post*, Oct. 12, 1782.
[2] Quoted *ibid.*, July 13, 1782.
[3] A. A. Giesecke, *American Commercial Legislation before 1789*, (Univ. of Pa., 1910), pp. 125 *ff.*
[4] Champion, *Considerations on the Present Situation*, p. 151.

"Those infamous paricides, the Refugees and English Factors,"
said one of them, "are permitted quietly to contaminate the
air of a land of *Freedom* — to impede the wheels of government
with their gold — and to ruin our Merchants and Tradesmen
by their Importations, our Trade is suffering every restriction,
and as a nation we are treated with every indignity and insult
that ignorance, ingratitude or voraciousness can invent." [1]
The following week the picture was painted with more detail.
Ruin was coming. Our money had all gone to pay for European imports of the past three years. The whale fishery, which
formerly placed £800,000 in England, was ruined by the English
duty of £18 sterling per ton of oil, depriving Massachusetts of
half her means of remittance. The regulations prohibiting
American shipping in the West Indies and elsewhere closed all
vents for the commodities produced in New England. American credit in England had gone completely, but a swarm of
British agents, British factors, and British merchants were
sent among us and were daily increasing. [2] A few days later
a meeting of protest was held by the American merchants
at Faneuil Hall, at which drastic resolves were adopted.
It was voted that, as there was no commercial treaty with
Great Britain, a petition be sent to Congress "for laws
putting our commerce on an equality," and it was planned to
communicate with committees in other seaports. The merchants pledged themselves to buy no goods from the English
factors, to prevent, as far as they could, others from doing so,
and not to lease them any warehouse or to employ any persons
who helped them with their carting. [3]

These resolutions, however, seem to have been of little effect,
and a fortnight later an article appeared advising violent
methods of coercion. "We have *assembled!* We have passed
our *resolves*," it proclaimed, in the style of 1765. "We have
declared our determinations! But my countrymen, are *words*
our only weapons? Is the flame extinct which roused us to
assemble? . . . Was our danger real or imaginary — if real,

[1] *Massachusetts Centinel*, April 9, 1785.
[2] *Ibid.*, April 13, 1785.
[3] *Ibid.*, April 20, 1785.

the question is have we remedied the evil? While our resolves are treated with indignity! . . . We threatened the British Factors; but now we are in duty bound, not only to threaten but to execute on all those daring individuals of our own, who with the most consummate arrogance daily violate our resolutions!" [1]

Even the merchants from the neighboring colony of Connecticut were threatened. Is it not hard, another article continued, when the Boston merchants are pledged to buy nothing from British factors, "to see the Connecticut Gentry in and out (in swarms) at their stores every hour of the day? . . . A word to the wise is sufficient. Let them keep their names from the public and themselves from ——." [2]

It is interesting to trace this spirit of intolerance and forcible coercion that appears again and again throughout the entire history of Massachusetts. Whether the questions in dispute were religious, political, or economic, whether they were as real as Land Banks or as metaphysical as witches, the people of that state have always shown a much greater tendency than in any other part of New England to descend to the arguments of threatenings, intimidation, physical violence, bloodshed, and mob action. It is a psychological trait that must be admitted, though it cannot be explained.

Massachusetts, Rhode Island, and New Hampshire continued their experiments in legislation discriminating against British vessels, and at one time no such vessels were allowed to land goods in any of the three states. [3] By 1785, however, the financial crisis had become acute. Elbridge Gerry wrote that "the scarcity of money in consequence of our excessive and extravagant importations of British frippery has occasioned stagnation of trade, stopping discounts at the bank, and other embarrassments and confusion." [4] The bank was undoubtedly the Massachusetts Bank, which had been incorporated the previous year and which was the first in the state.

[1] *Mass. Centinel*, April 30, 1785.
[2] *Ibid.*, April 23, 1785.
[3] Giesecke, *Commercial Legislation*, p. 137, *note*.
[4] Austin, *Gerry*, vol. I, p. 470.

It is probable that the strong anti-English agitation had its ground partly in the political campaign that was then under way, but of the genuineness of the financial crisis there is no doubt. The state treasury was almost empty, large arrears of taxes were due, and mutterings were beginning to be heard from the distressed people of the rural counties as well as from the seaport merchants and state creditors. John Hancock, who had retained the Revolutionary popularity which he always carefully fostered among the masses by a judicious use of his wealth, was Governor. Sensing a coming storm, he resigned at the end of January 1785, with the intention, apparently, of having the Lieutenant-Governor, Thomas Cushing, whom he could control, elected to his place in the spring.[1] The plan failed, and after an extremely abusive campaign James Bowdoin was chosen Governor. As neither candidate received a majority, the election had been thrown into the legislature. The lower House gave a large majority to Cushing as the "popular party" candidate, whereas Bowdoin was chosen by the Council, and in this the House subsequently acquiesced. Bowdoin, owing to his English connections, was calumniated as a Tory, and the real contest was between him as the leader of the conservative lawyer-merchant party and Hancock as the idol of the people. It is probable that the latter, who was neither very able nor courageous, felt that his party was going too far, and had no desire to ride out the storm at the helm. Bowdoin seems to have been put in by the conservatives, who were becoming alarmed by the unrest that was rapidly developing.

In his first message to the legislature the new Governor suggested that a convention should be called from all the states to grant greater powers to Congress, including that of regulating foreign commerce. The legislature, in compliance, passed a series of resolutions advocating the Governor's recommendation, and Bowdoin forwarded them to the Massachusetts delegates in Congress. Those delegates, however, S. Holten, Gerry, and King, took the extraordinary step of not presenting

[1] Gerry thought he never intended that the resignation should be accepted but that he would be pressed to remain in office. King, *Rufus King*, vol. I, p. 76. *Cf.* A. E. Morse, *The Federalist Party in Massachusetts to the Year 1800*, (Princeton, 1909), pp. 27 ff.

them but, instead, of remonstrating with the Governor.[1] In a long letter they stated their objections to the course pursued and evinced their dread of a stronger Federal government. They admitted that "more power in Congress" had indeed been the cry from all quarters, but feared that "plans have been artfully laid, and vigorously pursued which had they been Successful, we think would inevitably have changed our Republican Governments into balefull Aristocracies." [2] The whole letter was strongly anti-Federal, and the lines in Massachusetts were already thus being drawn for the later battle over the Federal Constitution. Nathaniel Dane, a member of the legislature, in a letter to the delegates stated that that body had suggested the proposed convention because it seemed to be the general opinion that the present federal compact was defective, more particularly as regarded the powers of taxation and regulation of trade. "But," he continued, "how far the yeomanry or the body of the people of this State would accede to any proposition that might be proposed by a Convention for enlarging the powers of Congress in matters of taxation in any form, I have mighty doubts." The cause of the original suggestion, he said, was "the embarrassments our gentlemen in trade have for some time experienced," mainly due to Great Britain. The more the legislature considered, however, the less sanguine they felt as to the people being willing to agree, and therefore they dropped the matter.[3] The explosion of the forces of economic discontent in the next two years was to broaden the desire for a stronger government, which at present was felt mainly by the wealthier merchant class, and which, as Dane points out, was first brought about by the external pressure from England.

The question of the national finances had already brought about serious dissension in two of the New England states. The old system of requisitions, to which the colonists had clung so desperately when still dependent upon England, had proved as frail a reed for public finance to lean upon under the confeder-

---

[1] Morse, *Federalist Party*, pp. 30 f.
[2] King, *Rufus King*, vol. I, pp. 63, 65.
[3] *Rufus King, op. cit.*, vol. I, p. 69.

acy as under the empire.   In 1782 South Carolina was the only
state in the Union that paid her full quota of the national expenses.   Rhode Island paid but one fourth of hers and New
Hampshire only one one hundred and twenty-first part of hers.[1]
In 1781 Congress had recommended to the states that it was
absolutely necessary that it should be empowered by them to
lay a duty of five per cent *ad valorem* on all imports, — with
certain exceptions, — in order to discharge the principal and
interest of the public debt.

Connecticut and New Hampshire acquiesced within a few
months, so urgent did the necessity appear.   Massachusetts
gave her consent the following year; but Rhode Island refused,
and it is from this point that her opposition to the Federal
government may be dated.   Most of the leaders in that state
realized the need for parting with a certain portion of the state's
rights if the general government were to survive, but the people
were narrowly parochial in their views, and found a champion
in the person of David Howell, a professor in Brown University.[2]
His objections were for the most part economic.   He feared
that the merchant and consumer would pay all the tax, that
Rhode Island, from her peculiar position as mainly an importing
state, would pay more than her proportion, and that she would
suffer from the high prices charged by her neighbors.   He
admitted the duty of the state to pay taxes, but claimed that
only its own legislature could prescribe the method of raising
them.[3]   The members of Congress from the state, who had
been favorable to the impost, were retired and Howell and
John Collins, the future paper-money governor, were among
those chosen.   In October 1782 the Assembly voted unanimously against granting Congress the power that it had asked.
Howell declared that the opposition of the people to British
oppression would not rank the state higher in the annals of the
country than this resistance to the impost, and he was probably
sincere.

[1] W. G. Brown, *Life of Oliver Ellsworth*, (New York, 1905), p. 87.
[2] F. G. Bates, *Rhode Island and the Formation of the Union*, (Columbia Univ.
Studies, 1898), pp. 72 *f*.
[3] *Ibid.*, pp. 76 *f*.; Staples, *R. I. in the Cont. Cong.*, pp. 387 *f*.

The people of Rhode Island throughout all their history had developed a strong individualism. It was not surprising, therefore, though unfortunate, that the state's most popular delegate in Congress should have been the strongest proponent in that body, at this period, of states' rights. Howell more and more inveighed against the danger of centralization. His constant refrain was that "if the states give up to Congress the power of raising money from them, and of disposing of that money, their particular sovereignty will, in fact, be all absorbed in one mighty sovereignty, against the abuses of which they will retain only the power of complaining, and receiving for answer that they have no remedy." [1]

The question of the impost became mixed with that of the cession of the public lands, from which it was hoped that the national debt might be paid. The friends of the impost kept up the fight and finally, in 1786, when the position of the Confederation was absolutely desperate, they succeeded in forcing consent from the Rhode Island Assembly. The conditions of trade were largely responsible for the altered point of view, and also the changed membership of the House. The long fight, however, had made much bitterness and divided the people into strongly opposed parties.

This partisan feeling was continued in the contest over paper money, which rent the commonwealth, destroyed her economic structure for a time, and ruined her reputation with her neighbors. In all of the colonies there had always been to some extent a conflict between the landed and mercantile interests, and in the preceding volume we have traced its appearance at times of crisis. In the little colony of Rhode Island the contrast between the small farmer and the rich merchant of Newport had been particularly marked. The farmer had suffered much during the war and the British occupation, and the merchant class had sustained a severe loss in the emigration of many of its leaders, particularly the group of rich Hebrews who had been largely responsible for the growth and importance of Newport, and of whom few remained at the end of the war. The resisting power of the mercantile element had thus de-

[1] Bates, *Rhode Island*, p. 93.

creased, whereas the demands of the ignorant "country party" had become more radical owing to very real distress. On the return of peace, creditors began to demand payment of debts. In October 1781 paper money had been declared by the legislature to be no longer legal tender for taxes or debts to the state.[1] The formation of associations against payment of taxes, with occasional rioting, which now became the order of the day in the other New England states, affected Rhode Island also. In that state, however, owing to the fact that a majority of the people were of the radical party, they were able to seize the government and carry out their wishes by legal means, whereas in the other states the discontented minorities were controlled by armed force. The granting to Congress of the power to levy the impost brought about the most violent phase of the struggle. The towns voted petitions and instructions dealing with their troubles, and the clamor for paper money became insistent. It was said that the combination of an extreme scarcity of cash and the lack of any market for real estate combined to raise the interest rates on farm mortgages to anywhere from thirty to sixty per cent.[2] In March 1786 the demand for paper was defeated by forty-three to eighteen — the same division as occurred on the vote against the impost at the same session. The public demand grew, however, and in the April election there was a complete overturn of the legislature, half the upper House and forty-five Assemblymen out of seventy being new men.[3]

At once an act was passed emitting £100,000 in paper, which was to be loaned at four per cent in equal shares to all freeholders, on landed security of a value of twice the face of the loan. The mercantile town of Providence protested vigorously against the danger, but without avail. The new paper was made legal tender, and if any creditor should refuse to accept it, the debtor was permitted to deposit the amount of the debt with a judge of his county and thus wipe out the debt. In less than two months the new bills had depreciated so greatly that a new act was passed, levying a fine of £100 on anyone

---

[1] Bates, *op. cit.*, p. 116.   [2] *U. S. Chronicle*, Oct. 26, 1786.
[3] Bates, *op. cit.*, p. 123.

refusing to accept it or to sell any article at its coin value for paper of the same face amount. Newport, Providence, and Bristol all sought to avert the consequences, but the bill was passed by a majority of six.

Merchants closed their stores rather than ruin themselves by selling goods on these terms, farmers from the neighboring states refused to bring in their produce, business came to a halt, and the question of food supply became a serious one. An attempt was made to introduce measures in the legislature that would save the situation, but the country party merely increased their wrath against the mercantile element. Delegates from sixteen towns met in a convention in August and voted that they would withhold their farm produce from all those who violated the paper-money act, and recommended to the Assembly to redeem the state's debt in paper at a fixed price.[1] The Assembly then convened in special session and passed a forcing act, making the paper legal tender for the state's Continental obligations as well, — a repudiation of good faith with regard to the Confederation, — and forcing anyone who violated the money act to appear before a court of three county judges, within three days of any complaint, for trial. The right to a jury was abolished and the decision of a majority of the three judges was to be final and without appeal.[2] Other laws in favor of debtors against creditors were also passed.

Fortunately the judges of the Superior Court, although some of them were paper-money advocates, were better defenders of constitutional rights and simple honesty than were the legislators of the popular party. In the case of Trevett *vs.* Weeden, — an action brought against a poor butcher of the latter name for refusing to receive paper money at a par with specie, — the court decided that "the information was not cognizable before them," the effect of this decision thus being that paper could not be forced upon unwilling takers.[3] The radical members of the legislature were furious, and efforts were made to force the court to subservience to the legislative will, but without success. Moreover, in view of the conditions of trade and

[1] Bates, *op. cit.*, p. 128.   [2] *Ibid.*, p. 129.   [3] *Ibid.*, p. 134.

sustenance, public opinion was slowly undergoing a change and was less violently in favor of paper. The legislature, however, took further action tending to ruin the good name of the state by enacting the law that the state securities should be liquidated in paper, thus repudiating a large part of the state debt. Gradually the power of the paper-money party declined, and at last the Legal Tender Act of 1786 was repealed in 1789.

The resumption of specie payments throughout the nation — eight years earlier, in 1781 — had occurred with such apparent ease that there seems to have been an overestimate of the amount of coin then in the country. It was generally assumed that the payments made by France and England for the troops here must have been very great, and that the money had remained on this side of the water. Sheffield was probably more correct in figuring it at a much smaller amount than was currently estimated. France, he thought, had sent in all only about £600,000 sterling, while England had financed her operations largely by bills and by only occasional remittances of specie after the first years of the war.[1] Trade with Havana had brought in some more, but the total amount was certainly not nearly so large as its sudden appearance in all the colonies seemed to indicate. There was, however, considerably more than before the war, so that the stoppage of the customary pre-war supply of specie or bills on England due to the West India trade was not felt at the very first, as it would have been formerly. The resumption of specie payments, although thus seemingly carried through so easily as to have affected many historians as well as some contemporary observers, did work considerable hardship at the time. Certainly the discussions of the period regarding it show ill-feeling between classes and a fear of the situation. "Nothing so scarce as money" was the general cry, said the *Massachusetts Spy* of Worcester, quoting from the *Boston Gazette*.[2] "There is nothing a lawful tender but hard money and that exceeding scarce," complained the *Massachusetts Gazette* of Springfield, and spoke of the difficulty

[1] *Observations on the Commerce of the American States*, pp. 168 ff.
[2] *Mass. Spy*, June 20, 1782.

debtors were already facing.[1] The *Connecticut Courant* during
1779, when resumption was under discussion, revealed in its
articles a marked bitterness between the debtors and creditors
of that state.   In the two or three years following peace, specie
seems to have become scarcer in general circulation.   A member of the Massachusetts legislature figured that probably
at one time during the war there had been from double to treble
the amount in the country which there had been in 1774, but
that this surplus had all been drained away in the adverse
trade balance and that what remained was being hoarded.
"Monied men will not part with their cash until necessity or
self-preservation draw it from them," he noted, and added that
the farmers and laborers disliked to give up all their little supply
of hard money for taxes.[2]

Everywhere there was bitter complaint of the taxes, and they
unquestionably bore heavily on the poorer people.   In 1774
Massachusetts had been out of debt, and the Province tax had
been less than fifteen cents per capita; but by 1786 her debt
had risen to £1,631,789, and in addition her share of the Continental debt was £1,565,831.   It was impossible to collect taxes
sufficient to carry this load and liquidate any of the principal.
Of the £1,407,895 of direct taxes levied between 1780 and
1785 about £280,000 remained uncollected.[3]   In Connecticut
there was the same complaint.   The people, it was said, were
at the end of their tether.   Not only were the post-war taxes
unbearably heavy, but their incidence ruined the poor man.
The fact that lands were taxed regardless of the quality might
take from the owner of an inferior farm almost the value of the
property, some lands selling at that time for only five shillings
an acre.[4]   The poorer farmers were disposing of their farms
and emigrating to states where the taxes were lighter, and
mechanics were forsaking their trades and going to sea.   In
New Hampshire the conditions were similar; there were the
same demands for paper money; a riot occurred at Exeter;

[1] Issue of Sept. 3, 1782.
[2] *National Arithmetic*, pp. 26, 82.
[3] C. J. Bullock, *Historical Sketch of the Finances and Financial Policy of Massachusetts,
1780–1905*, American Economic Association, *Publications*, Ser. III, vol. VIII, pp. 5, 8.
[4] Stuart, *Trumbull*, p. 633.

and at Keene the court was forced to suspend all cases when overawed by a mob.[1]

It was in Massachusetts, however, that discontent assumed its most dangerous form, finally threatening the existence of the state. Much of it centred in the western counties, though by no means wholly confined to them. The social unrest was evidenced not only in organized movements but in an unusual outbreak of crime in what was generally a law-abiding community. In a single issue of a newspaper we find notices of a horse stolen, a house broken into and robbed, and three other robberies and holdups.[2] A few months later the robberies had become so numerous around Northampton that the citizens of that town formed themselves into a society to run down the perpetrators.[3]

In Hampshire County in 1782 and 1783 no less than seven conventions were held to discuss the grievances of the day. Of the first, that at Hadley in February 1782, we have no records, but at a second, held at Hatfield in April, thirty-six towns were represented. The action was fairly conservative, and on a vote to request the inferior court to forbear giving judgment in cases for debt except under certain conditions, the towns voted twenty-one against and only fifteen in favor.[4] It was requested that a committee be appointed by the legislature to visit the county and consider grievances, and Major Hawley, who was one of the conservatives attempting to guide matters, was much in favor of this. Various men, such as Samuel Ely, were trying to stir the people up to violent methods of coercion of the creditor class, and it was felt that the situation was becoming dangerous. In a letter to Caleb Strong, a member of the legislature, Hawley said that, without some such measure as a committee of investigation, "there is the utmost hazard that the government will take such measures as may vastly endanger the whole American cause. You would be astonished to know with what amazing rapidity the spirit of the Insur-

[1] W. Plumer, Jr., *Life of William Plumer*, (Boston, 1856), pp. 67 ff.
[2] *Mass. Gazette*, (Springfield), Sept. 24, 1782.
[3] *Mass. Gazette*, Dec. 10, 1782.
[4] D. W. & R. F. Wells, *History of Hatfield*, (Springfield, 1910), p. 198.

gents propagates. Many are infected with it of whom you would never have the least suspicion. We are not certain who besides the Devil sprang Ely at first. But we are not at a loss who ventilates the flame for the fire is now become such a flame as I cannot describe to you. The General Court have not had any affair of greater magnitude before them since the Revolution."

Ely was a disqualified clergyman who had had a church at Somers in Connecticut, and appears to have been a man of no education or judgment. In April he and a mob threatened the sitting of the court at Northampton but were dispersed, and Ely gave himself into custody. When presented to the jury for sedition, it was stated that he had said that "we must throw up our constitution"; that "the constitution is broke already, the Governor has too much salary, the Judges of the Superior Court have too much salary; we can get men that will ride the circuit for half the money . . . that the General Court should not sit; we will pay no more respect to them than to puppies." He also said that he had "been to all the towns on the lower part of the county and that they were all for breaking the Courts up," and that he could raise two thousand men if he could get somebody to lead them.[1]

On June 15 a mob of several hundred assembled for an attack upon the jail at Northampton, where Ely had been confined. The jail was broken and Ely was rescued, but three of the Members of the mob were captured. Another mob of about three hundred then gathered to rescue these three and assembled at Hatfield. General Elihu Porter, the sheriff of the county, called out twelve hundred militia for the protection of the jail, but after negotiating for several days he finally capitulated to the mob and delivered up Ely to the rioters, on their word of honor that he would be surrendered when required by the General Court. That body soon afterward pardoned all the insurgents with the exception of Ely, who fled from the state and in September was reported to be in jail in Westminster, Vermont.[2]

[1] *Mass. Gazette*, (Springfield), May 14, 1782.
[2] *Ibid.*, Sept. 24, 1782.

In July the legislature passed an act making neat cattle and certain other articles legal tender for the payment of debts, and also suspended the collection of taxes pledged to pay installments of the public debt. These and other measures, however, did not go to the root of the matter, and did not prevent the spread of disaffection. Forcible resistance to tax-collecting became frequent. The deputy-sheriff at Pittsfield, for instance, in September took a yoke of oxen from a farmer on an execution for debt. The owner, Enoch Marvin, and seven others rescued the cattle from the sheriff, who then raised a posse of forty men. At Marvin's house he found a party of thirty to defend it under the lead of Thomas Lusk, who was a substantial man in the community. These thirty had covenanted together to resist all sheriffs and collectors in levying taxes and collecting debts, but after a short battle they fled.[1]

Petitions for redress of grievances began to come from Berkshire County as well as Hampshire.[2] Conventions and town meetings continued to give voice to the troubles of the debt-ridden farmers, and at Westfield the town voted, fifty to forty, in January 1783, to pay no "Rates by Distress" until June.[3] To the real grievances were added others in the minds of the people that had little or no foundation, but that undoubtedly had some influence in creating a feeling of distrust and resentment. These are summed up by a writer who signed himself "Examiner" in the *Massachusetts Gazette*. Answering a series of weak letters which had been appearing for the conservative side, he said, after mentioning the oppressive weight of taxes, that "there are not a few who have already fled from them into the state of Vermont, where the taxes are lighter. I know of others who are preparing to follow them and I myself am afraid that I shall be obliged to bear them company. . . . The public demands are so great, that I see no way to discharge them unless I make sale of my farm. I have a few small debts, but government have incapacitated me for recovering them. . . . However the complaint is not barely that taxes are heavy;

---

[1] *Ibid.*, Oct. 8, 1782.
[2] *Ibid.*, July 30, 1782.
[3] J. H. Lockwood, *Westfield and Its Historic Influence*, (Springfield, 1922), p. 59.

but that they are heavier than they need be: That due regard has not been paid to economy: That multitudes have been supported at the public expence who did no service: And that the New England States, and especially this State, are taxed beyond their proportion both in men and money: That we in this Commonwealth pay a heavier tax than men of the same estates do in any other of the United States, and double to what they do in the State of New York: That the great, extensive, populous and rich State of Virginia, though fully officer'd, have not more than 150 rank and file with Gen. Washington: That there are few save New England men in our army: That raising so many men has cost us a vast sum, and that most of our towns are still greatly in debt on that account: That the taxes of the county of Hampshire are higher than in any other county in the State, in proportion to our numbers and estates: Further that our friends, brethren, and children in the army are unpaid: That we know but little about the expenditure of the money we have advanced, and that the little we do know rather increases our uneasiness: That we have no security that what we have paid will ever be refunded: That the balance of power lies to the southward, and that the northern States will be in danger of being oppressed by the southern: That Philadelphia being the seat of Government, it may be expected the cash of the United States will center there: and that there is not cash enough in this State to pay the taxes lying upon us." [1]

In May 1783 there was an attack by an armed crowd on the court then sitting at Springfield, but the rioters were repulsed. A "Shorter Catechism", that appeared in the *Massachusetts Gazette* and many other papers in several of the states, contained some questions and answers that proved very popular and indicate the feeling of the times. We give a few of these as symptomatic of public opinion. Question, "What is law?" Answer, "A servant to the rich and a taskmaster." Question, "What are courts of justice?" Answer, "Executioners of the law." Question, "What are lawyers?" Answer, "Rods of corruption." Question, "What is patriotism?" Answer, "An

[1] *Mass. Gazette*, (Springfield), Sept. 10, 1782.

hobby horse." Question, "What is independence?" Answer, "Dependence on nothing." Question, "Do we enjoy it?" Answer, "Yes." Question, "Who gained it for us?" Answer, "The army." Question, "How shall we reward them?" Answer, "Cheat 'em." Question, "What is public credit?" Answer, "Soldiers notes at 30 per cent discount."

The unsettled state of the public mind was reflected in many conflicting currents of migration that set in after 1782. The more settled portions of all the New England states poured forth swarms of emigrants seeking to better their condition in less crowded places. Some went into the wilderness of Maine. The infertile tracts yet unoccupied in New Hampshire were slowly taken up by those who had been forced thither by debt and discouragement. Settlers poured into Vermont from all the surrounding states. Although northern New England filled rapidly, the greatest emigration of New England people after 1781 was to states outside the section — to Pennsylvania, New York, and Ohio.[1] The western lands were said to be filling up "with amazing rapidity," and were affording a vent for many of the discontented elements who were suffering severely from the effects of the war. Without this safety valve there would undoubtedly have been explosions of resentment far more powerful in the older settlements than actually occurred. Rapid as was the draining away of the more adventurous and courageous of the poorer people, however, it was not sufficient to avoid a crisis of the first magnitude in Massachusetts.

[1] L. K. Mathews, *The Expansion of New England*, (Boston, 1909), p. 147.

CHAPTER VI

REBELLION

Distress among the Poor — Mob in New Hampshire — Views of Ruling Class in Massachusetts — Debtors — Reform Demanded and Refused — Holding of Conventions — Shays's Rebellion

IT is evident from what has been said in the preceding chapters that the economic situation was seriously disturbed in the years following the end of the war, and that dangerous conditions had arisen. The changes in business and agriculture during the struggle; the rapid rise of a new wealthy class; the simultaneous depression of many who had formerly been rich or well-to-do; maladjustment between the returns from various occupations; the chaos of paper money; the lack of specie, that quickly succeeded its sudden appearance in 1781; the load of debts, public and private; the harsh laws relating to debtors; the burden of taxation and its unequal incidence; the spirit of a people who had just passed through an agonizing struggle to win for themselves liberty of political action — all made up a situation that was threatening in the extreme. The Federal government was too weak and too remote to serve as a bulwark against local disturbance, and the only forces that could be relied upon to keep society together were the state governments and the political sense of the people. The latter had been developed to a remarkable extent in New England, but there was, nevertheless, much ignorance among the poorer elements and much of prejudice and selfishness not only among them but among the rich, who pretended to a superior breadth of mind.

It is impossible to determine to how great an extent the poor had been led into debt and folly by the prevailing extravagance and heightened scale of living to which allusion has already been made. As to the folly, the rich set the example and shared in it equally with the poor, and it is unquestionable that it was upon the latter that the burdens of the war had fallen heaviest. By 1786 their extreme distress had become a fact that could not be ignored, although it received scant sympathy from the rich and the leaders of public opinion. The condition was common to all the New England states. "A Cursory Perspective" which made the rounds of the newspapers in 1786 described New Hampshire as "complaining of her late tender act and her poverty"; Massachusetts as "possessed of little cash and a stagnated trade"; Rhode Island "happy in her new paper money"; Connecticut as "complaining of hard times but do not yet express great uneasiness"; and Vermont as "young: lost in the woods; crying, I can't get out." [1]

Vermont was indeed young and as yet unrecognized, but that did not prevent her sharing in the general misery. One great cause of dissatisfaction and injustice had, it is true, recently been removed in that commonwealth, which has always cared more for common sense and a rough justice than for precedents and logic. In addition to the cloud on many land titles in that state, owing to the conflict with New York, there had been an immense amount of swindling of settlers by persons who sold lands to which they had no title at all. The emigrants would improve the land and build houses, only to find later that they were liable to ejectment by the real owners, with no compensation for their labor and improvements. One of the most active of these land-swindlers was a fellow named Simeon Sears, and so notorious were his operations that when certain citizens of Bennington, who had been confined by the New York authorities in the City Hall at Albany, thirty miles away, were discussing attacking and destroying that building, Ethan Allen remarked that the better way would be just to get "Sim Sears to sell the D——d thing." [2] In 1785 a bill was passed by the legislature to provide for such cases of fraud and eviction, that gave the honest but gulled tenant, when dispossessed, the full

[1] *U. S. Chronicle*, June 15, 1786.
[2] D. Chipman, *Life of Nathaniel Chipman*, (Boston, 1846), p. 63.

value of his improvements and half the increased value of the land.[1]

This was a great step in advance and did away with much injustice, but the economic evils of the neighboring states were also felt in Vermont. In August 1786, Governor Chittenden, in an address to the people, spoke at some length of the troubles that beset them. During the war, he said, "we were obliged to follow the example of Joshua of old, who commanded the sun to stand still while he fought his battle; we commanded our creditors to stand still while we fought our enemies," and this had distressed great numbers. Owing partly to this, and partly to the growth of luxury and the lack of specie, the cost of lawsuits, mainly for unquestioned debts, had in two years nearly equaled the entire cost of the war in any two years of its continuance. The popular remedies called for, which included paper money, a legal-tender act, and the killing of all lawyers and deputy sheriffs, were in his opinion but temporary palliatives. If he had to choose one of them, he would take paper money, to be made tender only for· such debts as should be legally sued for, with the idea of preventing suits.[2]

On August 15 a meeting of about two hundred farmers, from ten towns, was held at Rutland, and manifested a "spirited resentment" against the harassing of so many good people by the "banditti" known "by the name of Attorneys." A notice of the meeting ended with the warning: "Take notice how you impose upon those who have passed thro' the wilderness, and endured fire, famine and the sword towards obtaining their own rights, and the liberties of mankind."[3] At the October session of the legislature petitions were presented from nine towns, setting forth grievances regarding taxation and lawsuits for debt. Taxes, they said, were now laid mainly on the "middling farmer and labouring poor man," whereas they should be "paid by owners of property in proportion to its true value."[4]

Two acts were passed for the relief of debtors. In an effort to stave off radical legislation, further action was delayed until

[1] D. Chipman, *Life of Nathaniel Chipman*, pp. 63 f.
[2] *Records of Governor and Council*, vol. III, pp. 359 f.
[3] *Ibid.*, p. 362.   [4] *Ibid.*, pp. 362 f.

the sense of the people could be taken in town meetings; but, impatient of the delay, mobs in both Windsor and Rutland counties tried to prevent the courts from sitting. In February of the following year the returns were made by the towns as to the questions submitted to them, and it is noteworthy that the project for paper money was defeated by nearly twenty-two hundred votes against, as opposed to less than five hundred in favor, although a general tender act was carried by a large majority. At the next session of the legislature it was voted without a dissentient voice that Jonathan Fassett, who had been a leader in the threatened insurrection, should be deprived of his seat in the Assembly. Acts were passed for the suppression of riots, for the fulfillment of contracts according to intent, for the tender of certain articles in payment of debts, for the reorganization of the courts, and for the remedy of other grievances. Vermont was essentially a frontier state. The general level of education was probably lower there than elsewhere in New England. With its manhood suffrage and single legislative chamber, it was far the most democratic of all the states. Nevertheless, it handled the delicate situation better than did any of the others, and by forcibly suppressing the rioting at the beginning and at the same time harkening to the voice of the people and taking active measures for the redress of grievances, it avoided the appeal to arms which was at the same time racking the political structure of its most powerful neighbor, Massachusetts.

Connecticut seems to have suffered somewhat less from the economic ills of the period than the other states, though there was much suffering and uneasiness. David Humphreys, on his return from France, painted too bright a picture of his native colony in a letter to Jefferson, but even he ended with the statement that "many people appear to be uneasy and to prognosticate revolutions they hardly know how or why." [1] The course of events in the neighboring Bay State, to which we shall soon turn, was being closely followed. "The dispersion of the insurgents in Massachusetts is happy for us," wrote "a

[1] F. L. Humphreys, *Life and Times of David Humphreys*, (New York, 1917), vol. I, p. 354.

gent in New Haven" to the *Massachusetts Gazette*. "The sons of fraud, rapine and licentiousness in several towns, and in several counties in this State, were waiting with anxious expectations to see Shays and his banditti victorious; had this event taken place, a rebellion would in all probability have speedily ensued; but now scarcely a man mentions the word grievance."[1]

In Rhode Island we have already seen how armed conflict was avoided by the issuing of the paper money demanded by the people. They got what they wanted, although the effects were not what they had anticipated. The mercantile and conservative class had been so depleted by the Revolution that they could not control legislation, and armed resistance by them was out of the question. The situation, therefore, worked itself out without bloodshed, though with much unnecessary suffering and injustice.

In New Hampshire there were the same scarcity of hard money, the same demand for paper, and the same difficulties over debts and lawsuits.[2] Almost every town held meetings to consider the distress of the people which was said to have reached an "alarming" degree.[3] A satirical treatment in the press of the people's demand for paper money called forth a reply that is indicative of much of the feeling beneath the surface at this time. "The good people mark the men and their measures in every town," wrote "A Tradesman," "and know the secret springs or moving causes." He complained of the stockjobbing that was rampant and declared it to be "truly a melancholy sight to see the people under such pressure of fortune as to implicitly submit to an oligarchical government, which puts it in the power of a few rich men to speak, write, and even think for the multitudes, whom they esteem as asses of

---

[1] *Mass. Gazette*, April 3, 1787.

[2] A resolve of the town of Derryfield was typical of the views of the more ignorant farmers. It was voted that "the Genral Court macke as much money in Bills of Credit as pay the whole of thies States Securetes In three monthes from thies Dat and Shall be a Lawfull tender in all Payments both Publicke and Privite also Death to Countrfit Said money and Said Money not to Carye any Intrist and in Case any person Shall Refuse or neglect to Bringe in ther State Securities by the first Day of Apreel nixt and Recive ther money the Intrest to Case from that Dat." *Early Records of the Town of Derryfield, now Manchester*, (Manchester, 1906), vol. II, p. 121.

[3] *Mass. Gazette*, Aug. 14, 1786.

burthen." But "the people," he adds, "are not such fools as their honours take them to be, which time will discover." [1] A tender Act, passed in 1785, by which every sort of property became legal tender at an appraised valuation, merely made hard money scarcer than ever and did not relieve the situation. [2]

Committees from thirty towns petitioned the legislature in August to issue irredeemable paper. A plan of issue was drawn up and submitted to the towns, but in September a mob of about two hundred men marched upon the legislature at Exeter and threatened that body unless immediate action were taken. For some hours they held the legislators prisoners, but the governor ordered out the militia and the crowd was dispersed. The people generally rallied to the side of government, and it was deemed politic and safe to discharge the prisoners taken by the troops. [3] The courthouse at Plymouth was burned on December 5, but that does not seem to have been part of any organized movement, and the New Hampshire papers could boast that the inhabitants were enjoying peace and tranquillity while their neighbors in Massachusetts were fast approaching "the horrors of civil war." [4]

In that latter state, from the beginning of settlement in the seventeenth century, the ruling class had shown itself singularly impervious to ideas. The few concessions which had been won from them, looking toward freedom of thought or action for any outside their own group, had been so only by prolonged and sometimes bloody struggles. Of toleration in religion they had no conception. In political thinking, the beliefs of John Winthrop and John Cotton that democracy was "the meanest and worst of all forms of government" and that "if the people be governors who shall be governed?" had become ingrained in the majority of the later leaders. [5] The keynote in the colony had always been rigid suppression, and it is possible that this explains to some extent the fanaticism that has

---

[1] *New Hampshire Spy*, Nov. 14, 1786.

[2] "We are drained of our hard cash in the northern states for remittance to our quondam connections with Great Britain." *N. H. Spy*, Dec. 1, 1786.

[3] Plumer, *William Plumer*, pp. 75 f.; Belknap, *New Hampshire*, vol. II, pp. 360 f.; *Mass. Gazette*, Sept. 26, 1786.

[4] *N. H. Spy*, Dec. 5, 1786.   [5] Adams, *Founding of New England*, p. 143.

characterized movements among its people and the constant tendency of minority opinion to find expression in violent mob-action. The petty aristocracy of clergy, lawyers, and merchants scorned the poor, had no belief in their political wisdom, and at the same time was thrown into periodic panics on account of fear of them.

It was all very well, when the common people were to be goaded into action in the war, for the "well-born," in John Adams's oft-reiterated phrase, to talk about all men being created equal, and of the rights of all to life, liberty, and the pursuit of happiness; but once the war was won, the old doctrines of the peculiar rights of the "well-born" to govern and the peculiar sanctity of their property came once more to the fore. At the time of the adoption of the Constitution of 1780, as we have seen, much was made of the distinction between property and persons, and the necessity of giving both representation. But although property became fully represented, that right was denied to a large part of the population which had hitherto possessed it, even under the limited franchise of the old charter. The property qualifications for that franchise had been doubled in Massachusetts at the very time when New Hampshire was giving the vote to every male over twenty-one who paid a poll tax and when Vermont had abolished all restrictions on the voting by males of legal age.

The attitude toward the poorer elements in the Massachusetts population is well shown by that part of the address of the Constitutional Convention defending the franchise clause. All those not possessing the required property qualification, it ran, "are either those who live upon a Paternal estate, expecting the Fee thereof, who are just entering into business, or those whose Idleness of Life and profligacy of manners will forever bar them from acquiring and possessing Property . . . men who will pay less regard to the Rights of Property because they have nothing to lose." [1] The people had been under the delusion that they had fought an eight-years war for the rights of man, and at the time of the formation of the Constitution, as we saw in an earlier chapter, many towns objected strenu-

[1] Quoted by Morison, Mass. Hist. Soc., *Coll.*, vol. L, p. 390.

ously to this further limitation of the franchise. Dorchester claimed that men might be "usefull and respectable members of Society" even if they did not possess sixty pounds. It was argued — oh, shades of 1776! — that taxation and representation went together, and that if the Senate represented property there was no reason why the lower House should not represent persons. This, however, now that the war was over, was considered dangerous radical doctrine. Property must be protected, whatever happened to "persons." It was protected so well that by 1786, the year of the rebellion, forty per cent of the state taxes were levied solely on polls.

In the preceding year no taxes at all had been laid, owing to unsettled conditions and the supineness of the legislature; but as a result of a vigorous message from the new governor, Bowdoin, in 1786 a tax of £311,000 was voted, of which £145,000 was for the state's quota of the Federal needs and £100,000 for the partial payment of the notes which had been given to the soldiers for pay.[1] In October Rufus King wrote to John Adams that the taxes for that year "for the purposes of the union, the state, and the counties & towns, including the support of the clergy & the town schools" would not be less than a million and a half dollars, about four fifths of which would have to be directly levied upon polls and estates, and would equal about one third of the total income of the citizens. He considered it "beyond what prudence would authorize."[2] The population of Massachusetts, including Maine, was then approximately four hundred thousand, so that, on a per capita basis, the taxes would have averaged about twenty dollars to every household of five. "But to have the Collectors call for twenty dollars taxes at a time is more money than we ever see at once," complained "A Farmer" in a letter to the *Massachusetts Centinel*, advocating indirect taxes that could be more easily borne.[3]

[1] Bullock, *Finances of Massachusetts*, p. 9.
[2] King, *Rufus King*, vol. I, p. 190.
[3] Quoted by Joseph P. Warren, Appendix II, in "The Shays' Rebellion," a manuscript thesis in Harvard University Library. This thesis has been of great value to me in the preparation of this chapter. In quoting from the sources, however, my own references are usually to the newspapers of the day, as being more readily accessible, whereas Dr. Warren's are from manuscripts in the Mass. Archives for the same material.

The excessive taxes, combined with the mass of personal debt, the amount of which cannot be ascertained, were too great to be borne. Farms could not even be sold to clear their owners.[1] In Concord, for several years, suits for debt had averaged about fifty annually, or one to every five families in the town.[2] In Groton, from 1784 to 1786, every fourth if not every third man in the town was subjected to from one to twelve suits for debt.[3] In Worcester County in 1784-85 there were four thousand lawsuits in a population of fifty thousand, or one to nearly every head of a family.

The abuse that was heaped on the lawyers was probably not deserved, though historians have not hesitated to repeat it. That the members of the bar in Massachusetts were at least men of education is shown by the fact that, of the seventy admitted to practice from 1776 to 1786 inclusive, fifty-seven were graduates of Harvard, one of Princeton, one of Brown, and three of Yale.[4] They were merely instruments employed by the creditors to execute the laws passed by the legislature, but these laws were unjust and inhumane. When judgment was entered against a debtor, there was no property, save the clothes on his back, that could not be seized. Not only his farm but his live stock, his bed, and even the last bit of food in the house could be sold by the sheriff for a fraction of their actual value. If the proceeds of these at forced sale were not sufficient to satisfy the judgment, the unfortunate debtor could be thrown into prison and thus be deprived of all opportunity of working off the debt. In Concord in 1786 the jail records show that three times as many prisoners were confined for debt as for all other causes combined, and in Worcester County twenty times as many.[5]

[1] "If we would sell our farms to pay our debts, the distresses are so great in other states there are no purchasers." Address of Governor Chittenden, Vermont, 1786. *Records of Governor and Council*, vol. III, p. 360.

[2] Reverend Grindall Reynolds, *A Collection of Historical and Other Papers*, (Concord, 1895), p. 97.

[3] S. A. Green, "Groton during Shays's Rebellion," Mass. Hist. Soc., *Proceedings*, 1884, p. 298.

[4] Jonathan Smith, "Features of Shays' Rebellion," Clinton Hist. Soc., *Papers*, vol. I, p. 13.

[5] Reynolds, *Historical Papers*, p. 199; Smith, *op. cit.*, p. 12.

In May there was an election for members of the General Court, and the widespread dissatisfaction of the people was shown by a fairly complete overturn of the members, although the poorest part of the population was disfranchised and could not thus give expression to their grievances. Few lawyers were returned to the new legislature. The suggestion to issue paper money was voted down, very wisely, but practically nothing was done to relieve the distress. From that time on, the discontented classes took matters into their own hands. In June a town meeting was held at Groton to choose a "Committee of Correspondence," quite in accord with Revolutionary precedent. This committee was to communicate with other towns and endeavor to secure the removal of the legislature from Boston; to have it limit the number of attorneys to one for each county; to stop all lawsuits until money should be more plentiful; to issue sufficient paper money to pay all foreign and domestic debts; to provide that temporarily no distress be made for debts or taxes; to pay interest to the holders of the public securities not on their par value but only on the price the holder had paid; and to "see that there is no more Infringements made on our Injured Rights and previledges." [1] In the same month began the series of county conventions which were the notable feature of the peaceable side of the rebellion. Bristol County held one at Taunton on July 27, at which a petition for paper money and relief for debtors was prepared for the legislature. The following day a paper was circulated throughout the county, stating that the suits for debt threatened "to involve great part of the people in beggary and misery," and as the legislature was doing nothing for their relief, that the signers would engage to oppose by force all courts that might sit in that county for suits against debtors, until a redress of grievances could be legally secured. [2]

On the seventeenth of August a convention of delegates of thirty-seven towns in Worcester County met at Leicester— Willis Hall, a deacon of the church at Sutton, being chosen moderator. Among the grievances named were the sitting of the legislature at Boston; the abuses of the law and exorbitant

[1] Green, *op. cit.*, p. 300.   [2] Text in *Mass. Gazette*, Aug. 14, 1786.

fees; the administration of the Courts of Common Pleas; too many officials at high salaries; excessive grants to individuals; paying money to the Federal government while the accounts of amounts due the state from Congress were still unsettled; and the payment of interest on the state debt. It was also voted to correspond with other county conventions, to oppose all mobs and riots, and to try to obtain redress by constitutional means only.[1]

The failure of the reform legislature to do anything to redress the very real grievances of the people could not fail to create trouble. There was nothing illegal about meeting together in peaceable conventions and petitioning the legislature. The conservatives, however, refused to recognize the real situation and gave vent to much stupid and dangerous nonsense in the press. "Instead of chearfully paying, as far as they are able, their own private debts, retrenching their idle, unnecessary expenses, and contributing their portion to support a government of their own making," wrote "A Citizen," "we see them assembling in conventions to do acts treasonable to the state." Their leaders, he said, are "destitute of property, without reputation, hardy and factious in their tempers, and eminent only for their vices and depravity," or maybe are only "vile emissaries of haughty Britain." The conventions, he added, amount to "a reassumption of the power to govern into the hands of the people."[2]

A few days later "An other Citizen" continued in the same strain. He scoffed at the possibility that such men as attended the conventions should know anything of governmental affairs or finances. "Though all power originates *from* the people," he said, "it does not remain *with* them." "We have a government of our own establishment, equal to all the powers for which government is established; and laws of our own making; we annually choose the officers of that government; they are answerable to us; and they are bound to alter the laws or to make new ones, according to the exigences of the people."[3]

---

[1] Text in *Mass. Gazette*, Aug. 25, 1786. Several towns in the county refused to send representatives, among them Worcester and Bolton. *Ibid.*, Aug. 22 and 29.
[2] *Mass. Gazette*, Aug. 22, 1786.   [3] *Ibid.*, Aug. 25, 1786.

It is evident that if such talk as this represented the attitude of the conservative leaders, a clash could hardly be avoided. Necessary as it undoubtedly was to adopt the Constitution of 1780, it cannot be said that it was wholly the people's choice. As we have seen, it was adopted only by juggling the returns, and from one third to one half of the people of the state had been opposed to it, or at least to a considerable part of it. This was a minority formidable enough in the establishment of a new government to call for considerate treatment. Moreover, a large portion of the people who were suffering from the grievances complained of did *not* have a voice in the choosing of officers and making of laws, as asserted. Although the trouble started in eastern Massachusetts, the rebellion assumed its most serious form in those counties that had been most strenuous in opposition to increasing the property qualification for the franchise.

Fisher Ames, who well represented the reactionary element in the state following the Revolution, said that a more popular form of government "could not be contrived nor could it stand." [1] This, of course, was false. The old charter had been more popular in the franchise, and of the more democratic states, which surrounded the reactionary Massachusetts on every side, at least two passed through the post-war crisis with less disturbance than did the Bay State with its distrust of the people and its "strong" constitution. The attitude of the conservative element and their utter lack of sympathy with or understanding of those who were smarting under wrongs is shown not only by such anonymous letters to the press as quoted above, but by the writings of such men as Ames. When the long-brewing trouble finally broke into open opposition to the government, he could talk only of "the desperate ambition of the worst men in the commonwealth"; "the convenience of bankrupts and sots, who have gambled or slept away their estates"; "the sophisms of wrong-headed men of some understanding"; and "the multitude of tavern-haunting politicians." [2]

Faced by genuine grievances, denied to a great extent the

[1] *Works of Fisher Ames*, (Boston, 1809), p. 3.   [2] *Ibid.*, p. 3.

right to express themselves at the polls, with a legislature that showed itself unable or unwilling to devise remedial measures, and with the leaders of the state utterly unsympathetic, what was left for the discontented but violent action? Even Alexander Hamilton, who certainly cannot be accused of popular leanings or of countenancing uprisings, wrote the following year, in defense of the new Federal Constitution, that "if the representatives of the People betray their constituents, there is then no resource left but in the exertion of that original right of self-defence which is paramount to all positive forms of Government," and that in single states where the subdivisions had no distinct governments to oppose the legal authority "the citizens must rush tumultuously to arms, without concert, without system, without resource; except in their courage and despair." [1] If a man like Hamilton could voice such sentiments, is it any wonder that the farmers and artisans of remote rural districts and small towns, faced by a recalcitrant legislature and an obstinate group of reactionary leaders, and without organized political parties to espouse their cause, could find no recourse save in armed action?

Until comparatively recently, most historians have followed to a great extent the contemporary utterances of the reactionaries in vilifying the characters and motives of the malcontents, but a sounder judgment and a more sympathetic attitude are now coming to prevail. There is something peculiarly irritating in the self-complacent outpourings of such a man as Fisher Ames. He was eighteen in 1776, and twenty-five when peace was declared. Yet during the entire Revolutionary struggle he stayed comfortably at home, studying law and reading poetry. His laudatory biographer tells us that he "watched its progress with patriotick concern . . . though too young to take an active part." [2] The men whom this conservative young statesman designated in 1786 as sots and bankrupts and the worst men in the commonwealth, had not been too young from eighteen to twenty-five to take an active part in the defense of their country. If they were less versed in poetry

---

[1] *The Federalist*, (ed. New York, 1897), pp. 184 *f.*
[2] Ames, *Works*, pp. vi, x.

and the classics than the young Boston lawyer, they had served through the grueling years of Valley Forge and Saratoga and Stony Point.

The mass of those who broke into rebellion were, indeed, yeomen farmers, mechanics, and laborers, and so of no account in the eyes of the merchants and professional classes of aristocratic Massachusetts society. They were many of them without votes under the "most popular form of government" that — in the opinion of those same classes — could "be contrived," and so without interest, perhaps, for the legislators. But they were far from being a mere rabble, and they were led by men who had been officers in the late war. The nominal leader, Daniel Shays, although not a man of ability, was by no means the craven coward and mere agitator that his opponents painted at the time. He had responded to the alarm at Lexington, when he had served for eleven days. He was in the battle of Bunker Hill and was promoted then for brave and gallant conduct. He was in the expedition against Ticonderoga in 1776, and during his career in the army fought at Saratoga and Stony Point, raised a company, and was made a captain. This is a war record that certainly bears comparison with that of the supercilious young Ames, reading poetry in Boston and watching the progress of the struggle "with patriotick concern." Shays was poor, and was much criticized for his lack of fine feeling in having sold a sword that had been presented to him by Lafayette. He was, however, elected to local offices such as town warden, for some years after the war.[1] A number of men who served with him in the contest have left their opinions on record. Henry Hallowell, in his diary, speaks of having served in Shays's regiment, and says that he was "respected as a very good officer, and was very good to his men."[2] Captain Park Holland, who had also been under Shays in the Revolution and who served under General Lincoln in the rebellion, wrote of his former superior that he was "a brave and good soldier, or officer, and I can truly say that it was with no regret on my part that I had not reached here in season to see him

[1] Smith, *op. cit.*, p. 17.
[2] H. K. Sanderson, *Lynn in the Revolution*, (Boston, 1909), pp. 177, 180.

and his mistaken followers fired upon as enemies." Of the malcontents generally he added that "we who stood by the side of these men, in many hard-fought battles with a powerful enemy and witnessed their hardships and sufferings borne without a complaint would much rather remember the good service they rendered their country" than dwell upon their later mistake in trying to right their wrongs by force.[1]

Of the other men who were prominent enough in the movement to be indicted for treason in 1787, fifteen out of twenty-one were described in the indictments as "gentlemen" and only six as "yeomen." All of Shays's captains, so far as is known, had been soldiers in the Revolution. Captain Wheeler, for example, had served in both the French and Indian and later wars, had been a captain in the Revolution, was a deacon in the church, and a man of high standing in his community. Out of forty names taken at random from indictments in the rebellion twenty-eight are known to have been Revolutionary soldiers, and the rest cannot be traced, as their addresses are not given.[2] The numbers engaged, also, show that the movement could not have been confined to a mere rabble. General Knox, the Secretary of War, writing to Washington, stated that the numbers of insurgents amounted to "one-fifth part of several populous counties,"[3] and the numbers of those in sympathy with the movement in the western part of the state has been placed at a much higher ratio.

Immediately after the meeting of the convention at Leicester, Governor Bowdoin issued a proclamation to revive the spirit of the militia, which had grown very slack, and earnestly recommended that every town immediately take steps to see that they were furnished with the full complement of powder and ammunition required by law.[4] On the twenty-second of August a convention of fifty towns of Hampshire County met at Hatfield, with Colonel Benjamin Bonny in the chair. Among the grievances complained of were the existence of the

---

[1] "Park Holland's Narrative," given as Appendix I in Warren's Mss. thesis, *op. cit.*
[2] Smith, *op. cit.*, p. 16.
[3] F. S. Drake, *Life and Correspondence of Henry Knox*, (Boston, 1873), p. 92.
[4] *Mass. Gazette*, Aug. 22, 1786.

state senate; the method of representation; the Court of
Common Pleas, lawyers, and high fees; the sitting of the legislature at Boston; the mode of taxation and of paying the state
debt; the unequal incidence of taxation; and the lack of a circulating medium. It was voted that the representatives of all
the towns in the county be instructed to vote for an issue of
paper money, to be legal tender and to be exchanged for the
state debt. It was further resolved that the constitution
should be revised, that the legislature should meet at once to
consider grievances, and that the people should abstain from
all mobbing and unlawful assemblies.[1] As the "conventions"
were continuing bodies, it was also agreed that copies of the
resolutions should be sent to those of Worcester and Berkshire
Counties. The following day a convention of delegates from
a majority of the towns of Essex County met at Concord and
voiced a number of the same grievances as had the other conventions. In addition, complaint was made of "taking men's
bodies for debt, and confining them in jail, when they possess
property sufficient to answer the demands of their creditors";
of the accounts of the United States with Massachusetts
remaining unsettled; and of the method of choosing jurors.[2]
Loyalty to the constitution was proclaimed, and mobbing dis-
countenanced.

The meeting of these various conventions, representing
several hundred towns, was evidence that the demand of the
people was widespread and that the failure of the legislature to
act on grievances was bringing a new force of public opinion
into action. Although at all the gatherings the use of lawful
means only had been recommended, an outbreak could no
longer be staved off, and it occurred on the twenty-ninth of
August at Northampton. A mob said to number about fifteen
hundred, of whom five hundred were armed, headed by a
captain of militia, seized the courthouse when the court was
about to sit, and prevented it from conducting its business.
The reports agree that the crowd exhibited much sobriety and

[1] *Mass. Gazette*, Sept. 8, 1786; G. R. Minot, *History of the Insurrections in Massachusetts*, (Boston, 1810), pp. 33 f.
[2] *Mass. Gazette*, Sept. 5, 1786.

good order and that there was no violence.[1]   The governor at once issued a proclamation calling upon all civil and military officers to suppress such outbreaks, and stating that he had instructed the Attorney-General to prosecute and bring to punishment the ringleaders and abettors of this and any similar violations of law.[2]

A meeting was held a few days after at Portland, Maine, to consider the holding of a county convention, but the conservative element retained control and the plan was negatived.   It was said, however, that it made no difference whether the General Court considered the conventions illegal or not; the Parliament of Great Britain had considered the General Court illegal, but that had not prevented the people from supporting it, and it mattered not to them now whether they were injured by the government of Britain or that of Massachusetts.[3]   A convention of the towns of the three counties of York, Cumberland, and Lincoln was held at Portland September 6, and expressed the opinion that no redress of grievances could be had until Maine was made an independent state, separate from Massachusetts.   There would be no difficulty then, it was naïvely said, because "government is a very simple, easy thing." [4]

The attack on the court at Northampton led to fears for the one to be held at Worcester on September 5.   The governor called on the sheriff of that county to prevent a repetition of the Northampton episode, and also instructed Major-General Warner, who commanded the county militia, to give aid. Many of the militia, however, flatly refused to turn out, and those who did showed little desire to oppose the insurgents. The latter numbered about two hundred at first, and during the several days in which they were parleying with the court, were reënforced to double that number.   The court was finally compelled to adjourn until the third Tuesday in November, and the insurgents were successful.[5]

---

[1] *Mass. Gazette*, Sept. 5, 1786.   [3] *Ibid.*, Sept. 8, 1786.
[2] *Ibid.*   [4] *Ibid.*, Sept. 22, 1786.
[5] Warren, *op. cit.*, fols. 39, 43.   The folio references are to a typewritten copy which I was permitted to have made.

At Great Barrington, on the twelfth, although the militia had also been ordered out there, the mob was ahead of them and held the courthouse all the night before the sitting. These fifteen hundred "stubborn Jonathans," as they were described, overawed the militia and court, prevented the latter from sitting, and released all the debtors held in jail.[1] They also drew up a paper declaring that no more courts should sit until the constitution had been revised, and they actually got three of the four judges to sign the document.

Disaffection was by no means confined to the western counties, and trouble was expected at the meeting of the courts at both Concord and Taunton. It was decided by the governor and his advisers to send militia to protect the Middlesex Court at Concord, but on the tenth two of the judges advised the government that the people were much excited and that lenient measures would better secure the end. At the same time a petition from twenty-four towns in that county expressed loyalty to the government, coupled with fears of the possible results of stern measures.[2] The governor, therefore, — unwisely, as it proved, — countermanded his orders to the militia. The court was to meet on the twelfth but before that date a meeting was held in Faneuil Hall in Boston at which Samuel Adams was presiding officer. The meeting declined to consider "whether the grievances, mentioned by the conventions in some of the counties of the state, really exist or not," — which was certainly the fundamental point, — and confined itself only to the question of armed insurrection. Adams, who had been the leading agitator and revolutionist in the colony a decade and more previously, when the revolutionary party was in a decided minority, now gave his voice for the absolute right of a majority to rule, and the forced submission of a minority, however large.[3]

[1] *Mass. Gazette*, Sept. 29, 1786.
[2] Warren, *op. cit.*, fol. 48. The letter from the town of Concord, offering to act in concert with the neighboring towns for the purpose of mediating between opposing parties should they meet, was published in the *Mass. Gazette*, Sept. 12, 1786.
[3] I see no reason to doubt his biographer's belief that the "Address" published by the meeting was written by him. W. V. Wells, *Life and Public Services of Samuel Adams*, (Boston, 1865), vol. III, p. 225.

The picture of the arch-conspirator and manipulator of the Boston mobs now deprecating "tumultuous methods" and the rights of minorities has a certain sardonic humor. Evidently he himself felt the need of explanation, and the address contrasts at length the justification for revolution in 1776 and the presumed absence of it in 1786. The legislature, he said, — ignoring the fact that a large part of the people was disfranchised under the new constitution, — is elected by the people, and so controlled by them. The minority may not always get what they want but, naïvely asked the ex-revolutionist, "is not this always the case when in society the compact is for the minority to submit to the majority? Let the majority be ever so much in the wrong, is there any remedy, within the reach of nature, compatible with the ideas of society and government? To say, the majority shall not govern, is saying either that we will reduce ourselves to a state of nature, or reject the ideas of civil liberty." Of course the malcontents might claim, as they did in Maine, that it made no difference whether evils were suffered from the government of Britain or from that of Massachusetts, but Adams was no longer on the opposition bench. Refusing even to consider the grievances of the people, — which the town of Concord voted on the same day were not groundless, — he declared that the trouble came solely from British emissaries and from "wicked and unprincipled men" who sought only their own emolument.[1]

Meanwhile, the court at Concord had been left unprotected. About seventy armed men, under the lead of Job Shattuck of Groton and two others, appeared and were unmoved by the attempted moral suasion of the Concord mediating committee. This mob appears to have been a rather disreputable lot, but they were soon joined by about ninety men of better calibre from Worcester, and, increased to about three hundred in all, they forced the justices to agree that the court should not be opened.[2] The government was thus set at defiance within the near neighborhood of Boston. In Bristol County it was left to the discretion of the sheriff and the justices whether the militia should be used or not, although the Governor and

[1] *Mass. Gazette*, Sept. 12, 1786.   [2] *Ibid.*, Sept. 15, 1786.

Council rather advised against it. General Cobb did use the soldiers to protect the court. Nevertheless, the insurgents were in such large numbers that, in spite of the presence of two troops of militia, the justices adjourned until December without doing any business. There was also trouble in Essex County, though the court sat, somewhat timidly, at Newbury.

So far, the efforts of the insurgents had been directed to prevent the hearing of cases for debt by forcing the courts to close. Fearing, however, as a result of their acts, indictments against themselves in the Supreme Court, the leaders now decided that they must close the court for their own safety. This court was to meet at Springfield on September 29, and Major-General William Shepherd, of the Hampshire militia, prepared to defend it. On the day of the sitting about seven hundred to a thousand insurgents were faced by eight hundred militia. The former passed resolutions that the court be allowed to deal with all criminal cases except the indictment of insurgents by the grand jury, that judgments in civil cases be suspended until a redress of grievances could be had, and that the militia be disbanded at once. Captain Shays, as chairman of the committee that presented these resolutions to the court, now made his first appearance as a leader. It was agreed that both militia and insurgents should disband, and the court then adjourned.[1] It was to meet next at Great Barrington on October 3, but did not dare go there. Bands of several hundred insurgents collected, and perpetrated a number of abuses against private citizens — a phase that was rare until the very last stage of the rebellion. On October 4 the town of Stockbridge passed resolutions denouncing the attempts to close the courts and promising support to the government.[2]

Meanwhile the legislature was in special session at Boston, and the Governor called for energetic measures. For three weeks the members talked and passed vague resolutions, but the two houses could not agree and did nothing either to uphold the government by strong measures or to redress the grievances of the disaffected. At the end of October the court at Taunton had again to be protected by troops who, this time, faced only

[1] *Mass. Gazette*, Oct. 3, 1786. [2] *Ibid.*, Oct. 10, 1786.

a weak body of insurgents.   On the twenty-first the legislature advised the Governor that they would take steps to protect the Supreme Court scheduled to meet at Cambridge, and four days later passed a riot act.   This strengthened the Governor's hands, and, protected by over two thousand troops, the court held its session undisturbed.

Finally the legislature provided that the payment of back taxes might be made in specified articles instead of money, passed a tender act for a limited time, and offered a plan for lessening the business that had to be brought before the Court of Common Pleas.   Import and excise taxes were laid in order to reduce direct taxation, and an indemnity act was passed giving full pardon to anyone who had been in insurrection since June 1, provided he would take the oath of allegiance before January 1.   A long debate on suspending the Writ of Habeas Corpus, however, had ended in its suspension November 10 and this further irritated the insurgents.   The Governor and Council were also given the power, up to July 1, 1787, of imprisoning without bail any person they considered dangerous to the state.   The Courts of Common Pleas and General Sessions, with the exception of that to meet at Worcester in November, were temporarily suspended.   Having voted an address to the people the legislature then adjourned.[1]

The real troubles, however, had been left practically untouched.   Nothing of importance had been done as to the scarcity of money, the seizure of person as well as property for debt, and the grievances as to the courts.   The dislike of the Court of Common Pleas seems to have had a sound foundation.   An article in the *Boston Magazine*, several years before, had asked, "What real service are the Courts of Common Pleas in deciding causes in the method they are usually conducted? Not one cause in ten that is disputed is finally issued there, nor one in five perhaps has a trial there of any kind. . . .   The time and expense usually attending a suit in Common Pleas is only preparatory to a trial; and very frequently the preparation is incomplete in the first instance."   The defendant did not make his real answer until the case had been taken to the

[1] The address is in *Mass. Gazette*, Nov. 28 and Dec. 1, 1786.

Supreme Court, and the time and money were all wasted.[1] The Worcester County convention in October, in a petition to the legislature, said truly that these courts were "an amazing expense" to the people, with no conceivable good whatever; that not one case in forty before the judges was really designed for trial; and that no dependence could be placed upon the decisions.[2] Yet the legislature made no resolute attack upon this problem, and the Senate insisted that the courts should be retained. In a word, the legislature had neither undertaken to suppress the rebellion by force nor had it redressed grievances in such a way as to bring about a peaceable and voluntary settlement.

Washington, at Mount Vernon, was keenly interested in the situation, and his comments on the Massachusetts government are terse and illuminating. "For God's sake, tell me," he wrote to David Humphreys in October, "what is the cause of these commotions? Do they proceed from licentiousness, British influence disseminated by the Tories, or real grievances which admit of redress? If the latter, why were they delayed until the public mind had become so agitated? If the former, why are not the powers of government tried at once?"[3] A few days later, writing to Henry Lee, he said: "You talk, my good sir, of employing influence to appease the present tumult in Massachusetts. . . . *Influence* is no *government*. Let us have one by which our lives, liberties and properties will be secured, or let us know the worst at once. . . . Know precisely what the insurgents aim at. If they have *real* grievances, redress them if possible; or acknowledge the justice of them, and your inability to do it at the present moment. If they have not, employ the force of government against them at once."[4] When judged by the standard of this vigorous sanity, it is no wonder that the blind obstinacy of the Massachusetts conservatives, the refusal of such men as Sam Adams even to consider the grievances, and the shilly-shallying of the legislature moved Washington to yet stronger comment.

[1] The article was reprinted in the *Mass. Gazette*, Oct. 6, 1786.
[2] *Ibid.*, Oct. 17, 1786.
[3] Quoted by J. C. Fitzpatrick, "Some Sayings of Washington which Apply To-day," *Daughters of the American Revolution Magazine*, vol. LV, p. 61.
[4] *Ibid.*, p. 62.

On November 28 court was held at Cambridge under protection of the militia, and in spite of rumors of attack, no rebels appeared. This emboldened the government, and warrants were issued for the arrest of Job Shattuck and four other insurgent leaders of Groton and Shirley. Two escaped, but Shattuck, Page, and Parker were captured, the first after a severe fight in which he was badly wounded.[1] They were placed in Boston jail, and in Middlesex County this practically ended the rebellion, which was also over by the first of December in the other eastern counties, in spite of anxiety and minor disturbances.

Trouble, however, was expected in Worcester County when the court should meet there on December 5. The Governor sent the usual orders to the sheriff and General Warner of the militia to protect the court, but later lost heart and directed Warner to desist from action unless the militia had already turned out in sufficient numbers to ensure success. The court was instructed to adjourn if there was any opposition, and, as a thousand insurgents appeared, it promptly did so. The insurgents disbanded in a few days, after having sent a petition to the legislature for pardon, reciting the usual grievances, including the recent suspension of the writ of habeas corpus.[2] The court at Springfield was next attacked on the twenty-sixth and forced to suspend.[3] It may be noted that just at this same time, in the democratic state of Vermont, with manhood suffrage, the courts were being kept open and any who interfered with them were being promptly landed in jail by the militia and sheriffs.[4]

With the beginning of the new year the situation changed. The disaffected gave up hope that the legislature would honestly redress their grievances. The town of Rehoboth in Bristol County adopted a novel expedient by stopping the pay of its representative, it being the sense of a town meeting that there was no reason for being at the expense of keeping him at Boston

[1] Warren, *op. cit.*, fols. 76 *f.*
[2] *Mass. Gazette*, Dec. 8, 15, 1786.
[3] Bowdoin and Temple Papers, Mass. Hist. Soc., *Coll.*, Ser. VII, vol. VI, pp. 121-4.
[4] *Conn. Courant*, Dec. 25, 1786.

another eight weeks "to make laws which in our judgment are not consistent with republican principles," and "because this town do not entertain the most distant idea that the present administration will relieve our distresses." [1] On the other hand, the government seems by this time to have resolved to suppress the revolt by force.

About the first of January, General Benjamin Lincoln was appointed to lead an expedition to crush the insurgents. It was an excellent choice. Lincoln had a good record in the Revolutionary War, was energetic, and had sound judgment in political as well as military matters. The Governor and Council also planned to raise a force of forty-four hundred men, with four companies of artillery. There were, however, no public funds with which to meet the expense and the state treasurer was unable to negotiate a loan. At this point we must turn to consider the question that had been secretly agitated for some months of the use of Federal troops in the emergency.

Congress had two interests in the insurrection — the possible overthrow of the state government with its effects on other states, and the protection of the Federal arsenal at Springfield from the insurgents. On September 26 General Henry Knox had warned Congress of the coming storm. [2] Knox, who like many of the Massachusetts conservative leaders had all the stubborn timidity of middle-class wealth, was in a panic over the danger to established order and property and could see nothing else. He refused to consider the possibility that the people had real grievances, and painted the situation and the insurgents in the blackest colors. In his eyes they were merely "twelve or fifteen thousand desperate and unprincipled men" who were determined to seize and divide the property of the rich. [3] History never repeats itself in all its details, but it is enlightening to observe how true to form the post-war psychology of the various classes always runs after every great conflict.

---

[1] *Mass. Gazette*, Jan. 9, 1786.
[2] J. P. Warren, "The Confederation and the Shays Rebellion," *American Historical Review*, vol. XI, p. 44.
[3] Drake, *Knox*, p. 92.

Knox had been at Springfield during the trouble there, and proceeding to Boston he took up the matter with Bowdoin and his advisers. It was finally agreed that, without referring to the insurrection, Congress should be asked to furnish the state with a quota of Federal troops. Nothing was to be said to the legislature, and the matter was left to Knox and the state's representatives in Congress to handle. The real danger that existed at that time of an Indian war on the western frontier was used as a cloak, and Congress, agreeing to the secret plan, called for recruits. Most of these were to be raised in New England, and a requisition was to be made on all of the states for $500,000 for the expenses of the campaign. On October 22 Bowdoin laid the requisitions before the legislature, enlarging on the Indian danger. The legislature immediately passed a bill raising the troops, but the real object soon began to be suspected. A loan of £2500 was authorized but only £500 was subscribed. On December 11, Jeremiah Wadsworth wrote to Knox that "the Deacons of Massachusetts" had not raised a man, whereas Shays had seven or eight hundred. "Had you not better employ them than wait for the Deacons?" he inquired sarcastically. "I begin to think he will govern the State, as I see no disposition in any body else to do it." [1]

Lincoln, when ordered to proceed against the insurgents without any money being provided, adopted prompt measures which proved effective. He went to a club of Boston gentlemen, warned them that it would be best to loan part of their wealth to save the rest, and within twenty-four hours had financed his own expedition.[2] His orders required him to protect the sittings of the courts, to proceed to the western counties if he deemed it advisable, and to apprehend any persons attempting "the destruction or annoyance" of the commonwealth.[3]

[1] Quoted from Knox Mss., *Am. Hist. Rev., op. cit.,* p. 59.
[2] Letter from Lincoln to Washington, Dec. 4, 1786 and subsequent dates, Washington Papers, Library of Congress, fol. 6. Warren, when writing his thesis, used the transcript in the Sparks Papers at Harvard and evidently did not know of the existence of the original. Lincoln did not state the amount he raised, but it was said to be $20,000. *Am. Hist. Rev., op. cit.,* p. 43.
[3] Lincoln letter, *op. cit.,* fols. 7 *f.*

There was no trouble at the court at Worcester, whither Lincoln marched first. On the twenty-fourth of January, the day after the sitting of the court, it was learned that Shays and his forces had taken a position at Wilbraham, six miles south of Springfield, while Luke Day and another band of insurgents were at West Springfield.[1] Lincoln at once set off to the relief of General Shepherd, who was defending the Federal arsenal, it being understood that the rebels were planning to attack it on the twenty-fifth. Owing to a failure of communications between Shays and Day, Shays made the attack alone on the appointed date, expecting support. Four insurgents were killed, and Shays's force dispersed for the moment.[2] Meanwhile, Lincoln and his troops had reached Springfield by forced marches.

The General did not rest his troops even overnight, but immediately set them in motion to prevent the union of Day and Shays, and to cut off the retreat of the former. Day's force was found, attacked, and broken up with little attempt at resistance. Shays at once retreated to Amherst, where he was joined by stragglers from the other rebel party.[3] After one day's rest Lincoln followed him, and as he entered Amherst on the twenty-eighth Shays with his followers marched into his native township of Pelham. Lincoln refused to follow him into this wilderness, and Shays moved on to Hadley and Hatfield. On the twenty-ninth Lincoln sent word to the insurgents that any privates who would surrender themselves to a justice of the peace, deliver their arms, and take the oath of allegiance within three days, would be recommended to the General Court for pardon.[4] The next day he wrote to Shays, pointing out the danger of his situation and offering to recommend him and his followers for mercy if they would surrender.[5] Shays replied

[1] *Ibid.*, fol. 9; *Mass. Gazette*, Jan. 26, 1787.

[2] Lincoln letter, *op. cit.*, fol. 9; Shepherd's report of the engagement was in *Mass. Gazette*, Jan. 30, 1787, and has been reprinted in *Am. Hist. Rev.*, vol. II, p. 694, and by W. L. Smith, "Springfield in the Insurrection of 1786," Conn. Valley Hist. Soc., *Papers*, vol. I, pp. 86 *f*.

[3] Lincoln to Bowdoin, *Mass. Gazette*, Jan. 30, 1787, reprinted in *Am. Hist. Rev.*, vol. II, pp. 695 *ff*.

[4] Warren, thesis, *op. cit.*, fol. 95.

[5] Lincoln letter, *op. cit.*, fol. 11; *Mass. Gazette*, Feb. 2, 1787.

that, however unjustifiable the rebellion may have been, it had been due to real grievances; that the people would disperse if a general pardon were granted to them; and asked for an armistice until petitions for redress could again be presented to the legislature.[1]

Lincoln replied to this and a later letter that he was without authority to delay operations. On the evening of February 2 he heard that Shays had suddenly abandoned his position and had marched towards Petersham. Lincoln at once started in pursuit at eight o'clock, marched thirty miles through a blinding snowstorm, and reached Petersham at nine next morning. This now famous march took the rebels completely by surprise. A hundred and fifty were captured and the rest scattered in every direction. Shays himself fled to Vermont, and the organized phase of the revolt came to an end. The legislature, at Lincoln's request, had declared the existence of a state of rebellion, and strengthened by this action, Lincoln and Warner now proceeded to stamp out the remaining embers in the western counties — a matter that took some weeks. The scattered bands became desperate, and the lawlessness of the movement belongs mainly to this period. The trouble lasted longest in Berkshire, and on February 13 Eli Parsons, one of the rebel leaders, issued a circular calling on the people to rise and "to Burgoyne" Lincoln and his army.[2] The rebellion, however, was at an end. Even the neighboring states, with the exception of Rhode Island, offered no refuge, and at the request of Massachusetts the governors of one after another issued proclamations for the capture of the refugees.

The first week in February the legislature again met, and the Governor reported the progress of Lincoln's arms. Forty thousand pounds were appropriated to pay the expense of the campaign and bounties were offered for enlistments. The request for pardon, which had been transmitted through General Lincoln, was also considered. Petitions from various towns begging lenient treatment for the rebels were ignored and their own petition refused.[3] Samuel Adams, as chairman

---

[1] Lincoln letter, *op. cit.*, tol. 12.   [2] *Mass. Gazette*, Feb. 27, 1787.
[3] *Ibid.*, Feb. 9, 1787.

of the committee which was appointed to consider it, made a report that to a considerable extent consisted of futile quibbling. Considering the gravity of the situation, the real evils of the times, and the ignorance of many of the rebels, the third and fourth reasons given by the committee for refusing to consider the petition were typical of the legislative mind at its worst. It could not be accepted, they said, because the petitioners, although they acknowledged their "error," considered that it was only a "failing," and because they appeared "to view themselves *on equal if not better standing* than the legislature by proposing '*a reconciliation.*'" [1]

The legislature, whose stupidity and vacillation had been largely responsible for the rebellion having assumed the proportions it had, now proved itself not only stupid but vindictive. General Lincoln felt that there was nothing further to fear from the former rebels, but it is notorious that the men who have fought an enemy show magnanimity afterward, whereas the splenetic vindictiveness of the stay-at-homes is apt to rise as the danger diminishes. On February 16 the legislature passed an act refusing pardon to all in the rebel ranks who were above the grade of non-commissioned officers, who were citizens of other states, who had ever been members of the legislature, held any civil or military commission, or who had ever attended any of the state or county conventions. Even the remnant who might be admitted to amnesty were to be forbidden to vote, hold any office, serve on a jury, teach school, keep an inn, or retail spirits, for three years.

Lincoln wrote to Washington that as the rebellion was now crushed and the opposition to government hourly decreasing, the most critical moment of the movement had been reached. He approved of the punishment of a few leaders as an example, but said that the legislature had included such large classes that many towns would be wholly disfranchised, and the people would properly declare that no constitutional way had been left to remedy their real grievances. He thought, therefore, that there might be renewed trouble.[2] With this view Wash-

---

[1] Wells, *Samuel Adams*, vol. III, p. 240.
[2] Lincoln letter, *op. cit.*, fols. 36 *ff.*

ington wholly agreed.[1] Fortunately the legislature, a month later, mitigated the rigor of its measure to some extent and appointed a commission of three persons, consisting of General Lincoln, Samuel Phillips, Jr., and Samuel A. Otis, to receive applications from the western rebels and pardon them without the conditions formerly required. Certain leaders, such as Shays, Parsons, Day, and Wheeler were exempted from this concession.

The general voice of the state was loud against the harsh measures of the legislature. "The people in this State are exceedingly soured," wrote James Sullivan to Rufus King. "Boston has its usual prudence. Every countryman who comes in and offers to apologize for his son or brother deluded, is railed at and called a Rebel. . . . The people think the disqualifying Act &c to be measures to keep in office those who are now in; the effect will be known in the spring." [2]

On the other hand, the legislature now undertook partially to redress certain grievances the existence of which it had formerly denied. The salary of the governor, which before had been stated not to have been excessive, was reduced nearly thirty per cent, although Bowdoin vetoed this on constitutional grounds. The fees to civil officers were also reduced, as were the number of sittings of the Courts of Common Pleas and General Sessions. Some inconveniences in legal procedure were remedied, and it was admitted that the long journeys necessary to register deeds had been a genuine grievance. Three registry offices instead of one were provided for the large county of Hampshire.[3] Meanwhile, the harsh treatment of the rebels had resulted in raids of scattered parties from over the borders of the other states where they had attempted to take refuge, and the general election in Massachusetts was approaching.

John Hancock, who had characteristically recovered his health coincident with the suppression of the rebellion and the passing of the political storm, ran in opposition to Bowdoin.

---

[1] Fitzpatrick, "Some Sayings of Washington," *op. cit.*, p. 64.
[2] King, *Rufus King*, vol. I, pp. 214 *f.*
[3] Warren, thesis, vol. II, fol. 6.

Sullivan's prediction that the effect of the governmental measures would be known in the spring was amply fulfilled. Of the twenty-four thousand votes cast, Bowdoin received only six thousand and Hancock eighteen thousand. Only one quarter of the members of the new House of Representatives had been in the former one. A number of the late rebels were elected, and the three western counties, which on account of the expense had sent only sixty-eight members in 1786, showed their interest and resentment by returning one hundred and eighteen.[1] The legislative overturn amounted to a revolution in government.

Meanwhile, the commissioners were dispensing pardons wholesale. The Supreme Court, however, condemned six men to death in Berkshire County the first week of April. Henry Gale was condemned on the second of May and Shattuck on the twenty-second. The insurgents who had fled to Vermont made a daring effort to save some of the condemned men from their fate, and by a raid captured two peaceable citizens of Hampshire to hold as hostages for the lives of the rebels. The new legislature passed an act to raise troops for the protection of Hampshire and Berkshire counties, but at the same time swept away the disqualifying act of the previous legislature and, with a few exceptions, granted amnesty to all who would take the oath of allegiance. The only exceptions were those still under sentence of death and nine newly named, including Shays, Day, Parsons, and other leaders. On June 18 these were also pardoned. With the Amnesty Act all opposition to the government ceased. In the holding of the county conventions and in the attempts to delay the sitting of the courts the rebels had merely followed revolutionary precedent established by the "patriots" of a few years before. These measures had been considered legitimate then, and probably appeared far less revolutionary and illegal to the more or less ignorant insurgents than they did to the reformed revolutionaries of Boston or to subsequent historians. There is no reason to doubt that the unanimous expressions of a desire to avoid force and use legal methods only, which were universally heard at the beginning of the movement, were genuine. Even after

[1] Minot, *History of the Insurrections*, p. 176.

the second phase of the rebellion was reached, such conservatives as were not wholly blinded by fear or hate commented upon the remarkable orderliness of the rebel forces. For the most part there was no personal violence or pillage of property until the end, when many of the rebels had been rendered desperate by the failure of their cause and by the acts of the legislature. The neglect of that body to levy any taxes in 1785 and its attempt to collect far more than the people could bear in 1786 were typical of its unstable policy, which ran alternately from one extreme to the other and which caused a total loss of confidence in its good faith and ability. Had the lawmakers followed either of Washington's suggestions, and either firmly repressed the movement by force in its initial stage or made a genuine attempt to redress acknowledged grievances, the movement would probably have been handled as easily as it was in New Hampshire or Connecticut or Vermont. It is noteworthy that the state in which the doctrine of government by the "well-born" was carried to its furthest point and in which the government had the narrowest franchise was the one which had the most trouble with its people.

CHAPTER VII

ADOPTION OF THE FEDERAL CONSTITUTION

Need for Federal Union — Constitution Adopted in the Several States — Economic Factors — Parties — Conservative Reaction — Separation of Maine Discussed — Recalcitrancy of Rhode Island — Vermont Admitted to the Union

THE decade following the disturbed period with which we have dealt in the past few chapters was one of great progress toward stability. In it we find movements and tendencies taking the definite shapes which they were long to maintain. The Federal government was formed; the independent state of Vermont was admitted to the Union; trade expanded and shifted to a considerable extent from its colonial channels to new ones that were to prove enormously profitable in the nineteenth century; banks were founded; and manufacturing began to transform New England industry and life. Immigration commenced to pour in from Europe for the first time in the eastern states since 1640; and, on the other hand, New England emigrants of the old stock began to transform the new West.

The failure of the Continental Congress to secure from the states adequate powers of taxation and the right to regulate commerce had finally resulted in the calling of a general convention, which was to meet in Philadelphia in May 1787. The rebellion in Massachusetts and disturbed conditions in several other states gave timely suggestion of the need for a stronger central authority. Of the five New England states only three were represented in the convention. Vermont had not yet become a member of the Confederation, and Rhode Island, as we shall note later, declined to participate. New Hampshire

— it was said from lack of funds — at first took no action, and it was not until John Langdon, a wealthy merchant, offered to pay the expenses of a delegation that the situation was relieved. The members consisted of Langdon himself and Nicholas Gilman, a man of no special ability. Massachusetts sent Elbridge Gerry, Nathaniel Gorham, Rufus King, and Caleb Strong, a moderately good delegation of which King was the ablest member. The strongest delegation was that from Connecticut, which sent William Samuel Johnson, regarded as one of the most learned men in the country, Roger Sherman, and Oliver Ellsworth. All three were opposed to a strong central government, and did their most valuable work in upholding the rights of the states and individuals.[1] It has been claimed that Sherman was the author of the great compromise of the Constitution, by which each state has equal representation in the Senate, whereas representation is according to population in the House.[2] Perhaps, however, Connecticut's share should not be overstressed, for although her representatives were in favor of the plan and Sherman was undoubtedly one of the leaders who thus solved the most perplexing problem before the convention, we know little of the discussion in the committee which reported on the matter, and of which Sherman was not a member.[3]

Following the completion of the convention's labors came the necessity for ratification by the several states, and a lively campaign at once began, the newspapers being filled with articles for and against the proposed instrument. In Connecticut there was a greater unanimity of opinion than in any other section of New England,[4] and Humphreys wrote to Washington that the merchants and all the men in the liberal professions, as well as the ex-army officers, would be in favor of the new Constitution. He added that much had been done to prepare the minds of the people and he himself claimed to "have had

[1] Max Farrand, *The Framing of the Constitution*, (Yale Univ. Press, 1913), p. 200.
[2] See, *e.g.*, Boutell, *Sherman*, p. 165.
[3] Farrand, *op. cit.*, p. 98.
[4] The vote in the Connecticut convention was 128 yeas, and only 40 nays. B. C. Steiner, "Connecticut's Ratification of the Federal Constitution," Am. Antiq. Soc., *Proceedings*, N. S., vol. XXV, p. 124.

no inconsiderable agency in the superintendence of two Presses from which more newspapers are circulated I imagine, than from any others in New England," noting that the press was particularly efficacious in forming public opinion "in this quarter of the Continent." [1]

Although there were ample discussions held in all the states regarding the political aspects of the new Constitution, the economic factors were in reality the determining ones in its adoption. In his first article in defense of the Constitution in the *Connecticut Courant*, Ellsworth, writing under the pseudonym of "A Landholder," stressed the economic point of view and held that the financial interests of the farmers were identical with those of the merchants. A Federal government of energy, he said, was the only one which could preserve their "liberty and riches." [2] Naturally all those holding the obligations of the government in one form or another were in favor of a strong authority and taxing power, and three years later Chauncey Goodrich of Hartford wrote that even in Connecticut it was possible that without the aid of these creditors the government could not have been formed.[3]

In one respect, however, the situation in Connecticut was favorable to a sentiment for adoption even among classes that in most states were opposed to the new plan of government. The state had practically no European commerce of its own and was dependent upon the imports of its neighbors for its European goods. Both New York and Massachusetts had laid import duties to provide part of the funds for their shares of the Federal burdens, and it was estimated that New York raised in this way from £60,000 to £80,000 a year, of which Connecticut paid one third.[4] That state claimed, therefore, that it not only had to raise its own taxes but was paying a considerable part of its neighbors', and that only a strong

---

[1] Humphreys, *David Humphreys*, vol. I, p. 424.

[2] Reprinted by P. L. Ford, *Essays on the Constitution of the United States*, (Brooklyn, 1892), p. 141.

[3] Geo. Gibbs, *Memoirs of the Administrations of Washington and John Adams*, (New York, 1846), vol. I, p. 38.

[4] O. G. Libby, *Geographical Distribution of the Vote of the Thirteen States on the Federal Constitution*, (Univ. of Wisconsin, 1894), p. 16.

Federal government, with the power of general trade legislation, could save it from ruin. In a special convention at Hartford the Constitution was adopted easily by a vote of one hundred and twenty-eight to forty on January 9, 1788.

In New Hampshire the situation was more complicated. "So confident were we," wrote a Federalist in February 1788, "of the prevailing voice in favor of the Constitution that no pains were taken to counteract the intrigues of a few notoriously vile characters, who were too successful in the dark and dirty business of seducing a great number of the interior towns by false representations to fetter their delegates with positive instructions to vote in all events against the Constitution." [1] Rather than risk a vote under those conditions, the convention was adjourned until June.

Speaking broadly, the state was made up of three sections — that along the seacoast, which included the largest towns and most of the professional men and wealthy merchants; that in the interior; and that along the Connecticut River. This last section was distinct in interest from the others and closely allied to Vermont and the Connecticut River region of Massachusetts. In this section the same argument was used in favor of the Constitution that had been effective in Connecticut. It was said that all imports came by way of the Connecticut River from New York or Boston, and consequently paid the import duties of other states. This argument, combined with adroit leadership of such men as Judge Livermore, swung the section into the Federal column. It was the middle section, made up largely of small farmers of narrow views and limited experience, that opposed the ratification. However, at the second convention, held at Concord, the seaboard and Connecticut Valley towns succeeded in overriding those of the middle section, and the Constitution was adopted by a vote of fifty-seven to forty-seven. The only speech in the convention that has come down to us was that by Joshua Atherton, opposing slavery and the slave trade. [2]

For Massachusetts we have much more ample information, and the full text of the debates in the convention. At first, as

[1] Quoted by Libby, *op. cit.*, p. 72.   [2] Elliott's *Debates*, vol. II, pp. 202 *f.*

in New Hampshire, the Federalists felt that sentiment was overwhelmingly in their favor and that adoption would be a simple matter.[1] They were soon disillusioned. The opposition, strengthened by Anti-Federal pamphlets and articles in the press, made the most of debatable points, of the fact that the members of the Federal Convention had been by no means unanimous, and of the arguments advanced by Elbridge Gerry, who, although one of the representatives of Massachusetts in the convention, was opposed to the Constitution. Samuel Adams was also strongly against it, and although his influence was far from being what it had been in the earlier years, he could use the press effectively. The most popular leader, John Hancock, as usual, refused to commit himself until he saw which way the popular wind blew, and his influence was lost in favor of ratification until the last moment.

Most of the articles in the press originated in or near Boston, both during and after the sitting of the state convention. Some of those on the Anti-Federalist side were of considerable ability, especially those which have been assigned to the authorship of General James Warren and James Winthrop.[2] Space does not permit a detailed discussion of the controversy, but in general the points made by those opposed to ratification were that the whole method of procedure in the writing and submission of the new frame of government had been unconstitutional according to the Articles of Confederation; that the plan would tend inevitably to the creation of an aristocracy; that it favored unduly the wealthy elements of the population; that it contained no bill of rights; that it would impair the sovereignty of the individual states; that it would create a swarm of Federal officeholders who would overrun the country; that the Federal courts would overrule the State courts; that the general laws enacted by the new government could not be fairly applied to states so different in their internal culture as, for example, Massachusetts and Georgia; that the basis of representation was unequal; and that the control of the people over their representatives was insufficient.

[1] Harding, *Contest in Massachusetts*, pp. 16 *ff*.
[2] *Ibid.*, *op. cit.*, pp. 28 *ff.*; Ford, *op. cit.*, pp. 51 *ff*.

In the only article of importance written in the western part of the state, the old fear of the west for the east comes out clearly. It says that in the proposed Constitution "a foundation is laid for throwing the whole power of the Federal government into the hands of those who are in the mercantile interests; and for the landed, which is the great interest of the country, to lie unrepresented, forlorn, and without hope." [1] From a private letter of the outspoken editor of the first newspaper in Maine we get the point of view of another frontier section. "The vast Continent of America," wrote Thomas B. Wait of Portland, "cannot be long subjected to a Democracy if consolidated into one Government — you might as well attempt to rule Hell by Prayer." [2]

The fact is that, whereas the opinions of the common people had remained largely unchanged, there had been a marked reversal in that portion of the conservative element which had been carried away temporarily by the revolutionary stream. Administration had been found to be a far more difficult problem than revolution. Few of the leaders at any time had been genuine believers in democracy, and the chaotic condition of the Federal government and such outbreaks as Shays's Rebellion had substantially cooled the ardor of many liberals. It is true that in the ablest papers written in defense of the Constitution, such as those comprised in the *Federalist*, the popular doctrines of a decade before were still tacitly accepted. [3]   But the freedom and equality of all men and the inherent right of "the people" to rule, which had been so glowingly spread before them in the war propaganda, were now quietly shelved in favor of a government that could command obedience, protect the established order, and secure property. Elbridge Gerry spoke for a large class when he admitted that he had been "too republican heretofore," but that he had been "taught by experience the danger of the levelling spirit." [4]   In fact, as has lately been pointed out the doctrine of popular sovereignty merely gives "a specious

---

[1] Quoted by Harding, *op. cit.*, p. 34.
[2] *Ibid.*, *op. cit.*, p. 39.
[3] *Cf.* C. E. Merriam, *A History of American Political Theories*, (New York, 1918) pp. 100 *f.*
[4] Quoted by Merriam, *op. cit.*, p. 99.

xactitude of form to that principle of consent for which, in
ome fashion, room must be found in the modern state."[1]
his was being borne in upon the leaders of the new states and
efenders of the social order — which to them meant the order
o which they had been accustomed, and that in which they
ould continue to rule.

On the other hand, as the author just quoted has also said,
the social rights which are translated into legal rights are
most always the rights of a limited group of men."[2] This
uth was unconsciously realized by those who, however ig-
orant and wrong-headed, had glimpsed a better order in which
e poor and debtors should not be exploited by law. When
1776 they had been told that all men were born free and
qual and entitled to life, liberty, and the pursuit of happiness,
ey had believed it and fought for it. In 1787 they saw a
oor man kept in jail for a year with no hope of release, because
f a small debt to a creditor in the same line of business, who
us freed himself from competition. They saw others lan-
uishing with no prospect of ever again being at liberty to
pport their families, because of debts of a few shillings only.[3]
he "life, liberty, and pursuit of happiness" which they had
een promised thus took on for them a different coloring from
at which it had for the doctrinaire leaders of the more fortu-
ate classes.

In the years of agitation and propaganda those leaders had
inned in the ears of the multitude the dangers of tyranny
om a despotic government. Now the same leaders, for the
ost part, asked for a strong central government just at a
me when the poor had suffered severely for several years.
ll this should be kept in mind in considering the opposition
hich was manifested toward the new Constitution. That
strument reversed the popular trend and was less democratic
an many of the new State constitutions. Moreover, we
ust remember that, as we have said, the question was largely
n economic one. Those who claim that the Constitution is
acrosanct on high political grounds and should never be altered

[1] H. J. Laski, *The Foundations of Sovereignty*, (London, 1921), p. 226.
[2] *Ibid.*, p. 229.   [3] Nevins, *American States*, pp. 456 *f.*

in spite of social injustice should recall that originally it was
— to a great extent — adopted as a remedy for the evils of
a specific economic situation, that of the disturbed post-revolu-
tionary decade of a century and a half ago. "I conceive, Sir,
that the present Constitution was dictated by commercial
necessity more than any other cause," said Fisher Ames in
Congress, after having been one of its warmest defenders in the
Massachusetts convention.[1] It was based on the antagonism
of the mercantile and agrarian groups of the day, as is clearly
brought out in the *Federalist*, and both groups fought for their
own interests.

Massachusetts, like New Hampshire, was divided politically
and economically into three sections. First, there was the
coast district, that of oldest settlement, largest urban population, greatest wealth, and leading mercantile interests. The
second, or middle, section was that of the small farmers, tilling
poorer farms than in other portions of the state, and without the
advantage of water communication. In connection with the
influence of poverty on politics, Professor Libby notes that
fifty-six of the Anti-Federal towns of that day now show 30,318
acres of abandoned farms, whereas thirty Federal towns show
only 8556.[2] The third section was that of the rich Connecticut Valley, of which the northern farming districts proved
Anti-Federal and the southern ones, with their trading towns,
Federal.

The convention met at Boston January 9, 1788. It numbered three hundred and sixty-four delegates and every shade
of opinion was represented. Governor Hancock was elected
chairman on account of his popularity with the masses. The
Federal leaders formed a remarkably strong group, including
Caleb Strong, Rufus King, ex-Governor Bowdoin, General
Lincoln, Theophilus Parsons, Fisher Ames, and Theodore
Sedgwick. Elbridge Gerry, who opposed ratification, was
not a member of the convention, and the Anti-Federal leaders
could muster no such array of talents as their opponents. Indeed, some of them were so obscure that we know little o

[1] Quoted by Beard, *Economic Origins*, p. 7.
[2] *Geographical Distribution of the Vote*, p. 12.

nothing of them beyond their record in the debates. There was no question but that a stronger Federal government was a necessity if the Union were to be maintained, and this was obvious at the time to the educated and prosperous in Massachusetts. The difficulty was that a very large proportion of the population was neither educated nor prosperous. The leaders of this class might make a poor showing, but that the class itself was large and of considerable influence upon public opinion was indicated by the vote on ratification.

Had the question been submitted, as it was in Rhode Island, to votes of individual town meetings, or even had it been submitted to the convention as soon as assembled, it is unquestionable that Massachusetts would have defeated the Constitution. The Federalist leaders first secured the convention method, and next, they avoided an early vote by wisely passing a resolution that the document should be considered by paragraphs before any vote should be taken on it as a whole. In general the discussion dealt with the same topics that had already been dwelt upon at length in the press. Two minor points indicated certain trends of opinion of the day — the lack of a religious test for office and the section relating to slavery. As to the first, it is noteworthy that the absence of any such test was upheld by the clergymen who were members of the convention, and objected to only by some of the more narrow-minded lay members.[1] Slavery, which had been virtually forbidden in the Constitutions of New Hampshire, Vermont, and Massachusetts, was roundly denounced by several of the members, and the clause relating to it in the Federal constitution severely criticized.

A careful reading of the entire debate and of much of the controversial writings in the press reveals that the objections of the Anti-Federalists in Massachusetts had three important bases. One was the mistrust and disbelief in delegated powers, another was the conflict of interest between the commercial and agrarian groups, and the third was a similar conflict between the democrats and those who believed, like John Adams, in the right of the cultured and well-born to govern the state.

[1] Elliott's *Debates*, vol. II, pp. 118, 120, 148.

It has been claimed, indeed, that this last difference of opinion underlay the main part of the opposition in the state.[1]

After two weeks of debate, the Federalists realized that they were not strong enough to secure a vote unqualifiedly ratifying the Constitution.   They therefore decided to introduce amendments which would meet the main objections of their opponents, but which could be passed as recommendations to Congress without invalidating the ratification of the main body of the instrument.   However, the distrust which the people felt for the advocates of adoption was so great that it was deemed necessary to secure someone who was not of their party to introduce the resolution.   The opposition, King wrote to James Madison, "seems to arise from an opinion that is immovable, that some injury is plotted against them — that the system is the production of the rich and ambitious . . . and that the consequence will be the establishment of two orders in Society, one comprehending the opulent and great, and the other the poor and illiterate." [2]

There was at that time no immigrant problem in Massachusetts.   There had been practically no immigration of new stock since 1640, and the population was remarkably homogeneous.   Practically every family in the state had been there for a century and a half.   It may be pointed out, under these conditions, that if more than one half of the elected delegates from all the towns in the state were firmly possessed of the notions that King attributed to them, — and they seem to have been so, — all things could not have been so well with the governmental and educational systems of the commonwealth or with the social activity of the Puritan gentry as the panegyrists of the purity and simplicity of colonial days would have us believe.

Up to January 30, Hancock had not taken his seat as chairman.   The gout — which, as John Adams said, always conveniently prevented the popular idol from being about when there was anything unpopular to be done — had prevented

---

[1] Harding, *Contest in Massachusetts*, p. 76.
[2] King, *Rufus King*, vol. I, p. 317; *cf.* [Jonathan Jackson] *Thoughts upon the Politica. Situation* . . . (Worcester, 1788), p. 118.

his appearance. King wrote a few days before the end of the month that "as soon as the majority is exhibited on either side I think his Health will suffice him to be abroad."[1] It was pointed out to him that the Constitution could be ratified if the recommendatory amendments were added. He was offered the opportunity to introduce the resolution ratifying the Constitution and suggesting the amendments, thus gaining for him the prestige of apparently having been the one who had composed the differences between the two parties. He was also promised the support of the Bowdoin following for the governorship in the next election, and apparently he was told that if Virginia did not come into the Union, which was then doubtful, he would be considered as the candidate for the vice-presidency.[2]

The scheme succeeded. Hancock arose in the convention at the appointed time and read as his own the amendments which had been prepared by Theophilus Parsons.[3] The farce was played out, Samuel Adams was won over, and when the final vote was taken it was in favor of ratification by the slight majority of nineteen in three hundred and fifty-five votes. The distribution of the vote is even more instructive. Of the three sections into which we have noted the state to have been divided by economic interests, the eastern one was seventy-three per cent in favor and twenty-seven against; the western, forty-two per cent in favor and fifty-eight against; whereas the middle was only fourteen per cent in favor and eighty-six against.[4]

When Massachusetts recorded her decision only five states had accepted the Constitution.[5] Along the whole seaboard the Federal leaders felt that the decision would determine the result in New York and the whole question of adoption. There is no doubt that ratification by Massachusetts was actually the turning-point in the contest, and that the Constitution would

---

[1] Quoted by Harding, *op. cit.*, p. 85.
[2] There seems to be no reason to doubt the authenticity of this deal. *Vide* Harding, *op. cit.*, pp. 84 *ff.*; Morse, *Federalist Party*, pp. 50 *ff.*, 212 *ff.*
[3] Parsons, *Theophilus Parsons*, pp. 65 *f.*
[4] Libby, *Geographical Distribution of the Votes*, p. 12.
[5] Delaware, Pennsylvania, New Jersey, Georgia, and Connecticut.

not have been adopted had her vote been adverse. Whether chaos and civil war between the states would have resulted, as many statesmen believed, it is impossible to say. Certainly the subsequent political development of America would have been different from what it has been. Almost to the last minute the majority was against it. The scheme evolved by a small but shrewd and able group, utilizing the vanity of a popular idol, saved the day. It is an instructive example, when we are led to consider "social forces" only as determining the historic process, and individuals as negligible.

In Rhode Island, as we have seen, during the paper-money agitation the mercantile-town party had lost control of the government, and the country party was firmly in the saddle. The question of appointing delegates to the Federal Convention came before the legislature in March 1787, the same session at which the state repudiated its financial obligations to the Confederacy. By a majority of twenty-three the legislature refused to participate in the convention. The minority were furious, and the other states bitterly condemned the stand taken by Rhode Island. To her paper-money frauds and her repudiation of her obligations was now added refusal to cooperate with the rest of the continent in the endeavor to form a more perfect government. At once she became a pariah among her sister states. Talk was heard of forcing her to join; of not letting her in under any circumstances; and even of dividing her territory among her neighbors.[1]

When the convention finished its labors and the Constitution was submitted to the states, some notice had to be taken of it. There was a strong minority in Rhode Island in favor of ratification, led by such men as Marchant and Champlin of Newport, and Arnold and Bowen of Providence, but the great majority, both within the legislature and without, were opposed. It was felt by these opponents that the surest way to defeat ratification was to submit the Constitution to the town meetings rather than to the legislature, and this was accordingly carried out. Instead of voting, however, the towns of Newport and Providence both gave instructions to call a

[1] Bates, *Rhode Island*, pp. 152 *ff.*

convention for the purpose. The Federalists, in order to show their disapprobation of the method of voting by towns, abstained for the most part from voting at all, and the popular vote when taken showed, therefore, 2708 against ratification and only 237 in favor in an electorate of over 6000.[1] In March and October the legislature twice refused to consider a convention. By this time New Hampshire had ratified as the ninth state to do so, and the Constitution was accordingly declared in force. By the time eleven states had assented, the Rhode Island legislature met in March, but for a fourth and a fifth time defeated the demand for a convention. The mercantile element realized what it would mean to the prosperity and commerce of the state to be outside the pale of a Union that could cut off her trading with all parts of the continent and which, in view of her attitude on money, credit, and the violation of contracts, would be likely to do so. As we have said, however, the Tory emigration had removed many of the most able men in the state, and the Federal party lacked leaders. The farmers could not yet see the result of their acts, and the demand for a convention was defeated for the sixth time. In July 1789 the new Federal Congress passed an Act by which all imported articles received into the Union through Rhode Island should be considered as coming from foreign ports. The Assembly began to weaken. By January 1790 North Carolina had ratified, and Rhode Island was the only state that had not done so. Meanwhile, Congress had prepared the amendments to the Constitution which had been generally demanded, and these factors, together with the new revenue laws, were of influence on the minds of the Anti-Federalists.[2]

Finally, a convention was agreed to and met in March 1790, but failed to act and was adjourned to May. The state election which intervened was a complete victory for the Anti-Federalists. Coercion was now freely discussed in Congress by representatives of the other states, who were losing patience. The feeling was that the maritime situation of a small state like Rhode Island would not permit her to be left out of the

[1] Bates, *op. cit.*, p. 164. [2] Bates, *op. cit.*, p. 177.

Union, and that her recalcitrancy should not be allowed to jeopardize the success of the whole. "Enemies they must be, or fellow citizens, and that in a very short time," wrote one Congressman.[1] At last a bill passed the United States Senate prohibiting all commercial intercourse between any part of the Union and Rhode Island, and demanding payment by that state of a part of her share of the Federal debt. This meant that the way would be paved for armed coercion; but the House was not yet ready for so strong a measure. The struggle within Rhode Island continued, Newport threatening to secede from the state and inciting other towns to do so and to join the Union should the state not ratify. At last, on May 29, ratification was carried by the close vote of thirty-four to thirty-two, with unquestionably the great majority of the people of the commonwealth against it.[2]

At the time of the adoption of the Constitution by Massachusetts, the fear that it might lessen the chances for eventual separation of Maine from that state had probably accounted for some of the opposition manifested in the province, and in 1791 the agitation for seceding and setting up a separate government was renewed. Among the reasons given by those in favor of the movement were the inconvenience of having all the papers in suits in the Supreme Judicial Court kept in Boston, the unequal operation of taxes, the expense of having to travel to Massachusetts across the intervening state of New Hampshire to attend the legislature, and the difficulty of procuring legislation favorable to the peculiar interests of the province. It was pointed out that the population of Maine was already greater than that of Vermont and nearly double that of Rhode Island or Delaware, and that the assumption of state debts and the financial situation at the moment made the time peculiarly opportune for separation.[3] In a referendum held the next year, however, the vote was only two thousand and eighty-

---

[1] Bates, *op. cit.*, p. 187.
[2] The story is given with many documents, by Staples, *R. I. in the Cont. Cong.* pp. 574 *ff.*
[3] *An Address to the Numerous and Respectable Inhabitants of the Great Extensive District of Maine*, March, 1791. [Broadside] *cf.* [Daniel Davis] *An Address to the Inhabitants of the District of Maine*, (Portland, 1791), pp. 8 *ff.*

four in favor of seceding, whereas twenty-four hundred and thirty-eight voted against it, and the matter was not seriously agitated again until 1815.[1]

During all this time Vermont had continued a sovereign state outside the Union and with no connection with any other power. Levi Allen had maintained negotiations with the British government, largely for his personal advantage, it appears, and when he was in England in 1784, claiming to have a commission from the state, he was actually possessed of no such document, although he received one for the purpose of furthering the project of a canal two years later.[2] In July 1788 Ethan Allen, then in Quebec, wrote to Lord Dorchester representing that Vermont had serious objections, on account of economic interests and fear of embroiling herself in the inter-state quarrels, to uniting with the rest of the new nation.   The leading men, he said, were not in favor of a republican form of government, and desired reunion with Great Britain.[3]

Meanwhile, New York had changed her attitude, and in her anxiety to add another northern state to the Union in order to strengthen the power of the North in Congress, was willing to come to an adjustment with Vermont over all matters formerly in dispute. Commissioners were appointed from the two states, and in 1790 finally agreed that New York should relinquish all claims to lands within the boundaries of Vermont for the lump sum of $30,000.[4] This paved the way for the entrance of Vermont into the Union should she so desire, and in January of the following year a convention was held at Bennington to debate the question of adopting the Federal Constitution. It was pointed out by those in favor of doing so that the position of Vermont as an independent country was an impossible one. Forming as she did a wedge running into the new powerful Union of states, and occupying a posi-tion on the frontier of the British, it would be impossible for the United States to leave her out permanently. Should the

---

[1] E. Stanwood, "The Separation of Maine from Massachusetts," Mass. Hist. Soc., *Proceedings*, Ser. III, vol. I, p. 131.

[2] *Records of Governor and Council*, vol. III, pp. 408 *f*.

[3] *Report on the Canadian Archives*, 1890, pp. 210 *f*.

[4] *Records of Governor and Council*, vol. III, pp. 421 *f*.

nation wish to exert itself, it had ample military and commercial powers to force her to unite whether she desired it or not; and should she be shut out from all the ports and commercial advantages of the United States, her own commerce would be smothered, as Canada did not afford sufficient markets for her produce and was difficult of access from large parts of the state.   Ratification was voted almost unanimously, there being only four dissentient votes out of one hundred and nine.[1] This cut the ground from under the feet of Levi Allen, who had continued negotiations with the British and was in their pay.[2] Affirming to the British authorities that he had always been a Loyalist, he received from them £100 a year, claiming at the same time that he was in close touch with Governor Chittenden. On January 20, 1791 Congress passed an act admitting Vermont to the Union as the fourteenth state, and the New England section was once more united.

[1] *Records of Governor and Council*, vol. III, pp. 464 f.
[2] *Report on the Canadian Archives*, 1889, p. 53.

CHAPTER VIII

THE ECONOMIC STRUCTURE, 1790–1800

Question of Sectional Strengths after Revolution — New England Declines in Comparative Importance — Economic Character of the Population — Lack of Markets for Agricultural Produce — Conditions of Agriculture — Movements of Population — Land Companies — Manufactures — Opening of the Oriental Trade — Speculation

In order to understand the political and social movements of the end of the eighteenth and the beginning of the nineteenth century in New England, it is necessary to make a brief survey of the economic basis of that section. First of all we may note that the Eastern States had been steadily declining in importance as compared with the other parts of the Union, and under the new conditions this fact began to acquire a significance which it had not had under the imperial administration before the Revolution. It is true that there had always been jealousy between the different colonies, as well as between the loosely compacted groups into which the colonies naturally coalesced. At the opening of the struggle there may be considered as having been five such groups: Canada and the Far West, New England, the Middle Colonies, the South, and the West Indies. So long as any conflict of interest between them — as notably in the case of the economic relations between New England and the West Indies — was finally determined by the Parliament across the sea, the question of their own comparative strength in wealth and population was more or less negligible. After the achievement of independence by some of them, however, the situation altered entirely. As the interests of the different sections of the new American nation were diverse, or at least were considered so, and as national sentiment was weak, it seemed obvious that each state or section would have to depend upon the strength it could muster to protect its own prosperity and welfare. As colonies within the British empire, it had made little difference, save to provincial pride, whether or not Virginia had a larger population than Massachusetts; but the question assumed a new aspect when England was no longer the arbiter, and when any conflict of interest between states or sections had to be determined by votes in Congress, in which body representation was based upon population.

As compared with the rest of the colonies, the decline in population in New England had been steady from the beginning. In 1650 the people of that section had numbered, in round figures, fifty-two per cent of the whole. By 1700 they formed only thirty-eight per cent, by 1750 twenty-eight per cent, and by 1790 but twenty-five per cent. A New Englander in 1790, studying the figures of the first Federal census taken in that year, together with such other statistics as might be available to him, could have found no hope anywhere.

We have already noted the almost stationary population of Boston, increasing perhaps two thousand only in a half century, as contrasted with the rapid growth of both New York and Philadelphia, which, both numbering about thirteen thousand in 1750, gained thirty-three thousand and forty-two thousand respectively in forty years.[1] Isaac Weld, speaking of the Massachusetts capital about 1800, wrote that "though it has a most excellent harbour, and has always been inhabited by an enterprising and industrious people, yet it is now inferior both in size and commerce, to Baltimore, which was little more than the residence of a few fishermen thirty years ago." [2] This statement, although somewhat exaggerated, was not so far from the truth as to population at least. Weld recognized

---

[1] The figures, when no other source is indicated, are taken from the tables in *A Century of Population Growth*, (Washington, 1909). Although these are not wholly accurate and should be checked with other compilations, they are sufficiently so for our present purpose.

[2] *Travels through the States of North America, 1795, 1796, 1797*, (London, 1807), vol. I, p. 56.

FORT WARREN AND BOSTON HARBOR, 1853

From an unpublished water-color sketch by Thomas Kelah Wharton; original in the New York Public Library

that the trouble with Boston was that it had no navigable river and no hinterland from which to draw. Salem was growing more rapidly, but Newport had fewer residents than it had had forty years earlier.

Comparing the largest two states of the Northern and Southern sections, we find that the white population of Virginia had come to outnumber that of Massachusetts by over twentyfive thousand. To this we have to add one hundred and seventy-five thousand votes more, or three fifths of the slaves, that being the ratio allowed by the Constitution for slave representation. Apparently, moreover, in spite of the large families which we think of as characteristic of New England at this period, the whites were increasing more rapidly in Virginia than in the Bay State, for whereas in the latter there were eighty-one hundred fewer white boys under sixteen than there were adults, in the former there were fifty-five hundred more.

An interesting side-light on the two sections, partly economic and partly social, may be derived from the figures of receipts at the various post-offices, the period taken being the three months ending January 5, 1790. Boston was the only office in New England in which the income was over $100, the receipts there being $665, at Worcester $11, Springfield $12, Salem $81, Hartford $74, New Haven $47, and Norwalk $3, to name a few of the more typical communities. On the other hand, in Virginia, Richmond took in $482, Petersburg $322, Alexandria $290, Fredericksburg $237, and such practically unknown places as Dumfries and Cabin Point exceeded Hartford and Worcester respectively.[1]

The steady rise of the Middle States and the South at the expense, comparatively, of the influence in the future of his own section, stirred deep anxiety and jealousy in the breast of the New Englander of that day. There was also the bugaboo of the possible rise of a new West beyond the mountains, threatening to upset still further the balance of power between what were regarded as merely federated states. The states of New England were ancient and, for the most part, well defined, and it may be added, well filled, for the industrial

[1] *American State Papers, Post Office*, pp. 9 ff.

revolution, with its possibilities of enormous increase in population, was yet undreamed of.   The great bulk of the people, as in all the states, were farmers, and there were reasons, which we shall discuss presently, why the limits of an agricultural population in New England appeared to have been reached.

The anxious observer might, indeed, have found some comfort in the return of the people at this time to their old habits of industry, and the gradual disappearance of the extravagance of the war period among those who could not afford it. "Habits of industry and frugality are taking place of those of luxury and dissipation, more generally and with more celerity than I expected," wrote Stephen Higginson from Boston. "It is a growing Idea, that the manners contracted during the War must be done away; and that every Class of Citizens must expect only to thrive by the means comonly succesful in a time of peace." [1]   Homespun was once more replacing imported finery in farmers' houses, and spinning-bees were becoming as popular as they had been in Stamp Act days.[2]   But in 1790 both the influence and the welfare of the section were menaced, and as the problems of New England were largely peculiar to that portion of the country, it came to pass in the troubled years which were beginning that it should be forced into an attitude which was violently sectional.

In 1790 about eighty-five per cent of the entire New England population lived in towns of less than three thousand inhabitants; nor must it be forgotten that by "towns" were meant not the compact communities of modern days but the New England "townships," which averaged more than forty square miles in extent and in some instances were considerably larger. Only nine had a population of between four and five thousand, three between five and six thousand, and only six numbered more than that.   Outside of a very few of the largest centres, such as Boston and Salem, it may be said that practically every family lived in whole or large part from the profits or

[1] "Letters of Stephen Higginson," American Historical Association, *Report*, 1896, vol. I, p. 781.
[2] R. M. Tryon, *Household Manufactures in the United States, 1640-1860*, (Chicago, 1917), pp. 123 *ff*.

products of agriculture. The only commercial towns were those along the coasts and the Connecticut River, and in some of these there were small classes of citizens who had become wholly divorced from the soil and who were therefore dependent upon the farmers of the surrounding country within a transportation radius of approximately twenty miles, or upon those who could ship by water. This, of course, was notably true of Boston. Even twenty years later in many of the maritime towns of from three to seven thousand population, such as New Haven, New London, and Hartford, apparently about one half of the inhabitants were farmers, so that the demand for agricultural produce in such towns could not have extended far beyond their own borders.[1]

In rural communities — and in 1790 practically the whole of New England may be considered as one vast community of that type — there is no local market for agricultural produce unless division of labor has progressed so far as to cause the emergence of a class that does not raise its own food but devotes itself to other forms of activity. There was indeed, at this time, a certain amount of specialization. But even in the case of artisans such as shoemakers, business men such as millers and storekeepers, professional men such as doctors, lawyers, and clergymen, there were few members of any community who were without enough land of their own to make them independent, as to their food supplies, of their neighbors who devoted their entire energies to their farms and household industries. The markets for any agricultural surplus were therefore limited to the small ones of the maritime towns or such as might be built up by an export trade.

There were three regions to which the farmer who was located near enough to water transport could ship his surplus: the city of New York, the Southern states, — in which agriculture was more specialized, — and the West Indies. The first was a limited market and open to keen competition from Long Island and New Jersey. A careful analysis of the second, which was mainly confined to the coastal plain of South Caro-

[1] P. W. Bidwell, *Rural Economy in New England at the Beginning of the Nineteenth Century*, (New Haven, 1916), p. 292.

lina and Georgia, indicates that even twenty years later that market was also very limited and subject to competition by the farmers of the Southern highlands. As Bidwell says, the fact that the comparatively few New England farmers who were in a position to ship to so distant and small a market did so is the best evidence of the utter lack of any market nearer home.[1]

Of the three export markets, by far the most important was the West Indies, although it is impossible to reach any accurate estimate of the amounts of farm produce which were shipped thither from New England. We have spoken many times of the importance of the West India trade to the circle of New England commerce, but it must be considered that three of the most valuable items of export were fish, lumber, and horses. With the first two of these the farmer would have little or nothing to do, while the export of horses had declined very heavily during the Revolution and the trade was never recovered.[2] After Jay's treaty was signed, moreover, the size of the vessels was limited to seventy tons, about one half their former capacity, and these usually made but two trips a year. If from the total figures of exports from the whole United States to all the West India Islands we deduct the items mentioned and others which were not the produce of farms, as well as the large shipments of wheat and flour from the Middle and Southern States in which New England had no share, it becomes evident that the market afforded to the farmer of that section could have been only a moderate one.

Whatever the total exports to all three of these markets may have aggregated, they afforded an outlet for surplus production only to those farmers who were located within a few miles of navigable waters; for, with a few exceptions, the roads were so bad as to preclude the transport of articles over them in any considerable bulk at a cost which would make their sale profitable. This absence of markets for the only

[1] P. W. Bidwell, *Rural Economy in New England at the Beginning of the Nineteenth Century*, (New Haven, 1916), pp. 294 *ff*., 300.
[2] Deane Phillips, *Horse Raising in Colonial New England*, (Cornell University, 1922), p. 927.

produce of by far the largest part of the population had far-reaching effects. Having nothing to sell, the purchases of most of the farmers were of necessity limited to the smallest number of articles possible, and for these they bartered their corn or hay or wood or even their labor, at the country store. Everything of all sorts, clothes, tools, furniture, that could be made on the farm was manufactured there by old and young, hardly any member of the household of whatever age escaping some appointed task in the family economy. This naturally tended to retard division of labor in the community. The period was, it is true, an era of transition, and the making of hats had already become a shop industry, while shoemaking had entered the capitalist stage, with the craftsmen, however, still working in their homes.[1] But for the most part even those who specialized in some handicraft were still itinerants, going from house to house to ply their trade, and in most of New England there was no whole-time occupation by which a man could earn a living for himself and his family save farming.

Although the versatility thus enjoined upon the members of a farmer's household and the need of making that household almost wholly self-sustaining bred in the New England farmer that "Yankee ingenuity" which has become proverbial, it also had other and less desirable effects. For one thing, it kept agriculture at a very low level of efficiency, and the population at a low standard of living.[2] All the implements were of primitive type, clumsy and indescribably costly in the expenditure of labor required. The wooden "Old Colony plow," for example, which was in use in New England until 1820, had a ten-foot beam and a four-foot landslide, and it has been said that "it made the furrows stand up like the ribs of a lean horse in the month of March." There was no real labor-saving farm-machinery in general use until 1850, and the only invention in the period covered by this chapter that foreshadowed a later successor was a cast-iron plow, invented in New Jersey in the

[1] For the latter, vide Blanche E. Hazard, Organization of the Boot and Shoe Industry in Massachusetts before 1875, (Harvard University Press, 1921), pp. 24 ff.
[2] Bidwell, op. cit., pp. 352, 368.

1790's. Even this was for long rejected by the farmers because they feared it would injure the fertility of the soil and poison the land.[1]

South Carolina and Pennsylvania both had organized societies for the promotion of agriculture before the Massachusetts Society for that purpose was founded in 1792.[2] For many years, however, these societies had little or no influence upon the great mass of farmers, who considered any new ideas as impractical, but the fundamental factor making for inefficiency was the lack of a market. With his love of money and his versatile ingenuity, the Yankee farmer would undoubtedly have become a much better agriculturist had he had an outlet for any surplus production which new methods might have brought him. When, however, by producing a surplus he could do nothing to improve his position or scale of living, he preferred to cultivate his acres wastefully rather than to trouble himself with new and more intensive methods. In the absence of a market he could have been induced to incur the risks of "newfangled notions" only by pressure of population; but at this time the line of least resistance from this evil was emigration to new and usually richer lands.

Although the life of the average farmer's family produced strength of character, versatility, and a sense of self-reliance, it also induced narrow-mindedness, intellectual stagnation, and an economy that too often became mere sordid meanness. It is easy for those who have attained to a standard of living which provides them with leisure and release from a numbing round of daily toil to talk of "plain living and high thinking." But anyone who, either from personal experience or from intimate contact with others, has been able to observe the effects of too long hours of labor, cannot but realize that overfatigue is fatal to intellectual development. The small farm of the old type was an unsurpassed school for boyhood but an intellectual prison for manhood. A farmer's boy was

[1] H. W. Quaintance, "The Influence of Farm Machinery on Production and Labor," American Economic Association, *Publications*, Ser. III, vol. V, pp. 4, 7. The cotton gin was in use only in the South.
[2] C. L. Flint, "A Hundred Years' Progress," *Report*, U. S. Department of Agriculture, (Washington, 1872), p. 282.

well equipped for success, but he achieved it only on condition of leaving the farm before it became too late.

The extraordinary movements of population which set in after the Revolution — to which we have already alluded — showed that discontent with these conditions, — pressure on the soil from an agricultural standpoint, and the lack of opportunities for making a livelihood other than by farming, — were beginning to be widespread. It has been estimated that between 1790 and 1820 the natural increase in population in Massachusetts, Rhode Island, and Connecticut would have been 1,681,673 persons, had they all remained within those states. As it was in fact only 881,594, approximately 800,000 persons must have emigrated.[1] The movement is well illustrated by analyzing the changes of population in such a community as Middlefield, a small hill-town in western Massachusetts. In 1770 there were only two families living in this territory, increasing to thirty by 1780. In the next decade nearly a hundred families, consisting of six hundred individuals, took possession of farm lands. It is noteworthy that these early settlers came from fifty-four different towns in Massachusetts and Connecticut, one from New York, the origin of eighteen families being unknown.[2] As the amount of desirable land was limited, and as there was no occupation but farming, there was also a continuous and increasing exodus of young men. Forty of these had left by 1790, fifty-eight more by 1800, ninety-five more by 1810, and ninety-one more by 1820. In spite of this there was an increase in the population of the town of over two hundred between 1790 and 1810. Of those who left, about one half settled temporarily or permanently in other Massachusetts towns, about a quarter in New York, and the remainder in Ohio and other parts of the West.[3] The movement illustrates how the mobile population was taking up every corner of the available land in the older states, and how the more energetic, ambitious, or restless were moving out of those states altogether.

---

[1] Bidwell, *op. cit.*, p. 387.
[2] E. P. & P. M. Smith, *History of the Town of Middlefield*, privately printed, (1924), pp. 27, 393.   [3] *Ibid.*, pp. 27, 111, 395.

Before the Revolution the population of Rhode Island and Connecticut had been increasing at the rate of over twenty-eight per cent in every decade.   In that between 1790 and 1800 the population of the former remained stationary and that of the latter increased only five and one-half per cent.   A further analysis enables us to realize the results of a lack of markets for agricultural produce and the absence of any division of labor as affording means of earning a living.   There was no difference in the fertility of the soil or inhabitants in the two towns of Lebanon and Greenwich, yet between 1790 and 1810 the population of the former decreased twenty per cent, whereas that of the latter increased twelve per cent.   The explanation would seem to be that whereas Greenwich was within easy access of the New York market, Lebanon was fifteen miles from the nearest water transport.   The same results may be found by examining counties occupying similarly contrasted locations.   If we approach the problem from the other standpoint, that of division of labor, we may take the two towns of Farmington and Danbury.   The former had about twenty per cent more land than the latter and both were equally good for farming, but in the two decades from 1790 the number of people in Farmington, which was purely an agricultural community, increased less than two per cent, whereas that in Danbury increased twenty per cent, the explanation being that the manufacture of hats in the latter gave employment to a large number of persons not engaged in farming, and also enlarged the market for those who were.[1]   It was becoming obvious that unless new markets could be created at home or abroad New England had reached its limit of wealth and population as an agricultural section.   We shall see in later chapters how the development of manufactures both enlarged the farmers' markets and permitted a vast increase in population by opening new means of making a living.

Undoubtedly the hard times immediately following the Revolution, and the financial confusion in Rhode Island owing to paper money, had much to do with bringing about the extraordinary shifts in population.   It has been estimated that

[1] Bidwell, *op. cit.*, pp. 399 *ff*.

within six weeks after the collapse of Shays's Rebellion over seven hundred families emigrated from western Massachusetts into Vermont.[1] Brissot de Warville, speaking of conditions in Rhode Island in 1788, said that if paper money were not speedily abolished he thought the whole state would "be unpeopled," and that "nearly all the honest people of Newport would quit the place if they could sell their effects."[2] As the movement increased it came to embrace all classes, and grew to be almost a mania. First there went the restless and debt-ridden, low in the economic scale; then the farmers looking for good land at low cost; and lastly the mechanics and professional men seeking openings in localities of rapidly increasing population.[3] Mingled with these streams were many sons of families which were well-to-do, or which had been — for it is a mistake to think of early New England as wholly a land of frugality and steady habits. "It has been observed frequently," said a writer in the *Norwich Packet* in 1792, "that estates, in this part of the country do not often last in a family more than three generations, and frequently not so long. A man by his industry and economy gets a large estate for his son, his son lives in affluence and brings up a family of children in idleness and dissipation, who think the wealth of their father can never be spent."[4] Thus early began the American tradition of "three generations from shirt sleeves to shirt sleeves."

The western shores of Lake Champlain and the older towns of the Hudson River Valley became largely transformed by the influx of New England men. The present city of Hudson was changed in four years from a mere Dutch farm in 1784 to a New England commercial town with a considerable population, warehouses, wharves, and shipping.[5] Visiting the new settlement of Whitesborough on the Mohawk in 1788, Watson reported that "settlers are continually pouring in from the Connecticut hive," and that there were already three hundred "Yankees on their muster list."[6] Binghamton was settled

[1] Morse, *Federal Party*, p. 183 note.
[2] *New Travels in the United States* . . . *1788*, (London, 1794), vol. I, p. 120.
[3] Mathews, *Expansion of New England*, p. 166.   [4] Issue of Jan. 5, 1792.
[5] Elkanah Watson, *Men and Times of the Revolution*, (New York, 1856), p. 266.
[6] *Ibid.*, p. 271.

from Connecticut and Massachusetts, and in the places just mentioned and many others New England ideas and type of social structure were being carried westward in the course of expansion, although the intermixture of men from so many different localities bred a new diversity of opinion and a broader outlook. Even within New England the ferment must have meant the breaking down of many old prejudices and narrow points of view. The men of Middlefield, for example, coming from over sixty different towns, must have acquired a broader vision and a new tolerance when acting together in their own town meeting and in exchange of experiences in the evening's talk beside the roaring fires.

The movement was largely an individualistic one, resulting from the simultaneous desire on the part of thousands to better their condition in one way or another; but capitalists soon saw attractive opportunities for speculation and began operations on a scale undreamed of before the war. In 1786 the state of New York ceded to Massachusetts, in friendly settlement of that state's western claims, the title to about six million acres near Lake Ontario. Two years later, Massachusetts sold the preëmption claims to this land, for a million dollars, to Nathaniel Gorham and Oliver Phelps, representing an Association which secured by purchase the Indian title to about one half of it. The proprietors then offered the land for sale to settlers in townships, of which fifty had been sold by 1790, and the immigration from Connecticut, western Massachusetts, and Vermont was said to be beyond belief.[1]

Another association, the Ohio Company, operating in southeastern Ohio, was not a typical land company but largely an attempt to secure for the revolutionary soldiers of Connecticut their dues by means of a sale of western lands by Congress.[2] General Rufus Putnam was the leading spirit in it at first, later being joined by the Reverend Manasseh Cutler. The relations of the Association to its settlers were unique, and it has been said that no other land company in America can match its rec-

---

[1] O. Turner, *Holland Purchase*, (Buffalo, 1850), pp. 326 *ff*.
[2] A. B. Hulbert, *Records of the Original Proceedings of the Ohio Company*, (Marietta, 1917), vol. I, p. xlviii.

ord in laying the foundations of an American state.   Through
its efforts New England influence advanced yet farther into the
frontier region of the new West.   Cutler's relations with Congress had been extremely close and influential just at the time
when the Northwest Ordinance was being considered, and it
may have been partly due to him that the New England township system was that which was adopted as the basis of the development of the enormous territory embraced under that Act.[1]

The speculations of the Duer group in New York had also
extended into lands, and in 1791, in company with Generals
Henry Knox and Henry Jackson of Boston, they bought two
million acres in Maine from the Massachusetts government, at
ten cents an acre.   Efforts were made to bring in immigrants
from France, but the scheme failed with the general financial
crash that occurred the following year.

The relations between agricultural prosperity, efficiency,
value of land, and growth of population on the one hand and
an adequate market for surplus agricultural produce on the
other were well understood by such men as Alexander Hamilton.   "It is evident," he wrote in his great Report on Manufactures in 1791, "that the exertions of the husbandman will
be steady or fluctuating, vigorous or feeble, in proportion to
the steadiness or fluctuation, adequateness or inadequateness
of the markets on which he must depend, for the vent of the
surplus which may be produced by his labor; and that such
surplus, in the ordinary course of things, will be greater or less
in the same proportion."   Considering how rapidly the population was increasing and new settlements were being formed,
with the consequent increase in agricultural produce, he pointed
out that a market for the surplus was a matter of first importance, and that, with the economic and political ideas of the
times as affecting international trade, a domestic market was
greatly to be preferred to a foreign one.   Such a market, he
clearly foresaw, could be secured only by building up manufactures and by the creation of a class divorced from the soil,
who would consume the products of the farmer.[2]

[1] W. P. Cutler, *Manasseh Cutler*, (Cincinnati, 1888), vol. I, pp. 124 ff.
[2] *American State Papers, Finance*, vol. I, p. 127.

There were several factors, however, tending to retard the growth of manufactures after the abnormal requirements and conditions of the war had passed. Skilled workmen were scarce; the technique of England was far ahead of that in America; machinery was difficult to obtain and there was much ignorance as to its use; raw materials were often high-priced; the dictates of fashion called for foreign materials in many cases; and English competition was keen. It has often been stated that high wages were another deterrent, but this is questionable. George Cabot wrote to Hamilton that, although the wages of farm labor were much higher in America than in England and artisans received slightly higher wages than agriculturists, yet the artisans did not ask so much as similar workmen in the old country, where the discrepancy between the two classes was much greater.[1]

The other adverse factors come out frequently in the current discussions. Elisha Colt, writing of the attempt to establish a "Woolen Manufacture" at Hartford, said that when the promoters began they were "not only totally unacquainted with the various parts or subdivisions of the Labour; but equally destitute of every kind of Machinery and Labourers for executing such a project." They managed to collect a number of men, chiefly soldiers who had deserted from the British army during the war and remained in the country. These had some knowledge of the work, but none of them knew very much and their experimenting cost the company dear. In addition, he said, they had had to struggle with every sort of embarrassment attending the setting up of a new business, "either from the Ignorance, the Knavery or the fickleness of the Workmen; the high price of materials; the smallness of our Capital; and the prejudices of the Community against *home made* cloths, and the interested views and Jealousy of the British Factors."[2]

In New Haven a button factory had been started and reached the point where it was turning out two hundred different sorts, when the English manufacturers sent over large quantities at

[1] H. C. Lodge, *Life and Letters of George Cabot*, (Boston, 1877), p. 47.
[2] Letter of Elisha Colt to John Chester, Hartford, Aug. 20, 1791. Hamilton Papers, Mss., Library of Congress.

one third less than the accustomed price, in order to stifle this infant competition.[1]   One of the hat-making plants at Danbury complained of the difficulty of securing furs and the high prices of the raw material, due to the fact that almost the whole fur trade was engrossed by one person in New York, who shipped all furs to England so that the Danbury hatters had to purchase them after being shipped back.[2]   Another trouble, reported by a traveler, was that New England manufacturers invariably invested too much money in buildings and machinery, resulting in heavy mortgages on the property.[3] There were many paper mills, but the complaint was made that the oldest of these, those at Milton, had "fallen into the common error of our Manufactories, to get a good name, and not to labour to keep it, turning off their articles." [4]

Nevertheless, a beginning was being made, and, in spite of the increase in population, the importation of foreign manufactured goods had decreased by one half, due mainly to home production, though a large part of this was carried on in the households.[5]   In 1791 about ten thousand dozen of cotton and wool cards were being turned out in Massachusetts, of which two thirds were exported to other states, the business employing about twenty-five thousand persons, mostly women and children.   One of the most important attempts to establish a new industry was made in Rhode Island through the combined efforts of Samuel Slater, an Englishman, and the Providence firm of Almy & Brown.   In spite of the fact that there were stringent laws in England against the emigration of skilled workmen or the exporting of any models or drawings of machinery,

[1] Letter of J. & J. Mix to John Chester, New Haven, Sept. 30, 1791.   Hamilton Papers, Mss., *ibid.*

[2] Letter of O. Burr to John Chester, Danbury, Sept. 12, 1791.   Hamilton Papers, Mss., *ibid.*

[3] Henry Wansey, *Journal of an Excursion to the United States, 1794,* (Salisbury, 1796), p. 85.

[4] *Diary of William Bentley,* vol. I, p. 246.

[5] [Tench Coxe] *A brief Examination of Lord Sheffield's Observations,* (Philadelphia, 1791), p. 117.   *Cf.* letter of Nathaniel Gorham to Alexander Hamilton, Boston, Oct. 13, 1791.   Gorham says that the European imports into Massachusetts had declined fifty per cent in twenty years; that Connecticut had transferred its trade to New York; but that this was not enough to account for the decline, and that the reason must be sought in the increase of domestic manufactures.   Hamilton Papers, Mss., *Ibid.*

Slater, in furtherance of his own career, determined to acquire such knowledge of the Arkwright system of cotton-spinning as would enable him to reproduce it from memory in America. He finally left England, disguised as a farm hand, and after a short stay in New York made arrangements with Moses Brown to establish a mill at Providence. The enterprise was successful, the first cotton thread made either in Europe or America being manufactured there in 1793.[1]

With the type of mill introduced by Slater new problems arose in connection with labor, of which we shall have more to say in later chapters. It had been expected that manufacturing would make a market by giving work to persons divorced from the soil, but the first nine operatives employed by Slater were children, seven boys and two girls, all from seven to twelve years of age. Two years later he established a Sunday School for them, and it has been claimed that he treated them well.[2] In 1801 the number of children employed in the cotton mill at Pawtucket was over one hundred, ranging from four to ten years of age. Josiah Quincy, who visited the plant, said that the superintendent was eloquent on the usefulness of such a business in employing so many children of the poor. "But an eloquence was exerted on the other side of the question," Quincy adds, "more commanding than his, which called us to pity these little creatures, plying in a contracted room, among flyers and coggs, at an age when nature requires for them air, space and sports. There was an air of dull dejection on the countenances of all of them." [3]

The first tariff act of the Federal government, that of 1789, was intended to be partly protective in its effect, but was of comparatively little influence.[4] The early legislation of the new state was directed to the encouragement of trade rather than manufactures, as the commercial and trading elements dominated the economic life of the country until after the

[1] W. R. Bagnall, *Samuel Slater and the Early Development of the Cotton Manufacture in the United States*, (Middletown, 1890), pp. 28 *ff*., 50.
[2] *Ibid.*, pp. 49 *f.*; G. S. White, *Memoir of Samuel Slater*, (Philadelphia, 1836), p. 117.
[3] "Account of Journey of Josiah Quincy in 1801," Mass. Hist. Soc., *Proceedings*, Ser. II, vol. IV, p. 124.
[4] F. W. Taussig, *The Tariff History of the United States*, (New York, 1914), p. 14.

beginning of the new century. The adoption of the Constitution and the formation of the Union marked the beginning of a new era in commerce for all New England. Trade, it is true, had begun to improve in 1787, and the two years of Shays's Rebellion covered its lowest ebb. In 1788 Humphreys, writing to Jefferson, noted that the balance of exchange had actually turned in favor of Massachusetts, and that the East India trade had contributed not a little to that result.[1] Many articles began to appear in the papers regarding expanding commerce and the increase in shipbuilding.[2]

The old triangular trade of Europe, the West Indies, and New England was not indeed regained, and as the West India trade did not increase materially from 1786, it was necessary to find new routes and markets.[3] At the end of 1786 the West India merchants presented a memorial to Parliament, complaining of the increased cost and the precariousness of their supplies on account of the exclusion of American carriers.[4] Their contention was well founded, if we may accept the figures given by a contemporary American statistician, according to whom oak staves shipped from the United States to the British islands cost there from $24 to $31 as against prices for the same articles shipped to the French islands of $12 to $16; pine boards were from $24 to $30 for the British against $11 to $16 for the French; and so with an extended list of articles.[5] Parliament, however, turned a deaf ear, and it was claimed in the House of Commons that the regulations had increased British shipping by seven hundred vessels and four thousand seamen.[6]

New England merchants, meanwhile, had tapped a new source of wealth. In 1784 the New York ship Empress of China, with Major Samuel Shaw of Boston as one of the joint supercargoes, reached the country for which she had been

[1] Humphreys, *David Humphreys*, vol. I, p. 440.
[2] Quoted by Morse, *Federalist Party*, p. 61 *note*.
[3] E. Channing, *History of the United States*, (New York, 1916), vol. III, pp. 414, 422.
[4] "Memorial of the General Meeting of the West India Planters," *The Political Magazine*, (London, 1787), pp. 15 *f*.
[5] Coxe, *Brief Examination*, pp. 100 *ff*.
[6] *Parliamentary Register*, vol. XXI, p. 117.

named.[1]   The year before, the little fifty-five-ton sloop Harriet, of Hingham, had started on the same voyage, but meeting some British East Indiamen at the Cape of Good Hope had made a profitable deal there and returned.   Shaw, after coming home from his first trip, went back to Canton in 1786 and established the first American mercantile house in China.[2] In May 1787 the Salem vessel The Grand Turk arrived safe in port from the Far East, bringing enormous profit to her owner. Some months later John Brown of Providence sent the General Washington to the East Indies, the vessel returning a year and a half later with a cargo valued at approximately $100,000.[3] The same year saw also the beginning of the voyage of the Columbia, which ended after three years in the summer of 1790, when the ship returned after having been the first to fly the American flag in circling the globe.   It was this ship that in the course of its voyage opened up the fur trade of the Northwest coast at Nootka Sound, which was to provide the Boston merchants with goods to be exchanged for the riches of China.[4]

Meanwhile, fourteen other vessels, of which four belonged to Elias Haskett Derby of Salem, had preceded the Columbia to Canton, bringing home silks, chinaware, and tea, and by 1792 the "Boston-Northwest-Canton-Boston" route was fairly well established.[5]   The Oriental trade was divided between Boston and Salem, the merchants of the former for the most part sending their ships westward around the Horn to China, whereas those of the latter sailed eastward around the Cape of Good Hope to the East Indies.

For the years 1785 and 1786 the shipping lists show scarcely any vessels other than those in the American coasting trade, with occasional entries from the West Indies,[6] but by 1790 the

---

[1] Thomas Randall of New York was the other supercargo, although not mentioned in New England accounts of the voyage.   Some years later Randall wrote a long letter concerning it to Alexander Hamilton.   Letter dated Aug. 14, 1791.   Hamilton Papers, Mss., Library of Congress.

[2] Morison, *Maritime History*, pp. 44 f.

[3] G. S. Kimball, *The East-India Trade of Providence from 1787 to 1807*, (Brown University, 1896), p. 10.

[4] Morison, *op. cit.*, pp. 45 ff.

[5] *Ibid.*, p. 50.

[6] *Boston Gazette* for those years, *passim*.

SHIP HAZARD OF SALEM
From the original in the Peabody Museum

coming change was conspicuously manifest. In twenty days in the early summer of that year the customs books at Salem show not only such familiar entries as brigs and schooners from Cadiz, Port-au-Prince, and Martinico, with cargoes valued at $114, $56, and $101, but the harbingers of new wealth in the brig William-and-Henry from Canton, with a cargo of nearly $10,000, and the ships Lighthorse and Astrea from the same port with cargoes of $16,000 and $27,000.[1] By 1805–06 the American imports at Canton had risen to $5,000,000. The pepper trade with the Malay Archipelago was also opened up and America, which had exported only 492 pounds of that spice in 1791, became, largely through Salem, the world market by 1805, with exports of over seven and a half million pounds.[2]

The decline in New England commerce during the Revolution and down to the Federal period is indicated by the fact that, whereas in 1772 one hundred and twenty-three vessels were built, only eleven keels were laid in 1789.[3] In that year, however, the Federal government in a tariff act gave protection to American shipping in competition with foreign carriers, and the proportion of American vessels in the foreign trade rose from seventeen and one-half per cent at that time to ninety-four per cent in 1796, the tonnage engaged rising from 123,000 to 576,000.[4] In this gain New England, as the chief shipping section of the country, shared to the full. Federal aid was extended not only to the merchant marine but to the New England fisheries as well. Charles C. Pinckney of South Carolina had declared that in the Revolution "the eastern states had lost everything but their country and freedom," and that the South was called upon by "every tie of justice, friendship and humanity, to relieve their distress."[5] From 1789 onward a series of Acts were passed giving bounties or otherwise encouraging the fishermen, and the industry slowly recovered.

It was the riches from the Far East, however, rather than from the fishing banks, that reëstablished the maritime supremacy

[1] Morison, op. cit., p. 82.
[2] Ibid., p. 91.
[3] Report of the Lords of the Committee of Privy Council, Jan. 28, 1791, p. 44.
[4] W. W. Bates, American Marine, (Boston, 1895), pp. 96 f.
[5] Quoted by McFarland, New England Fisheries, p. 132.

of Massachusetts. Fabulous wealth for those days flowed in from ventures sent thither, and fortunes were made and families founded in this new trade, to which the Yankee merchants had been driven by the restrictive West Indian policy of the British government. Elias Haskett Derby, who died in 1799, left an estate of a million and a half. Israel Thorndike of Beverly and Simon Forrester of Salem both left about the same, while William Gray had accumulated three millions a few years later.[1] In Boston and Salem and Newburyport beautiful houses, many of them to-day constituting the finest examples of domestic architecture in America, were built to accommodate this new class of mercantile magnates. Few of their owners represented old families. Some had started as laborers or sailors, and many were only one generation from such an origin; but they lived lavishly and somehow managed to display most excellent taste in housing and furniture. Not all of the new-rich of this period came to fit into their new places so admirably.

The decade was one of great financial activity, of a broadening of the investment field, and in its earlier years of a speculation that culminated in 1792. With the assumption of the state debts and the refunding of the Continental debt, a large advance occurred in the prices of all sorts of governmental obligations, those of the Federal securities quadrupling between October 1789 and December 1791.[2] In 1789 the *Massachusetts Gazette* began to print security quotations regularly. The stockbroker appeared as a distinct type of business man, and trading on margin and other elements in our modern markets came into vogue. The formation of banks both afforded a new vehicle for speculation and furnished liquid funds for its furtherance. The incorporation of the Massachusetts Bank in 1794 was followed by the Providence Bank in 1791 and five others in the year after.[3] The public press and private letters

---

[1] Morison, *Maritime History*, p. 119.

[2] Davis, *American Corporations*, vol. I, p. 195. The state debts in New England were approximately $300,000 in New Hampshire; $5,226,000 in Massachusetts; $510,000 in Rhode Island; and $1,951,000 in Connecticut. Nevins, *American States*, p. 542. When the Federal government assumed the greater part of these, it greatly strengthened the credit of the individual states.

[3] They were located at Portsmouth, Hartford, New London, New Haven, and Boston. Davis, *op. cit.*, vol. II, p. 333.

of the day all testify to the universal participation in the speculative mania that centred at New York but spread all over the country districts of New England in the early years of the decade.

A correspondent at Worcester wrote to the *Norwich Packet* that "as fast as one bubble of speculation breaks another is blown up, — we are in the high road of becoming the greatest sharpers in the universe, — lottery bubbles, bank and tontine bubbles, — and many others, the rage of the present day, are most absurdly anti-republican, — they strike at the roots of industry and economy." [1]

With the rapid fortunes made in the rise of securities, land, and other commodities, a new class arose to join the war-rich of the decade before and the somewhat aloof magnates of the Massachusetts coast. There was much current comment on these newcomers, and bitter feeling on the part of the less fortunate portion of the community. Connecticut had the deserved nickname of "the land of steady habits," yet the speculation was as wild there as elsewhere. One paper noted with regret that "the professors of honest and useful occupations [were] made the butt of ridicule to the imaginary *Noblesse of yesterday*"; and Oliver Wolcott wrote from Litchfield of the "pretty pungent dislike" with which was viewed "the unrivalled opulence of certain people, of low cunning and ostentatious display of grandeur" in the larger towns.[2] The crash came in 1792 and innumerable smaller folk were involved in the ruin of the more spectacular figures such as Colonel Duer of New York.

In a New England that was rapidly altering, all these economic factors became closely related to European affairs and to politics and religion at home. These relations will form the subject of the next chapter.

[1] *Norwich Packet*, March 15, 1792.
[2] *Norwich Packet*, April 4, 1792; Gibbs, *Administrations of Washington and Adams*, vol. I, p. 74.

CHAPTER IX

THE REVOLUTION EXTENDED

The European War — Effect on Domestic Politics — Enthusiasm for France — New England Federalism — Democratic Clubs — Jay's Treaty — Dominating Political Groups — Clergy in Politics — Growth of Religious Dissent — Rise of the Democrats — Talk of Disunion — Beginning of Irish Immigration

For over two hundred and fifty years the American colonies had formed an integral part of the complex European system of states and their dependencies. Not only had they been economically and politically dependent upon England, but whenever the smouldering hostility between that country and France had flashed into the flames of open war they had inevitably been drawn in as active participants. When independence was won, it was felt that a new era had opened and that America should keep out of entanglements with European affairs — a feeling to which Washington gave expression in his Farewell Address. Independence, however, had been merely political. Americans, both mentally and economically, were still enmeshed in the European system in a thousand ways. It must be remembered that that system embraced practically the entire world with which America was in relations of any sort until the China trade was opened. If New England vessels went to South America, there they found Spain; if to the East Indies, there was Holland; the West Indies were Swedish, Danish, French, or English; if traders or settlers went overland north to Canada or west of the Lakes and the Alleghanies there were British garrisons; if they went south to Florida there again was Spain. Indeed, it may almost be said that in

Ship Hercules of Salem Cap! Edward West passing the Mole Head of Naples coming to an anchor 13 Sept 1809

Ship Australia of Salem Nath! J. Thissun Commander entering the New harbour of Marseilles June 1809

SALEM SHIPS HERCULES AND AUSTRALIA
From originals in the Peabody Museum

the world of ideas, of political relations, and of trade, the infant nation on the Atlantic seaboard was entirely surrounded by the all-embracing European system.

By 1793 the war in Europe, which had followed upon the Revolution in France, had become general, involving not only that country but England, Holland, and Spain, and the interests of New Englanders were deeply divided between the two leading antagonists. The West Indies, as we have stated, were but parts of Europe as far as commercial policy was concerned, and we have already spoken of England's regulations covering American trade with her possessions there. The French had shown no more willingness to allow free trade than had the English, but the great bulk of the commerce had gone to the French islands, over 101,000 out of 167,000 tons of shipping entering America from the West Indies in 1790 being from French ports.[1]

When war was declared between England and France in 1793, the French opened the ports of the West Indies to neutrals, owing to economic necessity. England, however, soon undertook the conquest of the islands and issued orders to capture any American or other neutral vessels trading with them. In order herself to gain benefit by the neutral trade, she relaxed to some extent the regulations covering that with her own islands. The strain of war, with the need of largely increasing the personnel of her navy, made her willing to decrease her commerce in order to release merchantmen for naval service. It was also imperative that no British seaman should escape that service by serving on foreign vessels, and consequently wherever her officers found British seamen on captured American vessels they were seized, and thus to the captures of vessels was added impressment of their crews, to serve as legitimate grievances of American merchants.

On May 9, the French government issued its decree to the effect that neutral vessels under certain conditions might be seized by French ships of war or privateers and carried into

[1] A. T. Mahan, *Sea Power in Its Relations to the War of 1812*, (Boston, 1905), vol. I, p. 85. In 1795 the imports into America from the British West Indies were $6,426,091, and from the French islands $15,751,758. T. Pitkin, *Statistical View of the Commerce of the United States*, (New York, 1817), p. 251.

French ports, and the seizures thus permitted began at once. Both governments continued from then until the end of the war in 1801 to harass American commerce by a series of orders or decrees, and by seizures which were outside the limits of international law as then established, and which had profound effect on American domestic politics. Meanwhile, Washington had issued his Proclamation of Neutrality on April 22, 1793. The country, however, was in a ferment. Both France and England were violating our rights, but Americans overlooked the acts of one or the other as their sympathies were engaged in favor of English or of French.

But it was not alone from the great European Powers that Americans suffered humiliation and spoliation. They were helpless even before the depredations of the Algerine pirates in the Mediterranean, and American vessels scarcely dared venture into those waters save under the protection of the Portuguese navy.[1] Although John Adams and Gouverneur Morris preached the need for a small naval force of our own, and although in the opinion of the ablest naval critic of the present day such a force would have been sufficient to make us respected and would have prevented the War of 1812, it was felt that the finances of the government did not permit of it.[2] Diplomacy was resorted to, and John Jay was dispatched to England in 1794 to settle the long outstanding differences left since the Peace of 1783 and the new questions which had arisen.[3] Jay did not succeed in protecting American seamen from impressment, nor in asserting the doctrine of free ships, free goods; whereas he yielded to the British Admiralty's doctrine of contraband and accepted, in practice though not in principle, the Rule of 1756.[4] On the other hand, he did procure some con-

---

[1] Mahan, *Sea Power in the War of 1812*, vol. I, pp. 73 *ff.*; G. W. Allen, *Our Navy and the Barbary Corsairs*, (Boston, 1905), p. 15.

[2] Mahan, *op. cit.*, vol. I, pp. 71 *ff.* Henry Adams took the opposite stand in writing in 1879 of Gallatin, but his arguments must fall before Mahan's superior knowledge. *Life of Albert Gallatin*, (Philadelphia, 1879), p. 171.

[3] S. F. Bemis has made a definitive study of the whole negotiation in *Jay's Treaty*, (New York, 1923).

[4] Bemis, *op. cit.*, pp. 269 *ff.* In brief, the Rule of 1756 was that "neutrals would not be permitted to engage in time of war in a trade from which they were excluded in time of peace." J. B. Moore, *A Digest of International Law*, (Washington, 1906), vol. VII, p. 383.

cessions, and the fact that England was at last willing to sign any commercial treaty at all with the United States in the dangerous and unstable condition in which their nationality then stood, was a matter "of far greater import than the technical recognition of independence forced from George III." [1]

Friction with England continued in spite of the treaty, but before the end of the decade the depredations of France increased so greatly as to involve the United States in what was virtually unacknowledged war with that country. Decree had followed decree, and the spoliations and maltreatment of our vessels, cargoes, and crews had become unbearable by 1798.[2] Congress acted at last, and in April of that year organized the Navy Department and increased the army. Among other measures, an Act was passed authorizing American merchant vessels to arm and to repel by force any attack upon them by the French, as well as to recapture any American ships that might have been taken. War was not declared, but commercial intercourse was declared suspended. From that time until the end of the European war there were many conflicts, not only between our merchant vessels and the French but between the armed naval vessels of both countries. After this very brief and inadequate account of what was an extremely complex international situation, we must turn to consider the effects of these developments upon the political and social conditions in New England.

In discussing the adoption of the Federal Constitution we noted at some length the division into parties that occurred at that time — or if the word "parties" connotes too much of organization and machinery in the modern sense, the two groups of conflicting opinion into which men had divided. To a great extent we found this division to have been an economic cleavage between those whose financial interests demanded a strong central government and those who feared such a government, or, in general, between the mercantile elements and the agrarian elements, between the rich and the poor.[3] Until

---

[1] Bemis, *op. cit.*, p. 270.
[2] G. W. Allen, *Our Naval War with France*, (Boston, 1909), pp. 29 *ff*.
[3] *Vide supra*, chap. VII.

comparatively recently it had always been considered that the parties formed at that time were continuing and that the Federalists and Republicans whom we have now to discuss were the successors of those who were in favor or opposed to the adoption of the Constitution. This has now been denied by some, but the older view appears to be the more correct one, based upon both contemporary evidence and the facts of human nature.[1] It is true that there was no party machinery and, judging by the small numbers throughout all New England who voted as compared with those entitled to do so, that there was but slight interest in contesting elections.[2]

Those among the people, however, who had voted for the Constitution had had very definite reasons for doing so. They wished to protect their financial interests and to provide a curb for what they considered the dangerously mobbish or democratic elements, such as had come to the surface to spread terror and threaten the state in Shays's Rebellion. When the new government had been formed, this same group wished to see policies pursued such as that exemplified by Hamilton, which would continue to secure these objects. Made up of most of the men of wealth in all the New England states, bound together by business, social, and family ties, this general group, or Federal party, knew what they wanted, and the leaders were in sufficiently close touch with one another to bring about concerted action for securing their objects. On the other hand, those elements who had been opposed to the Constitution had no such cohesive forces among them. They belonged for the most part to the poorer part of the population; lived scattered in the country rather than in cities; had no powerful group of leaders in close touch with one another; lacked means of communication; and their wishes were negative rather than positive. They did not want tariffs or shipping subsidies or what-not. They wanted to be let alone and have the government impinge upon them as little as possible — a much less

[1] *Cf.* C. A. Beard, *Economic Origins of Jeffersonian Democracy*, (New York, 1915), pp. 10 *ff.*

[2] W. A. Robinson, *Jeffersonian Democracy in New England*, (Yale Univ. Press, 1916), pp. 2 *ff.*

tangible object to work for. They were an unorganized collection of elements in opposition. The term "Republican,"
said the *Columbian Centinel* in 1792, has "so often been
applied . . . to Anti-Federalists, Insurgents, State Dema-
gogues and professed enemies to the union of our common
country, that it is difficult to ascertain its precise meaning." [1]
Although the remark was made by a political opponent, it
contained much truth. Under the strong pressure of the international situation, these two more or less inchoate groups
were each to be firmly welded into an organized political
party.

Even in New England, where under the lead of Samuel
Adams the propaganda of Revolutionary days had been most
rabid and bitter, the feeling of hostility toward England as the
former enemy had softened much more rapidly than might
have been expected. In that land, which has always loved
public anniversaries, it is enlightening to read in Dr. Bentley's
Diary for 1792 on the provocative nineteenth of April that
"the recollections of the events of this day [are] almost lost.
Few observed to recall it." [2] Apart from sentiment, however,
the most influential group in New England, the merchants, who
were also the leaders of the Federalist party, were bound by
the closest of ties to London. Not only did the imports from
England after independence continue greatly to exceed those
from any other country, but the credit extended by English
bankers to New England merchants was absolutely essential
to the carrying on of their business with almost any part of
the world, even the newly developing Northwest-Coast-China
trade. Bills on London were good virtually anywhere, whereas
those on American banks were not. Supercargoes could sell
merchandise at any port where a favorable market offered,
receive London bills, and use them elsewhere to purchase other
goods wherever most desirable. Business relations with France
had grown closer than before independence from England was
won, but after 1792 these became dangerously speculative,

---

[1] Quoted by Robinson, *Jeffersonian Democracy*, p. 7.
[2] W. Bentley, *Diary*, vol. I, p. 361. He adds that "there was a sermon at Lexington for several years, but it has long since ceased."

and the more conservative merchants were driven to almost complete dependence upon their London connections.[1]

The New England merchants who had worked so hard for the adoption of the Constitution had been well rewarded during the first few years of the new government. When the first senators were chosen in Massachusetts, Caleb Strong of Northampton was selected as one, to placate the western counties, but as to the other it seems to have been admitted, as James Sullivan said, that "the merchants made the Constitution and they should name the candidate." [2]   Various Acts regarding the fisheries, duties, shipping, and warehouses, passed during the first two administrations, all redounded greatly to the benefit of the merchants.   Many of these Acts were sectional measures, which were of advantage to the North rather than the South, and when the depredations of England on American commerce began, a new rift appeared between the feelings of the two parts of the nation.   Whereas in New England the richer element was in favor of England for the reasons noted above, in the South the debts which the planters had owed to English bankers before the Revolution and which had never been paid exerted an influence in the opposite direction.   A fortnight after Washington's proclamation of neutrality Oliver Wolcott wrote from Connecticut that he did not believe that there were fifty persons in all New England who would not support the government, and that if the Southerners were ever inclined to dissolve the Union they would have to count on the Potomac as the dividing line.[3]   A little later Timothy Dwight wrote that New England absolutely would not enter into a war with England, and that ninety-nine in a hundred there would sooner separate from the Union.[4]

These statements, which were not true even of New England, could by no means be applied to the country at large.   In March of the next year, even after the notorious actions of Genêt, the French representative in the United States, had

[1] Morison, *Maritime History*, p. 169.
[2] Quoted by Morison, *ibid.*, p. 164.
[3] Gibbs, *Administrations of Washington and Adams*, vol. I, p. 102.
[4] *Ibid.*, p. 107.

cooled the ardor of many Francophiles, Fisher Ames wrote from Congress that he "would not justify the insolence and injustice of the English: they are not to be justified; but our fury for the French, and against the English, is more natural than salutary. France has stopped more than an hundred sail of our vessels at Bordeaux. We sit still; we say nothing; we affect to depend on their justice; we make excuses. England stops our vessels with provoking insolence; we are in a rage." He went on to say truly that this discrimination was in no wise deserved by the French.[1]

Not only had France been our ally in the War for Independence, but her own revolution had been watched with the deepest interest and sympathy by the majority of Americans. When the French Republic was proclaimed a thrill of joy ran through all America, and at the end of 1792 and the beginning of 1793 celebrations took place everywhere to signalize the defeat of the Allies. A great civic festival was held in Boston, and demonstrations occurred throughout the towns of New England.[2] Sympathy with France became a veritable frenzy on the part of a large section of the American public, not to be chilled by any acts of the new government until — and then only partly — the Revolution entered upon its most bloody and irreligious phase at the end of the decade.

The Americans are a sentimental people, but so violent did the pro-French feeling become that its foundation must be looked for beyond the mere sentiment for a former ally or a disinterested rejoicing over the apparent spread of democratic ideas. We have had occasion, time and again, in the three volumes which comprise this history of New England, to point out the evidences of class feeling and the bitterness of economic and social clashes in what used to be considered a homogeneous social structure. We have touched upon the very large body of discontent which was left over after our own Revolution. We have seen the strong opposition that was felt against the adoption of the Constitution. That instrument had been

[1] *Works*, vol. I, p. 139.
[2] C. D. Hazen, *Contemporary American Opinion of the French Revolution*, (Johns Hopkins Univ. Studies, 1897), pp. 164 ff.

adopted, however wisely, as a result of a strong reaction on the part of the most conservative elements against the democracy which had been preached to the people during the war with England.   That firm hands were needed to guide the new Ship of State is unquestionable, but this did not make it any more palatable to many of the "common people" and others who had fought for the "rights of man," when they found that their government had been organized in the interests of the merchants and the "rights of property."   As we saw above, it has been claimed that the real struggle over adoption in Massachusetts was the conflict between those who believed in democracy and those who believed in John Adams's doctrine of the right of the well-born to govern.

There may be said to have been two strong feelings among the stubborn citizens of New England of that day, one or the other being shared by almost every man.   One was the feeling that he was just as good as anyone else.   The other was that he was a good deal better.   The first may be considered at the bottom of Republican doctrine and the second of Federalist. The national leader of the Federalists was Alexander Hamilton, but the dominating group, not only in New England but in the nation, was the Essex Junto which we have already mentioned.   The doctrines of New England Federalism were based solely on the opinions, wishes, and prejudices of George Cabot, Timothy Pickering, Fisher Ames, Theophilus Parsons, John Lowell, Jr., and a few others associated with them, all lawyers and merchants of Essex County.   All of these men had the utmost contempt, and at times dread, of all such people — naturally the great majority of the state — as were outside the charmed circle of the rich or well-born.   In the latter alone did the members of the Junto conceive that wisdom or even virtue could lie.   In their private correspondence or public utterances it is always the rich about whom all virtue centres. We find constantly such expressions as the "wise, rich, and good," the "rich and able," the "wise and rich," or the "wise, the good, and the rich." [1]

Their hatred of democracy exceeded even that felt by John

[1] Ames, *Works*, vol. I, pp. 310 *f*., 316.

Winthrop or John Cotton. "Democracy is a troubled spirit, fated never to rest, and whose dreams if it sleeps, present only visions of hell," wrote Ames to Timothy Dwight.[1] "It has never happened in the world, and it never will," he wrote again some years later, "that a democracy has been kept out of the control of the fiercest and most turbulent spirits in the society; they will breathe into it all their own fury, and make it subservient to the worst designs of the worst men."[2] Finally, almost in the words of Winthrop in 1630, he asked, "Ought we not to consider democracy as the worst of all governments, or if there be a worse, as the certain forerunner of that?"[3] They had little respect for that vaunted New England institution, the town meeting, and objected to other meetings for the expression of public opinion. "Take the people of any one place, the more general their meeting," wrote Pickering, "the greater will be the proportion of members incompetent to judge of the subject discussed." He admitted that in small towns the people might understand their own petty local affairs, but in the larger ones, such as New York or Philadelphia, he declared that he "never knew a large meeting of the citizens that was other than a mob."[4] "Where is the boasted advantage of a representation system over the turbulent mobocracy of Athens," asked Cabot, "if the resort to popular meetings is necessary?"[5]

This was far removed from the doctrines on which the leaders had fed that same "mobocracy" when they had had to call its members from their plows and firesides on thousands of New England farms in the years of sanguinary struggle. It is true that the poorer people still to a great extent looked up to the leading families of their small communities and to the clergy for political guidance, but a vision had been given them at the time of the Revolution of a larger life in which they were to share, and here and there all through the land individuals felt that they had been defrauded of the fruits for which they had

---

[1] *Ibid.*, vol. I, p. 337.
[2] *Ibid.*, vol. II, p. 356.
[3] *Ibid.*, vol. II, p. 364.
[4] Pickering, *Timothy Pickering*, vol. III, p. 182.
[5] Lodge, *Cabot*, p. 85.

fought. It was too obvious, moreover, that many of the new-rich, fattened on war contracts or speculation in public funds, were not the sole founts of wisdom and virtue in their communities. Discontent may not have been organized or vocal to any great extent in 1790, but that it was fermenting under the surface there can be little doubt.

Upon this situation, the news of the French Revolution, of the overthrow of the monarchy and the establishment of a republic, wrought a sudden and marvelous effect. Once more the heavens had opened and a vision had been vouchsafed to the common man. Here was an opportunity not for sullen and dumb discontent but for open and unbounded rejoicing. Enthusiasm for everything French suddenly knew no bounds. Not only were the festivals and celebrations spoken of above held in many New England towns, but French fashions, French modes of speaking, French holidays, and French ideas became all the mode among her sympathizers. Even street names in Boston were altered and Royal Exchange Alley became Equality Lane.[1]

Suddenly, all over the country, this enthusiasm took more tangible — and what was considered by some an extremely ominous — form in the shape of secret societies modeled on the Jacobin Clubs of Paris. Many of these societies were called "Democratic" Clubs, a word, incidentally, which was introduced from France at this time. In the "Declaration" sent out by the one formed in Boston it was stated, after noting that under the American Constitution citizens had the "right in an orderly and peaceable manner to assemble and consult upon the public good," that the members had agreed to meet and converse together "for the purpose of gaining and communicating information on the affairs of their country; to express with decency and firmness, their sentiments respecting the measures adopted by their Delegates, and to offer their opinions with candor on matters of political concernment."[2]

In some cases, as in that of the society in Chittenden County, Vermont, hatred of England was openly avowed. Among other places where the clubs were formed were Bennington

[1] Hazen, *Contemporary American Opinion*, p. 216.   [2] *Ibid.*, pp. 193 *f.*

Addison, Rutland, and Cumberland counties, Vermont, and Portland, Maine, and it is probable there were others elsewhere. In any case, the effect of their organization was far-reaching. Wherever they were formed they threw themselves into the local political situation with extraordinary vigor. In Boston in the autumn of 1794 the election for members of the state legislature was hotly contested. Dr. Charles Jarvis, who had always supported Republican measures, was nominated against the redoubtable Fisher Ames, who wrote of the members of the new Club who were actively campaigning, that "they poison every spring; they whisper to every gale; they are everywhere, always acting like Old Nick and his imps. . . . They will be busy as Macbeth's witches at the election, and all agree the event is very doubtful." [1]

Ames finally retained his seat, but this springing of the despised democracy into organized action instilled both hate and fear into the hearts of the Federalists and the "rich and good." Every diabolical motive possible was attributed to members of the Clubs. At last, in a speech before Congress, Washington attacked them as secret and "self-created societies," connecting them with the recent Whiskey Rebellion in Pennsylvania and heartily condemning them. It was pointed out by their defenders that they were no more "self-created" than the Order of the Cincinnati; but Washington's authority was too great with the country at large to be withstood and the clubs began to wither under his censure. By March 1795, Wolcott wrote from Connecticut that he trusted "the demoniacal societies" were sinking into contempt. [2]

The extremists in democracy, however, had made themselves heard, and a new rancor entered into party strife. Rhode Island and New Hampshire were little affected as yet, but the withdrawal from public life of Governor Samuel Adams in Massachusetts and the death of Governor Chittenden in Vermont opened the way for more violent contests. Samuel Dexter, one of the ablest Federalists in Massachusetts, was

---

[1] *Works*, vol. I, p. 148. *Cf.* Robinson, *Jeffersonian Democracy*, pp. 10 *ff.*; Morse, *Federalist Party*, pp. 148 *f.*
[2] Gibbs, *Administrations of Washington and Adams*, vol. I, p. 179.

defeated by Joseph Varnum in 1795 for the legislature, and in
Vermont the following year, that extraordinary Irishman,
Matthew Lyon, was elected to Congress as a Democrat.[1]   Dr.
Bentley noted in his Diary that electioneering was going on
actively in Massachusetts and New Hampshire, even extending
in Boston to petty town-officers, and that this was "the Commencement of a new Career."[2]

Just at the time of the suppression of the Democratic Clubs
there came another opportunity for democratic sentiment to
express itself with violence over a national event.   The Democrats, having allied themselves in sympathy to France, were
naturally opposed to England, and when the terms of Jay's
apparently humiliating treaty with that country were made
public a howl of rage went up from their ranks.   In fact, not
a few of the merchants and Federalists were inclined at first
to join in the condemnation themselves, but for the most part
these were soon made to see how subtly linked were the interests of the shipping group to the other groups of capitalists
and how these were all linked to national finance.[3]   Some,
however, were never reconciled.   Ames, who was rabid against
the merchants who joined with the Democrats in denouncing
the treaty, could not disguise his "contempt for the blindness
and gullibility of the rich men who so readily lend their strength
to the party which is thirsting for the contents of their iron
chests."[4]

A town meeting in Boston condemned the treaty as injurious to commerce, derogatory to national honor, and dangerous
to the peace of the citizens.[5]   At Portsmouth a meeting of the
people expressed their "most hearty disapprobation."[6]   In
western Massachusetts Caleb Strong reported the people quiet,
and Wolcott said there would be no trouble in Connecticut,
where the people were "calm and hard at work."[7]   Boston,
however, was by no means calm, and the opinion of certain

[1] J. F. McLaughlin, *Matthew Lyon*, p. 212.
[2] *Diary*, vol. II, p. 174 [1796].   [3] *Cf.* Beard, *Economic Origins*, p. 295.
[4] Gibbs, *Administrations of Washington and Adams*, vol. I, p. 210.
[5] *Treaty of Amity, Commerce and Navigation*, (Philadelphia, 1795), p. 155.
[6] *Ibid.*, p. 159.
[7] Pickering, *Timothy Pickering*, vol. III, p. 199; Gibbs, *op. cit.*, vol. I, p. 215.

sections there took the usual expression of mob violence. A British privateer was attacked and destroyed at its dock, and other vessels threatened.[1] Throughout the summer effigies were burned and mobs paraded the streets, much to the fear of the more timid inhabitants, some of whom took refuge in the country. Effigies were also burned at Newport, and some efforts were made from New Haven to foment trouble in Connecticut.[2]

The Boston Chamber of Commerce met in August and approved the treaty, and by that time the merchants generally had rallied to its support. Partly from the reaction against the more violent acts and speeches of the Democrats, and partly by the efforts of the Federalist leaders and particularly the clergy, public sentiment shifted, and the next year, when the treaty was ratified by the United States Senate, it met with no opposition in New England.

The Congregational clergy, occupying a privileged position and with vested interests, were the natural allies of the rich and conservative elements in New England. The backbone of the Federalist party was made up of the merchant-lawyer-capitalist group, the clergy, and the local magnates who, in the small villages and towns, had been accustomed to a position and a political influence similar to those of the country gentry in England. John Adams always saw clearly the many social and economic conflicts of interest in New England society, which for long escaped the more modern historians of that section. "The state of Connecticut," he wrote in 1808, "has always been governed by an aristocracy, more decisively than the empire of Great Britain is. Half a dozen, or, at most, a dozen families, have controlled that country when a colony, as well as since it has been a state. An aristocracy can govern the elections of the people without hereditary legal dignities, privileges, and powers, better than with them. In the Massachusetts, many of our prime men were banished in the Revolution. Most of our present rulers are new men. But these have been promoted by an aristocracy." In America he saw that this aristocracy was based solely on money. Two parties, he said, have always existed in every country, the rich and the

<hr>

[1] Morse, *Federal Party*, pp. 153 ff.   [2] Gibbs, *op. cit.*, vol. I, pp. 226, 229.

poor.   Land speculation had always been rampant in America, and Adams, well knowing the answer, queried whether "this spirit has not become a rage, from Georgia to New Hampshire, within the last thirty years?   Whether foundations have not been laid for immense fortunes in a few families for their posterity?   Whether the variations of a fluctuating medium and an unsteady public faith have not raised vast fortunes in personal property, in banks, in commerce, in roads, bridges, &c.? " [1]

These compact governing groups felt themselves governing by divine right.   They also felt themselves almost impregnably entrenched, as indeed they were.   An examination of the interrelations of the governing group in Connecticut, for example, is most illuminating.   Dr. Timothy Dwight, the leading clergyman of the state, known as "the Pope," and United States Senator James Hillhouse had married sisters.   In 1800 Theodore Dwight, brother of "the Pope," was candidate for Congress.   Congressman Morris married Dwight's sister.   Congressman Hosmer was related to Hillhouse by marriage.   Congressman Chauncey Goodrich had married a sister of Oliver Wolcott, Secretary of the Treasury.   Roger Griswold, a candidate for Congress in the same election·of 1800, was a cousin of Hillhouse; and so the relations could be continued with other members of the dominating group.[2]

On the other side, Adams saw "the common people," as he called them, the "farmers, tradesmen and laborers, many of the smaller shopkeepers and merchants" who, when they could not by the utmost industry and frugality in a life of seventy years do more than support a family and lay up four or five thousand dollars, must think it very hard when they saw mushroom fortunes springing up, and would be ready to throw themselves into the arms of a party who would oppose the existing order.[3]   Naturally, those in control of the purse and politics of society wanted no opposition, and Hillhouse, who to a great extent did both in Connecticut, called the new party spirit "a demon and a fiend." [4]

---

[1] *Works*, vol. VI, p. 530.
[2] Quoted from *The Aurora* by Beard, *Economic Origins*, p. 364.
[3] *Works*, vol. VI, p. 531.   [4] *Ibid.*, p. 540.

The fear thrown into the hearts of the conservatives by the secret Democratic societies and the mobbish spirit of those who had so violently opposed Jay's Treaty had done much to embitter the relations between the two sections of society. But as the French Revolution advanced, threatening to destroy all established society and to overthrow the Christian religion, the Democrats, who had so frenziedly espoused its cause and to a great extent still maintained it, came to be regarded with an abhorrence that is almost impossible to realize to-day. The clergy needed no inducement other than their obvious interest to become Federalists, but in the religious excesses of the Revolution they found a weapon made to their hand with which to confound their Democratic enemies. At first many of the clergy had been in favor of the overthrow of the monarchy and friendly to the Revolution, just as many of the merchants had at first been opposed to Jay's Treaty; but a reversal took place in the one case as completely as in the other, and by the end of 1795 there was not a clerical voice raised in New England except in denunciation of the atheism of the French Revolutionists and American Democrats. The clerical reaction to the confiscation of all church property by the French, to the installation of "the Goddess of Reason," and to the abolition of the Christian Sabbath so venerated in New England, was all natural enough. In addition the clergy were at this time deeply stirred by what they considered as an engulfing wave of atheism in New England itself. Paine's *Age of Reason* appeared in 1794 and created an unprecedented sensation. Yale and Harvard were hotbeds of infidelity. The events of the years from 1793 to 1795 in France thus brought flocking to the standards of Federalism in New England all those who placed the rights of property above those of man, and the claims of orthodoxy and an established church above those of free-thinking. In spite of the fact that the power of the clergy had been slowly undermined for many decades, it was still great, particularly in the rural districts, and, largely as a result of their efforts, Federalism had become completely dominant in New England by 1797.

Democratic feeling, however, was also rising, and although

the New England Democrats did not dare or perhaps wish to attack religion itself as in the Middle States, nevertheless they did not hesitate to oppose bitterly this advance of the solid phalanx of Congregational clergy into the political arena. Although the bitterness with which the Democrats complained of the political activity of the clergy is an indication of dread of their power, it is also an indication of the altered position of the latter. It was admitted, by both their friends and foes, that "that servile awe, which in a royal government, was felt both towards magistrates and ministers" had been much dissipated by the American Revolution. The growth in democratic spirit had affected the social position of the clergy, and poverty, with resulting quarrels over salaries, had tended to lessen the respect felt for the minister in many of the country parishes.[1]

Among the laity, apart from the inroads of actual infidelity, there was rapidly developing a liberalizing of the older Calvinism and an indifference to doctrine. This movement was felt even among the clergy themselves in the larger centres, and in Boston a visitor wrote in 1791 that the ministers there were so diverse in their views that they could not agree on any one point in theology. Ten years later there was but one minister in that city who accepted the doctrine of the Trinity.[2]

In Connecticut, where some of the bitterest political opposition to the clergy was found, there were also special forces at work. There, as elsewhere, the Anti-Federalists were the advocates of wider suffrage and religious toleration, but equal religious rights were not secured until after the dissenters had joined with the Republicans to secure a majority of the popular vote.[3] Throughout this decade and the next, however, dissent steadily increased, the Baptists especially becoming active in the attack on the injustices of the standing order. One of these was the fact that the lower schools were practically parochial schools of the Congregational church, but the authority of the government was also being seriously ques-

---

[1] Morse, *Federal Party*, p. 123.
[2] G. W. Cooke, *Unitarianism in America*, (Boston, 1910), p. 75.
[3] Purcell, *Connecticut in Transition*, p. 47

YALE STUDENTS ON THE GREEN
From *Leslie's Weekly, 1856*

tioned in such matters as compulsory church attendance on Sundays and the taxation of every person for some form of worship. A reactionary law was passed in 1791, changing the requirements as to the certificates which every dissenter was obliged to take out, so that thereafter they had to be signed by two civil officers or a justice of the peace, and this provoked a storm throughout the state. The justices were for the most part members of the Congregational church, as were most political officeholders, and this backward step entrenched the church more strongly than ever. Although the law was repealed, the substitute did not give the dissenters the relief to which they felt they were entitled.[1]

Another grievance was that involved in public taxation for the support of Yale College, a Congregational institution. In 1793 another storm was raised over the sale of some of the state's western lands and the appropriation of the proceeds in a manner that the dissenters believed would inure almost wholly to the benefit of the established church.[2] About the same time the governor issued a proclamation ordering that a contribution be taken up in every parish for the support of the Presbyterian missions in the west, to which the dissenters naturally objected strongly.[3] In 1794 a Baptist, the Reverend John Leland, addressed a great throng which had assembled in front of the capitol at Hartford, coming from all parts of the state, and almost threatening civil war. He proclaimed absolute liberty of conscience; denied that the civil government had any right to regulate religion; asserted that Church and State should be separate; and advised that the constitution be remedied so that the dissenters could secure their rights in a constitutional manner.[4] In this speech he foreshadowed the union of the dissenters and Republicans to secure control of government by the ballot and the downfall of the

[1] Greene, *Religious Liberty*, pp. 372 ff.

[2] *Ibid.*, pp. 381 ff.

[3] From the time of the Saybrook Platform the churches in Connecticut had been largely Presbyterian in character, and the terms Presbyterian and Congregational were used at this period interchangeably. *Ibid.*, p. 150.

[4] *Ibid.*, pp. 387 ff.; Purcell, *Connecticut in Transition*, pp. 76 f. The law as to lands was repealed, and the proceeds were appropriated to the maintenance of schools, thus laying the foundation of the School Fund.

established church, both of which were to be witnessed within a few years.

Centring around the years of the election of 1800, feeling on both sides took on an intense bitterness. The clergy indulged in vitriolic diatribes against the Republicans, from their leader, Thomas Jefferson, down to the humbler members of the party in country villages. In his Fourth of July oration in 1798 Timothy Dwight attacked at once the freethinkers, French, and Democrats. "For what end shall we be connected with men of whom this is the character and the conduct?" he asked. "Is it that our churches may become temples of reason, our Sabbath a decade, and our psalms of praise Marsellaise hymns? Is it that we may change our holy worship into a dance of Jacobin phrenzy and that we may behold a strumpet personating a Goddess on the altars of Jehovah? . . . Is it that we may see our wives and daughters the victims of legal prostitution . . . the loathing of God and man? Shall we, my brethren, become partakers of these sins? Shall we introduce them into our government, our schools, our families? Shall our sons become the disciples of Voltaire, and the dragoons of Marat; or our daughers the concubines of the Illuminati?" [1]

The innumerable letter-writers to the newspapers who rallied to the support of the clergy when attacked for political interference by the Republicans indulged themselves in similar vein. "Jacobinism exclaims against the influence of the clergy," wrote one; "and why? Because Jacobinism wishes to see mankind *without moral restraint or bias*. It exclaims against every object which thwarts the *natural* appetites of war, or which tends to the moral connection of human society. How boldly does it deny the propriety of the marriage covenant, of the tender connexions of life, of the obligation of a promise, and the quiet possession of *individual property!*" [2]

---

[1] Quoted by Beard, *Economic Origins*, pp. 365 *f*. The Illuminati was a secret order that had been instituted many years before in Germany, and which some of the clergy believed had been transported to New England. It had not, but the excitement raised over the question added to the ferment of those days. *Vide* V. Stauffer, *New England and the Bavarian Illuminati, cit. supra.*

[2] *Conn. Courant*, Sept. 28, 1801.

Another wrote, "Shall we find them [Republicans] affectionate and *faithful* husbands? Are they men, who patiently wait for the freemen to elect them into office, as they may deserve? Do they practice the meek, and pious duties of Religion, by doing justly, loving mercy, and walking humbly? . . . Do they not wish, by introducing their unsettled, and turbulent practices, which are so diametrically opposite to our old habits, to get themselves into those places, which they cannot obtain under the present regular, and settled course of proceedings, and then to force out of office, the honorable, and virtuous men, who now fill our Counsels with singular wisdom, integrity and talents?" [1]

Around none of the rising local Democratic leaders in New England did the windy words of controversy swirl more wildly than round Abraham Bishop of New Haven, and he did not hesitate to give as good as he received. The American Revolution, he said in a speech at Wallingford, had promised much in favor of freedom of mind and conscience, but the blow had to be followed up. The Revolution would never be accomplished until Church and State had been separated. Moses and Aaron found it too profitable to walk hand in hand. "The clergyman preaches politics, the civilian prates of orthodoxy, and if any man refuses to join the coalition, they endeavor to hunt him down to the tune of 'the church is in danger.'" This, he said, bred hypocrisy throughout the whole community. "We are taught hypocrisy from our cradles," as he put it, and "those who live in the midst of this deceitful union, will feel the force of these remarks; those who do not, can but very imperfectly conceive what it forms to the introduction of any truth, which can diminish the power, wealth or infallibility of the fraternity." He denounced the "family alliances, producing patriarchs in opinion and the general habit of whole towns committing to a few individuals the power to dictate to them opinions on all subjects. . . . Steady habits," he contended, were made use of to arrest the progress of truth, to maintain an obsequious subservience to the clergy in place of genuine religion, and to keep in office, by manipulation of nominations,

[1] *Conn. Courant*, April 6, 1801.

the self-perpetuating oligarchical group of rulers instead of allowing the people to choose their own.[1]

The economic issue, however, was also well in the forefront of discussion. In Connecticut, Bishop attacked the financial system of the Federalists, denounced commerce with its requirement for an expensive navy to protect it, and upheld the interests of the farmers as the backbone of the State.[2] On the other hand, the Federalists predicted certain ruin for all holders of the public funds, for stockholders in the banks, insurance companies, and other corporations, if Jefferson and the Democrats should be elected.[3] That the two parties represented two opposed economic blocs in the state, in the main the capitalists and merchants against the agrarians, was well recognized on both sides at the time.

As the last years of the century passed, the confusion and bitterness grew. The firm attitude displayed by the Federal government toward France was a wise one, though it angered the Democrats. When, in 1798, however, the Alien and Sedition Laws were passed, they deserved the storm of protest with which they were greeted by the opposition.[4] Nevertheless, when Kentucky and Virginia passed their resolutions, the Federalist legislatures of the New England states promptly and unequivocally sustained the constitutionality of the two Acts and denounced the states'-rights doctrines advanced by the two Southern states.[5] The legislature of Massachusetts, for example, declared that if the states had the right to pass on the constitutionality of the acts of the Federal government it would reduce the Constitution to a nullity, and that they firmly believed that the various states were connected by a common interest that ought to render the Union indissoluble.[6]

As we shall see in the next two chapters, the extremists among the New England Federalists were quite willing to change their

---

[1] *Oration Delivered at Wallingford, March 11, 1801,* (New Haven, 1801), pp. v, 13, 17.

[2] *Connecticut Republicanism, An Oration,* (Philadelphia, 1800), *passim.*

[3] *Cf.* quotations from Boston papers, Beard, *Economic Origins,* pp. 358 *ff.*

[4] Johnston and Woodburn, *American Political History,* (New York, 1910), vol. I, pp. 182 *ff.*

[5] H. V. Ames, *State Documents on Federal Relations,* (Philadelphia, 1906), pp. 15 *ff.*

[6] *Ibid.,* pp. 19 *f.*

note entirely within a few years, and to conspire to dissolve the Union which they now so strongly upheld. In fact, throughout all the early years of the republic there was constant talk of dissolution, both North and South. In the years 1796 to 1798 a series of letters were published in the *Connecticut Courant*, claiming that the economic and moral differences between the two sections, and above all the presence of slavery in the South, were bound to cause a forcible and final separation of the states.[1] The articles were very violent in tone, and the morals of the Southern planters were bitterly attacked, whereas New Englanders were held up as models of religion and virtue. In his inaugural address in 1801, Governor Trumbull repelled the idea of secession with deep aversion, but said to the legislature that he heard much too frequently from many quarters doubts expressed as to the continuance of the Union.[2]

It is in this decade also that we get our first glimpse of a movement which was later to transform New England political life — the foreign vote. In 1794 Oliver Ellsworth wrote to Wolcott that there was much to be apprehended "from the great numbers of violent men who emigrate to this country from every part of Europe."[3] In New England it was the Irish who were at this time giving special concern to the Federalists, for not only were they coming in considerable numbers, owing to the recent disturbances in Ireland, but they all or nearly all joined the ranks of the Democrats; and it must be remembered that the conservative Federalists regarded the latter much as we have lately looked upon the Bolsheviks and other Reds. Rufus King, who was in England in 1798 after the Irish Rebellion had been suppressed, was much exercised over the possibility of heavy emigration from that island to the United States, and particularly the disposal of the state prisoners. He wrote to Pickering, who was then Secretary of State, that probably thousands of fugitives would seek an

---

[1] Some of these letters were signed "Pelham" and some "Gustavus." *Conn. Courant*, Nov. 12, Dec. 12, 1796; July 31, Aug. 21, 28, Sept. 11, 1797; April 9, 1798.
[2] *Ibid.*, Oct. 12, 1801.
[3] Gibbs, *Administrations of Washington and Adams*, vol. I, p. 136.

asylum in America, and that their principles and habits would exercise a pernicious effect.[1]

The Irish rebels were supposed to have been in close touch with the French revolutionists and to have the same views. King remonstrated with the English Government against any of them being allowed to leave for America, and his course was approved by President Adams. Mr. King feared particularly those who belonged to the higher social and professional classes and who might for that very reason exercise a greater influence upon the New Englanders. In answer to a letter from him, William Bingham replied that these would undoubtedly be far more dangerous than the ordinary disaffected Irish, for "they will join the party in opposition to Government and will vent their resentments against Great Britain by attacking those [the Federalists] who are disposed to be on friendly terms with her. They will be discontented and disorganizing characters whose residence among us cannot be otherwise than injurious in the present moment of political agitation." [2]

Nevertheless, many Irish came, and by the creation of "The American Society of United Irishmen" formed a compact body which threw its whole political weight with the Democrats against the Federalists. It was a secret society and thus aroused all the fears that the Jacobin Democratic Clubs had three or four years earlier. Although its members were pledged primarily to the emancipation of Ireland, their constitution also proclaimed that they would strive for "the attainment of liberty and equality to mankind in whatever nation they resided." [3] At this time, though the figures were probably greatly exaggerated, it was computed that there were thirty thousand French and fifty thousand Irish refugees in the United States, and the fear of these refugees had been one of the motives for the passage of the Alien Act. Writing some years afterward, William Sullivan noted that these Irish immigrants hated England and were devoted to France, and that they were easily led into hatred of the government of the

---

[1] King, *Rufus King*, vol. II, p. 637.   [2] *Ibid.*, pp. 639 ff., 644.
[3] J. C. Hamilton, *History of the Republic of the United States*, (Philadelphia, 1864) vol. VII, p. 158.

United States — by which latter he apparently meant the Federal party and its policies. He therefore thought that these newcomers merited "punitive measures" by the government.[1]

Fisher Ames complained that the patriots of '76 never "contemplated the claim of the imported united Irish, that a mob should govern us." [2] That the Irish did not all vote the Democratic ticket, however, is indicated in an article analyzing the reasons for the increased Federal vote in Boston in 1800, which attributed it in part to the vote of a bloc of "forty men of color" and the fact that "the United Irishmen" did "not yet *all of them* perceive" that by supporting the Federalists they were voting for the same maxims in government from which they had fled.[3] A few years later a traveler, writing from Boston, reported that the Irish were exceedingly useful, performing a great part of the heaviest labor, and although without money or education were happy, independent, and attached to the government.[4]

By 1798 the acts of the revolutionists in France had so far alienated American sympathy as to react seriously upon the Democratic cause in New England, and that year marks the highest point to which Federalism attained in that section. American politics still traveled in the wake of European happenings, and the Federalist party was soon to be split into two antagonistic sections by events connected with the country which had kept America in a ferment for nearly a decade. The Federalist leaders had been loudly demanding war with France, and the country was felt to be on the verge of proclaimed hostilities, when President Adams suddenly sent an envoy to Paris without even consulting his Cabinet, and avoided the war so heartily desired. The breach thus made between the Federalist President and the more extreme leaders of his party weakened it for the presidential election of 1800. Nevertheless, when the election was over four out of five

[1] *Familiar Letters*, Boston, 1834, p. 127.
[2] *Works*, vol. II, p. 212.
[3] *Independent Chronicle*, Nov. 3, 1800.
[4] John Melish, *Travels through the United States . . . in 1806*, (Philadelphia, 1815), vol. I, p. 93.

New England governors were Federalist, the Federalists controlled all of the legislatures, and a large majority of the representatives in Congress and all of the senators were of the same
party.[1]   It was a curious reversal that the western counties of
Massachusetts, which had been most radical during the period
of Shays's Rebellion, had now become the stronghold of conservatism, and for years after 1800 continued to roll up large
Federal majorities.[2]

Nevertheless, Republican strength was growing, and the
movement against the established order in religion, politics,
and finance had acquired a momentum that nothing thereafter
could stop.   The opposition elements were no longer scattered,
without leaders and without cohesion.   They had learned how
to use political machinery and to make public opinion.   The
"steady habits" of Connecticut seemed to make that state
impregnable to the onslaughts of the radical party, it being, in
Aaron Burr's judgment, so hopeless to change anything there
that one "might as soon attempt to revolutionize the kingdom
of heaven." [3]   But even in Connecticut a Federalist writer to
the *Courant*, oblivious of the way in which the clergy had made
their pulpits into political platforms, complained that, if one
would see the Democrats at work, "let him follow them to their
Democratic Thanksgivings, where, under the masque of public
worship, they are practising intrigue, and disorganization;
where the state is divided into departments, and each man has
his task assigned him, to deceive, and ensnare the unwary,
and to breed swift destruction to our happy country.   There
he will find midnight plottings to destroy our government, to
corrupt our morals, to debauch our youth, and trample under
foot our Religion." [4]   This was merely the Federalist way of
saying that the Democrats were becoming dangerously active
in practical politics.   Indeed, it was complained that "for the

[1] Robinson, *Jeffersonian Democracy*, p. 35.
[2] I have seen no adequate explanation of this, and can offer none.   It may be said
however, that the clergy had an unusually strong hold there, and that after the rebellion
many hundreds of the more radical citizens migrated to Vermont and elsewhere
Vide Morse, *Federal Party*, pp. 180 *ff*.
[3] Quoted by Robinson, *cit. supra*, p. 28.
[4] *Conn. Courant*, April 8, 1801.

first time they have had the audacity in the state of Connecticut to circulate printed tickets" when drawing up nominations.[1]

Moreover, the discussion at the time of the Revolution and later in the voting on the State and Federal Constitutions had bred a love of politics and public discussion among the people at large. "The Americans are all politicians, and every man a federalist or a democrat," wrote a traveler in Connecticut in 1806.[2] He commented on the universal reading of newspapers, and stated that there was "scarcely a poor owner of a miserable log hut, who lives on the border of the stage road, but has a newspaper left at his door." The Democratic news-sheets were undoubtedly becoming effective agents in influencing the people, and the Federalists were alarmed. "Public opinion must be addressed," wrote Ames in 1802, "must be purified from the dangerous errors with which it is infected. . . . The federalists must entrench themselves in the State governments, and endeavor to make State justice and State power a shelter of the wise, and good, and rich, from the wild destroying rage of the southern Jacobins." [3]

[1] Robinson, *op. cit.*, p. 28.
[2] John Lambert, *Travels through Canada and the United States, 1806, 1807, and 1809,* (London, 1814), p. 10.
[3] *Works*, vol. I, p. 310.

CHAPTER X

PROSPERITY AND RUIN

Democratic Victory — Political Methods and Machinery — Suffrage Agitation in Connecticut — Acquisition of Louisiana — Secessionist Plot — Commercial Prosperity — Renewed European Complications — Chesapeake Affair — Impressment of Seamen — The Embargo

IN the country at large, the Democratic party had been successful, and Thomas Jefferson was elected President in 1800. He himself declared, some years later, that the election was as genuine a revolution as had been that of 1776.[1] The Federalist party, wise as many of their measures had been and much as the country owes to them for piloting the State through the first troubled years, had represented a natural conservative reaction from the philosophy of the Revolutionary period. Now, for the first time, the nation was to be governed by a man and a party who still believed in that philosophy; and in this sense Jefferson's words were true. Federalism had been, as Henry Adams termed it, but "a halfway house between the European past and the American future."[2] The people had at length come into possession of what they had believed themselves to be fighting for a generation earlier; and that fact, which seemed to "the wise, the good and the rich" a portent of all imaginable horrors, sent shudders up their spines.

To the clergy of the established church in New England, the accession to the presidency of a man who believed neither in priests, a state church, nor revealed religion, appeared to herald the approach of Antichrist. The removal of many

---

[1] J. P. Gordy, *History of Political Parties*, (New York, 1900), vol. I, p. 382.
[2] *History of the United States*, (New York, 1889), vol. II, p. 76.

Federalists from office in order to replace them by Democrats was regarded as an effort to sweep away all bulwarks of established order. Dr. Dwight poured out his wrath and fears in language so frenzied as to be almost insane. The object of "Jacobinism," he said, was to destroy every trace of civilization in the world. "We have now reached the consummation of democratic blessedness. We have a country governed by blockheads and knaves; the ties of marriage with all its felicities are severed and destroyed; our wives and daughters are thrown into the stews; our children are cast into the world from the breast and forgotten. . . . Can the imagination paint anything more dreadful on this side hell?" [1]

If a man of Dwight's distinguished position and talents could be led to such utterly unfounded outbursts as this, the tone and feelings of lesser partisans may well be imagined. At first, indeed, Jefferson's statements and policies were so much more conservative and reconciling than had been anticipated that many were led to realize that the dangers had been overestimated. His removals from office, however, particularly in the case of the collectorship at New Haven, and his attitude — easily to be sympathized with — toward the clergy in New England who attacked him so violently, brought about a bitterness of partisan feeling in New England that had never before been equaled.

It was no longer the views of the opposing parties that came to be roundly denounced by either side, but the methods used by both in developing their influence and machinery. The Democratic Clubs formed in Connecticut were execrated for being as wicked as those of France. "A number of the most vicious men in the world," wrote a Federalist, "who are pampered by large salaries and incomes from the public money, have established revolutionary committees thro' the state, to co-operate in the avowed design of overturning the government"; and added that if they ever obtained control of the legislature they would introduce complete anarchy. [2] On the

---

[1] Quoted by Adams, *Hist. of U. S.*, vol. I, p. 225.
[2] *Conn. Courant*, March 30, 1803. *Cf. The 6th of August or the Litchfield Festival*, (n. p. 1806).

other hand, the Democrats complained in no uncertain terms of the methods of the Federalists. "An Election Day is the season of tyranny, and almost of usurpation," we read in one attack. "At this period every petty nabob exercises his powers and influence. Every avenue is thronged with hirelings, sycophants, and cringing supplicants, who live on the smiles, patronage and drudgery of their employers : a long list of vote distributors are published in the *Gazette*" (he added), and these are placed about the city. "Why are these men so active in inspecting every man's vote? and by frowns and menaces terrifying those who may not readily accede to their candidates ? Will any person presume to deny the influence which such a formidable combination produces; or say, that many individuals are not intimidated when acting under the immediate eye of those who have it in their power to injure them in their various occupations?" [1]

It was claimed, apparently not without reason, that the banks also acted for the Federalists. Under their direction, we find in one article, "the middling interest were controlled by impending ruinous checks on their renewals. This is not conjecture, it is fact. Men were told, if they expected their notes should be honored at the bank, they must be federalists." [2] Within a few years following the "revolution of 1800" the Federalists organized their machinery in all the New England states on the basis of a legislative caucus, with local committees reaching down through the towns. It was done with extreme caution, owing to the dislike of the New Englanders for giving up their apparent freedom of choice in the matter of candidates.[3]

[1] *Independent Chronicle*, April 19, 1804.

[2] *Ibid.*, April 19, May 3, Sept. 6, 1804. *Cf.* Morison, *Otis*, vol. I, pp. 260 *f.*

[3] For the development of the system in Massachusetts, with notes on New Hampshire and Rhode Island, *vide* Morison, *Otis*, vol. I, pp. 286 *ff.* The following "Address to the Freemen of Connecticut" describes the inception of the system in that state. "The members of the House of Representatives and a number of persons from various parts of the State have thought proper to meet at the State House and consider the political situation in view of the organized system of the Democrats."

"It could not escape the consideration of any person present, that a proceeding of this nature was a deviation from the ancient practice of the State. That it would be far better, that all the freemen should exercise their elective rights without any interference whatever. But although the result of the late election had proved, that a large

The keynote of Federalism was distrust in the common man. Belief in him was the battle cry of the Democrats. It was natural, therefore, that one of the earliest issues raised in New England should have been that of the restricted suffrage. Owing to the fact that Vermont had no property qualification at all, and that in New Hampshire every adult male who paid a tax or did militia duty could vote, the struggle was confined to the three southern states of the section. It is noteworthy that in Connecticut, where the people had least voice in their affairs, the programme of the Democrats assumed its most radical form. In Massachusetts there were said to be twenty-seven thousand men unenfranchised for lack of sufficient property, though twenty thousand of them paid taxes.[1] The question in that state, however, did not become the burning one which it did in Connecticut, and in fact did not attract much attention until 1809.

In Connecticut the Federalist party, alarmed by the increase in Republican votes, passed an act in 1801, known as the "Stand-up Law" from the fact that among other provisions it required that the freemen in voting, instead of depositing ballots, should stand up to be counted. The whole law was aimed at increasing the undue influence of the "wise and rich," and created a paroxysm of anger among the Republicans. The Federalists denied that taxation and representation were reciprocal, and did their best to nullify the effects of the slogan of 1776.[2] Noah Webster declared flatly that "our laws

and decided majority of our fellow citizens were determined to support the Government of the State, yet the form of our election was known to be such, that the will of the majority might ultimately be defeated, should they not unite on their candidates. . . . But how to form a list of Candidates, which should be unexceptionable with respect to the manner of making it, and which would probably unite the suffrages of the freemen, is a subject novel in this State and of great difficulty. . . . Any attempt by a few individuals to direct the public attention to a particular list of Candidates might be considered as an officious interference with the right of suffrage. But under the peculiar circumstances of the times, it was believed, that the people of the State would not deem it improper for the Representatives of the towns, with such other persons as were present, during the session of the Legislature, to submit to the freemen, a list of candidates to compose the nominations for Assistants in September next. In this proceeding, it must be evident that we are acting only on the defensive. Those who are attempting to destroy the government of the State, have led the way. They form their lists and they unite to a man." *Conn. Courant*, June 8, 1803.

[1] *Independent Chronicle*, Aug. 23, 1804.   [2] *Conn. Courant*, March 2, 1803.

principally respect property; that is their great object"; and that to give all men the suffrage would be to prostrate "the wealth of individuals to the rapaciousness of a merciless gang."[1] In 1802 a bill proposed by Colonel Ephraim Kirby, providing for written ballots, was defeated by one hundred and twenty to fifty-nine in the legislature, and all attempts of the Republicans to safeguard or extend the suffrage broke in vain against the solid opposition of the Federalist majority.

As has been pointed out several times, the machinery of elections was so devised as to keep perpetually in power those who already exercised it, and the prospect therefore appeared hopeless for the opposition, which although growing in numbers was likely to remain a minority for a long time. It was natural that the lack of a written constitution and the question of the legality of that under which the state was functioning should again be agitated. On the twenty-ninth of August, 1804, after much discussion, a convention of Republican delegates from ninety-seven towns met at New Haven and voted an address to the people.[2]

Starting with a quotation from the Declaration of Independence, the address proceeded and stated that by that declaration the sovereignty had been vested in the people, but had never been exercised by them. Although every state in the Union except Rhode Island and Connecticut had adopted written constitutions based upon the consent of the people, in Connecticut there was no constitution — only a government that had never received the approval of the electorate. This government, excellent as it might seem to those who exercised it, was in reality a bad government because it gave the power to a group, tended to the increase of aristocracies, and was unfriendly to the principles of the American Revolution. It had been said that all had gone well in Connecticut; but "what prudent farmer among us," the address asked, "is contented with the abundant crops of his farm, while he has no title deed on record?" The grievances of the times were indicated by the points that should be looked for in a new constitution. This,

---

[1] Purcell, *Connecticut in Transition*, p. 225.
[2] *Conn. Courant*, Aug. 15, 22, 29, Sept. 5, 19, 26, Oct. 3, 1804.

it was stated, should declare that taxation and representation were inseparable; that all men should be free in the exercise of their religion; that judges should be dependent on the will of the people; that the qualifications of freemen should be determined so that the legislature could not alter them at will; and that a separation of the executive, legislative, and judicial powers should be effected, so that the legislature should not combine them all.[1] The address denied that a constitution was desired in the interests of party, and pointed out that the "interests of a legislature in power and those of the people may be at variance; but the interests of a [constitutional] convention and those of the people are the same."

In Federalist pamphlets the New Haven meeting was denounced as "a daring outrage against order and civil society," and it was claimed that if the people generally had been "as violent and desperate as some of those factious leaders, the whole state would have become an *aceldama* or field of blood." [2] The elections of 1805 were fought over this issue of a constitution. The wealthy towns of the Connecticut Valley and elsewhere were Federalist, whereas those in which religious dissent was a force were Democratic; but in the new legislature the Federalists continued to outnumber the Republicans nearly two to one, in spite of gains at the polls by the latter.[3] Nevertheless, the leaven was at work.

In 1803 a far greater question had been injected into party strife by the unexpected acquisition by Jefferson from the French government of the ill-defined territory of Louisiana. For obvious reasons the Federalists were in arms at once. Threatened as they were on every side with the destruction of their party by the rising tide of Democracy, even in the conservative strongholds of New England, the prospect of a large addition to the Union of Democratic and slave territory was indeed alarming. As has been pointed out again and again, the Federalists viewed with the utmost abhorrence and genuine

---

[1] *Address to the People of the State of Connecticut,* Broadside in the Library of Congress.

[2] [David Daggett] *Steady Habits Vindicated,* (Hartford, 1805), p. 9.

[3] Purcell, *Connecticut in Transition,* pp. 265 ff.

fear the democratic doctrines on which the Revolution had rested philosophically. Moreover, although up to 1800 the Federalists had been a national party, they were losing ground faster in the South than in New England, and had practically no foothold at all in the now rapidly expanding West. In addition, the compromise in the Federal Constitution by which the slave states had been given additional representation of three fifths of the slave population had always rankled in the free states.[1] In Congress the New England representatives in both houses were almost solidly against the purchase. Although the constitutional aspects of the problem came in for much debate, Uriah Tracy of Connecticut, in what was perhaps the ablest speech on the Federalist side, put his finger on the main point: "The relative strength which this admission gives to a Southern and Western interest is contradictory to the principles of the original Union." [2]

The accession became an accomplished fact by the votes of the Republicans, and at once some of the New England Federalist leaders entered upon the path of threatened secession from the Union which they were to follow at intervals during the next decade.[3] Of the United States senators from that section, Plumer and Olcott from New Hampshire, Pickering and Adams from Massachusetts, Tracy and Hillhouse from Connecticut, all but two — Olcott and Adams — believed secession to be inevitable.[4] In the House, Roger Griswold and Calvin Goddard of Connecticut and Samuel Hunt of New Hampshire were of the same belief. In January 1804 Pickering wrote a long letter to George Cabot on what he called the "delicate subject." Everything, he said, pointed to the necessity of separation, and he believed the sooner the better. When and how were the only questions. Federalism was

---

[1] There were some slaves held in the Northern states. According to the first census, in 1790, New Hampshire had 157, Rhode Island 958, Connecticut 2648, New York 21,193, New Jersey 11,423, Pennsylvania 3707, and Delaware 8887. The overwhelming sectional difference, however, is shown by the figures for the rest of the Union — 645,234. *Century of Population Growth*, pp. 201 *f.*

[2] Adams, *Hist. of U. S.*, vol. II, pp. 107 *f.*

[3] The suggestion appeared as early as August 1803, although the main agitation occurred in the next year. *Vide Conn. Courant*, Aug. 17, 1803.

[4] Adams, *op. cit.*, vol. II, p. 160; Plumer, *William Plumer*, pp. 283 *ff.*

crumbling, even in New England, and he thought there was no time to be lost. He felt sure that the concurrence of all the New England states could be secured, but that New York would have to be made the centre of the new confederation.[1] Pickering pointed to the spring sessions of the several legislatures as the time for action, and as the weeks went by a plot took definite form. In March, Griswold wrote from Washington that there could be no safety for the Northern states without a separation, and that the project the conspirators had formed was to induce the legislatures of the three New England states which had remained Federal, beginning with Massachusetts, to call for an independent reunion of the Northern states, and then to be governed by circumstances.[2] As the plot matured, others were approached, among them Aaron Burr, whom it was planned to make the head of the new nation. Alexander Hamilton, whom it was hoped to draw in, disapproved of the scheme, which he thought had great practical disadvantages while at the same time "administering no relief to our real disease, which is Democracy." That poison, he thought, would be only the more virulent if the Union were broken into smaller divisions.[3] Rufus King, George Cabot, and others of the less rabid leaders of the Federalists also disapproved.

When the Massachusetts legislature met in June, William Ely of Springfield introduced a measure which was passed by a strictly party vote, to amend the Federal Constitution so that representation and taxation should be apportioned on the basis of free white population only. This, of course, would never have been agreed to by the Southerners, who had been induced to enter the confederation only on the basis of slave representation. It would appear, therefore, that this resolution had for its object the testing of Northern sentiment as to disunion; but every state, with the exceptions of Connecticut and Delaware, which took no action, promptly rejected the proposal.[4]

[1] Lodge, *Cabot*, pp. 337 *ff.*
[2] Henry Adams, *Documents Relating to New England Federalism*, (Boston, 1877), pp. 354 *ff.*
[3] *Ibid.*, p. 365.
[4] Morison, *Otis*, vol. I, p. 264.

Meanwhile the schemes of the disunionists had become public and a lively newspaper controversy ensued. The Federalist papers early did their best to sway public opinion, and such journals as the *Connecticut Courant* fanned the flames of jealousy between North and South over the question of slave representation. "Is there anything more scandalous in the abuses of the British Constitution," it asked, "than this mockery of representation? Are the rotten boroughs of England more infamous than our negro boroughs? . . . Who freed Virginia and the Carolinas from the British troops when aided by their slaves? It was the men of the North — now destined vassals of the South." [1] Of course nothing was said about the rotten boroughs in Connecticut, where the strongly entrenched Federalist machine was opposing the suffrage demands of their own "men of the North" when they happened to be political opponents.

The Republican press fought the issue on every possible ground from the first breath that was heard of it. As early as January, the *Independent Chronicle* in Boston was expressing its "indignation and contempt" with regard to the plot to sow discord and to divide the Union.[2] It was said that the Federalists, finding their power dwindling in the North and completely overwhelmed in the Middle and Southern States, were taking this desperate means of retaining their control.[3] The *Eastern Argus* of Portland, Maine, told the Federalists that their downfall could be traced solely to their un-Republican measures, to their "standing armies," their Sedition Bill, their theory of the public debt, their British treaty, and their "absurd attempt to introduce 'a Nobility in a hole,'" together with their "proud contempt of the Farmer and Mechanic." [4]

On the other hand, the Federalists made no secret of their wishes. The newly founded *New England Palladium* supported their views, and pamphlets and handbills were circulated to spread them. Even these, however, admitted public apathy

---

[1] Issue of May 23, 1804.   *Cf.* April 4 and Sept. 7.
[2] Issue of Jan. 9, 1804.   *Cf.* April 9, 23, June 11, 28, Sept. 6, 13, Oct. 1.
[3] *Independent Chronicle*, June 28, 1804.
[4] Issue of Sept. 13, 1804.   *Cf.* Sept. 20 and 27, Oct. 4.

toward those ills which only "the wise and rich and good" seemed to perceive. "The Commonwealth was never in greater danger," these latter proclaimed — danger of losing its sovereignty and of being taxed without its consent. "It is in danger of passing under the dominion of men who are strangers to the interests, and who deride the habits and institutions of New England. . . . Massachusetts is a cypher in the national councils, and the wishes and the policy of New England are known only as they furnish themes for the invective and the irony of those who rule the nation." The Eastern states are the "mere colonies of Virginia." "The danger is the more serious as it is not generally perceived, and approaches us in the midst of prosperity and avocations, too happy to fear, too busy to repel it." [1] The plot, indeed, disapproved of by many of the Federalist leaders themselves, met with no popular response whatever, and the killing of Hamilton by Burr in the famous duel ended the impracticable scheme. The Federalist party, however, had been deeply implicated, and the answer of the people came in the autumn elections, when Jefferson was reëlected President by every New England state except Connecticut.

New England was, in fact, exceedingly prosperous. In spite of the hindrances to commerce during the French War, a considerable part of the carrying trade of the world had fallen into American hands and the greater part was carried by New England ships, to the profit of the merchants and shipowners of that section. Commerce with the British West Indies alone increased from \$2,144,000 in 1792 to \$9,700,000 in 1801.[2] The peace proclaimed in that year enabled the European nations to some extent to restore more normal conditions and to regain their own colonial and other trade, so that complaints from the West Indies again became frequent as to restrictions on securing American goods — which were also heard after war was renewed in 1803.[3] For the first two years of the new war,

---

[1] *A Defence of the Legislature of Massachusetts or the Rights of New England Vindicated*, (Boston, 1804), p. 4.
[2] F. L. Benns, *The American Struggle for the British West India Carrying Trade, 1815–1830*, (Indiana University Studies, 1923), p. 20.
[3] G. W. Jordan, *The Claims of the British West India Colonists*, (London, 1804), pp. 39 f.; S. Cock, *An Answer to Lord Sheffield's Pamphlet*, (London, 1804), pp. 52 ff.

however, England appeared to be more inclined to respect neutral trade, and American merchants again began to reap a rich reward. Notwithstanding heavy losses, commerce flourished amazingly. America became almost the exclusive carrier for the world, and of the million tons of American shipping in 1805 exactly half was New England owned.[1] Under these circumstances, the Federalists had a difficult task in trying to persuade the people that Jefferson's rule was dangerous or that there was any practical need for dissolving the Union.

There were, indeed, grievances against England. There were the restrictions on the West Indian trade, and the old running sore of impressment of American seamen, which latter we shall consider more particularly later. But, on the whole, New Englanders were inclined to overlook such matters while they were driving a roaring trade, protected to a great extent by the British navy. Suddenly, however, the English ministry threw a bomb the explosion of which echoed all along the Atlantic coast. English merchants had been looking with jealous eyes on the absorption of their own business by Americans, due to war conditions, and the English government saw danger to the navy in the crowds of English sailors who escaped impressment for war service in English merchant vessels by serving in American ships. Based on the old rule of 1756, modified by the Orders of 1798 and 1803, it had been held that goods might be carried by neutrals from belligerent colonies to their own countries and if the domestic requirements for admission were complied with, that the goods might then be reëxported thence to any place, like any other neutral goods. The American merchants, however, when technically complying with this rule, had been receiving a drawback from the customhouses on goods reëxported; and in May 1805 the British decided, in a test case brought before Sir William Scott, — that of the ship Essex, — that such goods had not complied with the conditions of actual importation and therefore that the voyage was not actually a "broken" one. The motive for the decision was easily understandable; but on the other hand, the United

[1] Figures quoted in *Columbian Centinel*, Sept. 24, 1808. The total was 1,984,900, of which New England owned 534,692. Of this, 426,000 belonged to Massachusetts.

States had a right to make its own regulations as to what constituted bona fide "importations," and England undoubtedly put a strained interpretation on her rights. In the ablest defense of the decision which appeared in that country — and which was reprinted during the Great War in 1917, when the question of neutral trade was again a serious one — James Stephen said rightly that "behind the doctrine of contraband of war and blockades there was a larger principle of which they were only illustrations, the right of a belligerent to prevent the neutral from giving assistance to the enemy." [1]

As the British, in accordance with the new interpretation, rapidly began seizing American ships, wrath waxed hot in New England. A town meeting at Salem, for example, in a memorial to Congress declared that they wanted peace, but would have no hesitation in going to war if necessary.[2] There was, indeed, no option except war or submission. But on sober thought it was seen that war would ruin the merchants, instead of merely decreasing their profits. Popular feeling ran high, but in Boston the merchants were able to control the form of the memorial sent from that town, which was exceedingly moderate in tone.[3] George Cabot, who, much against his will, had acted as chairman of the meeting, expressed his own views in a letter to Pickering. No considerable party, he said, was willing to take the consequences of war, and as for England, whatever her motives might be, she was in reality defending the whole civilized world, and would be justified in "saying to neutrals, 'If you will not help us in the battle, you shall not hinder its success under a cover of neutral pretensions.'" [4] This view, maintained again a century later, was that held by most of the Federalists throughout all the complications, contentions, and war of the next decade.

Even more severe upon neutral commerce than the decision in the Essex case were the Berlin Decree issued by Napoleon

---

[1] James Stephen, *War in Disguise*, (ed. 1917, London), p. vii. The American answer at the time was by Gouverneur Morris, *An Answer to War in Disguise*, (New York, 1806).
[2] *Independent Chronicle*, Jan. 30, 1806.
[3] Adams, *Hist. of U. S.*, vol. III, pp. 143 *f.*
[4] Lodge, *Cabot*, p. 353.

and the British Orders in Council, promulgated in retaliation in January 1807.[1] American national feeling was already becoming highly incensed at the utter disregard paid to neutral rights by the two principal belligerents, when the attack occurred in July upon the American frigate Chesapeake by the British ship-of-war Leopard off the coast of Virginia. Many British seamen at Norfolk and elsewhere had been deserting and enlisting in the American service. Without orders from home, the commander of the British squadron decided to take matters into his own hands, dispatched the Leopard after the Chesapeake when the latter sailed, overhauled her, forced her to surrender, and took from her four of her crew, after killing or wounding twenty-one others. Of the four taken as deserters, one was hanged, one died, and the other two were eventually restored.[2]

As soon as the news spread the entire country was in an uproar, and for a brief moment even the bitterness of party strife was lost to sight. A public meeting at Portsmouth, New Hampshire, denounced the "unprovoked and dastardly attack" as "an act of hostility against the sovereignty and Independence of our country."[3] At Newport one of the largest meetings held in years, made up of members of both parties, expressed the utmost detestation for the "late insult on our National Flag" and pledged themselves to prepare for war.[4] At Providence a meeting resolved that the affair was "a flagrant insult on our national honor," and that if the government decided on war, they would support it with their lives and fortunes.[5] In an article headed "The Spirit of Seventy-Six" the local paper proclaimed that "No neutrality can now be tolerated. Those who are not for us are against us."[6] The *Massachusetts Spy*, at Worcester, in an article headed "The Nation Insulted," pledged the people to extreme measures.[7] The *Connecticut Courant*

---

[1] Adams, *Hist. of U. S.*, vol. III, pp. 389 *ff*.

[2] *Ibid.*, vol. IV, pp. 2 *ff*.; Mahan, *Sea Power in the War of 1812*, vol. I, pp. 155 *ff*.

[3] *New Hampshire Gazette*, July 14, 1807. The news first appeared in the issue of July 7 under the head of "British Outrage."

[4] *Newport Mercury*, July 11, 1807.

[5] *The Phenix*, July 18, 1807.

[6] *Ibid.*

[7] Issue of July 8, 1807.

spoke of it as a "wanton and unprovoked attack," and an indignation meeting was held at New Haven.[1]   In the interior parts of New Hampshire it was reported "that but one spirit animated all classes, which was to rally round the standards of the government, with the spirit of '75, and shew the world that we are but one people, and have but one interest when the nation is insulted."   The *Salem Gazette* said that the public mind was filled with resentment throughout the whole of Massachusetts.   "One thing is certain," it added; "an act of war has been committed upon us," and that measures to prepare for the worst should immediately be taken and were strongly desired by all who loved their country.[2]

In Boston, almost if not quite alone, was there hesitation. At first the Federalists refused to call a town meeting.   The Republicans then held one, at which John Quincy Adams was the only Federalist present, and passed resolutions denouncing the outrage and pledging support to the government "in any measures, however serious."[3]   Forced by public sentiment to call a meeting of the town, the Federalists did so, and some of the less extreme leaders, like Otis and Adams, were on the committee that drew up the resolves, which were milder in tone than those of the earlier meeting.[4]   The Essex Junto did not take part, and such men as Cabot, Parsons, and Pickering warmly maintained that the British were within their rights.[5]

Had war been decided upon at that moment, the country would have been united in its support.   Jefferson, however, preferred suspension of commercial intercourse; the nation entered upon the most disastrous experiment in its history; and when war finally came in 1812 the country had become split into bitter factions again.   Meanwhile, through the press, the Junto began to sway public opinion in favor of England. The *Salem Gazette*, which had been so hot for war on July 10, a fortnight later was deprecating the fact that the papers which "come to hand teem with the resolves of meetings" throughout

---

[1] Issue of July 8, 1807; *Conn. Journal*, July 9, 1807.
[2] Issue of July 10, 1807.
[3] *Independent Chronicle*, July 13, 1807.
[4] *Ibid.*, July 20, 1807.
[5] Adams, *Hist. of U. S.*, vol. IV, p. 29.

the state.[1] A series of articles by "Pacificus" contended that
war was neither necessary nor expedient, and rather defended
British impressment of sailors.[2] The *New England Palladium*
pointed out that war would ruin the farmers and merchants,
and painted a gloomy picture of bankruptcies.[3] The *Portsmouth Oracle* stated that if war came it would not be on account
of the Chesapeake affair, which was only being used to inflame
the public mind, but that "the great cause of war, is the protection of British seamen under the American flag." [4] Pamphlets taking the same ground began to appear, and as the
summer passed the indignation cooled, public opinion became
confused, and the discussion shifted largely to the question of
impressment.[5]

If the outrage on the American flag had shown, as in a lightning flash, nascent American nationalism, Americans were
by no means united in feeling aggrieved at the mere exercise
in merchant vessels of the British claim to impress her own
citizens when found. The question, in fact, was by no means
simple, but belonged to that category which is the most difficult
of fair adjustment, that of a long recognized prescriptive right
which comes into conflict with new conditions. In the first
place, the British doctrine of citizenship held that allegiance
could not be transferred — a doctrine which the United States
also occasionally asserted. Moreover, with the connivance of
American consuls and other officials, deserting British seamen
could buy American citizenship papers for nominal sums. The
right to reclaim her citizens to their duty when found on foreign
vessels had been traditional in England, and had never been
questioned by the other European powers. The smallness
of the number of those deserting to Continental services, together with the difference in race and language, made but
little difficulty in enforcing the practice. With the rise of the
United States to the position of the second maritime nation

[1] Issue of July 24, 1807.
[2] *Columbian Centinel*, July 29, Aug. 1, 5, 8, 12, 22, 1807.
[3] Issue of July 24, 1807.   [4] Issue of July 25, 1807.
[5] [John Lowell] *Peace without Dishonor, War without Hope*, (Boston, 1807). In the
issues of *The Repertory* (Boston) may be found some of the strongest articles inspired
by the Junto.

in the world the situation became entirely altered. Not only were deserting British seamen by thousands to be found on American vessels, but the frequent impossibility of distinguishing between Americans and British, on account of identity of race and speech, together with the conflicting doctrines of allegiance and naturalization, made it impossible that the practice should be exercised without endless errors and international complications. Even when the British naval officers tried to distinguish between the two nationals, — which was not always the case, — many genuine Americans were bound to be caught in the net. Here then was a wholly novel situation. On the one hand, Americans of strong national feeling were not willing to put up with what they considered an injustice and an insult to national dignity simply because it had always been recognized by European powers. On the other hand, England, fighting for her life, which depended on her naval man-power, did not see why she should handicap herself by giving up a long-established "right" because a new nation demanded it.[1] As Canning, the British Prime Minister, wrote to Monroe; "These rights existed in their fullest force for ages previous to the establishment of the United States," and it was difficult to contend that that latter fact should abrogate them.[2]

As to the extent of the practice and the numbers of American seamen actually impressed, it was impossible to reach definite conclusions at the time, and certainly is so now. Figures may never lie, but the people who manipulate them do, and both sides in America exaggerated their case. On the one side, lists were compiled showing that thousands of genuine Americans had been seized by the British and in many cases forced to serve for years in the British navy. On the other side, we have such statements as that made by James Lloyd in 1813, who testified that he had been in active mercantile business in Boston from 1793 to 1807 and a shipowner all those years, and that in the entire time there was not a single passenger or seaman taken from any vessel in which he was interested. Nor since he had been in Congress, from 1807 to 1813, had he ever received a complaint from any of his constituents with regard

[1] Mahan, *Sea Power in the War of 1812*, vol. I, pp. 114 ff.   [2] *Ibid.*, p. 115.

to impressment, although Massachusetts owned one third of the tonnage of the country.[1] In the latter year, a committee in Nantucket reported that, although the island had maintained from eight hundred to a thousand seamen for the past twenty years, it had been impossible to find more than twenty cases of impressed men, and of those only one had been taken from a Nantucket vessel.[2] A Massachusetts sailor swore in 1813 that he had followed the sea from 1783 to 1812, and that in all that time no man or boy had ever been impressed from any vessel he had been on, except one British seaman in 1799.[3] In 1813 a committee of the Massachusetts legislature, appointed to investigate the question, reported that only one hundred and fifty-seven men had been impressed from the whole state. On the other hand, it was said in Salem with regard to this report that more than the number named had been impressed from that one port alone.[4] A government report claimed that over six thousand American sailors had been taken from American vessels. James Madison, who was strongly opposed to the British contention, wrote that between 1797 and 1801 over two thousand cases had applied to the consul in London for relief; that of these eleven hundred and forty-two had been discharged as not British; and that it was his belief that not one in ten or twenty who were impressed were British.[5]

The real question, however, was not one of numbers. When Pickering wrote to Governor Sullivan that the number was very small, John Quincy Adams rejoined by saying: "Suppose the crime had been, in every instance, as by its consequence it has been in many, deliberate murder, would it answer or silence the voice of our complaints to be told, that 'the number is small'?"[6] It was a malignant crime, he said, to "a people having a just sense of personal liberty and security."[7] What-

---

[1] *Columbian Centinel*, March 6, 1813.
[2] Four of these were married in England, four were taken while in British ports, and of the rest no details were known. *Columbian Centinel*, March 27, 1813.
[3] *Columbian Centinel*, March 27, 1813.
[4] *Ibid.*, March 13, 1813; *Baltimore Patriot*, March 18, 1813.
[5] *All Impressments Unlawful and Inadmissable*, (Boston, 1807), pp. 8 f.
[6] *A Letter from the Hon. Timothy Pickering*, (Boston, 1818), p. 9; *A Letter to Mr. Harrison Gray Otis . . . by J. Q. Adams*, [1808], (Baltimore, 1824), p. 11.
[7] *Ibid.*, p. 11.

ever the facts may have been, it is nevertheless certain that, all through the years leading up to the war and during that conflict, the New England section, which owned one half of the shipping of the country, made little complaint and on every occasion minimized the importance of the issue. The cry was always heard there that the number of impressments was small and that most of the men taken were British deserters anyway. The one object of the merchant-Federalist party was to avoid war with England at any cost. Business was profitable and, with no pride in the nation or interest in the common man of their state, they regarded the matter as trifling so long as the number of British seamen enlisting in American ships was greater than the number of Americans taken out of them — and this seems usually to have been the case. The merchants, therefore, well content with the situation, belittled the issue, and sarcastically asked whether we were to go to war to protect British deserters.[1]

Meanwhile, there had been other causes of friction between the United States and the leading two European Powers. In December 1806, Monroe and Pinckney had negotiated a treaty with Great Britain which secured certain rights for neutrals, but yielded to the British on the point of impressment. Jefferson, on this account, refused to submit it to the Senate. At the same time, no preparations were made to put the country in a position to resort to force should negotiation fail. In May the British had proclaimed a blockade of eight hundred miles of the German, Dutch, and French coasts. Napoleon retorted with the famous Berlin Decree in November. A year later England issued an Order in Council prohibiting any direct trade from the United States to any European country from which the British were excluded, and ordering that all goods exported from this country to any European country, except Sweden, must be first landed in Great Britain and have duties paid on them before reëxportation. Napoleon then issued his Milan Decree of December 1807, making any vessel lawful prize which should touch at a British port. Obviously there was nothing for the United States to do in self-respect but to

[1] *Cf.* review of Madison's pamphlet, in *Boston Gazette*, July 20, 1807.

declare war. But American self-respect in these years was at the lowest ebb it ever touched. The Republicans had done nothing to prepare the country for hostilities, and there was little to choose between France and England as enemies. As Jefferson said later, England had become "a den of pirates" and France "a den of thieves." [1]

Meanwhile, the Federalist party had been badly defeated in New England in the 1807 elections. Even Massachusetts had elected a Democratic governor and a Democratic majority in the legislature. Governor Trumbull of Connecticut was the sole Federalist surviving the Democratic landslide to hold an important state office. In the United States Senate only Pickering of Massachusetts and Hillhouse and Goodrich of Connecticut remained as leading Federalists from that section, while in the House Josiah Quincy was almost alone. Jefferson could believe that his policy had won the support of the people, and his policy had always been against war. In the critical position in which the country was now placed he determined to try a substitute, one which America had experimented with on several occasions and which he hoped might avert war, which was dreaded by the Republicans not so much for its horrors as for its effect on government. That substitute was the Embargo. Its economic and political results reached far beyond anything dreamed of by those who initiated the experiment. In this chapter we shall consider only the former, leaving the latter to be noted later.

There has never yet been any adequate study made of American pacifism, but that the Americans are pacifists as a nation has been evident from the very earliest days. The Civil War, as well as others, proved that they could fight well and long when there was no other escape, but militarism has never appealed to them, and they have always avoided war whenever possible. In the decade prior to the Revolution they had made use of commercial coercion as a weapon and, to a minor extent, on several occasions subsequently. It was not unnatural, therefore, that Jefferson and the Republicans, who represented the feelings and desires of the "plain people" of

[1] Johnston and Woodburn, *American Political History*, vol. I, p. 295.

the country much more nearly than did the Federalists, should resort to similar means to avoid hostilities, when there seemed no other way out of the complicated and threatening situation in 1807.

According to an Act passed by Congress and which Jefferson signed on December 22 of that year, no American vessel of any sort was permitted to sail from an American port destined for any foreign country. Coasting trade was not, as yet, prohibited. The friends of the measure wrote that commerce could not be carried on with safety before the Act was passed; that it would tend to preserve peace by bringing the British to terms from economic necessity without resort to arms; that it would be far less costly than war in money, lives, and suffering; and that it would encourage domestic manufactures.[1] The opposition party, however, at once attacked the Administration. Jefferson was charged with being under the influence of Napoleon and of wishing to destroy American commerce. Heretofore, in spite of all dangers and obstructions, trade had been carried on, and profits had been great in proportion to the risks. The Federalists, who represented the shipping interests, felt that England had been singled out for special hostility, although in their opinion France had been the earlier and greater aggressor of the two. They also felt that their own section at home, New England, was to be ruined for the sake of saving the rest of the nation the expense or suffering of war.

Moreover, having embarked on an ill-fated policy, the government was to find it necessary, throughout the next year or more, constantly to pass supplementary measures to stop the gaps and enforce the provisions of the original Embargo Act. The first of these was passed within a few weeks, and called for the giving of bonds and procuring of licenses by all coasting vessels. Another, passed in February, prohibited certain trade with Florida and Canada, even if carried on by land. In April still another supplementary Act was passed, dealing largely with matters of administration and adding many annoying details, such as holding up for examination on the high

[1] W. W. Jennings, *The American Embargo, 1807–1809*, (University of Iowa Studies, 1921), pp. 42 *ff*.

seas by armed vessels of the United States any ships merely suspected of violating the Embargo. In January 1809 the longest and most drastic of all the supplementary Acts was found necessary by the government to prevent the smuggling and other evasions of the law which the earlier ones had called forth. In this the provisions regarding licensing were made much more stringent, and almost absolute powers were given into the hands of local customhouse officers. The President was also authorized to use the army, navy, and militia to suppress armed resistance to the enforcement of the several acts.

As far as any influence upon our European enemies was concerned, the Embargo did little or no harm to either. Its disastrous effects, like American produce during its continuance, were all consumed at home. It has been claimed that its results in New England were not so severe as sometimes stated in the past.[1] It has also been claimed that they were felt to a greater extent in Virginia and the rest of the South than in New England, although opposition centred in the latter section.[2]

The facts, however, point to severe economic distress throughout New England as an immediate result of Jefferson's policy. Skillfully as the Federalists may have taken advantage of the situation to rehabilitate themselves, they could not have affected the political situation as forcibly as they did had not the measure proven so universally unpopular; and it would not have been so unpopular had not the distress been so general. The total exports from Massachusetts in 1808 were only $5,100,000 as compared with $20,100,000 in 1807. Those of Rhode Island declined from $1,600,000 to $240,000, and the declines in the other New England states were in similar proportion.[3] The losses in exports, which amounted to about seventy-five per cent, were almost equally divided between domestic and foreign products. In shipbuilding the tonnage constructed in 1808 was but one third of that of 1807.

The losses were by no means confined to commerce and the

---

[1] This is Professor Channing's view. *Hist. of U. S.*, vol. IV, pp. 387 f.
[2] Adams, *Hist. of U. S.*, vol. IV, pp. 280 f.; Jennings, *American Embargo*, pp. 198 ff.
[3] Jennings, *op. cit.*, p. 214.

STAFFORD, **Mineral Springs,** *Aug* 8 1808

Mr. *Rice & Lady* — — — Dr.

	Dollars	Cents
To Board and Lodging	4	06
Horse at Hay		67
Horse at Pasture		
Oats		48
Corn		
Warm Baths		50
Cold Baths		
Shower Baths		
Madeira Wine		
Vidonia		
Dry Lisbon		
Port		
Claret		
Metheglin		
Brandy		
Gin		
Old Spirits		
Breakfast		
Dinner		
Supper		
Lodging		
Punch		
Lemonade		

Received Payment, *for S Willard* $ 5 71

P. G. Burnham 33

6 04

OLD HOTEL BILL, 1808

shipping trades.   The farmers felt the closing of foreign markets, and a severe slump occurred in the prices of their products.
That of beans declined forty-one per cent, of potatoes twenty-
three per cent, of corn fifty-five per cent, of pork forty-three
per cent, with other declines of smaller amount in other produce.[1]   On the other hand, the prices of many imported necessities and luxuries advanced by leaps.   The newspapers and
private letters of the period are full of descriptions of the
disaster.   "There is but little market for the productions of
our labor," wrote one commentator in Rhode Island.   "Our
crop of hay will but little more than pay for making.   What
last year brought twenty, will this, bring but ten dollars.
Pork, at the last market of it, was worth ten cents, now it will
command but little more than five."   In general all crops and
produce were worth but half the previous ones.   Even wood,
which had never been exported, had declined heavily in price
because the distress was so great among the commercial population of the towns that they could not afford to buy it.   The
writer estimated that $100,000,000 worth of property was
embargoed and perishing in the United States for want of
export.[2]   Cabot wrote from Boston, only a few days after the
Embargo was proclaimed, that the evil effects were already
beginning to be felt, and that several thousand persons would
be out of employment immediately.[3]   It is not necessary to
multiply contemporary notices, many of which were, of course,
for political effect.   The actions of the people, which will be
noted in the next chapter, speak louder than individual comments.   A certain amount of smuggling across all borders
undoubtedly brought in some returns, and the enormous decrease in imports naturally stimulated manufacturing for the
whole market.   In fact, the Embargo did far more for the protection of New England manufactures than any of the tariff
legislation yet passed by Congress.   Although this was an
alleviating factor, it nevertheless involved a certain dislocation
in the labor market; and such transfers of capital and labor

---

[1] Jennings, op. cit., p. 186.
[2] An Address to the Citizens of Rhode Island, (n. p., Nov. 1808), pp. 10 f.
[3] Lodge, Cabot, p. 474.

from one form of employment to another cannot be effected without much anxiety and hardship for individuals, whatever the statistics may show as to totals in volume of trade and industry.

In addition to the actual economic distress caused, the various Acts also inflicted petty hardships and an annoying submission to the prying and overbearing conduct of officials, to which the people were not used, and these added heavily to the popular resentment. For example, in the local coasting trade, the farmers of Greenwich, Connecticut, sold their produce in New York, thirty miles to the west. Before they could make that trip, however, the new regulations required them to sail twenty miles to the east to Fairfield to get clearance papers![1] In some cases owners of vessels had to travel several hundred miles merely to get their documents signed. The governors of the states were authorized to issue permits to import foodstuffs into one state from another, and it was claimed, particularly in the case of Governor Sullivan of Massachusetts, that these were liable to abuse. It was said that certain merchants were favored, and that the use of the permits also allowed smuggling on a profitable scale.[2]

Any law, as we have learned from prohibition, which comes into violent conflict with the habits or prosperity of a considerable part of the population, not only is difficult of enforcement but breeds contempt for law. In fact, the parallel between the struggle to enforce the Embargo restrictions, which proved a losing one, and that to enforce prohibition, is instructive. The Canadian frontier was naturally the scene of much of the smuggling and of the fighting between the people and the revenue officers. Rafts were floated down Lake Champlain, loaded with produce and armed smugglers. One of these rafts was said to have been half a mile long and to have carried a bullet-proof fort and five to six hundred armed men on board. At Middlebury a raft guarded by only twelve men was overpowered and captured by the government officers, but recaptured by a hundred and fifty Canadians who came to the rescue. There were constant encounters between the people

[1] Jennings, *op. cit.*, p. 112.   [2] *Ibid.*, pp. 107 *ff.*

and the revenue men, and at least one smuggler was executed for resisting the law. Ships occasionally put to sea from small ports after running fights with revenue cutters.[1] At Newburyport the officers were forcibly prevented by an armed mob from detaining a vessel. As the months went by, opposition and violence increased. "I did not expect a crop of so sudden and rank growth of fraud and open opposition by force could have grown up in the United States," wrote Jefferson to Gallatin in August 1808.[2] The passage was thus rapid from the enactment of the laws to armed resistance and the call for militia to enforce the will of Congress. New England had passed almost as rapidly from great prosperity and the mere clash of politics at the hustings or in print to the depths of an economic crisis, a state of semi-rebellion, and threatened secession from the Union.

[1] Jennings, *op. cit.*, pp. 113 *ff.*   [2] Adams, *Hist. of U. S.*, vol. IV, p. 257.

CHAPTER XI

SECTIONALISM AND THE WAR

Pickering and Disunion — John Henry's Reports — Protests against the Embargo — Secession Plot of 1808 — Rage of New England against the Enforcement Act — Repeal of Embargo — Threatened Secession — War with England — Opposition in New England — Government Loans — Militia — Washington Benevolent Societies

THE fortunes of the Federalists, as we saw in the last chapter, had been steadily sinking in New England until it appeared as though nothing could revive them. It seemed that "the wise, the good and the rich" had lost control of the government for good, and as though the destinies of the New England commonwealths were to be entrusted solely to "the mob." The unpopularity of Jefferson's Embargo policy gave the Federalists an opportunity to regain their ascendancy — an opportunity of which they were quick to avail themselves, but unfortunately under the leadership of men who if not traitors were at least narrow-minded and selfish political bigots.

Timothy Pickering, who was then Senator of the United States and who had been the most ardent of the disunionists in the plot of 1804, made an immediate grasp at power. Within a few weeks after the passage of the Embargo Act he was already engaged in a traitorous correspondence with the British minister in Washington, in an effort to influence British policy for the benefit of his political party at home. Under his own guidance, a decade earlier, such an action had been made illegal by Congress and subject to a fine of five thousand dollars and a term of from six months to three years in state prison.[1]

[1] Adams, *Hist. of U. S.*, vol. IV, p. 236.

Pickering must, therefore, have been fully aware of the nature of the crime which he was committing. Ambitious to be president, and firmly convinced that the destinies of the United States were safe only in his own hands and those of the small group of extremists among the Federalists, he was ready to break the laws, engage in rebellion, disrupt the Union, or take any step which would tend to keep himself and his little group in power. Probably those allied with him were influenced less by personal ambition than by the insane belief that they alone knew what was best for the country. In the early days of New England leaders similarly placed could banish or hang those opposed to them. It was the old spirit working under new conditions.

Regardless of the law, therefore, Pickering entered upon his negotiations with the British minister, Rose, and when the latter left the country, arranged for a go-between in London, who was to serve as an intermediary between' the Federal group and the British Government. Pickering assured the minister that "our own best citizens consider the interests of the United States to be interwoven with those of Great Britain, and that our safety depends on hers. Men thus enlightened, could they control the measures of their own government, would give them a direction mutually beneficial to the two nations." This Senator and ex-Secretary of State also informed the British Government that whatever his country might do to provoke a war, England need not fear that there was any disposition really to have one.[1]

He furthermore wrote a letter to the Democratic Governor of Massachusetts, Sullivan, which he requested might be transmitted to the legislature. In this he claimed that the secret motive behind the Embargo was Jefferson's infatuation for France; that the country was in imminent danger of being betrayed and subjugated by Napoleon; and that the maritime states should immediately consider how best to preserve themselves.[2] Sullivan refused to place this communication before the legislature, and replied in a public letter in which, unfor-

[1] Adams, *New England Federalism*, pp. 366 f.
[2] Adams, *Hist. of U. S.*, vol. IV, pp. 238 f.

tunately, he lost his temper and played into Pickering's hands. "If there ever was an attempt," he wrote, "in its nature and consequence tending to rebellion and sedition, this is one." Pickering's whole effort, he declared, was directed to the dissolution of the Union.[1] Meanwhile, Pickering had sent a copy of his letter to Cabot for publication, should the Governor refuse to give it to the legislature, and Cabot published it in the papers.[2] Cabot estimated that fifty thousand persons would read it in the next fortnight, which gives us an interesting insight into the extent to which prompt publicity was then possible.[3]

The letter was copied throughout New England and instantly created a furore.[4] Pickering, already perhaps the best-known Federal leader, was now in train to carry the party with him in his extreme views. Cabot and some of the more conservative leaders feared the danger of being known as a pro-British faction. John Quincy Adams, Pickering's colleague in the Senate, felt at once the disunion tendency again in evidence, and in an open letter to Harrison Gray Otis asked, "If the commercial States are called to interpose on the one hand, will not the agricultural States be with equal propriety summoned to interpose on the other? If the East is stimulated against the West, and the Northern and Southern Sections are urged into collision with each other, by appeals from the acts of Congress to the respective States, *in what are these appeals to end?*"[5]

Pickering, however, had adroitly played on the disgust which the Embargo had aroused, and, in the next election, although Sullivan retained the governorship by a small majority, the Federalists regained the control of the legislature, and well in advance of the necessary date elected James Lloyd to succeed Adams in the Senate. Adams, who had voted for the Embargo, at once resigned his seat. In Rhode Island the almost complete

---

[1] *Interesting Correspondence between His Excellency Governor Sullivan and Colonel Pickering,* (Boston, 1808), p. 6.

[2] Lodge, *Cabot,* p. 381. There were alternative suggestions as to publication of other correspondence with juggling of the dates.

[3] *Ibid.,* p. 387.

[4] Pickering, *Timothy Pickering,* vol. IV, pp. 129 *ff.*

[5] *A Letter to the Honorable Harrison Gray Otis . . . by John Quincy Adams,* ed., (Boston, 1808), p. 5.

Democratic control was broken and a Federalist legislature elected.[1] Connecticut, always safely Federal, increased her Federal representatives in the legislature by twenty-three, and in the autumn Vermont elected a Federal Council.[2]

Meanwhile, the British Government had another source of information as to the feelings of the Federalists, in addition to that furnished by Pickering's correspondence. In March 1800, John Henry, an Irishman, made a trip from Canada to Boston and wrote a series of observations to the private secretary of the Canadian Governor, Sir James Craig, which Craig forwarded to Castlereagh in England. Henry had a good acquaintance among the socially elect, but it is not likely that he came into possession of the secret plans — whatever they may have been — of the inner circle of Federalist leaders. Nevertheless, although his reports were based merely on general conversation, they tally so well with subsequent events that they may be taken as representing with fair accuracy the general drift of feeling. While in Vermont on his way south, he reported that the "sensibility excited by" the Embargo "is inconceivable"; that the roads were covered with sleighs hurrying produce over the border; and that a clash with the authorities would be inevitable. All feared a war with Great Britain. "The bold talk publicly of an organized resistance" to the Federal government, whereas the timid hoped for some sort of armed truce or even union with Great Britain in case of war, evidently following the Revolutionary precedent.[3]

In Boston he reported that, owing to the effects of the Embargo, "only men of large fortunes can now subsist. Everything by which personal exertion has been hitherto excited or rewarded has ceased to exist and the commercial cities present a dreadful spectacle of distress, despair and that abandonment of principle which grows out of poverty and disappointment." [4] The leaders were considering what measures to take, but "it is only within a few weeks that the men of talents and fortune could calculate on the co-operation of the mob." At a meeting

---

[1] Robinson, *Jeffersonian Democracy*, p. 81.
[2] *Ibid.*, p. 82; *Columbian Centinel*, April 23, 1808.
[3] *Report on Canadian Archives*, 1896, pp. 38 f.   [4] *Ibid.*, p. 42.

which he claimed to have attended it was decided that all the towns should send in memorials of protest to Congress, and that committees of correspondence should act with the central committee at Boston.[1] Henry considered this "confederacy of the men of talent and property" as important, though he could not say whether it might be regarded as likely to offer resistance to the Federal government in the event of war.

The memorials which Henry had stated were to be prepared and sent to Congress materialized through the spring and early summer. Northampton led the way as early as March 14, protesting against both the Embargo and the threatened war with England, and complaining of the lack of employment for seamen and the bankruptcies of merchants.[2] Others followed, and on August 9 Boston voted that the President be asked to suspend the Embargo either in whole or in part.[3] By the twenty-seventh similar resolutions had been passed by more than twenty other towns in the state, as well as by others elsewhere in New England.[4] Most of these were comparatively moderate in tone, and it remained for the debate and passage of the Enforcement Act in December to drive the New Englanders headlong on the path toward nullification and threatened secession.

It cannot be stated with certainty to what extent the leaders may have believed in the possibility or necessity of secession at this moment. That there had been a definite secessionist plot in the Northern States in 1804 is beyond question. Was there one in 1808 and 1809? John Quincy Adams wrote in 1829 that he believed there had been, and that it was the key to the whole policy of the Federalist leaders; and this is the view taken by his grandson, the distinguished historian of this period.[5] In his history he states unequivocally that "one by

[1] *Ibid.*, pp. 42 *f.* Morison thinks that these committees were merely the local Federalist committees. *Otis*, vol. II, p. 14 *n.*

[2] *Columbian Centinel*, March 30, 1808; *Boston Town Records*, vol. XXXV, p. 238.

[3] *Ibid.*, Aug. 10, 1808.

[4] A list of most of them, with the votes, is given in the *Columbian Centinel*, Aug. 27, 1808. *Cf.* issues of Aug. 10, 13, Sept. 14.

[5] *Correspondence between John Quincy Adams . . . and Several Citizens of Massachusetts*, (Boston, 1829), p. 33; Plumer, *William Plumer*, pp. 374 *f.*

one, the Federalist leaders gave their adhesion to the plan." [1]
Nevertheless, however strong suspicion may be, there is practically no direct evidence. Considering his record on this
matter both before and after, we need not take Pickering's own
disclaimer at the time with any seriousness.[2]   Otis, who was
always more cautious than Pickering and some of the others
in the inner circle of the Junto, wrote to Pickering saying that
"it would be a great misfortune for us to justify the obloquy of
wishing to promote a separation of the States," but signifi-
cantly added, "and of being solitary in that pursuit."   He
asked what might be expected of Connecticut, and whether a
convention to be held at Hartford of delegates from all the
commercial states might not be called to propose a mode of
relief "not inconsistent with the union of these states"; but
again added, "to which we should adhere as long as possible." [3]

William Plumer, who had been in the plot of 1804 but had
since come to disbelieve in secession, wrote in January that he
never had felt greater anxiety for the country than at that
moment, and rather from internal dissension than from European foes.   "Numbers who, a few months since," he wrote,
"would have revolted with horror at the fatal idea of the dissolution of the Union, now converse freely upon it, as an event
rather to be desired than avoided." [4]   Judge Story wrote that
he thought there was "great probability that the Essex Junto
have resolved to attempt a separation of the Eastern States
from the Union; and that, if the Embargo continues, their
plan may receive support from the yeomanry." [5]   At the same
time he wrote what was probably as near the truth as we can
get, that as to the spirit of rebellion in M   husetts, "the
Junto would awaken it if they dared, but it will not do." [6]   It
would be strange indeed, considering the views of Pickering and
certain others in 1804 and 1814, if they should have altered

---

[1] *Hist. of U. S.*, vol. IV, p. 403.
[2] In a speech he said: "With regard to the union of the States, Sir, no one ever
more ardently desired it than I, and, notwithstanding the insinuations to the contrary,
either respecting myself or my fellow-citizens of New England, we all still desire it."
Pickering, *Timothy Pickering*, vol. IV, p. 151.
[3] Morison, *Otis*, vol. II, p. 5.   Morison thinks there was no plot at this time.
[4] Plumer, *William Plumer*, p. 368.   [5] *Ibid.*, p. 369.
[6] W. W. Story, *Life and Letters of Joseph Story*, (Boston, 1851), vol. I, p. 192.

them so as to support the Union at the time when the public outcry was loudest against it.

With the passage of the Enforcement Act a veritable frenzy seized upon a large part of the New England population. In January 1809 the town of Bath passed resolutions which pointed directly at revolution, and proposed the formation of "committees of safety and correspondence" as in 1776.[1] A few days later Gloucester followed, also advising the appointment of the committees, and stating in the resolves that "some of the most important provisions of the constitution have been violated . . . that a standing army has been raised, and troops quartered among us in time of profound peace, to enforce at the point of the bayonet the most tyrannical laws; that the 'encroachments of the general government on the state governments' ought to 'be signals of general alarm' — one spirit ought to *animate the whole*, — and above all arouse the northern states to a real sense of their danger."[2] Worcester, Wiscasset, Hadley, Springfield, Newburyport, Rowley, Cambridge, Beverly, Brewster, Augusta, Yarmouth, and other towns quickly fell into line.[3]

The tone became increasingly violent. Oxford resolved, with regard to the Enforcement Act, that "it is our solemn opinion and conviction that the president of the United States, by approving a law delegating to himself this dangerous and unconstitutional power, has manifested a readiness for an act of usurpation, and is no longer worthy the confidence of a free and independent people," who may have to return to "that original right of self-defence which is paramount to all positive forms of government."[4] Boston presented a long petition to the state legislature, pointing out that the national administra-

---

[1] *Columbian Centinel*, Jan. 7, 1809.

[2] *Ibid.*, Jan. 14, 1809. The tone of many of these town resolutions is shown in the continuation of the Gloucester resolves: "That we will mutually watch and protect what little property we have still left — that we will use all lawful means 'to arrest disturbers and breakers of the peace; or such others as may (under pretence of authority from Goverment) go armed by night', or utter any menaces, or threatening speeches, to the fear and terror of the good people of this town; and that we will ever hold in abhorrence pimping spies and night-walkers, who strive to fatten on the spoils of their suffering fellow citizens." *Ibid.*

[3] *Ibid.*, Feb. 1, 15, 1809.   [4] *Ibid.*, Feb. 15, 1809.

tion "no longer conceal that the Embargo is 'War in disguise,' and is soon to be followed by open War." While professing attachment to the Union, the petition affirmed that Massachusetts "cannot admit the right, assumed by the National Government of compelling her to abandon the Ocean, to renounce commerce, to change the habits of her industry, and submit to be the victim of a desolating policy." It was resolved that all who should assist in enforcing the new Act should be considered as enemies to the people.[1]

When the legislature met in the same month, they gave immediate attention to the matter, and their various actions, including committee reports and a memorial to Congress, were soon published in pamphlet form.[2] The Enforcement Act was asserted by them to be unconstitutional, and amendments to the Constitution were demanded, among others the abolishing of slave representation. Although allegiance to the Union was proclaimed, it was evident that no such amendment could ever be passed without dissolving the Federal bond.[3] In an "Address to the People" the legislature undertook to defend their acts, and complained that "politicians of yesterday, from the back-woods and mountains vie with each other in the language of insult and defiance" to New England, which section had ceased to be of any weight in the national councils. The men of Massachusetts would have to choose "between the condition of citizens of a free state, possessing its equal weight and influence in the national government; or that of a colony, free in name, but in fact enslaved by sister states." [4]

In Connecticut, where the Federalist leaders were working in close harmony with those of Massachusetts, the legislature went a step further. Governor Trumbull had already been in communication with the Secretary of War when the legislature convened. As commander-in-chief of the state's military forces, he had declined absolutely to give any orders to the militia to assist the customhouse officers in suppressing riots or other disturbances arising from attempts to enforce what he

[1] *Boston Town Records*, vol. XXXV, pp. 241 ff.
[2] *The Patriotic Proceedings of the Legislature of Massachusetts*, (Boston, 1809).
[3] *Ibid.*, p. 127.   [4] *Ibid.*, p. 130.

declared to be an unconstitutional law.[1] In his address at the opening of the legislature he pointed out that when the Federal government overleaped the bounds of its constitutional powers it became the duty of the states "to interpose their protecting shield between the right and liberty of the people, and the assumed power of the general government."[2] The legislature then proceeded to adopt a series of resolutions approving the governor's refusal to employ the militia, and stating that it was the paramount duty of the legislature itself to "assert the unquestionable rights of this state [and] to abstain from any agency in the execution of measures which are unconstitutional and despotic."[3] In Rhode Island the legislature declared the Enforcement Act to be "unjust, oppressive, tyrannical and unconstitutional," and that a "dissolution of the Union may be more surely — and as speedily — effected by the systematic oppression of the government, as by the inconsiderate disobedience of the people."[4]

Each of the three legislatures whose actions have just been noted had made the suggestion, more or less openly, that they would coöperate with others in any action called for; and as we have seen, the Federalist leaders had mooted the point of assembling a convention of the New England states. This was not done, however, and in spite of all the froth on the surface, it was evidently considered that the time was not ripe for such a drastic move. The violence of language used in the memorials and resolutions must not blind us to the fact that New England was not unanimous in its opposition. The Rhode Island resolutions, for example, were passed by votes of seven to four in the Upper House and thirty-five to twenty-eight in the Lower. The New Hampshire Senate and House both voted in favor of the Embargo.[5] The numerous town resolves, which Jefferson said made him feel the foundations of government shaken under his feet, were probably inspired to a great extent from a central Federalist source.

[1] *The American Register*, vol. V, 1809, pp. 172 f., 177.
[2] *Ibid.*, p. 177.
[3] *Ibid.*, p. 182.
[4] Ames, *State Documents on Federal Relations*, p. 43.
[5] Jennings, *American Embargo*, p. 148.

Nevertheless, the detestation of New England for the Embargo and all the supplementary Acts had become so overwhelming that the repeal of the measure by Congress was finally forced in March 1809. Jefferson acknowledged himself beaten, and said that, instead of using the peaceful weapon of Embargo, "we must fight it out, or break the union." [1]   The Non-Intercourse Act, which was passed as a temporary measure, aroused considerable opposition in New England, but it allowed commerce with all nations except France and England and set the coasting trade entirely free.   There was a rumble from the legislatures again, and at the May session of that in Connecticut, Trumbull clearly pointed to armed resistance to the government.   After stating that it would be well to consider what measures it would be expedient to adopt for "securing the exercise of our future commercial rights" without the embarrassments of an embargo or similar acts, he suggested, with a pretence of reference to the disturbed condition of the world, that Connecticut should supply its militia with an adequate amount of small arms and increase its field artillery. [2]

Three days after the repeal of the Embargo, Jefferson retired from the presidency and gave place to James Madison.   The continued negotiations with the foreign belligerents which marked the diplomacy of the new president up to the final break with England belong to national history and cannot be detailed here.   In 1809 the folly of the Federalist leaders in taking up the cause of the discredited British minister, Jackson, resulted in their losing the influence which the Embargo had regained for them, and Connecticut and Rhode Island more than made up the former Republican losses, while Vermont elected a Republican governor and legislature.   By the following year Massachusetts also had a Republican governor and legislature, and New Hampshire was in Republican control.

The events of 1811 showed the same disunion and nullification spirit still at work among the Federalists.   In January came the debate in Congress over the admission of Louisiana as a State, and in the course of it Josiah Quincy made his

[1] Quoted by Jennings, *op. cit.*, p. 165.
[2] *The American Register*, 1809, p. 182.

famous and carefully premeditated speech. In well-weighed words he said that if the bill passed it would virtually dissolve the Union, free the states from their moral obligation; and that, "as it will be the right of all, so it will be the duty of some, to prepare definitely for a separation; amicably if they can, violently if they must." [1]

Almost at the same moment that the question of Louisiana was again bringing secession to the minds of the Essex Junto, the passage of a Non-Intercourse bill, directed against England, led to threats of nullification. The former non-intercourse measures had been dropped in the preceding May, but only with the proviso that if either France or England abandoned its hostile attitude toward neutrals, non-intercourse should be renewed against the other. At the end of 1810, Napoleon, by a characteristic lie, deceived Madison into believing that France was to cease her measures against our commerce, though almost immediately afterward every American vessel in French ports was illegally confiscated. As a result of the misconception, Congress passed in February a Non-Intercourse bill against England, though they had come into possession of the real facts before final passage of the bill. The reaction in New England was immediate. At a grand caucus held in Faneuil Hall in Boston, in March, the new measure was denounced in time-worn terms as "unjust, tyrannical, and oppressive," and it was resolved that "the only means short of an appeal to force" would be the election to all state offices of such men as would oppose "the execution of laws, which if persisted in must and will be resisted." [2]

The extreme views of the Essex leaders met with no popular response, and the Democrats carried the election. For four years, however, the Federalists had been preaching secession or nullification as cures for any ills arising from measures of which they disapproved. They had become thoroughly sectionalized and antifederal in outlook. They had sown the seeds of fear and hatred against both the South and West. They had preached the doctrine that the rest of the United States was

[1] Edmund Quincy, *Life of Josiah Quincy*, (Boston, 1868), p. 206.
[2] Quoted by Morison, *Otis*, vol. II, p. 24.

filled with tyrants jealous of New England and desperately bent upon destroying her.   Convinced that they alone knew how to govern, that the New Englanders were a breed superior to all others, and that there could be no glorious destiny for America in which New England Federalism was not the predominating influence, they had worked themselves into a state of mind which bordered on megalomania.   And they had done so on the eve of the first great war in which the new nation was to engage.

In the autumn of 1811 the Republican newspapers throughout the country began to cry loudly for war against England. Her refusal to abandon the Orders in Council, her interference with our commerce, including a practical blockade of New York, her malign influence over the Indians on our northwestern frontier, and — as an afterthought almost — her impressment of American seamen, were among the numerous causes alleged for declaring war.   It is true that our grievances against France were quite as genuine and serious, but those were overlooked. The Republican control of Massachusetts, so complete as even to have turned Pickering out of the Senate, seemed to have brought that state into line instead of its being under the thumb of the "British faction."   In the Congress which convened in November the younger group of Southern and Western "War Hawks" — such as John C. Calhoun of South Carolina, Felix P. Grundy of Tennessee, and Henry Clay of Kentucky — were in the saddle.   The West cared nothing for commerce, but it cared everything about the Indian question, and the Westerners felt that the only way to settle that was to drive the British out of Canada.   For that end war with Great Britain was essential, and plausible excuses had to be found.   These were to be discovered only, though amply, on the ocean.   Nevertheless, had all the other conditions remained exactly as they were, merely substituting France for England as the owner of Canada, the War of 1812 would undoubtedly have been fought against our former ally instead of our former enemy, so little had the alleged commercial reasons or impressment of seamen to do with the real situation.

Realizing that, under the influence of the "War Hawks,"

EMBARGO BY EXPRESS.

BOSTON, FRIDAY EVENING, APRIL 3, 1812..6 o'clock.

The following letter is this moment handed me by Express.

HARRISON G. OTIS.

" Mr. CALHOUN, of South Carolina, a member of the Committee of Foreign Relations, has this moment informed Mr. QUINCY, that the Committee of Foreign Relations have decided to lay a proposition for an EMBARGO on the table of the House of Representatives to-morrow. This information may be depended on from the respectability of the source from whence it is derived, and the measure to be recommended, it is understood, meets the approbation of the Executive.

James Lloyd,
Josiah Quincy,
James Emott.

" *Washington, Tuesday,*
     March 31, 1812, 2 o'clock, P. M. }

The Honorable H. G. Otis, Boston.

HANDBILL GIVING NOTICE OF EMBARGO, 1812
Library of Congress

war with England had at last become imminent, Quincy suggested to the other Federalist leaders a policy of openly favoring it, in the belief that it would be thoroughly mismanaged by the Republicans, who would be ousted in disgrace, and that the Federalists would then be called on to replace them. Astute from a wholly unmoral political standpoint as this suggestion may have been, the leaders had been too long and too deeply committed to their pro-British policy to be able to adopt it.[1] From that day the path to the Hartford Convention was straight. The debates in Congress dragged on through the autumn, winter, and spring, and finally, on June 18, 1812, war was declared against Great Britain.

A double war, one against both France and England, had at times been loudly called for. It was said that the devil himself could not tell which nation was the more wicked. The alleged arguments for the war were inextricably tangled, even by its ardent advocates. Grundy denounced impressment, but kept his more violent denunciations for England's hostile influence over the Indians. There was loud outcry against England's depredations, but even while the debates were continuing France was preying on our commerce even more ruthlessly than her antagonist. Indeed, when war was finally decided upon, no one knew exactly how or why. As Adams has said, "so complicated and historical had the causes of war become that no one even in America could explain or understand them, while Englishmen could see only that America required England as the price of peace to destroy herself by abandoning her naval power." In a life-and-death struggle with France, which was treating America quite as badly as herself, England preferred if need be to go down fighting, rather than to commit suicide by surrendering her strongest weapon while the enemy was allowed to retain hers.[2] In America the Federalists convinced themselves, and tried to convince others, that the country had been sold to France.

In March there had occurred an incident that served to embitter the Massachusetts leaders still more against Madison. John Henry, the English spy who had visited Boston and

[1] Cf. Morison, Otis, vol. II, pp. 34 ff.   [2] Hist. of U. S., vol. VII, p. 8.

reported on affairs there, had returned to America in company
with a young person who called himself the Count de Crillon,
and succeeded in selling to the Administration for fifty thousand dollars certain papers which it was represented would
implicate the Massachusetts Federalists in a treasonable plot
against the government. The papers proved, after purchase,
to be unimportant documents, but were transmitted to Congress by Madison. A violent newspaper controversy followed,
in which the Federalists naturally had the best of the argument,
Madison's action having been utterly foolish and unwise. The
expenditure of such a sum of government money for the purpose of besmirching the leaders of the opposition party was
inexcusable. The result, however, was to embitter yet more
the attitude of the leading Federalists, on the eve of a war when
the Administration should have done its utmost to conciliate
all sections and unify the sentiment of the nation.

When war was declared, Quincy and thirty-three other Federalist Congressmen at once issued an address to their constituents in which they stated that, although wrongs "very grievous
to our interests" and "humiliating to our pride" had been committed against us, there was nothing which made the resort
to war either necessary or expedient.[1] Yet Quincy had been
urging support of the war only a few weeks before, as a shrewd
bit of politics. In the May elections Massachusetts had again
chosen a Federalist governor, and on June 20 that official proclaimed a public fast on account of the war declared against
the nation "which for many generations has been the bulwark
of the religion we profess"! The Lower House of the legislature, in an "Address to the People," asked them to let the
sound of their disapprobation of the war "be loud and deep,"
and to let there be no volunteers for military service except for
defense.[2] John Lowell, the spokesman of the Junto, declared
in a pamphlet that the war was unjust, and that it was the
duty of citizens to abstain from taking any part in it.[3] This

[1] *An Address of Members of the House of Representatives . . . to Their Constituents,*
(Hanover, 1812), pp. 6 ff.
[2] Adams, *Hist. of U. S.*, vol. VI, pp. 401 f.
[3] *Mr. Madison's War*, (Boston, 1812), p. 5.

was the attitude that was, to a great extent, adopted; and although the Federalists controlled the greatest part of the liquid capital of the country, the whole of New England subscribed less than one million dollars to the war loan of eleven millions which the government had to float in May, whereas the citizens of New York and Philadelphia took about a million and a half for each city.[1]

The governors of the states of Massachusetts, Connecticut, and Rhode Island, when called upon to place the militia at the service of the general government, all declined, on the plea that it would be unconstitutional to do so.[2] Town and county meetings were held, and, at the one in Essex County, Pickering initiated again his favorite plan for a convention, but Samuel Dexter, breaking with the Junto, opposed it so vigorously that it was finally dropped.[3] At a convention held at Northampton in July, representing fifty-three towns in three counties, the war was declared to be "neither just, necessary nor expedient," and disunion was strongly suggested.[4] Pickering's private letters of this month show clearly that he wished a separation of the Eastern from the Western States, and that he desired that a New England convention should take a lead in the project.[5] The Republicans quickly countered the convention at Northampton with another representing fifty-one towns in the same counties, which strongly condemned the attitude of the Federalists.[6]

For the most part, however, the voice of New England was heard only in tones of angry condemnation and threatened secession. At a convention of fifteen hundred Federalists at Rockingham, New Hampshire, in September, a memorial drawn up by Daniel Webster denied emphatically that there was any cause for war. Impressment, he said, was the best of the alleged causes, but the situation as to that had not changed

[1] Adams, *Hist. of U. S.*, vol. VI, p. 207.
[2] Ames, *State Documents on Federal Relations*, pp. 12 *ff*.
[3] *Cf.* Morison, *Otis*, vol. II, pp. 60 *ff*.
[4] *Proceedings of a Convention of Delegates from the Counties of Hampshire, Franklin and Hampden* . . . (Northampton, 1812), pp. 8, 12.
[5] Adams, *New England Federalism*, pp. 388 *ff*.
[6] The meeting was held July 20. *Democrat Extra, July 21st, 1812,* Broadside in Library of Congress.

since the days of Washington, and the maritime states which alone suffered from it did not consider it a sufficient grievance. It was the voice of strangers "beyond the Western Mountains" that was raised so loudly, "while the fathers and brethren, the friends and relatives, the wives and children of these very sea-men, — nay even the seamen *themselves*, deprecate this War, as the greatest calamity that could fall upon them." [1] "From principle and habit," Webster said, they were "attached to the Union of the States. But our attachment is to the *substance* and not to the *form*. . . . We shrink from the separation of the States," he added, but if separation should come, it would be from an occasion like the present, when "one portion of the Country undertakes to control, to regulate, and to *sacrifice*, the interest of another." In the Resolutions the convention declared that the war had been undertaken in direct opposition to the will of the people of the state.[2]

With the purely military and naval aspects of the conflict this history need have little to do. No engagement of any importance took place within the borders of New England, and the part which that section played was singularly inglorious. The main interest, indeed, lies in the policy of obstruction which it was led to pursue by its leaders, and to which, perhaps, more than to any other one factor was due the partial failure of the war. If this chapter and the next are largely taken up with this unpleasant side of the matter, it must not be thought that the New Englanders were all traitors or that there was no patriotism or national pride among them. It is not an easy task to prescribe just what should be the conduct of a citizen toward his government when he believes it to be engaged in an unrighteous conflict, or how far the individual citizen may go in hampering the efforts of the nation. Governments have nearly always found it necessary, when possible, to abrogate the right of free speech at such times, in order to present a united front to the enemy. In the War of 1812, however, such a large and powerful section of the New England population

---

[1] *Speech of the Honorable George Sullivan at the late Rockingham Convention, with the Memorial, Resolutions and Report*, (Concord, 1812), p. 23.
[2] *Ibid.*, pp. 26, 28.

was clearly against the war that the government did not dare to interfere with the liberty either of the press or of individual utterance, and the opponents of the declared national policy carried all before them. That a majority was opposed to "Mr. Madison's War" is undoubtedly true; but that there was a large minority loyally supporting the government is also true. "A stranger to the existing state of parties in New England, but particularly in Massachusetts," said the *Independent Chronicle* in 1813, "would suppose, from reading the federal papers, that the people were united to a man, in opposition to the General Government and to the war . . . but the fact is far otherwise." It pointed out that in the May election there had been forty thousand votes cast for Varnum, who supported the war and the government, as against fifty thousand for his opponent, Governor Strong.[1]

The Federalists, however, were better organized. They constituted the great bulk of the wealthy social classes and the clergy. They controlled by 1813 all the state governments except Vermont, and were able to make their influence felt to a far greater extent than their mere numerical majority would indicate. That the love for the Union was strong enough to overcome all the desires and plottings of such men as Pickering, is evident from the course of events; but the fiery speeches of a Quincy still give the tone to the action of New England in those days, whereas the silent patriotism of a hundred farmers was of little influence then and yields no echo now.

So pronounced was the disaffection of the section that England was apparently hopeful that the Eastern States might elect to remain neutral during the conflict, and when the American coast was declared blockaded, the blockade was not extended to New England, whose ports were thus left open by the enemy. Moreover, when proclamations were issued prohibiting the importation of American products into the West Indies, the New England ports were again excepted, and the New Englanders had the profitable but invidious distinction of being treated as friends by the national enemy.[2]

[1] Issue of June 7, 1813.
[2] Adams, *Hist. of U. S.*, vol. VII, pp. 31 *ff.*

Nor, judging from the acts and speeches of the Federalist leaders, was such a hope a fantastic one. In January 1813 Congress was debating a bill providing that, if any man over eighteen enlisted in the military service, he should be retained during the term of enlistment — an act that would affect the relations of apprentices to their employers. Quincy denounced it as containing an atrocious principle. "Touch not private right," he said in his speech on the floor. "Regard the sacred ties of guardian and master. Corrupt not our youth. Listen to the necessities of mechanics and manufacturers. Have compassion on the tears of parents." And he added that if the New England states, but particularly Massachusetts, did not enforce against the Federal recruiting officers the old state laws against kidnapping and man-stealing, they "would be false to themselves, their posterity and their country." [1] The Republican papers sarcastically but truly pointed out in comment that impressment was assuredly kidnapping, but that, when it was done by the British, Mr. Quincy and his party were left wholly unmoved.

The New England newspapers now began to wage war on each other in what was practically an open debate on the question of the dissolution of the Union. Throughout January the *Columbian Centinel* in Boston ran a series of articles denouncing the Southern States. On January 13 it stated that, although it was considered criminal to utter the truth, it was a fact that "we are a divided people, and that the lines of our political and geographical divisions are nearly coincident. . . . North of the Delaware there is among all who do not bask or expect to bask in the Executive sunshine but one voice for *Peace*. South of that river, the general cry is 'Open War, O Peers!' There are not two hostile nations upon earth, whose views of the principles and polity of a perfect Commonwealth and of Men and Measures, are more discordant than those of these two great divisions. There is but little of congeniality or sympathy in our notions or feelings; and this small residuum will be extinguished by this withering war. The sentiment is hourly extending, and in these Northern States will soon be

[1] *Independent Chronicle*, Jan. 25, 1813; *Columbian Centinel*, Jan. 30, Feb. 3, 6, 1813.

universal, that we are in a condition no better in relation to the South, than that of a *conquered people*. . . . We must no longer be deafened by senseless clamors about a Separation of the States. . . . *The States are separated in fact* when one section assumes an *imposing Attitude*, and with a high hand, perseveres in measures fatal to the interests and repugnant to the opinion of another section. . . . Such a separation alone is matter of substance. The rest would be matter of form." [1]

Notwithstanding the expression of such views, the Federalists raised the cry in the spring political campaign that only if they were elected could the Union be safe.[2] Pickering's own idea was that the separation should be between the original seaboard states and the West, and this was warmly advocated in a pamphlet which appeared in April,[3] but in general the division suggested was between North and South. In May the *New England Palladium* urged that as all of the states east of the Delaware had chosen Federalist legislatures except Vermont, the time was ripe for the formation of a "Commercial League" among them that would be a "confederation" which could "defy the enmity and machinations of the slave holders and the backwoods-men." [4] The Republican *Chronicle*, commenting on this, said: if the division were necessary, let it be openly arrived at; and that if the people could vote on it, it was believed nine hundred and ninety-nine out of a thousand would be against it.[5]

Meanwhile, the government had again had to appeal for funds, and had attempted to float another loan. New England practically refused to subscribe, although the banks of that section held most of the specie of the country. Boston took only seventy-five thousand dollars, whereas Pennsylvania took seven millions. The New England Federalists were forever sneering at the "foreigners" in public life, but Astor, Girard,

[1] *Columbian Centinel*, Jan. 13, 1813.
[2] *Ibid.*, Feb. 20, 1813.
[3] *Thoughts in a Series of Letters in Answer to a Question Respecting the Division of the States*, (Boston, 1813). *Cf. Independent Chronicle*, July 29, 1813.
[4] Quoted in the *Independent Chronicle*, May 29, 1813.
[5] *Independent Chronicle*, May 27, 1813.

and Parish, three foreign-born citizens, subscribed to ten millions between them.[1]

The Federalist press did its best to discourage subscriptions and even suggested that the loan was an improper contract, not binding upon the people for repayment, as it was made for the support of a war which they abhorred. It was also suggested that if the Eastern States would dissolve the Union, the loan would never be paid.[2] In fact, it was claimed that the Constitution had already been broken and was no longer binding. In May the Massachusetts legislature adopted resolves declaring that the admission of Louisiana was a violation of the Constitution, and remonstrating against the war. In place of a vote of thanks to Captain Lawrence for his recent naval victory, Josiah Quincy, who had retired from Congress and was then a member of the State Senate, secured the passage of a resolve penned by himself that "in a war like the present, waged without justifiable cause . . . it is not becoming a moral and religious people to express any approbation of military and naval exploits not immediately connected with the defense of our seacoast and soil."[3] This action was bitterly denounced in Washington as "moral treason."

In November an event occurred in Vermont which echoed loudly beyond the borders of the state. Some of the state militia had been called to New York for the defense of the frontiers of that state and placed under Federal officers. In October Governor Chittenden in a speech before the legislature declared that this was unconstitutional, and the legislature adopted his view by a vote of ninety-six to eighty-nine. On November 10, he issued a proclamation recalling the troops within the limits of Vermont. They refused to obey; the Governor's representative was arrested, and a resolution was introduced in Congress to prosecute Chittenden for treason. The Massachusetts legislature at once pledged the support of that state to the Governor and people of Vermont. This drew

---

[1] Adams, *Hist. of U. S.*, vol. VII, p. 45.

[2] *New England Palladium*, April 27, 1813.

[3] Quincy, *Josiah Quincy*, p. 324; Ames, *Documents on Federal Relations*, pp. 65 f.; *New England Palladium*, June 22, 1813.

forth, in turn, resolutions from the legislatures of Pennsylvania and New Jersey denouncing both Massachusetts and Vermont, the expression used in the New Jersey resolve clearly indicating the passions which the times had excited.[1] The federal relations of the American states were fast threatening to descend to the level of a free-for-all fight, and the spectacle of the National Government and the several States yowling at each other like Kilkenny cats had at least the merit of affording amusement and comfort to the enemy. In fact, the Federalist press in Massachusetts was openly advocating the making of a separate peace with England by Massachusetts.[2]

The Federalist party by this time had changed completely from the original principles of Washington, Hamilton, and the other early leaders. With reference to the central government, it had become strongly antifederal. With regard to the Union, it was openly preaching secession. Instead of avoiding foreign alliances, it had become practically allied to the British government. With regard to another point it now made a reversal of its policy, in that it organized secret societies to forward its political aims — a policy that had been denounced as strongly by the Federalists as by Washington individually. In order to capitalize the influence of Washington's name, however, and with no regard for consistency, the new societies went by the name of Washington Benevolent Societies.

As we have seen, the Republicans had had their secret organizations in the last decade of the preceding century, clubs that had been roundly denounced by Washington and the Federalists because of their secrecy and possible baleful influence. In 1809, in order to bolster their falling fortunes, the Democrats of Rhode Island had organized Tammany Societies on the lines of those which had already become popular in Pennsylvania and New York. The first one in New England, that at Providence, was soon followed by others in Newport and Warwick, and were of considerable weight in the election of 1810.[3] It was

---

[1] Ames, *Documents on Federal Relations*, pp. 63 ff.; Morison, *Otis*, vol. II, pp. 64 f.
[2] Adams, *Hist. of U. S.*, vol. VII, p. 367.
[3] M. W. Jernegan, *The Tammany Societies of Rhode Island*, (Providence, 1897), pp. 10 f.

probably to combat the influence of Tammany that the Washington Benevolent Society was first formed in New York in 1808.[1]

So far as research has revealed, the first branch society in New England was formed at Providence on August 10, 1810, after several preliminary meetings had been held.[2] This antedated by nearly a year the Washington Benevolent Society of Berkshire County (Massachusetts), which was the first to be formed in the neighboring state. This county society had its local branches in Westfield, Springfield, Chicopee, Chester, Blandford, Granville, Wilbraham, Longmeadow, Northampton, Deerfield, and Becket.[3] The Hampshire County Society was organized some months later on the seventeenth of November,[4] and from that time onward county and town societies were rapidly formed throughout New England, the movement thriving especially in Vermont.[5] The Boston Society, which assumed the name of the Washington Benevolent Society of Massachusetts, was organized February 22, 1812, and its constitution and objects may be taken as typical of all the others. It was stated that the object was to cherish and inculcate the sound principles of government laid down by Washington, and to endeavor to "restore the reign of Washington principles and measures." Occasionally a fling was taken more directly at "democracy." The initiation fee of the Boston society was two dollars, and the annual dues one dollar, which were supposed to go to the relief of unfortunate members, it having been decided "to unite benevolence with patriotism" — an alluring

[1] Dixon R. Fox, *The Decline of Aristocracy in the Politics of New York*, (Columbia University Studies, 1919), pp. 89 *ff*.

[2] *Newport Mercury*, July 28, Aug. 10, 1810.

[3] H. H. Ballard, "A Forgotten Fraternity," Berkshire Historical and Scientific Society, *Collections*, vol. III, pp. 288 *f*.

[4] *Washington's Farewell Address . . . Published for the Hampshire Washington Society*, (New York, 1812). Library of Congress copy.

[5] Among other societies of which I have found mention were those of Windsor, Weathersfield, Harland, and Reading, Vt., and Cornish, Claremont, Charlestown, Newport, and Plainfield, N. H. (*The Washingtonian*, Feb. 27, 1815); Hanover, N. H., Lebanon, Lyme, Norwich, and Hartford, Conn., (*Ibid.*, Aug. 8, 1814); County of Franklin, Vt., (*Ibid.*, March 14, 1814); Gilmanton, N. H., (*The Text-Book of the W. B. S.*, Concord, 1812, Library of Congress copy); Plymouth County, Mass., (*Columbian Centinel*, Feb. 10, 1815); Nantucket, (*Ibid.*, March 27, 1813); Charlestown, Mass., (*Ibid.*, Feb. 27, 1813); Warren and Hamilton, Mass., (*Hampshire Gazette*, Dec. 28, 1814, Dec. 6, 1815).

party measure.[1]   The society had its committees in each of the
twelve wards of the town, and was evidently a most efficient
vote-combing machine.   The only list of names I have seen
contains about eighteen hundred members, including such
social and political leaders as the Otises, and such a varied
assortment of others as truckmen, hairdressers, ropemakers,
stevedores, blacksmiths, sailmakers, bakers, coopers, brick-
layers, tailors, and so on — a list that speaks volumes, in view
of the social distinctions of the era, for the efforts the Federal
leaders were making to build up their machine.   That the
social and financial magnates of the Federalist party in the
Boston of 1812, who loathed democracy from the bottom of
their souls, should hobnob and dine with such a motley crowd,
whose members they were forced to call "brother," calls for
no further comment on their "benevolence."

The great days for the Societies to make their public appear-
ances were Washington's Birthday and the thirtieth of April,
the anniversary of his inauguration.   Later the Fourth of July
was utilized in some places.   Dinners, parades, and speeches
were the favorite forms of celebration, and a somewhat elaborate ritual was developed, with banners and decorations.[2]   For
the celebration of the thirtieth of April 1813, in Boston, the
procession numbered over two thousand, including the Boston
Light Infantry, the Winslow Blues, the New England Guards,
and the Suffolk Rangers.   Besides the members of the Society
there were many of the clergy, "the government of Harvard
University," the Boston selectmen, two hundred and fifty
youths in blue-and-white uniforms, several bands of music,
and thirty-two standards and banners.   The oration was
delivered in the Old South Church by Josiah Quincy.   It was
on this occasion that the Society first displayed and carried in
the procession the gorget worn by Washington on the day of
Braddock's defeat.   This had been secured, through Quincy's
efforts, from Mrs. Peters, a granddaughter of Mrs. Washing-

---

[1] *A Directory Containing Names, Places of Business . . . of the Washington Benevolent Society of Massachusetts*, (Boston, 1813).

[2] The parades and other features varied little in detail.   *E.g., Columbian Centinel*
May 1, 1813.

ton.[1] This was an amusingly shrewd political move. The affiliated societies had spread as far south as Maryland,[2] and the echo of Quincy's cleverness was heard as far as Dixie. The "mantle" of Washington, said the *Baltimore Patriot*, certainly could never rest on these societies, but now his gorget, thanks to Quincy, does; and they are therefore relieved of all suspicion, past, present, and future. In their own words, "If ever, hereafter, we shall be overshadowed by the clouds of suspicion, or overpowered by the shafts of calumny, it will be sufficient to remember that we received the approbation of the family of Washington"![3] Political bunkum varies little from age to age.

It is no wonder that in one of the earliest attacks upon the "Benevolents" — the so-called *First Book of Knaves* — the venom should be expended upon "that deformed and blear-eyed hag, political hypocrisy."[4] A more interesting feature of this particular attack was the charge made that the Society had bribed a Negro named Prince, a former Republican, to become a Federalist and to work for the party for "two hundred pieces of silver" a year. Whether or not the charge was true, it has its interest, for it would have been pointless had not the colored vote in Boston become a factor worth considering by that time.[5] In the *Second Book* jibes were made at the Washingtonians' "benevolence" and an amusing comment was made upon "Massachusetts velvet, which by interpretation signifies tar and feathers."[6] It was claimed that all the dues were expended in making a show.[7] By the time the *Fourth Book* was published, the Boston society was evidently disintegrating, for it was noted that at the meeting on the thirtieth of April, although the "tag-rag" were present, Otis and other

[1] *Columbian Centinel*, April 21, 1813.
[2] *Baltimore Whig*, Feb. 24, 1813.
[3] Issue of April 23, 1813.
[4] *The First Book of the "Washington Benevolents" otherwise called the Book of Knaves*, [Boston, 1813], p. 3. This first book was followed by a second, 1813, a third, 1813, and a fourth, 1814. In the last, a fifth was promised to appear, but I have been unable to locate a copy and doubt if it was ever published. There are now original or photostat copies of the first four assembled in the Library of Congress.
[5] *The First Book, op. cit.*, pp. 12 *f*.
[6] *The Second Book, op. cit.*, pp. 6, 22.
[7] *Independent Chronicle*, May 6, 1813.

prominent members were not.[1] By 1815 the notices of meetings anywhere in New England become rare and I have found
none later than that year.

The societies were evidently a powerful agency in bringing
out the Federalist votes during the war.   Before elections the
papers contained many advertisements calling on the "Washingtonians" to work for certain candidates, and there are
ample evidences of great activity on the part of members.   As
representing the Federalist point of view they were, of course,
strongly opposed to the war, and the toasts and orations reveal
the spirit of the time.   For example, at the meeting of the
Franklin County Society at St. Albans on Washington's Birthday, 1814, such toasts were drunk as : "The present Misrulers
of our Country — ye have made a covenant with death and
with hell are we at agreement," and "The City of Washington
— How is the faithful city become an harlot."   The seventh
toast seems hardly appropriate to the celebration of the birth-
festival of the great Virginian : "the Southern Slave-Drivers, —
bawling 'Sailors' Rights' with a whip in one hand and Paine's
Rights of Man in the other — too contemptible to merit exe-
cration." [2]   The address, by the Reverend Mr. Booge, contained nothing on Washington, but was a violent diatribe
against the war, which, he said, was not for sailors' rights, but
was waged by the South from jealousy of Northern commerce.
He threatened the secession of the New England states, asserting that the North was being enslaved by the "Southern negro
made nobility and plantation tyrants," and the time had come
when New England must choose between "slavery and resistance." [3]   In fact, in most of the typical Washington Benevolent Society orations there is little of either Washington or
benevolence, but the object for which they were formed, and
which to a great extent they attained, is amply revealed.

[1] *The Fourth Book, op. cit.*, p. 8.
[2] *The Washingtonian*, March 14, 1814.
[3] *Ibid.*, March 21, 1814.

CHAPTER XII

PEACE AND THE HARTFORD CONVENTION

*Privateering — Trade with the Enemy — New Embargo —
Secession Again Threatened — Prosperity and Manufactures —
New England Absorbs Specie of Entire Country — Government
Loan — Conscription Act — Hartford Convention — Nullifica-
tion Resolves — End of the War*

IN spite of the embittered opposition which was shown in
New England toward the war, the struggle brought great
prosperity to that section as contrasted with the rest of the
Union. The wealth which it had poured into the Eastern
States, however, was derived in much smaller proportion from
the sea than would have been expected from the normal activities of the New England capitalists. Privateering undoubtedly brought large profits to some, but such instances as
that of the privateer America, which netted her owner over
a million dollars in sixteen months, or that of the Yankee, which
captured over five millions in prizes, were very exceptional.[1]
Privateering, indeed, was carried on upon an extensive scale
and caused heavy loss to the enemy, who complained that
even the home waters around the British Isles were no longer
safe for British vessels, so infested had they become with
American privateersmen.[2]

But New England participated in this activity to a lesser
extent than in previous wars, Boston and Salem together fitting
out only about seventy privateers as against a hundred and
thirteen from New York and Baltimore.[3] In the earlier years

---

[1] Channing, *Hist. of U. S.*, vol. IV, p. 527.

[2] G. Coggeshall, *History of the American Privateers*, (New York, 1856), pp. 302, 394.

[3] Morison, *Maritime History*, p. 199. Maclay, however, gives considerably higher
figures for Massachusetts. E. S. Maclay, *A History of American Privateers*, (New
York, 1899), p. 506. The available data are unreliable and the estimates vary greatly.

of the contest a fairly lucrative commerce had been maintained, but by 1814 this had been practically annihilated.[1] There was, however, a very considerable traffic carried on between the various New England states and the enemy, either by direct supply of British vessels, by the sending out of American ships clandestinely, or through trade over the Canadian border by land. It is impossible to estimate the total amount of this trade even roughly, but the fact of its existence was notorious throughout the war.[2] In 1813 and 1814 there are frequent mentions of it in the contemporary press. For example, we read that "the smuggling trade was never carried to so high a pitch as at the present day" in Boston, a town to which smuggling had never been a novelty.[3] Shortly after, smuggled goods to the value of twenty-five or thirty thousand dollars were seized at Portland.[4] A vessel from Boston, sailing under false Swedish colors and cleared for Fayal, was taken by the authorities for smuggling with Halifax.[5] Ten thousand dollars' worth of smuggled goods were captured at Buxton, Maine.[6] A brig, called Portuguese but actually Boston-owned, was taken at Savannah with a smuggled cargo worth twenty to thirty thousand dollars.[7] In March 1814 a mob in Boston beat a customs officer who had seized a wagon loaded with British goods, and in the same week at Cambridgeport a warrant was issued against an officer for "highway robbery," — the real offense being seizing smuggled goods, — for which he was landed in jail.[8] In April there was a fight, in which several persons were severely wounded, between smugglers and officers, when the latter tried to detain a dozen sleigh-loads of goods destined for Canada.[9] In June, Tyler P. Shaw of Northport, Maine, was tried for treason for supplying the British.[10] The *Plattsburg Republican* of June 18 had seven different advertisements of captured smuggled goods condemned

---

[1] Mahan, *op. cit.*, vol. II, p. 21.
[2] Adams, *Hist. of U. S.*, vol. VII, pp. 146, 368.
[3] *Niles Weekly Register*, vol. V, p. 214.
[4] *Ibid.*, p. 380.   [6] *Ibid.*, vol. VI, p. 36.
[5] *Ibid.*, vol. IV, p. 16.   [7] *Ibid.*, p. 36.
[8] *Independent Chronicle*, March 28, 31, 1814.
[9] *Ibid.*, April 4, 1814.
[10] *Ibid.*, June 27, 1814.

for sale.[1] At times the Washington Benevolent Societies were said to be implicated.[2] It is unnecessary to cite additional cases, for the whole traitorous trade was well known at the time and probably not overestimated as to its extent.[3]

It was with the intention of stopping as far as possible all maritime trade with the enemy that Congress, in December 1813, passed a new Embargo Act. Although, in effect, some trade still continued, it was made far more hazardous and costly, and naturally this added immensely to the Federalist hostility toward the Administration and all its works. Pickering felt that the time had at last arrived for New England to take forcible action, and so wrote Samuel Putnam from Washington, saying that Massachusetts should no longer passively endure her grievances. "The time is arrived," he wrote, "when *ordinary opposition* will prove futile. God forbid there should be any more *supplications* or *simple remonstrances.*" "On the spot you can best judge for what the people are ripe and what they will support." [4] He added that the New England states would now have to hold themselves "in readiness 'to right themselves.'" If Massachusetts led the way, he believed that the other New England states and New York would undoubtedly follow, and thought that a convention should be held with representatives from all of them.[5] Town meetings everywhere condemned the embargo, and at that held in Newbury the citizens declared themselves ready "to resist unto blood." [6] In the legislature, however, although the suggestion of a convention was held to be legal, it was stated that the time was not yet ripe, and the matter was held over until the next legislature should meet after election. This referred the decision to the people, and although the Federalists polled almost as many votes as before, the Republicans added enough to theirs to cut down the Federalist majority by about four thousand. On the other hand, in all

---

[1] *Niles Weekly Register*, vol. VI, p. 304.
[2] *Independent Chronicle*, March 31, 1814.
[3] Cf. *Documents Relating to Violations and Evasions of the Laws during the Commercial Restrictions and Late War with Great Britain*, (Bath, 1824).
[4] Adams, *New England Federalism*, p. 392.
[5] *Ibid.*, p. 393.   [6] Adams, *Hist. of U. S.*, vol. VIII, p. 6.

three states of Massachusetts, Rhode Island, and Connecticut, the more rabid Federalists had added to their strength. The result of the spring election in New York, however, was construed as condemning their plan for radical action.

Although the embargo was aimed at the shipping interest, one of the strongest supports of Federalism, the prosperity that had come to New England had been mainly derived from manufactures since the beginning of the war. In January 1814 they were estimated to have grown to a value of fifteen to twenty millions a year, and the New England banks were thought to be drawing a half million dollars a month from the banks of the South in payment for goods shipped. The spokesman even of the Federalists declared money was a drug, and the banks were at their wits' end to know how to lend it.[1] British bills were bought in large quantities at heavy discounts, partly in payment for goods sent to Canada. In 1809 the Massachusetts banks had held only $820,000 in specie. By the middle of 1814 the figure had risen to nearly $7,000,000. The banking capital of the New England section was about one third that of the entire country, and for the most part in Federal control.[2] When the need for new national financing approached, in the late winter of 1814, the danger of this situation was fully realized in Congress. In the letter already quoted from Pickering, he had expressed the idea that the citizens of Massachusetts should be cautioned against lending any of their money to the government or assisting it financially in any way, and this had been the steady policy of the Federalists.[3] In January the *Independent Chronicle* of Boston, in a long article on this topic, quoted a statement by Pickering in which he said, "Let the Federalists universally withhold their money and the war must soon come to an end." [4]

When the new loan was opened for subscription in April, the Federalist papers openly denounced it as an unsafe investment, and advocated making its failure as complete as

---

[1] Adams, *Hist. of U. S.*, vol. VIII, p. 15.
[2] *Ibid.*, vol. VII, pp. 387 *ff*.
[3] Adams, *New England Federalism*, p. 393.
[4] Issue of Jan. 3, 1814.

possible, in order to bring the government to a stand and end the war by stopping supplies.[1] The loan was largely a failure, New England being responsible for that result, and the position of the government became desperate. Controlling the major part of the specie of the country and one third of the banking capital, the New England Federalists had found the weapon with which they were to bring the government to terms before many months more. In August came the capture and burning of Washington by the British, which sent a panic through the nation. Practically all the banks outside of New England suspended payment, the New England banks alone remaining solvent by means of the specie which they had drained from all the rest of the country. New England, however, would afford no help to the administration, and the rest of the states had now become unable to do so. Madison, nevertheless, for a short time struggled on.

Throughout the year the Federalist papers became more and more outspoken on the subject of a possible dissolution of the Union. The governors of Rhode Island and Connecticut did not hesitate to more than hint at it in addresses to their legislatures.[2] Massachusetts, in so far as the leaders of the dominant party were concerned, had definitely made up its mind to end the war. In the autumn came Madison's last effort to strengthen the national resources in what had now become a hopeless contest with the enemy at home as well as abroad, and this effort produced the greatest crisis of the whole struggle in New England.

Until the last year of the war, that section had suffered no invasion by the enemy except for occasional minor incursions on the coast, with small damage. In the summer of 1814, however, the situation became more serious. In July, Sir Thomas Hardy sailed from Halifax with a formidable force for land operations and took possession of a considerable extent of the Maine coast, and more active operations were threatened on other New England borders. During that summer and autumn, the governors of three states took such action with

[1] E.g., Boston Gazette, April 14, 1814.
[2] Conn. Courant, March 8, Nov. 15, 1814.

regard to their militia forces as, whether or not due to an intentional plot to prostrate the general government, certainly had that effect, when combined with the financial crisis.[1]   On the very day when Washington was captured by the British, Connecticut withdrew her militia from the government service.   In September, when the British were threatening Lake Champlain, Governor Chittenden of Vermont refused to call out any militia from that state, on the ground that he had no constitutional authority to order them across the state border.[2]

Only a small proportion of the Federal troops had been detailed during the war for the defense of New England, owing to the deadlock between the Federal and State Governments on the subject of the use of the state militia.   When Governor Strong of Massachusetts at last ordered out about five thousand of the state troops to protect the coast, at the time of the invasion of Maine, he stated to the legislature that, relying on the Constitution, Massachusetts had paid her taxes with the expectation of protection from the national government.   As she had not received any, it now behooved the New England states to combine for their own defense.   This was echoed in a report made by the legislature, which then appointed a committee to call a "conference" of the states "whose interests is [sic] closest." [3]

The national government was sorely in need not only of money but of men as well.   Americans have never volunteered in sufficient numbers to make an efficient army in any considerable war in which the country has yet been engaged.   A certain number always enlist as a matter of patriotism or adventure.   An additional number have been tempted by high bounties.   But in the War of 1812, the Civil War, and the recent Great War, resort has always had to be made to drafts.   When Madison proposed such a measure to Congress, late in the autumn of 1814, it met with immediate opposition in that body and set New England in a blaze.   The Act was finally passed,

[1] Adams, *Hist. of U. S.*, vol. VIII, pp. 220 ff.
[2] This was not a case of factious policy, so far as he was concerned.   *Ibid.*, p. 223.
[3] Adams, *Hist. of U. S.*, vol. VIII, p. 225.

but instead of adding to the efficiency of the army, it ended the war by the increased opposition it engendered in the North.

The tone of public meetings, of articles in the press, and of discussions in Congress and the legislatures, testified to the depth of passion which had been aroused. In the Connecticut legislature not only the Federalists but twenty-three Republicans, among them the leader of the minority party, voted one hundred and sixty-eight to six that the Conscription Act was unconstitutional. They further called on the governor, in case it should be passed, to assemble the legislature again in special session, "to the End that opportunity may be given to consider what measures may be adopted to secure and preserve the rights and liberties of the people of this State, and the Freedom, Sovereignty, and Independence of the same." [1] In New Haven it was said that, if the law passed, it could not be enforced in the state "at less expence than half the blood of its citizens." At a large meeting of the men of the western Massachusetts counties of Hampshire, Franklin, and Hampden, it was resolved that "we dare not submit and will never yield obedience." [2]

In a "Letter to the President" which was widely published in various papers, the writer addressed Madison, saying, "If, by your violence and oppression, you drive New England off from this confederacy, you must answer for it. And you have already driven her to the very brink. One step more, and the union of the states is severed." [3] In another widely published series of articles, entitled "The Crisis," it was said that "the Crisis is come. . . . Every evil which we now endure — every danger which we fear, grew out of our want of foresight and firmness then. . . . Had we commanded and not prayed . . . we should not now see our cities tumbling into ruins, and our vessels at our wharves, naked as the woods of winter. . . . It is time to act. We have talked too long. . . . The sufferings which have multiplied about us, have at length aroused New England. She will now meet every danger, and go through every difficulty, until her rights are restored to the

---

[1] *Hampshire Gazette*, Nov. 16, 1814. [2] *Ibid.*, Nov. 23, 1814.
[3] *Ibid.*, Nov. 16, 1814.

full, and settled too strongly to be shaken." [1]   In the third article of this series it was demanded that New England make a separate peace with England; but even peace and the reopening of commerce, it was claimed, would not avail if it should leave New England "at the mercy of the Western States." "If we submit quietly, our destruction is certain.   If we oppose them with a high minded and steady courage, who will say that we shall not beat them back?"   The time was ripe, the author continued, and it would not do to wait until the United States army was filled by conscription, when New England should be beggared, and then have to fight against Federal veterans for her independence. [2]

Many articles also appeared discussing the abstract question of States' Rights, taking the ground to be occupied a half century later by the South.   In one of these, which first appeared in Connecticut and was reprinted elsewhere, as was the custom, we read that "the younger classes of our citizens who have come upon the stage since the commencement of our Federal Government, have many of them, considered it as one consolidated and not a confederation of independent sovereignties. This unjust conception has been the fruitful source of most of the errors which have led to our present unhappy condition, and nothing short of a correct understanding of our Federal Compact and the true principles of our civil and political liberty, can restore" the happiness the country enjoyed under Washington. [3]   Under stress of circumstances affecting their own personal or party interests, the Federalists and Republicans had each swung round a half circle and changed places with reference to the nature and required strength of the central government.

It was in the midst of excitement and passion, only faintly shadowed in the few extracts quoted above, that the call went out for the meeting of delegates from the several New England states which has since been known as the Hartford Convention. We may here reiterate a point to which we have frequently called attention in both this and the preceding volumes, which

[1] *Hampshire Gazette*, Dec. 21, 1814.   [2] *Ibid.*, Jan. 4, 1815.
[3] *Salem Gazette*, Oct. 21, 1814.

is that there are always two or more parties among the people
on every question. When we speak of Massachusetts or New
England, for example, as being opposed to the war, what we
mean and all that we mean is that an effective majority was
opposed to it. Naturally, the party or policy which becomes
effective is the one to which the historian has to give the more
attention; but there is always danger of losing sight of what
may have been very important minorities or policies which
did not fail of influence, although they did not win out at the
time. The characteristic feature in New England history
during the War of 1812 was the opposition and obstruction
offered to the national prosecution of the struggle by the powerful Federalist majority, and consequently we have dwelt at
length upon the sayings and doings of that majority. Nevertheless, during the whole war the Republican press and a considerable part undoubtedly of the members of that party supported the policies of the Administration in Washington, and
took a nationalistic view of the Union and of New England's
place in it. Such journals as the *Independent Chronicle* in
Boston were continually attacking the self-righteousness, conceit, and political ambition of the Federalists. As against the
steady campaign of abuse of the other sections of the country,
it pointed out that whereas the population of the Union was
nearly seven and a quarter millions, that of New England was
less than one and one half. "Is it not preposterous and absurd
then," it asked, "that these five states should expect to control
the other thirteen—or that less than one-fifth of the population
should control more than four-fifths?" It was admitted that
this argument could not convince the Federalists, who "assume
to themselves exclusively all the *wealth*, all the *religion*, and
all the *learning* of the nation," and who considered that they
had the exclusive right to rule. The Federalists, after all, —
it pointed out, — were only a mere majority, and when peace
should come and the passions aroused by the war should subside
they would undoubtedly become a "very 'contemptible'
minority."[1]

It is unnecessary to multiply such examples of extracts from

[1] *Independent Chronicle*, May 2, 1814.

the opposition press, but in considering the actions of the more extreme Federalist leaders it should be remembered that they must have been tempered to a considerable extent by the existence of a strong minority that was wholly opposed to their ideas. With all the contempt felt for democracy and "the people" by such men as Pickering and others, we yet find them questioning continually what the people may "be ripe" for, and how far they would follow a lead.

The extremists of lower position, such as the heady orators of local town meetings or mere members of the state legislatures, felt less responsibility and talked wildly, without thought of future courses to be pursued. During the winter session of the Massachusetts legislature the leaders, like Otis, felt themselves in a difficult position. They had, indeed, been playing a dangerous game. They wished to keep public feeling at high pitch against the Federal Government, and yet sufficiently in leash so that it should not be slipped until the leaders were ready for overt action. Speaking of the difficulty, Otis wrote to Noah Webster in May that it was impossible to say to the legislators, "'thus far may ye come but no further', without refrigerating the popular zeal," and yet the leaders could not sustain the town petitions and draft resolutions to afford a relief which could only be obtained "by avowed *nullification;* for which those leading persons were by no means prepared or desirous." [1]

As we have noted above, the question of holding a convention, when first proposed, had been postponed until the people should decide in the spring elections. By the time the spring session of the legislature was held, the Embargo had been repealed by Congress and the convention project was again put off. By autumn, however, the situation had wholly altered for the worse by the occurrence of the various events we have briefly noted above. In October the legislature passed a series of resolves, one of which provided for the appointment of twelve persons as delegates from Massachusetts to meet for conference in a convention with delegates from the other New England states, for the purpose of suggesting measures for the

[1] Morison, *Otis*, vol. II, p. 90.

common defense, and also for calling a constitutional convention from all the United States to amend the Federal Constitution.[1] The governor was authorized to send invitations to the other New England states to participate, and the delegates from Massachusetts were chosen.

Connecticut was the first state to accept, the Assembly passing a resolution to that effect by the overwhelming vote of one hundred and fifty-three to thirty-six. In Rhode Island the legislature had appointed a committee to report on the letter from the Secretary of War to the governor with reference to troops, and on the invitation from Massachusetts to join in the convention. Both these matters were considered in a single report which, after speaking of the oppressions of the national government, said that "we are not alone in these calamities. Our sister states of the south have been almost equally oppressed and abused. They are beginning to assert their rights, and with us they will never suffer our common rights, under the Constitution to be prostrated by a government we have ourselves created." This is a note I find nowhere else in the Federalist outpourings of the day. The resolution to accept the invitation from Massachusetts and to appoint four delegates to attend was passed by thirty-nine to twenty-three, the minority presenting a protest against the action, which was not entered upon the minutes "on account of its indecorous language and foul aspersions on the motives of the majority." [2]

In New Hampshire the legislature was not in session, and the Republican majority in the Council would not issue the call for a special session.[3] Nevertheless, the people of Cheshire and Windham counties, where the population was overwhelmingly Federalist, proceeded in meetings to elect delegates. In Vermont both governor and legislature were Federalist, and the former's attitude on the militia question has already been noted. The actual invasion of the New England states, however, had made him declare the war to be now a defensive one, and unlike

---

[1] Morison, *Otis*, vol. II, p. 103. The seven chapters devoted to the Convention in his volume give the best account there is.
[2] *Hampshire Gazette*, Nov. 23, 1814.
[3] *Niles Weekly Register*, vol. VII, p. 167.

the Massachusetts Federalists, he laid aside party distinctions in order to prosecute it. The legislative committee which reported on the invitation from Massachusetts were unanimous against accepting it, and it was officially declined. A meeting in Windham County, composed, it was said, "of a few Lawyers, Doctors and Merchants," chose a delegate, who attended the convention at Hartford and was admitted. The Vermont Secretary of State also went "without being sent by anybody," as the *Vermont Republican* said, but was denied a seat.[1] The convention was thus not representative of New England, but only of its three southern states.

As the date of its convening, December 15, approached, the newspapers were filled with articles regarding the objects which it might or should attain. The Republican press naturally attacked the very idea of holding a convention, and was almost a unit in declaring its object to be the breaking of the Federal Union. If this was good politics, the Federalists had certainly opened themselves to the attack, not only by their acts and speeches all through the war but by many of the articles which now appeared in the Federalist papers regarding the convention, by members of the extreme wing of the party.[2]

The *Boston Gazette* announced that "on or before the 4th of July, if James Madison is not out of office, a new form of government will be in operation in the eastern section of the union. Immediately after, the contest in many of the states, will be whether to adhere to the old or join the new government," and it discussed the terms of the new constitution to be formed.[3] A series of articles entitled "What is expected of the Convention at Hartford?" by John Lowell, the mouthpiece of the Essex Junto, was published in the *Boston Daily Advertiser* and reprinted throughout New England. Although signed "An Enemy to Separation," and paying respect to the Union in the

---

[1] *Records of Governor and Council*, vol. VI, p. 463.

[2] *Cf.* F. M. Anderson, "A Forgotten Phase of the New England Opposition to the War of 1812," Mississippi Valley Hist. Assoc., *Proceedings*, vol. VI, pp. 176 *ff.*

[3] Issue of Nov. 17, 1814. Suffrage was to be limited to free white native citizens; no new states could be admitted without the unanimous consent of the old; two thirds of both houses of congress was to be necessary to declare war; the president was to have a longer term but not be reëligible for office; slave representation to be abolished imposition of unlimited restrictions on commerce to be prohibited.

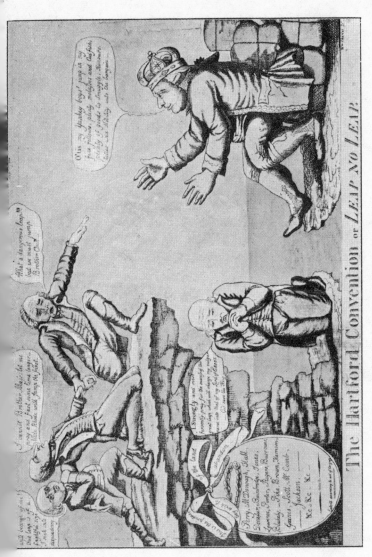

The Hartford Convention or *LEAP NO LEAP.*

CARTOON OF THE HARTFORD CONVENTION

Original in the New York Public Library

opening paragraph, the articles nevertheless pointed directly
at disunion, and in fact claimed that the union was already
dissolved or "at least so far suspended as to be the subject of
negotiation and arrangement," because of the acts of the other
sections and not of New England.[1] It was suggested that the
United States should not be allowed to collect taxes or enlist
men in New England during the remainder of the war unless the
government provided for the defense of that section, and also
that a declaration of neutrality might be wise.[2]

An article addressed "To the Members of the New-England
Convention," which appeared in the *Connecticut Courant* in
December, may be quoted as an expression of one type of ultra-
Federal conceit and sectionalism. After stating that the New
Englanders have always been "a peculiar people" who were
"the wonder of the world," it said that they fought alone the
first battles for independence and supplied more than half
the men and resources which supported the struggle throughout.
It was then prophesied that "this bold people" needed but
one century to control the destinies of Europe. "It was the
misfortune of this people . . . to be united with a race of men
in every respect their reverse; a mixture of all nations and all
colours; united by no common bond of language and religion;
ignorant, effeminate, and corrupt, who despise labour, and
destitute of everything which constitutes national or individual
wealth except what is wrung from the pitiful earnings of unwilling slaves. In a moment of unsuspecting generosity, while
the wounds were yet bleeding which we had received in their
defense, we admitted these men to a share in our Councils."
But it soon became evident that they envied the glory of New
England and were bent upon destroying her. "They began
by infusing into our population a poisonous democracy, which
at once corrupted the fountain of life and threatened the whole
social system with convulsion." The author of this diatribe
then recounted all the grievances of recent years, called for the
Spirit of '76, and suggested rebellion.[3] The above may be
considered as silly ranting, unworthy of quotation, but we

---

[1] *Conn. Courant*, Dec. 6, 1814.   [2] *Ibid.*, Nov. 29, Dec. 13, 1814.
[3] *Ibid.*, Dec. 20, 1814.

cannot understand the past if we consider only its wisdom and not its folly. Nor must it be ignored that the article was given considerable space in one of the leading Federal journals, at a time when contributed letters still largely took the place of the modern editorial.

If we turn from what the public was expecting or suggesting that the convention should do, to the opinions of its members on the same topics, we breathe a saner air. Otis, who more than any other man was responsible for the assembling of the convention, always claimed that it was intended to save rather than to destroy the Union, and that its two main objects were to defend New England against the enemy and to serve as a safety valve for the popular excitement.[1] Otis may have been sincere in these reminiscent ascriptions of motive, but his words would have a truer ring if his own record were a little better. In September, when the governor and the State Committee on Defense took no action beyond the calling out of the militia to save Boston from threatened British attack, many of the leading Federalists said that nothing should be done, and that the town should capitulate, as the British would respect private property.[2] The acts of the enemy at Norfolk and Washington, however, were not reassuring to some of the younger Federalists, and a town meeting was called to adopt more resolute methods of defense. Although Otis at the moment had a letter from Admiral Bainbridge in his pocket, begging that the forts in the harbor be strengthened, Otis did his best to oppose the patriotic energy of the younger element. In spite of his own statement in later years, his biographer is led to discard defense as one of the main objects of the convention.[3] Those that were really in Otis's mind at the time seem to have been to give strong expression to the grievances from which his section was suffering; to make some arrangement that would enable the Federal taxes hitherto collected for military operations in New England to pass to the local state treasuries, as part of a scheme for self-defense; and to secure, by means of a constitutional convention, certain amendments to the Federal

[1] Morison, *Otis*, vol. II, p. 110.   [2] *Ibid.*, p. 99.
[3] *Ibid.*, p. 113.

Constitution. Of the latter, the one especially aimed at in New England for some years past had had for its object the abolition of slave representation in the Southern States.

It is needless to point out that the South would never have yielded peacefully in abandoning the great compromise which alone had brought her into the Union.   It is difficult to see how the Federalist leaders could have failed to realize that insistence upon the point could only have meant either the forcible coercion of the South — which was never mentioned — or secession by New England.   Pickering, indeed, took a different view, though a politically fantastic one.   He would have forced the Western States to secede, and then argued that the common danger from the enemy would result in a closer union between the Northern, Middle, and Southern States, and that the latter two groups would have to concede whatever New England might desire in the way of constitutional changes, in order to secure her effective good-will in the struggle against England. We might smile at this wild scheme had it been suggested by some farmer-statesman who had never wandered a half-mile from his own acres, but it becomes almost incredible when propounded by a man who was one of the leaders in New England political thought, who had for years been a figure in national politics, and had been Secretary of State at Washington.   The utter intellectual isolation of New England could not be better shown.   Because of changes in population, New England was being outvoted.   That Pickering could believe that any remedy for the situation could be found by kicking the West out of the Union and retaining the South, but making it voluntarily divest itself of the strength guaranteed it by the Constitution, shows how little the Federalist leaders grasped the forces underlying any sectional feeling but their own, or those underlying the expansion of the nation.

The Essex Junto, with its extremist following in the Federalist party, undoubtedly wished for a more drastic plan of action in the convention than did Otis and the other moderates.   The *Columbian Centinel*, indeed, treated the convention as though it were itself being held for the purpose of drawing up a new Constitution.   Under captions similar to those it had used in 1788, when the Federal Constitution was being adopted by the several states, it announced the acceptance of the invitation to attend on the part of Connecticut as the "Second Pillar of a new Federal edifice raised," and Rhode Island's acceptance as the "third pillar." [1]

As Dr. Morison has pointed out, the Union was in danger of dissolution at the end of 1814, quite apart from the assembling of the Hartford Convention. The British held a part of Maine and were threatening an invasion by way of Lake George. At the other end of the country an expedition was on its way against New Orleans and — the Federalists, at least, believed — with every prospect of success. Washington had been burned, and the American navy destroyed. As he also points out, six states outside the borders of New England had taken steps to form state armies. The Federal government had exhausted its resources and lost the confidence of the people. Under the circumstances, any radical steps taken at Hartford, even though only three New England states were represented, might well have been the match to set the whole Federal edifice in flames. It certainly strengthened the resolve of the national enemy. In fact, its mere assembling was a menace, the force of which could not but be known to the men who took part in it, who had prepared the way by a constant fanning of discontent and sectional feeling, and who had done their best to paralyze the central government whose resulting impotency was one of the alleged causes of the meeting. It was an enormous responsibility, and one which they could not escape.

The convention met at Hartford on December 15, with twelve delegates from Massachusetts, three from Rhode Island, seven from Connecticut, and the two from New Hampshire, the others who were to make up the final number of twenty-six arriving later.[2] Among those from Massachusetts were George Cabot, H. G. Otis, Timothy Bigelow, Nathan Dane, and William Prescott. Daniel Lyman was there from Rhode Island, and Chauncey Goodrich, James Hillhouse, Calvin Goddard, and Roger Sherman from Connecticut. It was, in fact, a notable

---

[1] Issue of Nov. 9, 1814.

[2] Theodore Dwight, *History of the Hartford Convention*, (New York, 1833), p. 383.

gathering of men of high character among the ruling aristocratic class of New England. It is a fact worth noting that all but four were lawyers.[1] The delegation from Massachusetts comprised approximately one third of the members, and among these Bigelow was the only one who may be classed as an extremist of the Pickering type. Leaders like Cabot, Dane, and Otis might be counted upon to keep whatever action was taken within fairly moderate limits, as far as possible.

As soon as the convention was organized, Cabot was elected president, and Theodore Dwight of Hartford secretary. Among the rules adopted at the first session was one which aroused intense suspicion among the opponents of the convention at the time, and which for decades after served them best in their attacks upon the motives and acts of the members. This was that "the most inviolable secrecy shall be observed by each member of this Convention, including the Secretary, as to all propositions, debates, and proceedings thereof, until this injunction shall be suspended or altered." [2]

This was in accord with tradition, but was unquestionably a tactical mistake. Considering all that had been said and written about the disloyalty and desire for secession on the part of the Federalists, and indeed, considering the writings of some of their own prominent members, it would have been the part of wisdom had they come into the open and shown, if such were truly the fact, that they had nothing to conceal. It is probable that such was the fact, and that we may take at their face value the statements made later by leading members of the convention still living in 1828, when the Journal of the convention was published to put an end to public clamor as to what had gone on. These stated emphatically that there had never been any topic discussed except such as appeared in Dwight's minutes.

So far as the public was concerned, the results of the secret debating was the publication of a "Report" on the result of the conference.[3] This reviewed the state of the nation under

---

[1] Morison, *Otis*, vol. II, pp. 130 *ff.*   [2] Dwight, *op. cit.*, p. 385.
[3] *The Proceedings of a Convention of Delegates*, etc., (Boston, 1815). The references are to the third edition.

the recent administrations, and recognized that some of the more radical members of the party desired more drastic action than had been taken or recommended, but advised a course of "moderation and firmness" in order to save them "from the regret incident to sudden decisions."[1] "If the Union be destined to dissolution, by reason of the multiplied abuses of bad administrations," it continued, "it should, if possible, be the work of peaceable times, and deliberate consent."[2] It then gave reasons for considering that any measures tending to disunite the states in the midst of a war could "be justified only by absolute necessity." Unfortunately we do not possess the debates on this point, but know only the conclusion reached. It would have been well if the Federalists could have reached such a sane and common-sense decision without the preliminary of calling a convention in time of war, and have acted in accordance with it during the preceding two years. The Report also suggested, after discussing the questions of militia, drafting, and defense, that the states be allowed to assume their own defense individually, and that a reasonable proportion of the Federal taxes be apportioned to the states in which they were collected for that purpose.[3]

The amendments to the Constitution of the Federal government that were next considered were such as had long been the subject of controversy in New England. The first was to abolish slave representation; the second to prohibit any new state from being admitted to the Union without the consent of at least two thirds of both Houses of Congress; the third and fourth limited the power of the Federal government over commerce and the declaration of war; and the last had to do with the exclusion of foreigners from holding office, and the limitation of that of the president to one term.[4] It was also resolved, should peace not be declared and the defense of the states be further neglected, that it would be expedient to call another convention to meet in Boston in June, and Cabot, Lyman, and Goodrich, representing the three states, were empowered to call such a meeting.[5]

[1] *The Proceedings of a Convention of Delegates*, etc., (Boston, 1815), p. 4.
[2] *Ibid.*, p. 5.   [3] *Ibid.*, p. 12.   [4] *Ibid.*, pp. 16 *ff.*
[5] *Ibid.*, pp. 21 *f.*

The mild tone of the Report surprised the Democrats and enraged the more extreme Federalists. The Federalist press, however, to a very considerable extent altered its tone, and much less was heard of immediate secession or of a separate peace with the enemy. Within a few weeks after the convention adjourned, Massachusetts and Connecticut appointed commissioners to proceed to Washington to consult the Federal authorities on the propositions which had been made as to state defense. While these "ambassadors," as they were dubbed, were on their way, news came of the complete defeat of the British at the battle of New Orleans, and almost immediately after that of the treaty of peace between England and the United States. It was, indeed, none too soon for the cause of Union. After the adjournment of the convention some of the towns continued to pass resolutions practically nullifying the acts of the Federal government. Toward the end of January, Newburyport resolved that the time had come when "what is right, must be not only made known, but be made prevalent," and that "we have no hesitation in saying that we consider our State Legislatures as the sole, rightful, and bounden judges of the course which our safety may require, without any regard to the persons still assuming to be the national government," and that "the laws of the United States shall be temporarily suspended in our territory."[1] In Reading the town resolved that under God they would look only to the state governments, and that thereafter they would pay no Federal taxes.[2]

Meanwhile, Congress had passed an Act which received the President's signature on January 27, authorizing pretty nearly everything which the New Englanders had demanded as to defense and the military. It did not allow the states to collect the Federal taxes nor deduct any proportion from them, but it did receive into the national army and place on the national pay-roll units of troops raised by the states, which were to be employed only within the limits of such states severally, except with the consent of their governors.[3]

It is perhaps idle to consider what the course of events would

[1] *Hampshire Gazette*, Feb. 8, 1815.   [2] *Ibid.*, Jan. 18, 1815.
[3] Morison, *op. cit.*, p. 161.

have been, had the war continued. Would the second convention have been called? Would New England have made a
separate peace or seceded? It is probable that none of these
things would have come to pass, for it must not be forgotten
that even in the three states which took part in the convention
a considerable proportion of the population was opposed to the
policies and attitude of the Federalists, and that among the
latter there was a large element that would by no means have
followed their leaders over the brink of national suicide.[1]
Moreover, New Hampshire and Vermont would not have
joined in any such enterprise, and a confederacy of merely
Massachusetts, Rhode Island, and Connecticut would have
been impractical. That the majority of New Englanders had
been against the war from the beginning was an undoubted
fact, but, had they heartily coöperated with the rest of the
country and the national government after war was declared,
many of their later causes of complaint would not have arisen.
These were to some extent due, as was the growing bitterness
of feeling, to the policy and propaganda deliberately adopted
by the Federalist leaders. It may be conceded that national
feeling was a plant of slow growth and still in its infancy, but
there was such a feeling on the part of a large section of the New
England public, although not numbered among the "wise, the
rich, and the good." In fact, the higher one went in New
England at that period, the narrower and more restricted —
for the most part — did vision become, from either the social
or the national standpoint.

Had the Federalists had their way, the United States would
forever have been limited to a fringe of states along the Atlantic
seaboard, dominated by New England. John Quincy Adams
was notably lacking in the judicial temper, — to put it mildly,
— and we ought not to consider too seriously his statements as
to the motives of the Federalists of the Convention era; but
there can be no quarrel with his verdict as to the rôle they had
forced New England to play in the war, even after making
all due allowances for them. "As to our beloved New England," he wrote from London to William Eustis in July 1815,

[1] Cf. *Autobiography of Lyman Beecher*, (New York, 1864), vol. I.

"I blush to think of the part she has performed, for her shame is still the disgrace of the nation — faction for patriotism, a whining hypocrisy for political morals, dismemberment for union, and prostitution to the enemy for state sovereignty. You tell me they are ashamed of it themselves. I rejoice to hear it. As a true New England man and American I feel the infection of their shame, while I abhor the acts by which they have brought it upon us." [1]

Democracy has as yet been on trial for too short a time to determine with any degree of certitude whether it will prove any more permanently successful than any other form of government. We certainly can never again

> . . . recapture
> The first fine careless rapture

with which it was regarded as the beginning of the millennium during the late eighteenth and early nineteenth centuries. Nevertheless, if there has been much to cause sober pondering as to what the effects of democracy are likely to be, not only in the political but in the social and intellectual spheres, on the other hand it is well not to allow one's self to despair because of intelligence tests or the emergence of raw *mores* which may grate on the sensitive. In the case of the individual, we are coming to realize, as psychologists plumb the depths, that he is governed in his actions far less by rational motives than we used to think or than he himself believes. There is the whole array of "complexes," of compensatory actions, the vast field of the subconscious. In the larger sphere of social life, the life of nations, it may well be that we deceive ourselves in a similar way as to the ultra-importance of the rôle played by the rational intelligence. As to entrusting the power of government solely to a class composed of presumably the most intelligent members of the community, the history of New England shows us again and again, as a matter of practical statecraft, how the "wise, the rich, and the good" have shown less collective wisdom than the members of the despised lower orders, as well as a more bitter class spirit, a narrower intellectual outlook, and a less broadly human attitude toward life.

[1] *Writings*, ed. W. C. Ford, (New York, 1913), vol. V, p. 329.

CHAPTER XIII

A NEW OUTLOOK, 1815-1825

Effects of Peace — Shipping — Manufactures — Agriculture — The Tariff — Immigration and Emigration — Urban Development — Politics and Finance — Religious Societies — Overthrow of Old Order in Connecticut — New Constitution — Separation of Church and State — Revision of Massachusetts Constitution — Maine Becomes a Separate State — Missouri Compromise

PEACE had come with an unexpectedness that left the entire country gaping. Moreover, owing to the complications of her position in Europe, England had accorded terms that were far more favorable than the military events of the conflict had warranted the United States in expecting. The ground was wholly cut from under the feet of the Federalists and other opponents of the war, and the position of the Democratic party greatly strengthened. If the peace was sudden, the psychological transformation of the country was equally so. For the preceding twenty years America had been swirling with other countries in the European whirlpool. The British Government and Napoleon had almost more direct influence on the lives of the American' people than their own government and presidents. American political parties and passions had been but a reflection of those in Europe. The Union had been brought to the very brink of dissolution, not by purely domestic questions, but by the lawless contentions of the leading powers of the Old World. America had passed through a veritable nightmare, in which her soul seemed to have been ravished from her by powers three thousand miles away.

When peace came with the unexpectedness of a lightning

stroke, it was as though America suddenly emerged from an evil dream into the light of daytime actualities and activities. She awoke to a whole new range of ideas which had nothing to do with Europe. Domestic problems occupied her entire attention. The distempered passions of the preceding two decades subsided and an era of "good feeling" followed. At the beginning of 1815 every eye in New England was strained across the seas, following events in Europe with feverish interest, and our own great West was thought of mainly to be damned or, if possible, to be forcibly kicked out of the Union. By 1825 Europe was forgotten; attention was focused on problems at home. Along the Erie Canal, opened in that year, New Englanders were pouring by thousands to develop the new Northwest.

The end of the abnormal conditions produced by the war brought about a severe dislocation of the economic life of New England which was to have profound and lasting effect. Although all forms of business and industry at once felt the change, they were affected in diverse ways. Shipping, which had been the main producer of the accumulations of liquid capital in the section, was at first stimulated by the return of peace. As we have noted a number of times, the major part of the American ships engaged in the carrying trade were Massachusetts owned, and consequently the merchants of that state shared heavily in the extraordinary increase in that trade which occurred in the first two years of peace. Taking the country as a whole, the exports rose from less than seven millions in 1814 to nearly eighty-two millions in 1816, and imports from less than thirteen millions to over one hundred and forty-seven millions.[1] The increase in exports was largely due to the accumulation during the war of those American products, particularly agricultural, which were badly needed by Europe but which could not be shipped during the hostilities. The changing nature of the American export trade, however, and more especially the increasing importance of cotton, is shown by the fact that whereas the domestic exports of Massachusetts in 1818 were about five million seven hundred

[1] Johnson, *For. and Dom. Commerce*, vol. I, p. 32.

thousand, those from Louisiana were nearly twelve and a quarter millions.[1] The tremendous increase in imports was largely due to the dumping by British manufacturers of goods which had accumulated in England — and which we shall speak of again.

This situation was to a great extent temporary in character. As we shall see further on, protective tariffs were passed, which aimed at decreasing imports; and with the decline in the power of the Federal party the shipping interests lost powerful support in the Federal Legislature. In 1815 a series of reciprocity treaties were negotiated with England and other countries, which injured the carrying trade in several ways.[2] Even during the brief prosperity immediately following the announcement of peace, there was evident a distinct change in New England's interests. By 1816 the foreign trade of Massachusetts had, indeed, risen nearly to the high figures of the antebellum year of 1811, but in New Hampshire it was only a little over one third and in Rhode Island and Connecticut about one half of that before the war.[3] Manufacturing was beginning to absorb both the capital and the attention of former merchants — a situation which was true to a greater extent, as yet, in the smaller states than in Massachusetts. Even there, however, the new conditions in shipping were bringing changes in the geographical distribution of business, and the foreign trade was rapidly concentrating in Boston. Such smaller towns as Newburyport, Beverly, Salem, and Marblehead never recovered from the effects of the war until they followed the new trend into manufacturing.[4] By 1815 Salem had but fifty-seven vessels in foreign trade as against one hundred and eighty-two nine years earlier, and her leading merchants were moving into Boston. New Bedford alone, of the smaller ports, succeeded in rising to a new prosperity by specializing in one branch of trade, whaling, and became the leading whaling-port in the United States.

[1] Johnson, *For. and Dom. Commerce*, vol. I, p. 34.
[2] *Ibid.*, p. 36; K. Coman, *Industrial History*, pp. 181 *ff.*
[3] Pitkin, *Statistical View*, pp. 54, 56.
[4] Morison, *Maritime History*, p. 216.

Ship Rome of Salem Capt. Samuel R. Curwen, Leaving Marseilles March. 1846.

Ship Monk, of Salem Capt. John W. Allen 1813.

SALEM SHIPS ROME AND MONK
From originals in the Peabody Museum

Although the wealth of New England had been most conspicuous and fluid as concentrated in the hands of the merchant class, the great bulk of the population had always been, and was still, in the period covered by this chapter, engaged in farming. Even by 1820, when the new manufactures were absorbing a considerable part of the labor supply, for every fifty-one engaged in that pursuit and fifteen in commerce, there were one hundred and seventy-two who were farmers.[1] We have already spoken of the difficulties of transport and markets, which tended to keep agriculture on a low level of efficiency, and the war had done little to alter these conditions. From about 1810, however, there became evident the first beginnings of a revolution in methods, that were comparable in the final changes produced to those introduced by manufacturing.[2] There had been practically no change in the methods of domestic economy of the farmer since the earliest days. The farm was still to a great extent the almost self-sufficing unit it had always been, and every farm raised just the same crops in about the same proportions as all the others. The striking changes that occurred belong to a slightly later period, but in this one we may note the stirring of that new spirit which was evident in so many different directions in society at this time.

The few Agricultural Societies which had been established hitherto had been founded by men interested more or less theoretically in improvements, and had not appealed to the "dirt farmers," in the absence of any markets that would ensure a money return for the cost of experimenting. In 1811, however, the Berkshire plan of societies formed among the practical farmers themselves was inaugurated at Pittsfield, and in the next fifteen years spread into nearly every county in southern New England. Fairs and cattle shows became the order of the day, and the new organizations served the need for social contacts among the rural population as well as for the exchange of views among practical men. Elkanah Watson of

[1] W. P. Sterns, "The Foreign Trade of the United States from 1820 to 1840," *Journal of Political Economy*, vol. VIII, p. 3.
[2] P. W. Bidwell, "The Agricultural Revolution in New England," *American Historical Review*, vol. XXVI, p. 684.

Connecticut, who was among the most influential leaders of the time in working for improved agricultural methods and conditions, exhibited three merino sheep at Pittsfield in 1810, and although they occasioned a good deal of mirth and ridicule among the farmers, the exhibition was the germ of the Berkshire County Agricultural Society, whose regular annual exhibitions began in the year following.[1]   Three of the merinos had been imported from Spain in 1798 and given to a gentleman in Cambridge who, unaware of their value, calmly proceeded to eat them.   The first introduced for breeding purposes were brought over by Colonel Humphreys of Connecticut in 1802, and it is said that the Cambridge epicure, having discovered his error, paid a thousand dollars for a ram from the Humphreys flock.[2]   At any rate, the improvement in the breed of sheep was the foundation of the American woolen industry, and was indicative of the new spirit of enterprise at work. The development of agriculture, however, was still awaiting that of markets, and those in turn had to await the growth of a manufacturing population.

We have already noted how the Embargo and the subsequent war served almost as a prohibitive tariff would have done to stimulate domestic manufactures, and how capital was diverted from shipping to the production of goods, under stress of the abnormal conditions.   Nathan Appleton, for example, who had been an importer until 1807, played a prominent part in establishing the Massachusetts cotton mills.   P. T. Jackson, another new manufacturer, had been in the India trade.   Francis C. Lowell had been a merchant until 1810, when he found his business so reduced that he also turned to manufacturing.[3] These are but typical among numerous cases, and all the New England states shared in this transformation.   Even in Maine, between 1806 and 1814 fifty companies were incorporated for the manufacture of textiles, and in the latter year thirty were authorized for many different purposes.[4]   In Connecticut,

---

[1] Flint, "Hundred Years' Progress," p. 283.

[2] Humphreys, David Humphreys, vol. II, p. 345.

[3] M. T. Copeland, The Cotton Manufacturing Industry in the United States, (Harvard University Press, 1912), p. 5.

[4] C. D. Wright, History of Wages and Prices in Massachusetts, (Boston, 1885), p. 18.

Humphreys had incorporated the Humphreysville Manufacturing Company for wool manufacture in 1810, with a maximum capital of $500,000, and this was rapidly followed by many others.[1] The number of plants that sprang up in Connecticut was truly astonishing, as was the amount of capital invested. Even in 1810 the output of the state in manufactured products was estimated from about six to nearly eight million dollars, and this increased during the war. This was surpassed in New England only by the output of Massachusetts; but the textile mills of Rhode Island had also developed astonishingly. Almost all the mills had been for spinning yarn only and not for weaving, but just at the end of the war the power loom replaced the old hand-looms, and in the Waltham mill of Francis Lowell, who was the first to introduce this new method, the entire process of manufacturing the cotton into cloth was undertaken for the first time under one roof.[2]

The effect of the sudden peace with England upon the rapidly developing manufacturing business of New England was exactly the reverse of that upon shipping. In fact, to a considerable extent the two were closely related, and the almost complete ruin which overtook manufactures was linked with the sudden prosperity that came to shipping. As we have stated, it was the almost total cessation of commerce during the Embargo and the war which caused the demand for home products and also supplied the capital for the development of manufactures. When peace came and the ships of New England were once more free to sail the seas, the way was open for foreign merchandise to pour into the country. It came, indeed, in an amazing flood, as the figures quoted above prove. The end of the war in Europe had created problems there for the English manufacturers, who found the Continental markets demoralized and sought an outlet at any cost for the enormous surplus of goods on hand which had been brought about by the transition from war- to peace-time industry. Manufacturers, in order to meet their financial obligations, were forced to sell goods at almost any price in order to realize cash. In addition,

---

[1] Purcell, *Connecticut in Transition*, pp. 123 ff.
[2] Taussig, *Tariff History*, p. 29.

there was a deliberate policy of dumping on the American market, in order to injure the new competition which was threatening their future supremacy. In 1816 Lord Brougham, speaking in Parliament of the enormous exports to America, said that "it was well worth while to incur a loss upon the first exportation, in order, by the glut, to stifle in the cradle those rising manufactures in the United States which the war had forced into existence, contrary to the natural course of things." [1]

In the first year of peace America was inundated with English goods to the extent of more than twice the normal amount of consumption. These were sold at auction for excessively low prices and on credits extending to even a year's time. The public indulged in an orgy of extravagance and bought recklessly, as they do after the end of every great war. Credit was strained to the breaking-point; but for the American manufacturer the situation spelled ruin. Many of the new plants which had been built in New England and which had been making handsome profits at war-time prices had been carrying on their business on borrowed money. The collapse in prices and the sudden turn of the consumer from domestic to foreign goods left the manufacturers as stranded and helpless as fishes caught above the tide line. Specie was hoarded or went to settle foreign balances for imported goods. Banks closed down or cut their loans heavily with little regard for the needs of their clients. In Connecticut alone it was estimated that more than a million dollars were suddenly withdrawn from circulation either because of fear or because of speculation.[2] Industry came to a standstill.

Cotton manufacturing had another factor to contend with in the sudden advance in price of the raw material, due to the reopening of the European market, the staple rising from thirteen cents in 1814 to twenty-seven within two years.[3] A memorial to Congress in 1815 estimated the number of mills within thirty miles of Providence at one hundred and forty,

---

[1] A. S. Bolles, *Financial History of the United States*, (New York, 1894), vol. II, p. 359; E. Stanwood, *American Tariff Controversies in the Nineteenth Century*, (Boston, 1904), vol. I, pp. 167 f.

[2] Purcell, *Connecticut in Transition*, p. 109.

[3] Wright, *Wages and Prices*, p. 18.

with a hundred and thirty thousand spindles, although probably half of those numbers would be nearer the correct figures.[1] Yet when Lowell and Appleton made a visit to the mill district of Rhode Island, early the following year, they found that not a spindle was turning except in the old Slater mill.   Although they advised the owners to introduce the power loom, which would enable them to meet foreign competition even at the lower prices, the introduction of cheap India cottons at this time would have prevented this.[2] As a matter of fact, the Waltham mill, with its improved machinery and other advantages, was the only one of any importance to survive the deluge of foreign goods.

The distress of the manufacturers resulted in numerous petitions being presented to Congress, praying for the protection of the new industries.   As a result a Tariff Act was passed in 1816, levying duties of twenty-five per cent on cotton goods for three years, and affording additional protection to cotton manufacturing and other industries.[3]   As showing the lack of influence of the manufacturing as compared with the mercantile interests as yet in New England, it may be noted that the representatives of that section in Congress, with the exception of those from Vermont, in the main voted against the measure.

There was not at that time much knowledge of the effects of various rates of duties, and the tariff was not so effective as it had been hoped in affording real protection.   In Connecticut the state legislature gave additional assistance by exempting the cotton and woolen mills from taxation for four years, and their employees from the poll tax and militia duty.[4]   Nevertheless, imports continued on an enormous scale.   Niles estimated the excess of imports over exports for the years 1816 to 1818 for the entire country at over a hundred million dollars, and also estimated that between 1815 and 1820 American merchants defaulted on their foreign accounts to an equal amount.[5]   Although manufacturing recovered more rapidly

[1] [S. Batchelder], *Introduction and Early Progress of the Cotton Manufacture in the United States*, (Boston, 1863), p. 59.

[2] Stanwood, *Tariff Controversies*, vol. I, p. 141.

[3] *Ibid.*, pp. 136 ff.   [4] Purcell, *op. cit.*, p. 136.

[5] Sterns, "Foreign Trade of the U. S.," *op. cit.*, p. 38.

than might have been expected, the country entered upon a business crisis about 1822; and it was said at the time that as many of the factories had been built on bank loans, "bank and factory usually went over the same dam together."[1] Ninety or more failures, mostly small, occurred in Boston during the summer of 1822, and the specie in the banks of that city was reduced from $936,000 to $406,000 between January first and July first, although their circulation remained stationary. It is interesting to note that, of about $1,200,000 in specie exported from Boston in that period, all but $100,000 was shipped beyond the Cape of Good Hope.[2]

The crisis that occurred was felt in agriculture as well as in business. Not only had the farmers taken part in the general extravagance of the post-war period and bought more than they could afford of foreign fineries, but they had also been speculating heavily in lands. From about 1820 their always narrow markets had been somewhat seriously curtailed by the increased demand for cotton, which had been steadily making itself felt from Europe. The greatly increased number of ships employed in carrying cotton from the Southern States to England preferred to make very low return-freights rather than sail in ballast. Ships from Northern ports could not compete with these, and the result was that both manufactures and farm produce of the sorts formerly shipped from New England to the South were now sent to the latter direct from England.[3]

In 1820 the attempt to pass a new protective tariff was defeated in the Senate, and although New England senators were divided six to four in favor of the measure, the lingering traces of Federalism were sufficient to prevent its passage. Harrison Gray Otis, who voted against it, was publicly thanked by his constituents in Boston. An anti-tariff meeting, held in that city in October, was addressed by Daniel Webster, who at that time — partly on constitutional grounds — was opposed to protection, but who later was to change his position completely. In a long analysis of the proposed bill and of "the

[1] Review of *The Prospect Before Us*, in *North American Review*, vol. XVII, p. 190 [1823].   [2] *Ibid.*, p. 205.   [3] Sterns, *op. cit.*, p. 41.

American system" of producing at home all that the nation consumed, the *North American Review* attacked both vigorously. It estimated that in New England one seventh of the population was directly dependent upon shipping, and after admitting that many factories were injured and that some had failed, it asked whether it was reasonable that commerce should be called upon to pay their losses. "Because our villages here and there present a decayed manufactory, shall our cities be made to exhibit a similar spectacle in ruined wharfs, decaying warehouses, and rotting ships? . . . Shall the sea shore be deserted that the ignorance of some or imbecility of speculation may be repaired?" [1]

This opposition of the New England seaports continued in 1824, when the tariff of that year was enacted; but by that time the cotton industry had made great strides, and it was the southern New England states which saved the bill as far as that section was concerned. Maine had by then been admitted as a State, so that New England counted twelve senators, all of whom voted in favor of the measure except one from New Hampshire and the two from Massachusetts. Had the vote been full in the House, Maine, New Hampshire, and Massachusetts would have given only three in favor and twenty-three against, whereas Rhode Island, Connecticut, and Vermont gave twelve in favor and only one against.[2] From this time onward New England opinion turned in favor of protection. That opinion, Webster said, — speaking in the Senate four years later, — had up to 1824 been "founded in the conviction that on the whole it was wisest and best, both for herself and others, that manufactures should make haste slowly. She felt a reluctance to trust great interests on the foundation of government patronage." But after the policy of the country had been settled by the Act of 1824, she had to decide whether longer to resist what she could not prevent, or to accommodate herself and her pursuits to the new policy.[3]

[1] "Report of the Committee of Merchants and Others of Boston on the Tariff," *North American Review*, vol. XII, pp. 62, 82.

[2] Stanwood, *Tariff Controversies*, vol. I, p. 239.

[3] H. A. Hill, *Memoir of Abbott Lawrence*, (Boston, 1883), p. 29.

Writing many years later, in 1848, Abbott Lawrence combated the notion, then becoming prevalent, that the protective tariff system had been made by and for New England.   He pointed out that the earliest movement for protection for manufactures had been started in the South and West in order to build up an American market for their agricultural products, and that for long New England had resisted the movement because "we honestly believed [it] would greatly injure our navigation, and drive us from our accustomed employments into a business we did not understand."   Reluctantly as New England came into it, however, the men of that section, he said, "soon learned that with the transfer of their capital to manufacturing on a large scale, they acquired skill and knowledge in the use of it; that so far from our foreign commerce being diminished, it was increased, and that our domestic tonnage and commerce were very soon more than quadrupled." [1]   The farmers also by 1824 had come to consider that possibly their own unfortunate situation could be improved by the development of home markets due to manufacturing and by the lowering of ocean freights, so that the agricultural interest turned to the side of the manufacturing against the shipping. [2]

The economic changes following the war were beginning to be felt not only in opinion and politics but in the life of the people, though the full effects belong to a later period and only their beginnings need be noted here.   The rise of manufactures began a veritable revolution in the domestic economy not only of families in the smaller manufacturing villages and towns but on the scattered farms as well.   Home manufactures were fated to give place to the cheap goods made by the factories instead of by the families at the fireside, and we can trace the beginnings of the change in this period.   A somewhat more immediate effect, however, was upon the employment of considerable numbers of the population.   From the beginning, two "schools" of manufacturing arose, based upon the relations between the employers and their employees, which we may call the Rhode Island and Waltham systems. [3]   In Rhode

---

[1] H. A. Hill, *Memoir of Abbott Lawrence*, (Boston, 1883), pp. 150 *f.*
[2] Sterns, *op. cit.*, p. 46.   [3] Batchelder, *Cotton Manufacture*, pp. 73 *f.*

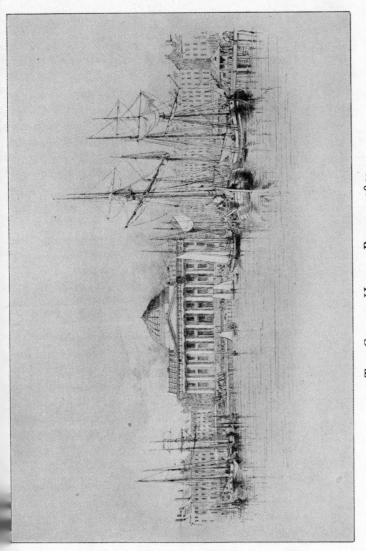

THE CUSTOM HOUSE, BOSTON, 1853

From an unpublished pen-and-ink sketch by Thomas Kelah Wharton; original in the New York Public Library

Island, Slater had introduced the English system of employing whole families, including the small children.   The consequence was that in that state the factory villages tended to be largely made up of families who were wholly dependent upon their work in the mills, and in some cases the parents were inclined to live on the labor of their young children.   This system also frequently included payment of wages in orders on the factory store instead of in cash.   As a result, the families of the operatives came to have no resources of their own to tide over bad times, and became wholly dependent upon their employers. On the other hand, at Waltham wages were paid in cash and the employees were accommodated in boarding-houses which cost them about half the wages of adult female operatives. This tended to preclude the employment of small children, who could not earn enough for board.   The operatives, therefore, were to a far greater extent than under the other system mature individuals, who had homes elsewhere and were not wholly dependent upon the mill-owners.

The difference between the two systems became more marked as time went on, the census of 1820 showing only the beginning of the differentiation.   At that time "boys and girls," presumably under sixteen years old, constituted forty-three per cent of the textile-mill operatives in Massachusetts as against fifty-five per cent in Rhode Island.[1]   It was only with the rise of the large mill-towns in the next two decades that the factory became a real problem in social life.   In 1813, however, the first step was taken to protect the welfare of the child worker by legislative enactment.   At the May session of the Connecticut legislature of that year it was enacted that children employed in factories must be taught to read and write, that their morals be attended to, and that they be required to attend worship.[2]   The law was very vaguely drawn and probably was merely to placate a certain amount of public hostility to the factory system as a whole.   There was no adequate means of

[1] P. H. Douglas, *American Apprenticeship and Industrial Education*, (Columbia University Studies, 1921), p. 57.
[2] *Legal Provisions Respecting the Education and Employment of Children in Factories*, (Hartford, 1842), p. 4.

enforcement provided, and apparently it was never invoked in a single case.

The decade covered by this chapter also saw the commencement of the larger movement of immigration that was destined to have great effect later upon the life of New England. The industrial development led to a demand for labor just at the time when emigration to the West was reaching hitherto undreamed-of proportions. Immigration was still but a trickling stream as compared with the great floods of the thirties and forties, and in 1825 only about fourteen hundred immigrants came to New England from foreign ports.[1] The emigration from New England westward, however, was startling. The war had brought a lull in the movement which in the preceding years of peace had already begun to assume large proportions. With the end of the struggle, and more particularly with the hard times that followed it, great numbers were induced to leave their homes and try their fortunes in the new lands. The various economic ills had greatly increased the number of debtors, as was the case after the Revolution, and many people found themselves in sore straits. Moreover, the ferment of thought on social and religious matters which was to alter society to a great extent in New England tended to drive many who were impatient of the old restraints out into the greater freedom of the West. Political reform and religious toleration, not merely legal but social, were moving too slowly at home for the more independent and restless spirits. This was recognized at the time as among the potent causes for the loss of population.[2]

Moreover, emigration was now not necessarily out to the real frontier with its hardships and Indian dangers. Western New York and Pennsylvania offered to the farmer or professional man opportunities for making a new start, without the loss of many of the advantages of fairly settled communities. The real "West" had advanced farther, to the line of new states, and the pioneers were pressing on to western Ohio, Indiana, and

---

[1] W. J. Bromwell, *History of Immigration into the United States*, (New York, 1856), p. 41.

[2] *Cf.* article from *Dedham Gazette* quoted by Purcell, *Connecticut in Transition*, p. 155.

Illinois. The upper tier of townships in Portage County, Ohio, were practically New England towns in appearance, social life, and population, and the Western Reserve was peopled almost wholly from Connecticut.[1] Occasionally an entire town moved from New England, preserving its church organization and membership, and gave the name of the old town to the new settlement, which became to all intents and purposes a bit of New England thrown down in the wilderness.

There are no statistics available which afford even approximate figures for the movement, but that it was on a vast scale is clearly enough indicated by contemporary accounts and by the serious alarm which it caused. Even more significant than the numbers of the poor who were leaving their old homes and depopulating New England villages were the character and standing of many of the richer men who were doing the same thing. To name a few of those who left Connecticut indicates the loss in intelligence and leadership which the older states were suffering. Gideon Granger, later Postmaster-General, Judge Hugh White, Governor Daniel Dickinson, Oliver Phelps, one of the greatest land-dealers of the day, Chief Justice Ambrose Spencer, General Peter Porter, Judge Frederick Whittlesey, and others of like calibre, all emigrated to New York, where they became prominent. Governor Samuel Huntington went to the shore of Lake Erie. Stanley Griswold became Governor of Michigan Territory, and Horace Holley president of Transylvania College. Even the Federalist Theodore Dwight moved to Albany.[2]

Efforts were made to stem the tide, but without effect; and the opening of the Erie Canal in 1825, just at the end of the decade described in this chapter, acted like an open sluiceway to drain off the population from New England. Aside from the changes wrought by this wholesale exodus, there were also changes in the distribution of population within the old state limits. As we have noted in Massachusetts, the smaller seaports were losing in wealth and size by the movement into Boston. This same tendency toward an urban development

---

[1] Mathews, *Expansion of New England*, p. 181.
[2] Purcell, *Connecticut in Transition*, p. 153.

was already noticeable elsewhere. In Connecticut, owing largely to manufacturing, people were leaving the country and moving into the larger centres such as Hartford, New Haven, New London, and Bridgeport, which were rapidly growing while the smaller towns were standing still or actually decreasing in population.[1] An urban wage-earning class was coming into being, with an outlook — social, religious, and political — quite different from that of the small farmer. The change was marked by the passing of Boston as a town in 1822, when the grant was made to it of a city charter.

The first election for mayor of the new municipality brought to light an interesting change that had been going on within the ranks of the Federalist party, which had survived as a governing power in Massachusetts alone of all the New England states. Harrison Gray Otis had accepted the suggestion that he take the nomination of the party as mayor, but to his intense surprise a new faction sprang up, known as the "Middling Interest," composed of the mechanics and petty shopkeepers, who refused to nominate Otis and turned to Josiah Quincy. As a matter of fact, neither secured a majority in the election; and the office, on a second balloting, went to John Phillips, who was a Federalist but persona grata to the "Middling Interest," which thus controlled the election.[2] In the state election for governor, the following year, Otis ran on the Federalist ticket but was easily defeated by his Democratic opponent. It is significant that both his participation in the Hartford Convention and his wealth proved heavily against him in the last, and what was generally considered the fairly safe, stronghold of the Federalist party. Nothing could more clearly indicate the trend of the times.

The alliance between the capitalists and the politicians is so natural a one that, as we have shown in the preceding volumes as well as this, it was in evidence from the very beginning of New England history, and there had been many outbreaks of resentment on the part of those outside the dominant groups. The period since the adoption of the Federal Constitution had

[1] Purcell, *Connecticut in Transition*, p. 131.
[2] Morison, *Otis*, vol. II, pp. 248 *f*.

been marked by the rise of a group of capitalists whose property was in more fluid shape than the landed estates or timber and shipping interests of the earlier days. After the beginning of the new century the rapid development of banks, manufacturing plants, and insurance companies, all in corporate form, brought a new influence into politics. This has been clearly traced in the case of Connecticut, but the story could be repeated in other states as well.

The earlier banks had been democratic in organization, but after 1800 became much less so. There was, for example, no longer any provision limiting the number of shares which might be held by any one individual, and the voting powers were also altered so as to do away with the advantages hitherto possessed by the smaller holders; and voting-strength came to depend wholly on the number of shares held. Moreover, the price of bank shares rose, thus tending to make them a rich man's investment. An examination of the names of stockholders of the leading Connecticut banks reveals the close connection — often the identity — of the stockholders and the leading politicians of the state. The Eagle Bank, for example, had among its directors Senator James Hillhouse, Theodore Dwight, Simeon Baldwin, Speaker Sylvanus Backus, Roger M. Sherman, and Timothy Dwight. As has been said, "a stronger combination in church and state or a group of more confirmed office-holders would be difficult to pick." Yet the same lines of influence can be traced in other institutions.[1]

By the Act of 1803 the connection between politics and finance had been made even closer by providing for the investment of the surplus funds of the state in bank stocks, giving the dominant party, in connection with the financiers, a powerful weapon. The rise of the insurance companies brought a new factor into the combination. Between 1803 and the end of the war there had been organized the Norwich Marine Insurance Company with a capital of $50,000–$100,000, the Middletown Marine Insurance Company with a capital of $60,000–$150,000, the Union Insurance Company with $100,000–$150,000, the Hartford Company with $150,000–$250,000, the New Haven

[1] Purcell, *op. cit.*, pp. 104 *ff.*

Company with $200,000, and the Middletown Company with $150,000–$300,000. These were all controlled by the same group who controlled the banks and dominated the legislature.[1] It may be noted that in 1818 the position of a corporation as such was greatly strengthened in the whole country by the decision in the Dartmouth College case, which Daniel Webster argued for his alma mater before the Supreme Court of the United States. The New Hampshire legislature had attempted to introduce certain changes in the management of the college and its funds, but the Supreme Court decided that a charter once given was a contract, and was therefore inviolate under the Federal Constitution.[2]

In spite of all the opposition to the clergy in politics and the decline in their power, they were still at this period the more important partners in the political alliance of the various "interests," and just as the banks, insurance companies, and other corporations introduced changes in methods of exerting influence by the capitalists, so the many moral and religious societies which now began to be founded were used as political levers. The Reverend Lyman Beecher discloses the process to some extent in his autobiography. Speaking of the organization of the "Society for the Suppression of Vice and Promotion of good Morals," he said that some of the clergy met in Judge Baldwin's office and invited some eight or more of the leading lawyers to be present. "That was a new thing in that day," he adds, "for the clergy and laymen to meet on the same level and coöperate. . . . The ministers had always managed things themselves, for in those days the ministers were all politicians. . . . On election day they had a festival. . . . And when they got together, they would talk over who should be governor, and who lieutenant-governor, and who in the Upper House, and their counsels would prevail."[3] The Missionary Society, the Connecticut Bible Society, the Ministers Annuity Society, the Charitable Society, and others seem all to have been mixed up with politics. The Bible Society and

[1] Purcell, *op. cit.*, pp. 112 *f.*
[2] G. T. Curtis, *Life of Daniel Webster*, (New York, 1870), vol. I, pp. 163 *ff.*
[3] *Autobiography*, vol. I, p. 259.

Ministers' Annuity Society, for example, used to meet at Hartford on election day. The lay trustees were the Federalist bosses, no Republicans appearing on any of the Boards. The leaders in the societies, lay and clerical, were the real rulers of the state, and at the meetings religious and political business went along merrily together.

Beecher was right, however, in noting an alteration in the attitude of the people at large. "The mass is changing," he said in a sermon about this time. "We are becoming another people. Our habits have held us long after those moral causes that formed them have ceased to operate. These habits at length are giving way." [1] We have already noted the demand from time to time for a new Constitution that should embody the broader views as to suffrage and religious toleration, among other ideas which had gradually been gaining ground. Events were now to move rapidly in a direction that would make such a change in the form of government possible. On February 21, 1816, a meeting was held at New Haven composed of Republicans and Episcopalians, for the purpose of establishing a new opposition party which should harmonize various factions. As a result of this movement a state ticket was placed in the field by what came to be known as the American or American Toleration and Reform Party.[2] The choice of Oliver Wolcott as candidate for governor by the new party showed clearly the breadth of its appeal. Although religious toleration was the main plank in their platform, other popular issues were also included. The new party gave the Federalists a close run, and the following year actually succeeded in defeating them and electing Wolcott in the heaviest voting ever cast in the state, indicating the extent to which the public had been aroused by the issues. The Tolerationists also secured control of the Council and had a large majority in the Assembly.

In a bitterly partisan review of the proceedings of the legislature, a writer in the *Courant* complained that of the twelve members of the Council only four had been members before, and of the eight new ones several had never held even the office of justice of the peace. There were six lawyers, four merchants,

[1] *Autobiography*, vol. I, p. 262.   [2] Purcell, *op. cit.*, p. 332.

and two doctors, of whom five only were Presbyterians, five were Episcopalians, one a Baptist and one "doubtful." These figures are more indicative of the overturn in the state than is the fact that of the twelve Councilors only five were Federalists and the rest Democrats.[1]   In spite of this composition of the Upper House, its aristocratic tendencies constantly thwarted the will of the lower, and it was not until the Tolerationists won an even more sweeping victory at the polls in September that the way was open to carry out reform measures, and when, in the spring of 1818, they secured one hundred and thirty-two seats to only sixty-nine held by the Federalists, the revolution was complete.[2]   The way was now open to secure a new Constitution for the state, and the legislature ordered that the freemen should meet on July 4 to elect delegates to a constitutional convention to be held in August.

Great public interest was shown, and there was much discussion of the questions at issue.   The grievances against the existing order and state of things were well summed up in a pamphlet called *The Politics of Connecticut*, in which the author demanded a constitution which should be an expression of the public will, and complained of the limitations on the suffrage. It "is the poor man's poor defence and only protection against the exorbitance and oppression of the rich," it said; "and yet the rich urge that the poor man's exclusion from his solitary privilege is the only security of *their* property against *his* depredations." [3]   Religious disabilities figured largely in the discussion, and particularly the disgraceful law under which profession of Unitarianism was made a felony.   Anyone lawfully convicted of professing this belief, as well as Deism, Atheism, or Polytheism, could be declared incapable of holding any public office, civil or military, and if convicted a second time was disabled from suing or maintaining any action in law or equity, acting as guardian of any child, or serving as executor of an estate.[4]

---

[1] *Conn. Courant*, June 16, 1818.
[2] Purcell, *op. cit.*, p. 367.
[3] [G. W. Richards] *Politics of Connecticut*, (Hartford, 1817), p. 13.
[4] *Ibid.*, p. 20.   *Cf. Public Laws of Connecticut*, (Hartford, 1808), title LXVI, p. 17.

The results of the reform movement were embodied in certain statutes passed by the legislature, but more particularly in the new constitution.   The suffrage was broadened so as to include all free white males twenty-one years old or more, who paid taxes or served in the militia, were of good moral character, and had been residents in their towns four months.   The color line had first been drawn by the legislature at the May session in 1814, at which it was enacted that in addition to all other qualifications for a freeman he must be "a free *white* male person."   This distinction was maintained in the law of 1818, and was the subject of debate in the constitutional convention of that year, which voted the disfranchisement of the Negro by one hundred and three to seventy-two.   It may be noted that the distinction was maintained in the constitutional amendment of 1845, and that it was not dropped until 1876.[1]   There was practically no public discussion of this matter, but the Negro was also disfranchised at about the same time in Rhode Island under the law of 1822, which declared that thereafter only white persons could be eligible as freemen.[2]

The most important reform achieved in the new Constitution was the complete separation of Church and State.   Every denomination of Christians was given equal rights with every other, no taxes for religious purposes could be collected by the state, and any member of a church organization who wished to withdraw from membership was no longer liable for any of its expenses.[3]   Naturally there was a terrific outburst from the clergy and members of the established church, yet even Lyman Beecher, who opposed the change tooth-and-nail, lived to confess that it was "the best thing that ever happened to the State of Connecticut."[4]   Although there was some temporary difficulty over finances, the church, so far from losing moral influence, gained.

---

[1] J. T. Adams, "Disfranchisement of the Negroes in New England," *American Historical Review*, vol. XXX, p. 545.

[2] *Ibid.*, p. 546.

[3] Greene, *Religious Liberty*, p. 489.   Reports of the debates of the Convention may be found in the *Connecticut Courant*, Sept. 8 and the following issues.   *Cf.* also *Journal of the Proceedings of the Convention of Delegates*, (Hartford, 1873).

[4] *Autobiography*, vol. I, p. 344.

That was not foreseen at the time, however; and all those who had constituted the ruling powers in church and politics in earlier days fought against what they considered the ruin of the commonwealth as well as the end of their own influence — two things which those in authority are very apt to consider as conveniently identical. Federalists fairly foamed with rage at what they declared to be the unseemly haste with which the Constitution was to be framed and passed upon. It is "unparalleled in the proceedings of any nation," wrote one, "unless it may be revolutionary France, in the maddest part of her bloody career." [1] Although it had been provided that the Constitution should be ratified by a mere majority instead of two thirds of the people, it secured a majority of only fifteen hundred and fifty-four votes out of a total of twenty-six thousand two hundred and eighty-two,[2] and it was claimed that many of these were fraudulent. Nevertheless, the adoption marked a new era and the culmination of the movement which had started in 1776, and which had been balked and delayed by the entrenched powers of the Congregational church and the old ruling families.

As marking the trend of the times, we may note that the following year, 1819, a law was passed in New Hampshire providing that no person should be forced to join any church or contribute to the support of any ecclesiastical institution without his consent, thus following the example of Connecticut in completely divorcing Church and State.[3] On the other hand, an amendment to the Constitution of Massachusetts, proposed by the convention held in that state in 1820 for the purpose of revising the Constitution, which proposed to annul the clause in the Declaration of Rights compelling church attendance, was rejected by a majority of over eight thousand.[4] With inexplicable carelessness, considering the high quality of the

---

[1] *Conn. Courant*, Aug. 4, 1818.

[2] *Ibid.*, Oct. 13, 1818. This gives the votes by counties and towns.

[3] *Some Remarks on the "Toleration Act" of 1819*, (Exeter, 1823). This was written by an opponent of the Act, who claimed it had resulted in a great decrease in church membership.

[4] *Journal of Debates and Proceedings of the Convention of Delegates*, (Boston, 1853), p. 633.

members of the convention, this amendment was offered to the
people as involving three separate matters, two of which were
in no way germane to the other; and perhaps the fairer test of
public sentiment is to be found twelve years later, when the
religious portion of the amendment was again offered in better
form and adopted.[1]

In 1820 the religious test for office was done away with, as
was also the property qualification for the suffrage, any male
citizen paying a state or county tax — with slight exceptions
— being made eligible to vote.   As a matter of fact, in Massachusetts, unlike Connecticut, the property qualification under
the old Constitution had long been a dead letter, and the technical widening of the franchise did not result in increasing the
number of actual voters.[2]

In the various legal and constitutional changes occurring
within the years just before and after 1820, we have clearly
discernible, behind the dry legalistic formulæ, the striving to
complete the revolutionary movement of the preceding century
and to give to the common man those equal rights and opportunities which had been held out to him as lures in the Revolutionary propaganda and then subsequently to a great extent
denied to him.   The separation of Maine from Massachusetts
and the creation of a sixth New England State was in direct
line with the desire of the individual for greater freedom of self-
expression.   It was this separation, which occurred in 1820,
that was one of the main reasons for the revision of the Massachusetts Constitution just mentioned.

There had been a revival of the project of separation in 1816,
but the suggestion had been voted down in that year owing to
a very practical business drawback.[3]   Under the Federal coasting laws, vessels were permitted to go freely from any port in a
state to another in the same or an adjoining state, but if the
port to which they sailed were located in a state not immediately adjoining, then they were required to clear at a custom-

---

[1] Frothingham, *Constitution of Massachusetts*, p. 41.
[2] Morison, *Otis*, vol. II, p. 235 *n*.
[3] E. Stanwood, "The Separation of Maine from Massachusetts," Mass. Hist. Soc.,
Proceedings, Ser. III, vol. I, p. 149.

house, which entailed loss of both time and money. The coasting trade of the Province of Maine employed about fifty thousand tons of shipping and between two and three thousand seamen, being one ninth part of the entire coasting trade of the United States.[1]   So long as Maine continued a part of Massachusetts, not only was Boston within "the same state" but New Hampshire, Rhode Island, Connecticut, and New York were all "adjoining" states; but if separation should occur, then the only free interstate trade left would be with New Hampshire.   Friends of Maine, notably Rufus King, secured the passage of a law in Congress in 1819, opening the entire coasting trade of the United States to vessels from any domestic port, thus preparing the way for Maine to become independent of Massachusetts.   The question came up for settlement immediately following this.[2]

The territory of Maine, which comprised five sevenths of the whole of Massachusetts as then constituted and was greater than all the rest of New England combined, had a population of about three hundred thousand, which was expected to grow with the rapidity of the new Western states.   It was pointed out that the government at Boston was practically an absentee one, and that, as the representatives of Maine were always in a minority, the affairs of that vast province were certain to be managed in the interests of Massachusetts proper rather than in those of Maine, which thus occupied almost a colonial status. A more interesting argument, strongly urged, was that of the influence of independence upon the development of individuality.   "The pride of place has no inconsiderable effect on character," wrote one advocate.   "Look at the new states of the west.   Have they not produced to their country, men of distinguished virtues and talents, who probably would have lived unknown, and 'blossomed unseen,' if they had remained in their colonial or territorial condition?"[3]

There was only moderate opposition on the part of Massachusetts, and the legislature passed an Act permitting Maine to separate, provided she voted to do so, adopted a constitution,

[1] King, *Rufus King*, vol. VI, p. 212.
[2] *Eastern Argus*, March 16, 1819.   [3] *Ibid.*, March 30, 1819.

and received the sanction of Congress.[1] The vote of the inhabitants was overwhelmingly in favor of separate statehood, and
Governor Brooks therefore issued a proclamation for a constitutional convention. The changed sentiment of the day was
evident in the two important points of religion and the suffrage.
In the Constitution as adopted, complete toleration was provided, Church and State were divorced, and the suffrage was
granted to every male citizen of twenty-one years and upwards
who had resided in the state for three months, practically without exception.[2] A suggestion was made in the debates to ex-
clude Negroes, but was promptly voted down.[3] In December
the proposed Constitution was adopted by the people by a vote
of nearly ten to one in favor.[4]

The question, however, was not to be terminated as a merely
local one. The Democrats of Maine might prefer a state of
their own, and the Federalists of Massachusetts might be willing to wish them God-speed, so as to "give us a snug little
Federal State for the rest of our lives," as one of them said;[5]
but the rest of the Union had their eyes fixed upon the implica-
tions of this new condition of affairs. Old Massachusetts, it is
true, would be reduced by the scission to a state of the second
rank, inferior to New York as the leading power of the North;
but the addition of a new state would give that section two
additional votes in the United States Senate. It was only five
years since the Hartford Convention and the threatened secession of New England, and since then new causes of sectional
strife had arisen. For two years the question had been agitated of the admission of Missouri to the Union, and whether
it should be allowed to come in as a free or a slave state.
The South had been struggling in vain against the growing
anti-slavery feeling of the North to secure the extension of
slave territory, and now if Maine were admitted as a State,
the Northern influence in Congress would be still further

[1] *Ibid.*, May 11, 25 and June 1, 22, 1819.
[2] *Ibid.*, Nov. 2, 1819.
[3] *The Debates, Resolutions and Other Proceedings of the Council of Delegates*, (Portland, 1820), p. 95.
[4] *Eastern Argus*, Dec. 14, 1819.
[5] Quincy, *Josiah Quincy*, p. 374.

strengthened. When, therefore, the question came up of admitting Maine, the Southerners at once seized upon the idea of making the admission of Maine, which of course would come in as a free state, depend upon the admission of Missouri as a slave state.[1]

As a result of the political manœuvring it was finally agreed to admit Maine and Missouri both, without conditions, but with the further proviso, which constituted the famous Missouri Compromise, that slavery should be forever prohibited north of the parallel of latitude of 36° 30′, which was in fact approximately the southern boundary of Missouri. Up to this time, although there had been more or less antislavery feeling in New England, there were few workers in the cause, no organized propaganda, and but little crystallized public sentiment.[2] The question raised by the admission of Missouri would have aroused much interest and discussion in any case, but the coupling of it with the admission of Maine brought it home to New Englanders still more vividly. "The feelings of the country are highly excited by the present debate in Congress on the subject of slavery. It is shameful," wrote the Reverend Thomas Robbins in an unusually long entry for his laconic diary, in February 1820.[3] Town meetings and legislatures passed resolutions. At a meeting at Salem, December 1819, while the bills were still being debated in Congress, Judge Joseph Story spoke passionately on the need for an express prohibition of slavery in all territories, and against admitting any new states except on condition of abolishing slavery within their limits.[4] The New Hampshire legislature passed a resolve almost unanimously that slavery was a great moral and political evil, and should be tolerated only as a necessity, and that any further extension should be absolutely prohibited.[5] The Vermont legislature declared that slavery was incompatible with the

[1] J. A. Woodburn, "The Historical Significance of the Missouri Compromise," American Historical Association, *Report*, 1893, p. 259.
[2] A. D. Adams, *The Neglected Period of Anti-Slavery in America, 1808–1831*, Radcliffe College Monograph, No. 14, pp. 66, 95.
[3] *Diary of Thomas Robbins*, Boston, 1886, vol. II, p. 811.
[4] Story, *Joseph Story*, vol. I, p. 360.
[5] F. B. Sanborn, *New Hampshire*, (Boston, 1904), p. 303.

principles of all free government, and that the admission of another slave state might endanger the freedom of the Union.[1] On the other hand, the South was aroused to a defense of its "peculiar institution," and although the conflict between the two sections was put off for another generation, the attempt of the North at this time to limit the further extension of slavery caused Southern sectional feeling to develop, and from this debate may be dated a new era in the relations between the states. Thus, only five years after the ending of the war with England, America had almost forgotten Europe. Not only was it busily engaged in its own commercial and social affairs, expanding rapidly westward, but the chief political issue had become wholly American and utterly unrelated to any of the affairs of the Old World.

[1] *Records of Governor and Council*, vol. VI, pp. 542 f.

CHAPTER XIV

A CHANGING SOCIETY

Character of Parties — Widening Gulf between Rich and Poor — Foreigners — Pauper Problem — Anti-Catholic Feeling — Destruction of Charlestown Convent — Riots in Boston — Suffrage in Rhode Island — Changes in Transportation — Effect on Capital and Labor — Character of Labor Movement — The Ten-Hour Day — Strikes — Trades Unions — Working-men's Party — Panic of 1837

As we have frequently pointed out in both this and the preceding volume, there were two distinct movements in the American Revolution, one for independence of the mother country, and the other for the overthrow of aristocratic control. That the latter struggle assumed, on the whole, a moderate and peaceful aspect and did not repeat the bloody scenes of the well-defined course of revolutions in other countries was probably due in the main to the presence of ample free lands, both within the old colonies and to the westward. These lands not only served to draw off the more restless, energetic, and turbulent elements among the people, but by proving a constant drain on the man-power of the older communities tended to maintain the economic position of labor in them and to enable the poorer portions of such communities, on the whole, to maintain a more or less even standard of living. The vast economic changes which occurred in the quarter of a century from 1825 to 1850 upset the equilibrium of the old social structure in New England, and brought in a period of seething unrest, which expressed itself in a multitude of minor and short-lived parties and groups advocating a bewildering diversity of "isms." The remaining chapters of this volume will reveal some of the aspects of this period, although it is impossible to display all its manifold variety. Almost all the movements in reality but express forms of a single contest — that of the common man against the privileged classes for a greater share in the good things of life, whether it was for the suffrage, higher wages, shorter hours of labor, better education, social recognition, or what not.

By far the keenest foreign observer of this period of American life, and one of the sanest who has ever commented upon America at any time, saw clearly what underlay the multitudinous struggles and movements of the day. "All the domestic controversies of the Americans at first appear to a stranger to be incomprehensible or puerile," wrote De Tocqueville of his impressions when here in 1831. But he adds that, after studying all the many parties, the deeper do we perceive that they are all connected with the fundamental divisions that have always existed in free communities, of which "the object of the one is to limit, and that of the other to extend, the authority of the people." [1]

This was also clearly seen by many Americans themselves. "There can be but two parties in politics in this country, for any length of time," we read in the *Boston Statesman*. "Minor divisions, arising from local causes and personal preferences, must be again, as they always have been heretofore, swallowed up in the two great natural divisions, *Democratic* and *Aristocratic*. It is of very little consequence what parties are called." [2] We shall not, therefore, attempt to trace the rise and fall of the many political movements of this quarter of a century, but merely discuss the social unrest in some of its broader aspects.

To a great extent the division was still between the country and the town — a continuation of the old parties which we have followed from early in the beginning of the eighteenth century.[3] The country folk felt themselves exploited by the town dwellers with their control of the banks, shipping, rail-

[1] Alexis De Tocqueville, *Democracy in America*, (Cambridge, 1862), vol. I, pp. 226 *f.*
[2] Issue of March 6, 1830.
[3] *Cf.* Adams, *Revolutionary New England*, pp. 94 *ff.*, 154 *ff.* The division ran back even to earlier times.

330 NEW ENGLAND IN THE REPUBLIC

roads, and manufactures, and it was this rivalry that was to be "the lifeblood of Jacksonian Democracy." [1] The doctrine of equality and the opportunities offered by free land and a rapidly expanding society in a new country restlessly stirred the imaginations of the poorer classes.   "I never met in America," says De Tocqueville, "with any citizen so poor as not to cast a glance of hope and envy on the enjoyments of the rich, or whose imagination did not possess itself by anticipation of those good things which fate still obstinately withheld from him." [2] In the decades now beginning, however, there were two tendencies at work which emphasized the gulf between rich and poor and between town and country.   One was the change in the nature of employment, due to the growth of manufactures, and the other was the rapid increase in luxuries which wealth could buy.   Of the former we shall speak both in this and in later chapters.   Of the latter innumerable illustrations might be given, but we may take, at hazard, that of ocean travel.

In the earlier days there had been comparatively little difference between the accommodations to be enjoyed or suffered by rich and poor.   After 1820 passenger travel became an important branch of ocean commerce, but even as late as 1850 the conditions under which poor immigrants crossed the sea were indescribable.   The lower deck of an emigrant ship was in many cases no better than a slaver.   The common height between decks was only four to five feet, so that the herded masses could not even stand upright.   The still lower or "orlop deck" was nothing but a black hole, too bad to use even for cattle. [3]   In the official report of a member of the New York Academy of Medicine, who inspected the Ceylon on her arrival from Liverpool in 1847, we read: "We passed through the steerage . . . but the indescribable filth, the emaciated, half-nude figures, many with the eruption disfiguring their faces, crouching in their bunks or strewed over the decks . . . presented a picture of which neither pen nor pencil can convey a

[1] A. B. Darling, *Political Changes in Massachusetts, 1824-1848*, (Yale University Press, 1925), p. 3.
[2] *Op. cit.*, vol. II, p. 157.
[3] F. Kapp, *Immigration and the Commissioners of Emigration*, (New York, 1870), p. 20.

full idea. . . . Some were just rising from their berths for the first time since leaving Liverpool, having been suffered to lie there during the entire voyage wallowing in their own filth." [1]

Let us compare this with the fashion in which the new-rich could make the same journey. "The packet ships between New York and Liverpool," wrote an English traveler by no means uncritical of things American in 1824, "are fitted up in a style of the greatest magnificence. Indeed, everything is lavished upon them that luxury can devise, or comfort require. Handsome carpets, ornamented lamps, silk curtains, a profusion of gilding, glass, and mahogany; a piano-forte and sofas in the ladies cabin; baths, &c., &c. 'The Paris,' a packet-ship trading to Havre, had a cabin fitted up in the most splendid style I ever saw in any vessel, except perhaps in the Royal Yachts of the King of England. The curtains of the berths were of rich straw-coloured silk, and the sides of the cabins were of rosewood, mahogany, and curled maple. Moreover, the intervals between the doors of the different state rooms, were panelled with mirrors, and would have reminded me of the appearance of the 'Café des Milles Colonnes,' if that glory of the Palais Royal had not been far inferior in cleanliness." [2]

If the above contrast is more vivid than might be found in much else as yet in the lives of rich and poor, nevertheless it serves to bring distinctly before us the fact that money was now coming to buy far more in the way of ostentatious luxury than it could have done a generation earlier, and we must remember that the moneyed class was larger and much richer, whereas the working classes — to denote what is commonly understood by that misused term — were steadily falling behind in comparative purchasing power. The advances which the farmer and the artisan were making in petty comforts were as nothing compared with the rapid strides which the new-rich were making in opulence and display. There had never been economic or social equality in New England, — far from it, — but also there had never been so wide a gulf as was now rapidly

[1] T. W. Page, "The Transportation of Immigrants and Reception Arrangements in the Nineteenth Century," *Journal of Political Economy*, vol. XIX, p. 739.
[2] Blane, *Excursion through the United States*, p. 351.

broadening for all men to see. The result was a great increase in the exodus of the poorer people from that section to the larger opportunities and particularly the more democratic atmosphere of the West. There was also an increase in the number of immigrants from Europe, to take the places left vacant by the native emigrants, and a ferment in the mixed population thus developing. So many were moving from their old homes to found new ones in a West where "equality" still possessed some meaning that it was said: "The East was breaking up." The numbers who now swarmed in from the Old World also began to cause great anxiety and bitter feeling.

It is impossible to arrive at accurate figures for either movement, but even the approximations possible show striking results as to the migratory movement of the New Englanders and the replacement of the old stock with foreigners. Had the population continued to grow at the normal rate of natural increase from 1790 to 1840, that of Massachusetts would have been 1,321,709 instead of the actual figure of only 729,031, and of the whole of New England 3,515,074 instead of 2,212,908. This difference — of 592,678 in the case of Massachusetts and of 1,302,166 in that of New England — represents the loss by emigration of New Englanders and their descendants, less what was made up by the immigration of foreigners.[1] Even if the estimate of natural increase is too high, it is evident, as we know from other indications, that the loss to New England ran into hundreds of thousands. On the other hand, in the twenty-five years between 1820 and 1845 approximately 3400 foreigners entered New England by way of Portland and Falmouth, 35,000 by way of Passamaquoddy, and 60,600 by way of Boston, as well as several thousand through other ports. Moreover, on account of certain port-regulations, it is probable that a far larger number of immigrants found their way into New England than through her own ports directly, these others coming by way of Canada or New York and thence overland.

For the entire country, the figures for the decade from 1830 to 1840 were quadruple those of the previous one, and the problem began to attract serious attention. The greater part

[1] Jesse Chickering, *Immigration into the United States*, (Boston, 1848), p. 31.

of those entering were from Ireland, owing partly in the later years to the famine conditions prevailing there in 1826,[1] and in New England the problem came to be mainly one of the Irish and Catholics. It was they who lingered on the seaboard and manufacturing towns and created a problem that was at once racial, social, political, and religious.[2]

The subject was "one of great delicacy," a writer pointed out in 1841, and "involves many of the conflicting tastes, passions, and prejudices of this great community. . . . We admit the subject has a sting in it."[3] It was complained that the two races could not possibly understand each other, that the treatment meted out to the newly arrived Irishman, full of romantic idealism as to what he was to find in the new land, embittered him from the start. Stigmatized as an alien, "he falls into the circle of his fellow-countrymen, becomes one of the mass of ignorance and intemperance, which disgraces our cities, and is soon, in fact, little better than a colonist, in the land which he sought with" reverence. The "cool New Englander" was said not to understand the Celtic temperament, to be enraged at the Irishman's vehemence in politics, while the laboring class disliked the Irish, as they did more work for less pay.[4] Easy and fraudulent naturalization was felt to be the real source of the political difficulty of the problem, and it was estimated in 1836 that fully one sixth of the naturalized voters in the election of that year had obtained their papers by fraud.[5]

The character of many of the immigrants and certain conditions of their emigration from home did create a serious social problem. Foreign nations, notably the small German States, but also Great Britain, discovered that it was cheaper to ship paupers to America than to maintain them in almshouses at home. Indeed, some of the German States and Switzerland not only emptied their poorhouses but shipped over convicts

[1] T. W. Page, "The Causes of the Earlier European Immigration to the United States," *Journal of Political Economy*, vol. XIX, p. 769.
[2] J. R. Commons and others, *History of Labor in the United States*, (New York, 1921), vol. I, p. 413; "Immigration," *North American Review*, vol. XL, [1835], p. 464.
[3] "The Irish in America," *North American Review*, vol. LII, p. 192.
[4] *Ibid.*, pp. 205 f., 208.   [5] Page, *op. cit.*, p. 689.

condemned to life sentences.[1] England never sent criminals
in this period, but there was a considerable export of paupers,
the consul at Liverpool reporting five hundred being thus sent
at the expense of their parishes in 1832.[2] Apparently, however, this was done on a small scale compared with the total
number of emigrants, and created international ill-will out of
all proportion to the actual extent of the evil. Some of the
English colonies were worse offenders than the mother country.
Jamaica passed a law that every foreign vessel under one
hundred tons, most of that size being American, had to carry
away one pauper or other undesirable person. On complaint
by President Van Buren, Lord Palmerston at once ordered this
practice to be stopped.[3]

The extreme poverty of many of the immigrants and their
inability to settle themselves promptly in their new surround-
ings created a serious problem for all the seaboard towns where
they congregated. In 1832 the South Boston Almshouse held
only 340 natives as against 613 immigrants. In the same year
the Free Dispensary in Boston treated 854 Americans and 1331
immigrants, of whom 1234 were Irish, 72 English, and only 25
of other nationalities.[4] Four years later, of the 866 paupers
in the Boston House of Refuge, 516 were foreigners.[5]

With the increasing number of Catholics, the Catholic Church
began to show signs of broadening activity, as was natural
enough. In the summer of 1829 a weekly paper called *The
Catholic Press* was started at Hartford, and some months later
another, with the somewhat provocative title of *The Jesuit*,
was founded in Boston, the name being changed later.[6] In
1831 the Reverend Lyman Beecher entered the lists, and in
four lectures delivered in Boston vigorously opposed Catholic

[1] Page, *op. cit.*, p. 1018. *Cf.* Message from President Van Buren on Foreign
Paupers, *House of Repres. Doct. No. 370, 25th Cong., 2d Sess.,* 1838, p. 14.
[2] Report of Secretary of Treasury Relative to Deportation of Paupers from Great
Britain, *U. S. Senate Doct. No. 5, 24th Cong., 2d Sess.,* pp. 3 ff.
[3] Message from President Van Buren, *op. cit.,* pp. 2 f.
[4] Page, *op. cit.,* p. 1012.
[5] Report of a Select Committee on Foreign Paupers. *House of Repres. Doct. No. 1040,
25th Cong., 2d Sess.,* 1838, p. 3.
[6] *Christian Register,* July 25, Sept. 12, 1829; "Destruction of the Charlestown Convent," U. S. Catholic Historical Society, *Records and Studies,* vol. XIII, p. 106.

doctrine, and denounced the influence of that church in politics. It had ever, he said, been opposed to freedom, had always supported the most despotic governments, and was incompatible with republican institutions. If the liberties of the nation were ever overthrown, it would probably be by the combination of unprincipled men with Roman Catholics.[1] The Right Reverend Bishop Fenwick answered in another series of lectures, defending his Church from Beecher's attack, and the controversy stirred up much discussion and bad feeling.[2]

A convent of Ursuline nuns had been established at Charlestown and had become very popular as a school for girls of prominent families, numbering many Protestants among the boarders and attracting pupils whose homes were scattered from Canada to New Orleans. From about the time of Beecher's first attacks, many stories were circulated among the lower classes as to ill-treatment both of nuns and of scholars. It was even said that one of the girls had been murdered. There was no foundation whatever for any of these rumors, but Beecher again opened attack on the Catholics in several fiery sermons and other clergy followed. The mob in Boston and Charlestown, always easily stirred to action, now resolved to take a hand.[3] Anonymous notices were posted, proclaiming that if there were not an immediate legal investigation before August 14, the nunnery would "be demolished by the Truckmen of Boston."[4]

Although the selectmen of the town made a thorough investigation of the convent and in an official statement declared that there was no foundation for criticism, the threat was carried out. A mob of about four thousand persons attacked the building at night and burned it to the ground, the nuns and their sixty-two pupils escaping to Roxbury.[5] A large meeting of leading Protestants was at once held in Faneuil Hall to

[1] Digests of the lectures were given in the *New York Observer*, Jan. 29, Feb. 5, 1831. I have been unable to find them in complete form.

[2] *Boston Statesman*, Jan. 22, 1831.

[3] "Destruction of the Charlestown Convent," U. S. Cath. Hist. Soc., *Records and Studies*, vol. XII, pp. 69 ff.

[4] E. Tucker, *The Burning of the Ursuline Convent*, (Worcester, 1890), p. 11.

[5] *Vide* the *Records and Studies, cit. supra*, and "The Roxbury Committee of Vigilance," Mass. Hist. Soc., *Proceedings*, vol. LVIII, pp. 325 ff.

express their detestation of the outrage, but the authorities did little more than to make a farce of the subsequent proceedings. Nothing was done to make good the property loss of over $20,000, although for many years the matter was occasionally brought up in the legislature.[1]   Of those who had taken part in the riot, one hundred were arrested but only thirteen were indicted, and of those none were convicted except one young man who was pardoned shortly after.[2]   A book was published just at this time purporting to be the experiences of a girl in the convent but which was obviously not written in the language that would be employed by such a person as the reputed author.[3]   The feeling aroused in the lower orders of the Protestants, however, was running so high it was feared the Catholics might retaliate, and the troops were called out. Bishop Fenwick behaved with extreme good sense and moderation throughout, and warned his people, through the parochial priests, against violence, advising them to await the course of justice.[4]

Anti-Catholic riots occurred in New York and other cities, and the agitation was kept up in various New England newspapers.[5]   In June 1837 a serious riot occurred in Boston, starting between some firemen and some Irish who were waiting for a funeral to pass.   The numbers on both sides rapidly increased, and the Protestant mob finally sacked a number of houses belonging to the Irish after the latter had quieted down and stopped fighting.   It was necessary to call out the militia,

---

[1] *Vide* Report of Committee to Consider Indemnifying the Proprietors of the Ursuline Convent, *Mass. House Doct. No. 30*, 1842; Report of Special Committee on petition of Amos Lawrence and 2000 others, *Mass. House Doct. No. 32*, 1844.

[2] The trial is given in *Boston Statesman*, Dec. 6, 13, 27, 1834, and Jan. 3, 1835.

[3] *Six Months in a Convent, or the Narrative of Rebecca Theresa Reed*, (Boston, 1835). *Cf. An Answer to Six Months in a Convent, by the Lady Superior*, (Boston, 1835), and *A Review of the Lady Superior's Reply to ' Six Months in a Convent,' being a Vindication of Miss Reed*, (Boston, 1835).   There is quite a little contemporary literature on this topic.

[4] J. B. McMaster, *History of the People of the United States*, (New York, 1910), vol. VI, p. 229.

[5] *Boston Courier*, March 30, 1835.   The *Providence Journal* had an article on a "cargo of priests" recently arrived.   Nov. 19, 1835.   The *Connecticut Courant* stated that two Roman Catholic bishops had pledged $1,000,000 to Mexico to be used against Texas, etc., Dec. 7, 1835.   The *Boston Courier* gives an account of a meeting held to show the dangers of Popery, Jan. 14, 1836.   *Cf.* June 13.

and it took several companies, preceded by the Lancers and a troop of horse, to dispel the rioters.[1]

Another indication of strong feeling against the Irish was given a few months later on the occasion of a muster of six companies of militia.   One of these, known as the Montgomery Guards, composed of naturalized and native Irishmen, had recently been formed, and in accordance with the orders of the Adjutant-General, this company marched to the place of meeting.   When they appeared, the members of the other five companies, with few exceptions, abandoned their officers and left the field.   When the Guards returned to their armory, they were mobbed and assaulted with bricks and other missiles, behaving with perfect self-control themselves.   A few days later the Adjutant-General issued general orders strongly condemning the action of the other regiments for conduct "unbecoming the citizen and the soldier," and praising "the exemplary behavior of the Montgomery Guards under the trying circumstances." [2]   Although all of the Guards were American citizens enrolled in the service of the state, the *New York Journal of Commerce* spoke of them as "foreigners" who had had "the effrontery" and "total want of decency" to appear with arms in their hands.[3]

The rioting that occurred in many of the states and the bitter racial and religious feelings aroused cannot be laid wholly at the door of the more ignorant classes.   If the clergy did not hesitate to stir up religious hatred from their pulpits, easily translated by the mob into arson and pillage, so also the conservatives, anxious to maintain the existing state of things inuring to their own advantage, did not hesitate to invoke racial antagonism to defeat the demands for any change. Manhood suffrage was so nearly attained in all the New England states except Connecticut, where Negroes were excluded, and in Rhode Island, where the suffrage was still archaic, that the general unrest of the times did not cause much discussion of the franchise except in the latter state.   There, however,

---

[1] *Independent Chronicle*, June 14, July 12, 1837.
[2] *Ibid.*, Sept. 13, 20, 1837.
[3] Issue of Sept. 13, 1837.

the demands of the people on the one hand and the opposition of the privileged class on the other were to develop into a bitter struggle, only the beginning of which lies in the period covered by this chapter. In 1829 a meeting attended by twelve to fifteen hundred persons was held at Providence, and a mildly worded memorial was drawn up to present to the legislature. Owing to the high property-qualification required, — a freehold estate worth $134, — the number of adult males entitled to vote was only 8400 as against 12,365 who were disfranchised, while the oldest son of a freeman was also a freeman, even though he did not possess the property qualification. The memorial protested against the "feudal absurdity" of the latter provision and against the high property-requirement. It was pointed out that the suffrage laws of Rhode Island were far less liberal than those of any other state, and although denying that the petitioners asked for any great change, the memorial requested that the laws be amended so that at least a majority of the adult males might be made voters.[1]

The committee of the legislature to which the memorial was referred brought in a report that was both stupid and insulting. It said that there was nothing in the memorial which required attention, and although the committee stated that they had "not thought it necessary to inquire particularly how many of the signers are native citizens of the state," they went on to denounce the signers as foreigners, and then drew a red herring across the trail of the real controversy by playing on racial antagonism against both Irish and Negroes.[2] Although the controversy died down for the moment, nothing could have been better calculated to embitter the unenfranchised than this substitution of insult and abuse for reason by the ruling class.

In 1834 a convention assembled at Providence to consider the matter again, and a committee, of which Thomas W. Dorr was a member, drew up an address to the people, in which it

---

[1] *Providence Patriot*, April 1, 1829; *Newport Mercury*, April 4, 1829; *Manufacturers' & Farmers' Journal*, Nov. 30, 1829.

[2] Report of the Committee on the Subject of the Extension of the Suffrage, *Rhode Island House Report*, June 1829.

was pointed out that Rhode Island was now the only state in the Union which did not have a written constitution, and that it was improper that the legislature should alone determine the right of the people to vote. Not only did considerably less than one half of the men of the state possess the franchise, but so unequal was the representation that of those who did, one half elected fifty-one representatives to the legislature and the other half only twenty-one. The new problem arising from the rapid urban growth was shown by the fact that although Jamestown elected one representative for every eighteen freemen, Providence had only one for every two hundred and seventy-five. But again the demands for reform were blocked.[1] The injustice of unequal representation, owing to changes in population, had become a crying evil throughout New England, but Vermont was the only state which attempted to remedy it.[2]

The change from rural to urban conditions of life was now well under way. Boston, which had a population of 43,298 in 1820, rose to 93,383 by 1840; and taking the country as a whole, the proportion of the total population living in cities of over 8000 people nearly doubled in the two decades. This made possible an increase in the feeling of solidarity among the laboring class, although it is a mistake to think, as yet, of a large manufacturing population crowded into industrial centres.[3]

The new transportation facilities, however, were beginning rapidly to transform the position and character of labor. The first great change came with the opening of the Erie Canal in 1825, by which the cost of transportation from Buffalo to New York was reduced from a hundred dollars a ton to twenty-five and even fifteen, and the time of passage from twenty days to eight. At first this served to tap only western New York, but with the extremely rapid rise of shipping on the Great Lakes a

[1] *An Address to the People of Rhode Island from the Convention Assembled at Providence,* (Providence, 1834), pp. 19 *ff.* There was little change made during the years immediately following, and Negroes continued to be disfranchised. *Rhode Island Acts and Resolves,* Jan. 1836, p. 3; June 1840, p. 26.

[2] *Journal of the Convention . . . together with the Amendments of the Constitution,* (St. Albans, 1836), pp. 25 *ff.*

[3] Commons, *History of Labor,* vol. I, p. 176; A. B. Darling, "The Workingmen's Party in Massachusetts, 1833-1834," *American Historical Review,* vol. XXIX, p. 84.

vast region was opened up, both as a source of agricultural products and as a market for manufactured goods.[1] The enormous success of this canal, which threatened to deprive Philadelphia of its trade to the West, forced Pennsylvania to construct a combined canal- and rail-system to Pittsburgh. New England remained more isolated than ever, and it was only about 1838 that by linking up several small railroads Boston was able to secure a through line to Albany, and thus tap the West by way of the Erie Canal. By that time there was war to the knife in railroad-building between New York and Pennsylvania for the Western trade, and Boston was struggling to exchange her oil, fish, and manufactured goods for corn and wheat at Oswego.[2]

This vast widening of the domestic markets had its effect on both capital and labor. It greatly increased the profits and power of the merchant capitalists as the farmers and manufacturers now looked to them to market their products and both became largely dependent upon them. The manufacturer, always short of capital, now began to appeal to the merchant for capital as well as for outlets for his products.[3] The merchant capitalists, in turn, competing with each other and anxious to secure as much as possible of the rapidly expanding but highly competitive markets, sought to reduce the cost of goods. They tried to hold down or lower wages and even to alter the whole scheme of production by the use of convict labor. Moreover, the increased means of travel, passenger as well as freight, made it more feasible to transport workers from one section to another, and made the manufacturer less dependent upon those in his immediate neighborhood.[4] In one respect the American worker was not opposed to what has come to be called the Industrial Revolution. There are practically no instances in which he objected to the introduction of machinery. What he did object to, and strenuously, was

[1] Johnson, *For. and Dom. Commerce*, vol. I, pp. 230 ff.; L. K. Mathews, "The Erie Canal and the Settlement of the West," Buffalo Hist. Soc., *Publications*, vol. XIV, pp. 189 ff.

[2] *Independent Chronicle*, Jan. 3, 1838. Cf. *History of Transportation in the United States before 1860*, ed. B. H. Meyer, (Washington, 1917), pp. 318 ff.

[3] Commons, *Hist. of Labor*, vol. I, p. 154.   [4] *Ibid.*, pp. 154 f., 440.

what he conceived as his exploitation by the new capitalist producers, who had acquired their wealth as distributors rather than producers, and who had suddenly arisen in a hitherto but little differentiated society.[1]

The conditions of the workers' lives, as well as many of their grievances, fall more properly into later chapters, and we shall here consider only their attitude and earlier struggles to free themselves from what they felt was a menace to their standing as human beings, deserving equality of treatment and opportunity. The workingmen of this period were fighting not only for wages and shorter hours but for all sorts of reforms in legal practice — education, temperance, land tenure, the treatment of women and children, and other matters. In short, they were fighting to maintain and improve a position they had held in a society which had been primarily agricultural and simple, and were not fighting as wage-earners forming a separate class in a highly organized industrial organization. In a Fourth of July address before the Democratic workingmen of Milford, Abel Cushing named "the pursuit of wealth, character, and consequence in the community," as the rights for which the Democrats were striving.[2] It was the last, the loss of "consequence in the community," due to the rapid rise of an extremely rich class and to the new conditions of labor, that troubled the mind of the laboring man more than anything else at this time. He was trying to save the social recognition — such as it had been — which he had received in the past, and to maintain his status, rather than to combat the specific evils of a new system. Organization was comparatively slow in New England, and little was done in that section before 1840, as compared with other parts of the country, to shorten the hours of labor.

There were, however, two notable strikes that we may consider for the light which they shed on the mind and methods of the capitalists at this period. The hours of labor varied in different employments. In manufacturing, the Eagle Mills at Griswold, Connecticut, for example, required fifteen hours

[1] Norman Ware, *The Industrial Worker, 1840–1860*, (Boston, 1924), p. xi.
[2] *Boston Statesman*, July 19, 1834.

and ten minutes actual labor per day, while another in the vicinity demanded fourteen hours.[1]   A report to the Massachusetts Senate noted that in that state the time of employment for children in the mills was usually thirteen hours a day, excepting the Sabbath, which "leaves little opportunity for daily instruction." [2]   In the trades and crafts the old custom of "from sunrise to sunset" still prevailed, having been taken over from agriculture.   Complaints of the evils of lack of leisure began to be heard, and in 1825 the first great strike for the ten-hour day was brought on by the carpenters of Boston.

The journeymen passed resolutions declaring that the existing condition was both unjust and inhumane, and that thereafter ten hours should constitute a working day.   The master carpenters at once countered with a set of resolutions in which they said that they learned "with surprise and regret" of the formation of a combination to alter the length of a day's work from "that which has been customary from time immemorial"; that the measure was calculated "to exert a very unhappy influence on our apprentices, by seducing them from that course of industry and economy of time, to which we are anxious to enure them"; that "it will expose the Journeymen themselves to many temptations and improvident practices"; that they dreaded the consequences upon the morals of society; that they would employ no journeyman who persisted in the demand; and would make no change in the hours.[3]

Back of the master carpenters, however, and still more important as opponents of labor, were the capitalists on whom the masters were dependent for work.   A number of these "gentlemen engaged in building the present season," as they styled themselves, at once came to the assistance of the masters in resisting the demands of the men for the same working hours that had already been accepted in New York.   They stated that they would support the masters to the extent, if necessary, of suspending all building for the entire season, and would not

---

[1] Seth Luther, *An Address to the Working Men of New England*, (Boston, 1832), p. 20.
[2] J. R. Commons and others, *A Documentary History of American Industrial Society*, (Cleveland, 1910), vol. V, p. 59.
[3] Commons, *Doct. Hist. Amer. Indus. Soc.*, vol. VI, p. 77.

employ any journeyman who persisted in the demand for the ten-hour day. Their resolutions were fully flavored with hypocritical cant, which was peculiarly galling to those who had not happened to make a fortune by speculating in land, by legislative favors, army contracts, or other and more legitimate methods. It was bad enough for the workman to feel himself inexorably slipping more and more into the power of the new-rich, but to be told that he belonged to a different order of humanity, that he was not entitled to leisure, and that he would go to pieces morally if he were not kept working for longer hours than the Southern Negroes, was a gratuitous insult.

It was this assumed moral superiority of the rich which accounted for much of the bitter feeling against them. The capitalists complained in their resolutions that if the "confederacy" to secure shorter hours should be countenanced by the community, the demand would spread to "all the Working Classes . . . opening a wide door for idleness and vice, and finally commuting the present condition of the Mechanical Classes, made happy and prosperous by frugality, orderly, temperate and ancient habits, for that degraded state, by which in other countries, many of these classes are obliged to leave their homes, bringing with them those feelings and habits, and a spirit of discontent and insubordination to which our native Mechanics have hitherto been strangers." The capitalists say that "all combinations by any Classes of Citizens, intended to regulate or effect the value of labor by abridging its duration, are in a high degree unjust and injurious to all other classes, inasmuch as they give an artificial and unnatural turn to business and tend to convert all its branches into Monopolies." [1]

Harrison Gray Otis was chairman of the capitalists' committee, and he and the other gentlemen evidently had no objections to monopolies or "artificial and unnatural turns" given to business by, for example, bank charters secured by political party influence, or benefits derived from the duties of a protective tariff for manufactures. Otis himself had endeavored quietly to secure a bank charter from the legislature so worded as to give himself and a few associates permanent

[1] *Ibid.*, pp. 79 ff.

control, regardless of the number of stockholders, and also, after having become a heavy investor in cotton mills, had turned from a freetrader to a protectionist — both surely "artificial and unnatural turns." [1]   That he and others of his class and outlook were honest in thinking that it was a very reprehensible matter for workmen to attempt to secure better hours or wages, whereas it was quite proper for themselves to secure special privileges from government, is probably true. That fact simply illustrates all the more clearly what government would become eventually, if entrusted wholly to any one class, and reconciles one somewhat to democracy with all its obvious and glaring faults.   It makes all the difference in the world whose ox is being gored.   When workmen combined to raise wages it was revolutionary, but when a few years later the Boston coal dealers combined to advance the price of coal fifty cents a ton, though "there was no reason but their avarice," the conservatives had no complaint. [2]

Although the carpenters' strike proved unsuccessful, a number of less important strikes followed, and the agitation for the ten-hour day was maintained. [3]   In 1831 an important step was taken in the formation at Providence of "The New England Association of Farmers, Mechanics, and other Working Men." The organization lasted only from December of that year to October 1834, but held three conventions at which delegates from five states took part.   It was pledged to the ten-hour day, and its activities were partly economic and partly political, leading to the reëntry of workingmen into politics in 1833 and 1834.   The note of resentment against the attitude of the rich appears quite as clearly as the demand for more leisure in the resolutions of the Association.   At the first convention complaint was made of "the low estimation in which useful labor is held by many whose station in society enables them to give the tone to public opinion." [4]   In the call

---

[1] Morison, *Otis*, vol. I, p. 260; vol. II, pp. 288 *f.*
[2] *Niles Register*, vol. LIX, p. 132 [1840].
[3] There were several strikes in Boston in 1830 and 1831, and one at Taunton, all for shorter hours.   Some of the employers looked favorably on the contention of the men. *16th Annual Report of the Commissioner of Labor*, 1901, p. 725.
[4] Commons, *Hist. of Labor*, vol. I, p. 303.

for the second convention it was pointed out that the learned professions were crowded, and that all those who could resorted to some means of living by their wits without hard physical toil, and effected various combinations to consolidate their position and advantages, "whilst the more industrious and useful portion of the community, who are too intent upon their daily occupation to form combinations for mutual advantage, or to guard against the devices of their better informed or more enterprising neighbours, are reduced to constant toil, stripped of the better share of their earnings, holding a subordinate, if not degraded situation in society, and frequently despised by the very men and women and children, who live at ease upon the fruits of their labour." [1]

In 1832 occurred the ship-carpenters' strike in Boston, and again it was the capitalists and shipowners, rather than the master carpenters, who took the lead in suppressing the strike, subscribing, it is said, $20,000 for the purpose and attempting to import workmen from other places as strike-breakers. They forced the master carpenters into line with themselves rather than with the workmen, and the strike was lost to the men in ten days, the capitalists stating that they would employ no man who was a member of any combination.[2] In the same year a strike occurred among the weavers at the Thompsonville Manufacturing Company's plant in Connecticut, which resulted in the company's bringing suit against the strike-leaders, whom they had imprisoned on a charge of conspiracy. Three separate trials took place, but in 1836 a verdict was rendered in favor of the men, the case having attracted much attention as the first of its kind in the country.[3]

The extreme lengths to which the owners of plants were willing to go to combat the new tendency to combination among the employees is shown by the extraordinary agreement which was drawn up by the Cocheco Manufacturing Company of Dover, New Hampshire, and which they required all their employees to sign. The workers were forced to agree to abide

---

[1] *Ibid.*, vol. I, p. 304.
[2] *Ibid.*, vol. I, pp. 312 f.; *16th Annual Rept. Comm. of Labor*, p. 725.
[3] Commons, *op. cit.*, pp. 313 f.

by all the regulations which the company then had in force or might thereafter adopt; "to work for such wages per week, and prices by the Job, as the Company may see fit to pay"; to be subject to all fines imposed; not to quit their jobs under two weeks' notice, and if they did, to forfeit two weeks' pay; not to enter into any combination "whereby the work may be impeded, or the Company's interest in any way injured," and if they did, to forfeit all pay then due; and to accept the monthly payment of wages.[1]

Two years later the first Trades Union in New England was formed in Boston, representing sixteen trades and their several organizations. It lasted only about a year, but is interesting as showing that the division between workmen and employer was not yet complete, and that the masters felt a certain solidarity of interest with their men — which feeling was being undermined by the capitalists, who were taking every means and opportunity to force the masters over to their own side. In admitting masters to the union, the workmen gave as explanation that "the interest of all who obtain their living by honest labour is substantially the same, since the boss is often brought back to journeywork by hard luck, and the journeyman may expect in his turn to become an employer, while both of them are invariably imposed upon and treated as if belonging to an inferior grade of society by those who live without labour. . . . There are in truth but two parties in the country," it continued, "the mechanics, farmers, artisans and all who labour, whether as boss or journeymen" and "the rich men, the professional men, and all who now live, or who intend hereafter to live, without useful labour."[2]

The economic cleavages which were to be formed in society by the Industrial Revolution were, in fact, but just beginning to appear. When the Workingmen's Party entered State politics in Massachusetts, in 1834, it made a strong appeal for the support of the workers in the mills and factories, but received scant encouragement from that quarter. A distinct factory population had not yet developed, and the party was not an

[1] Luther, *Address to the Working Men*, p. 36.
[2] Commons, *op. cit.*, vol. I, p. 378.

urban but a rural one, Boston contributing hardly one seventh
of its votes in its first campaign. Its urban element was
mainly made up of carpenters, masons, and other mechanics,
rather than of mill workers, who held more or less aloof. To
a great extent the party voiced the growing fear and dislike of
the country for the wealthy classes in the cities, who were
exploiting labor of all sorts and developing manufactures. It
may be said to have been merely the radical wing of the Democratic Party, itself a "country" party, and very soon merged
with it.[1]

"Who but the labourer, the mechanic, the farmer, the working men of every description" are the true democrats, a writer
asked. Others may be in the party, but "the working classes
of our country constitute the bone and sinew of democracy.
They feel their principles and their daily experience is calculated to fix and confirm them." They "are constantly insulted
and sneered upon by the rich and proud," and "must act with
more energy. They must first revolutionize the state by breaking down the usurped power of the Boston and Salem aristocracy, and the sprigs of nobility in other towns." [2]

The Democratic Party, as well as the great mass of the common people in New England, was greatly opposed to the protective tariff, and in the period covered by this chapter the
contest had not yet been settled among the capitalists themselves, although the manufacturing interest was becoming
steadily more powerful as compared with the shipping. There
is little in the arguments for and against protection appearing
at this time which we are not familiar with to-day, after a
century of discussion, and we need not be detained by arguments, threadbare and worn, but still current on both sides.
Most although not all of the merchants who gradually transferred their capital from ships to factories became acutely alive
to the necessity of protecting the American workingman —
and their own pocketbooks — against foreign competition,

[1] Darling, "Workingmen's Party in Massachusetts," pp. 81 *ff.* The organization
meeting of the party is reported in the *Boston Statesman*, Sept. 4, 1830.
[2] Quoted from the *Lynn Mirror and Essex Democrat* in the *Boston Statesman*, Sept.
11, 1830.

though the workingman himself clung stubbornly to free trade. In the vote on the tariff of 1828, the representatives of New England in Congress were twenty-four against to fifteen in favor of protection. The gradual shift is noticeable by 1832, when the actual votes were tied, seventeen to seventeen, with five absent.[1] The tremendous excitement which characterized the tariff controversy of 1832–34, with the threatened nullification by South Carolina, belongs rather to national than to sectional New England history.

This controversy, with the threatened action of South Carolina, appeared to be the only dark cloud on the business sky in 1832, when Jackson began his long contest with the United States Bank. When in midsummer of the following year that institution began to contract its loans, following the removal of the Government deposits, the money market distinctly felt the strain. By the end of 1833 and the beginning of 1834 the country was in the throes of panic. Forty failures occurred in New Bedford and ninety-three in Boston, to name only two points.[2] By October, however, the worst was over, and by 1835 the country had apparently wholly recovered. Speculation ensued on an enormous scale. The sale of public lands increased from $5,000,000 in 1834 to $25,000,000 in 1835. Vast sums had been spent on canals and other public works. In two years the excess of imports over exports had been over $111,000,000.[3] Nearly three hundred and fifty new banks were chartered between 1830 and 1837, of which New England had more than its share, Connecticut organizing twenty-two and Massachusetts seventy-two.[4] Speculation in real estate became a mania, not only in towns and cities but even in the wilderness. In five years the valuation of New York City real property jumped from $250,000,000 to $403,000,000. In a short period before the bubble burst, building-lots in such a place as Bangor, Maine, rose from $300 to $1000, and, on the

---

[1] *Speech of R. C. Winthrop in House of Representatives, Dec. 30, 1841,* (Washington, 1842), p. 9.
[2] McMaster, *Hist. of U. S.,* vol. VI, p. 198; *Boston Statesman,* March 29, 1834.
[3] Commons, *Hist. of Labor,* vol. I, p. 454.
[4] *Patriot and Democrat,* March 14, 1840; R. C. McGrane, *The Panic of 1837,* (University of Chicago Press, 1924), p. 13.

absurd rumor that the timber supply of that state was almost
exhausted, timber lands jumped upward from three to five
hundred per cent in price.[1]

By the spring of 1836, however, money was becoming tight,
and by April it was said that borrowers were paying a premium
of ten per cent a month in New York, while the prices of labor
and living were very high.[2]   The famous Specie Circular, issued
by President Jackson in July, greatly increased the financial
stringency, and when Van Buren took office in March 1837 he
refused to repeal it.[3]   Within a few weeks the crash came,
beginning with the failure of large cotton-houses in New Orleans,
with liabilities estimated at from $9,000,000 to $10,000,000.
Heavy failures of houses involved with these followed in New
York.[4]   On May 10 the banks of that city suspended payment,
followed about a week later by those in Philadelphia, Baltimore, Albany, Hartford, Boston, New Haven, Providence,
Mobile, Washington, and other cities.[5]   In all, during the
year six hundred and eighteen banks failed.   In April some
of the most important mills in Lowell were considering closing
down, and so rapid was the devastation wrought that by July
it was estimated that a hundred thousand laboring men were
idle in New England, with perhaps twice that number on half
pay.[6]   In what had become one of the leading industries of
Massachusetts, boot and shoe manufacturing, scarcely a manufacturer escaped bankruptcy, and it was said that fifty thousand persons were unemployed in the various branches of the
leather industry.[7]   By the same month, nearly one half of all
the spindles in Massachusetts had ceased operation, and it
was reported that a large part of them could not be started
again without raising new capital.[8]

By the spring of 1838 the financial situation was beginning
to clear.   Specie was pouring into the country from Europe,
in April of that year three ships bringing in about $1,000,000

---

[1] *Ibid.*, pp. 45, 47.   [2] *Independent Chronicle*, April 13, 23, 1836.
[3] Money loaned in Boston at from two per cent to four per cent a month. *Independent Chronicle*, Feb. 4, 1837.
[4] *Ibid.*, March 22, 1837.   [5] *Ibid.*, May 24, 1837.   [6] *Ibid.*, April 22, July 11, 1837.
[7] Hazard, *Boot and Shoe Industry*, p. 65; *Independent Chronicle*, July 11, 1837.
[8] *Ibid.*, July 15, 1837.

each in gold.[1] The banks of New England and most other sections resumed specie payments, but it was not until five years later that the country may be said to have recovered to any marked extent. As late as 1839 the state of Maine had in part to suspend payment, because the state treasurer found it impossible to borrow money either in Europe or America.[2] In fact, it was not until the discovery of gold in California reinvigorated the channels of trade that the hard times may be said to have ended.

In so far as the richer classes were concerned, there was, of course, a vast shifting of property. Some men went down; others gradually came up to take their places. The general social effects, including a changed outlook on the times, was more marked among the farmers and laborers of one sort and another. Although there was a great drop in the price of all articles and commodities, agriculture seems to have suffered most. A Western paper made the calculation that, before the panic, a farmer who carried a hundred bushels of wheat to market could buy a certain list of necessities and luxuries, and have $85.12½ left out of his $100, whereas in 1840, after selling the same amount of wheat and buying the same articles, he had only 12½ cents left.[3]

The effect on the frame of mind of labor was marked, and the long period of depression following on the panic brought about a feeling of social unrest that was hitherto unknown in similar intensity in America. Lack of employment created a far more bitter attitude toward immigration than we have already noted. Moreover, the first outbreak of panic, with the wholesale discharge of workmen, crushed out the nascent labor-movement, and trade organizations. Local societies, trades-unions, the national trades-unions, almost all organizations as well as the newspapers that labor had started, all disappeared.[4] In the following decade organized labor-movements became negligible, and in their place we shall have to deal with all sorts of humanitarian and speculative reforms, while labor turned more and more to politics and the ballot.

---

[1] *Patriot and Democrat*, April 28, 1838.
[2] *Kennebec Journal*, Sept. 3, 1839.
[3] McGrane, *op. cit.*, p. 175.
[4] Commons, *Hist. of Labor*, vol. I, p. 456.

CHAPTER XV

HUMANITARIANISM

Development of Literature — Unitarianism — Transcenden-
talism — Woman's Rights — Brook Farm — Education — School
Buildings — Teachers — Nonattendance — Imprisonment of
Debtors — Prisons — Blind — Deaf and Dumb — Insane —
Temperance — Peace Societies

THE War of the Revolution, the years of political turmoil following, and the two decades of entanglement with European affairs from 1794 to the end of our war with England in 1815 had left little inclination for the cultivation of literature in America. Almost insanely partisan politics, a bitter struggle for commercial life, and a hated military conflict were not conducive to fruits of the spirit. We have already noted, however, the extraordinarily abrupt change which came over the American mind with the signing of peace; and there were at that time a number of lads in different towns of eastern New England whose most impressionable years were to be influenced by the new outlook, and who a few years later were to bring about a marked literary movement in that section.

In the same year in which the war ended, 1815, the *North American Review* was founded at Boston, and although it was modeled on the British quarterlies, it was to serve for two generations as the vehicle for the expression of native American scholarship and letters. Seven years after its founding, three thousand copies were printed of each number, as compared with two thousand copies of the American editions of the *Edinburgh* and *Quarterly* together.[1] It was not, however, until the lads just mentioned grew into manhood that there occurred

[1] Blane, *Excursion through the U. S.*, p. 458.

the remarkable flowering of the New England spirit in literature which was a part of the new age both in Europe and
America — a flowering of native growth, though its roots were
in Europe.

Many of the leaders in what is frequently called — rather
grandiloquently and provincially — the "New England Renais-
sance" spent some years in Europe under the direct influence
of European thought before they began their work at home.
The year 1815 saw Edward Everett and George Ticknor
landed in Germany for study at Göttingen, and two years later
George Bancroft was also there. Prescott, Longfellow, and
Emerson had all three been abroad for shorter or longer stays
before writing anything at home. In the decade or so following 1830, after a half-century of almost complete intellectual
and artistic sterility in New England, there suddenly appeared
a first slender volume of verse by Whittier (1831), the first
volume of Bancroft's *History of the United States* (1834), Emerson's *Nature* and the other essays in that volume (1836), Hawthorne's *Twice-told Tales* (1837), Prescott's *Ferdinand and
Isabella* (1838), Longfellow's *Verses of the Night* (1839), and
Lowell's first volume of verses two years later. Many lesser
writers were following in the wake of these, while the rhetorical
orations of Webster and Everett held audiences enthralled.
It was as though, after an interminable succession of starless
nights, a wind had suddenly arisen, which, sweeping away the
clouds, allowed star after star to shine forth. It is true that
with the exception, perhaps, of Emerson none of them were
of the first magnitude. It is no part of our task here to appraise the permanent position of these men. Long over-
praised, due to the void surrounding them and the strong
national sensitiveness of their own generation, it is the duty of
the literary critic rather than of the historian to take their
just measure. What interests us is their sudden appearance,
as indicative both of the change that was coming over the mind
of America and of the influence they exerted.

Their emergence marked not America's maturity nor even
its coming of age, but its adolescence — the sudden discovery
of romance, of culture, of altruism, of optimism, of self-reliance,

and the sense of one's own individuality. These are all qualities of youth, and one is most struck by the youthfulness of
this whole period. It is the spirit of youth that is reflected in
the literature as well as in the life of the times. Bancroft sang
the praises of the new nation and of democracy until, as has
been said, his volumes "voted for Jackson." Longfellow ran-
sacked literature after literature of Continental Europe in
search of legend and romance to form the subjects of his poems.
Optimism, self-reliance, and the infinite possibilities inherent
in the individual were preached by Emerson and lesser men.
In the humanitarian movements with which the age was rife
we see altruism developing with all the enthusiasm of the
young and untried. In such experiments in living as Brook
Farm, the most significant note is the lyric one of youthful
buoyancy and confidence. The age had its dark side, a deep
shadow under which it lived, but at no other stage in our history either before or after do we find so much of the joy of living
translated into practice and genuine idealistic endeavor.

This was not an isolated phenomenon in America. We have
always shared in and been influenced by the currents of thought
and life in Europe, sometimes in turn, and — in more ways
than is often recognized — exerting our own refluent influence
upon the older world. At the same period which we are now
describing in New England there was in Europe, in the words
of John Morley, "a great wave of humanity, of benevolence,
of desire for improvement — a great wave of social sentiment,
in short," which "poured itself among all who had the faculty
of large and disinterested thinking."[1] This outburst ended
in several European countries in the revolutions of 1848. In
our country it ended in the Civil War. What we have to
trace, therefore, is only a local manifestation of a world movement.

The old strict Calvinism had been breaking down for several
generations, as we have seen in earlier chapters. Not only was
religious tolerance slowly growing as between sects, but even
within the Congregational Church itself there was a division
forming with little of the bitterness that would have been

[1] Quoted by O. B. Frothingham, *George Ripley*, (Boston, 1886), p. 109.

inevitable in the eighteenth century.   In 1805 the Hollis Professorship of Divinity at Harvard was given to a Unitarian ; but, in spite of opposition, strife between the liberal elements and the stricter Calvinists seems to have been more or less sedulously avoided on both sides.   The growth of the Unitarian movement within the old Church was, indeed, too obvious to escape all notice, and occasionally the fires of controversy burned brightly.   In 1815 there was a sudden flare-up in an attack upon the Liberals led by Dr. Morse, which was answered by John Lowell, one of the Harvard Corporation.   Against their will the Unitarians were forced to take a more independent attitude, which was reflected in a sermon preached by William Ellery Channing in Baltimore, Channing later becoming the leader of the movement in Boston.   A shock was also administered to the more strict Congregationalists by a court decision in 1820, which declared that when a majority of a church congregation should withdraw, — as they had done in the case under consideration owing to the election of a Unitarian clergyman, — the minority which might remain constituted the church, with all its property rights.[1]

In 1826 the controversy, which had been waged on neither side with any sustained bitterness, became more highly charged by the calling to Boston of the Reverend Lyman Beecher to take charge of the Hanover Church, on what came to be known as "Brimstone Corner."   How far Unitarianism had already spread at the time of Dr. Beecher's arrival is described by his daughter, Mrs. Harriet Beecher Stowe, who wrote that "all the literary men of Massachusetts were Unitarians.   All the trustees and professors of Harvard College were Unitarians. All the élite of wealth and fashion crowded Unitarian churches. The judges on the bench were Unitarian, giving decisions by which the peculiar features of church organization, so carefully ordained by the Pilgrim fathers, had been nullified." [2] Within a generation Unitarianism, instead of being a form of

---

[1] J. H. Allen, *The Unitarians*, (New York, 1894), p. 194.

[2] Lyman Beecher, *Autobiography*, vol. II, p. 110.   *Cf.* articles in *Boston Statesman*, March 26 and April 2, 1831, complaining of the undue influence of Harvard in politics, and that Unitarians held too many public offices, including the governorship and all but one of the Supreme Court judgeships.

dissent from an established church, with the social disabilities that such a position usually implies, became the religion of all the higher social circles of Massachusetts, and Calvinism occupied the lower social position of dissent.

There was, however, danger in this making Unitarianism the fashionable religion. It differed from the old Calvinism of New England in its belief in the fundamental goodness and soundness of human nature, not denying the existence of sin and suffering but minimizing them and looking upon both man and the world with perhaps a somewhat too easy optimism. Its tone was distinctly ethical and cool, rather than religious and emotional. These qualities, combined with the prompt adherence of the wealth and fashion of the state, tended to check the spirit of openmindedness and liberalism with which the movement had started, and to render it static. The innate conservatism of wealth and social position halted the advance, as tending to threaten the comfortable established order of things. That this was unconscious and not hypocritical did not lessen the effect. One of the most illuminating documents of the period, touching as it does upon almost every aspect of it, is the letter of resignation written by the Reverend George Ripley in 1840 — an action to which he had been led in part, he said, "by the present aspect of the times. . . . This is very different," he continued, "from what it was when I became your minister. In 1826 the Unitarian controversy was in the ascendant." The condition of religious thought at that time "promised well for the future. It awakened the brightest hopes in regard to the practical influence of religion in the community; to the spread of the pure, disinterested, and lovely spirit of charity in the various relations of society. . . . But this state of things it seems could not last forever. It passed away, and a new order of ideas was brought forward . . . A portion of the liberal clergy felt it their duty to carry out these views; to be faithful to their principles; not to shrink from their application . . . but in these conclusions they were divided from some of their brethren. It was thought dangerous to continue the progress which had been commenced. Liberal churches began to fear liberality, and the most heretical sect in Christendom to bring the charge of being so against those who carried out its own principles." [1]

So long as the Christian minister preaches vaguely and without in any way threatening the existing order of society, and above all the question of property, he is considered a pillar of society; but let him attempt to apply Christ's teaching to society rather than to the individual and it will be a rare congregation which will not draw back in fright. Ripley touched the sore point when he said that "the purpose of Christianity, as I firmly believe, is to redeem society as well as the individual from sin." As a Christian, he said that he believed it to be his duty to promote temperance, to "aid in the overthrow of every form of slavery"; that he held it to be a minister's duty to preach the gospel to the poor; and that his most frequent visits should be "not to the abodes of fashion and luxury but to the dwellings where not many of the wise and mighty of this world are apt to enter." He added that his "warmest sympathies should be with those who have none to care for them," and that he should "never be so much in earnest as when pleading the cause of the injured." [2] The church promptly accepted his resignation.

The Unitarian leader, Channing, himself realized the threatening danger as early as his Baltimore sermon in 1819. "Unitarianism," he said, "has suffered from union with a heart-withering philosophy. . . . Men will not be trifled with. . . . They want a religion that will take a strong hold upon them," as well as (he said elsewhere) "a poetry which pierces beneath the exterior of life to the depths of the soul." [3] This the more ardent souls and those who had, in Morley's phrase, "the faculty of large and disinterested thinking," were to find in that typically New England form assumed by the spirit of the age — Transcendentalism. It has recently been said that this was merely the intellectual and rather dry shape which European romanticism assumed in America,[4] but this is to miss somewhat of the real spirit of the movement.

[1] Frothingham, *George Ripley*, pp. 66 *ff.*
[2] *Ibid.*, p. 87.
[3] Quoted in *Cambridge History of American Literature*, (New York, 1917), vol. I, p. 331.
[4] Regis Michaud, *Autour d'Emerson*, (Paris, 1924), p. 139.

CITY OF BOSTON FROM THE HARBOR, 1853

From an unpublished pen-and-ink sketch by Thomas Kelah Wharton; original in the New York Public Library

It is, in truth, not easy of definition. There was nothing new in any part of its philosophical basis, which was mainly derived from Germany, in part directly and in greater part through the English writings of Coleridge. It also, to a lesser extent, had its roots in Greek and Oriental philosophies.[1] Interest in German metaphysics had been stirred by the return to Boston of the young men mentioned above who had studied at Göttingen, and also by the appointment of Charles T. Follen, a German political exile, as instructor at Harvard. The interest broadened, and in 1837 the Reverend Theodore Parker, in mentioning the additions to his private library in that year, noted that over a hundred of his new books were in German.[2] The word "transcendental" itself was derived from Kant, but came to be applied in New England in a broad and vague way to denote whatever was independent of, or transcended, the experiences of the senses. Ripley, speaking of the movement, said that its followers believed "in an order of truths which transcends the sphere of the external senses. Their leading idea is the supremacy of mind over matter, hence they maintain that the truth of religion does not depend on tradition, nor historical facts, but has an unerring witness in the soul. There is a light, they believe, which enlighteneth every man that cometh into the world . . . there is a faculty in all . . . to perceive spiritual truth when distinctly presented; and the ultimate appeal on all moral questions is not to a jury of scholars, a hierarchy of divines, or the prescription of a creed, but to the common sense of the human race." [3] This, of course, was not new, nor was the more or less Platonic form of its metaphysics, the conception of one vast Soul in the universe which embraces all life and with which the soul of the individual is identical, or the idea that Nature is merely the sense-garment of this one Over-Soul, or God.

But these somewhat inexperienced and naïve philosophers did not attempt to construct a definite system of philosophy, such

---

[1] *Vide* the earlier chapters in O. B. Frothingham's *Transcendentalism in New England*, (New York, 1876), and *Cambridge History of American Literature*, vol. I, pp. 346 ff.; Woodbridge Riley, *American Thought*, (New York, 1923), chap. VI.
[2] J. Weiss, *Life and Correspondence of Theodore Parker*, (New York, 1864), vol. I, p. 101.   [3] Frothingham, *George Ripley*, p. 84.

as those which were arising in Germany, any more than the poets followed the romantic lead of Wordsworth or Shelley in England. New England from the beginning had been deeply absorbed in the problems of conduct. Perhaps the two most characteristic products of that section, in tradition and the popular opinion of the country at large, have been wooden nutmegs and the New England conscience, incongruous as these may appear in their respective economic and spiritual spheres. As every wind of doctrine then blowing seeds of thought about in Europe blew across New England also, some of the seeds became planted in the fields of conduct and practical life; and it was in those fields that the new harvest was brought forth. Largely as reaction against the tenets of the earlier Calvinism, and with an intense belief in the goodness and perfectibility of man, in individualism, in optimism, in the immanence of God, and in defiance of authority, creeds, and codes, Transcendentalism called for "the spontaneous expression in every possible form of that individual human nature which Calvinism had thought deserving of confinement and rebuke." [1]

If there was no very definitely formulated system of philosophy in Transcendentalism, neither did any organization grow from it. In fact, extreme individualism was its keynote, and many of the leaders were opposed to organization of anything in any form. Even the so-called "Transcendental Club," at which a number of those interested in the new ideas used to meet, was simply a gathering of kindred spirits at irregular intervals. A mere list of those who shared in the movement in one way or another will suffice to show how broad and varied were its influences. Among those who attended, at one time or another, the meetings of the Club were Emerson, Bronson Alcott, James Freeman Clarke, Theodore Parker, Margaret Fuller, Orestes Brownson, Thoreau, Hawthorne, Follen, Elizabeth and Sophia Peabody, and William E. Channing, while Ripley, Charles A. Dana, and others appear in the Brook Farm days. The list, of course, could be greatly extended.

The intellectual and spiritual leader of the whole movement

[1] Barrett Wendell and C. N. Greenough, *A History of Literature in America*, (New York, 1904), p. 253.

was undoubtedly Emerson, though he held aloof from some of the practical — or impractical — experiments and from the vagaries of the "lunatic fringe." He resigned as pastor of his church because he had come to disbelieve in the administering of the Communion as other than a commemorative rite, but he was, nevertheless, through his lectures and writings, a preacher all his life rather than a philosopher. There is no reasoned system of thought in his work, but flashes of insight into the deepest and highest matters of the universe and of life, which lie scattered — and often bewilderingly disconnected — all through his essays. It was not so much his doctrines of the immanence or even the benevolence of God in the universe that moved his readers as it was his stirring message to the individual soul. In a generation in which society and convention were rigid to an extent we little realize now, such insistence upon self-development and self-reliance as we find in the essay by that title rang like trumpet calls to a new life. "There is a time in every man's education when he arrives at the conviction that imitation is suicide"; "What I must do is all that concerns me, not what the people think"; "My life is for itself and not for a spectacle"; "A foolish consistency is the hobgoblin of little minds"; "Insist on yourself, never imitate"; "Trust thyself: every heart vibrates to that iron string." [1] Emerson's note is a buoyant optimism. We should not look in his writings for system or for consistency; but they are a perpetual fountain of spiritual energy, to bathe in which is to reinvigorate the soul. Such phrases as "hitch your wagon to a star" have an electric effect on character and will, far beyond any meaning that may be assigned to them.

There was much fun poked at the Transcendentalists in their day, owing to the vagaries of the less balanced among them and more particularly to the "practical" man's humorous contempt for the dreamer. It is odd how seriously the "practical man" always takes himself. He feels that he is the atlas on whose shoulders all society rests. Yet it is to the man who is considered impractical in his day that society owes every advance it has ever made. Somehow the dreamers win

---

[1] *Works*, Boston, 1903, vol. II, essay, "Self Reliance," *passim*.

while the practical man, striving with all his might to keep things as they are, goes down to dust and is forgotten. He is the backbone of society; but in glorying in his own function he is apt to forget the far more important and delicate function of the brain. Among the very wildest ideas of the "cranks" of the 1830's and 1840's were the abolition of slavery, temperance, the right of women to speak in public, and the founding of a League of Nations. Yet, in the years that have passed, slavery has been abolished; prohibition, wisely or not, has been written into the Constitution; women occupy a position then undreamed of even by the cranks; and the League is functioning at Geneva, though America is not there.

The Woman's Rights movement, as an organized one, did not get under way in the period covered by this volume, and may therefore to a great extent be ignored, the first convention of suffragists being held in Massachusetts in 1850. Women, however, were beginning to take their place with men in the various social movements, and in so doing the question of their relative status was necessarily agitated. The advance made in the 1840's was in their winning the right not only to appear but to vote and speak at Antislavery meetings and those of the Peace Societies; in working on equal terms with men in such experiments as Brook Farm; and in the work of such women as the Grimké sisters and Dorothea Dix. Educational facilities for women, even in the higher branches, were also rapidly improving, evidencing a new sentiment as to woman's sphere and status.

Of the various efforts made by the Transcendentalists to translate their theory into practice, none other had quite the air of romance and of Arcadian simplicity possessed by Brook Farm. The idea of a community, in which a limited number of people might live on more or less coöperative lines and enjoy a better life than in the world of competition outside, was in the air in the second decade of the century. In 1825 Robert Owen, the English socialist, had founded his New Harmony Society by the Wabash River, and in the following year a dozen or more were established elsewhere.[1] In 1841 the Reverend Adin

[1] W. A. Hinds, *American Communities*, (Chicago, 1908), p. 139.

Ballou founded the Hopedale Community at Mendon, Massachusetts, which lasted for seventeen years.[1] This "miniature Christian republic," as its founder called it, caught up all the social and humanitarian ideas of the time. Essentially religious, although wholly tolerant and nonsectarian, it stood among other things for "tee-total temperance," antislavery, woman's rights, nonresistance, coöperation, and "Christian socialism." Started a year earlier and long outlasting Brook Farm, it had not, owing to its personnel, either the influence at the time or the romantic glamour since, which have attached to the more famous experiment.

The projects of communities had greatly appealed to the Reverend George Ripley, and when he resigned his pastorate his thoughts turned to the establishment of some form of society which might "insure a more natural union between intellectual and manual labor . . . guarantee the highest mental freedom, by providing all with labor adapted to their tastes and talents," and in which a more wholesome and simple life might be led by intelligent and cultivated persons than was possible under "the pressure of our competitive institutions."[2] After having bought Brook Farm at West Roxbury, Massachusetts, and gathered a few comrades, the association was organized in the autumn of 1841. Until it was altered in 1845 along the lines of Fourierism, it was hardly an organization at all, but a mere aggregate of kindred spirits who worked in the fields or about the cattle, did the housework, danced and sang, discussed every topic under the sun, and had what almost all of its members recalled in later years as the happiest time of their existence. There was a school for the children, a large number of the members were young unmarried people, and an air of youth hangs pleasantly about the whole experiment. Not a breath of scandal was heard about the life; only one death occurred; and one is impressed as much by the high spirits and joyousness of the place as by its earnest effort to labor happily with head and hand at once.

[1] *Ibid.*, pp. 232 *ff.*; Adin Ballou, *History of the Hopedale Community*, (Lowell, 1897), chaps. I-III.
[2] Lindsay Swift, *Brook Farm*, (New York, 1900), pp. 15 *f.*

Over two hundred persons were connected with it at one time or another, among them being Charles A. Dana, Hawthorne, George William Curtis and his brother, and others of lesser note though no less strongly marked personality. In the school, among the thirty scholars gathered by the second year were Margaret Fuller's youngest brother and the two little sons of George Bancroft.[1] Visitors trooped to see the experiment in action, it being said that there were over four thousand in one year. Among them were such distinguished persons as Emerson, Channing, Alcott, Margaret Fuller, Horace Greeley, W. W. Story, Lydia Maria Child, Parke Godwin, Orestes Brownson, Elizabeth Peabody, Albert Brisbane, Robert Owen, and many more, some of them having fairly close relations to the work, whereas others came only for a visit of curiosity.[2]

It is impossible as well as needless to relate the story of the Farm in detail. The reasons for failure were obvious. Ripley might find milking "eminently favorable to contemplation" when "the cow's tail was looped up behind," but Hawthorne, trailing at the end of a rope, at the other and controlling end of which was the insurgent "Transcendental heifer," found farm life less conducive to the intellectual. Nevertheless, in spite of the fact that the personnel of the membership became more commonplace after the industrial experiment of Fourierism was tried in 1845, the community was finally broken up with the same kindly feeling and good humor that had marked its whole course. Although from a practical standpoint the Farm may be put down as a failure, it cannot be considered as wholly so. The joy of living which seemed to come to all its members, the ease with which men of the working classes, of whom there were many, lived and mingled with their more intellectual fellow-members, the charm which even the visitors felt to hang about the place, the feeling of fellowship, all combined to form an influence which was felt then and is felt now as the story is read again. It may be that, just as many of the other dreams of the "cranks" of that time have become living realities in our lives to-day, so the dream of the Brook Farmers

[1] Swift, *op. cit.*, pp. 72 *ff.*; J. T. Codman, *Brook Farm*, (Boston, 1894), pp. 57 *ff.*
[2] Swift, *op. cit.*, pp. 206 *ff.*; Codman, *op. cit.*, pp. 80 *ff.*

of the dignity of labor and of a society based on plain living and high thinking, on mutual helpfulness instead of individual selfishness, may yet come to regenerate human society in some form which we cannot now foresee.[1]

On none of the evils of the day did the interest and efforts of reformers of all sorts converge with better and more immediate effect than upon those in the education of children. The complete inertia of those whose function it should have been to lead the community was attacked from two directions — on the one hand by those among the intellectual class who had been touched by the Transcendental and humanitarian currents of the day, and on the other by the labor leaders and organizations, whose every demand for better wages, shorter hours, or better education was considered "revolutionary" by a large proportion of the capitalists. It is not intended to make this generalization too sweeping, for there were some among the manufacturers who did take an interest in the welfare of their employees; but the chief pressure for bettering conditions came neither from the main body of the rich nor from the rural population, but from a few idealists and from the labor organizations.

New England has always prided itself upon its system of common schools, and to a certain extent justly so, for even at this period reading and writing were more widely diffused among the people of that section than in the rest of America or in England. But this should not blind us to the fact that conditions were atrocious. "It seems to be the destiny of New England, and eminently so of New Hampshire, to produce mind," said the Commissioner of Education of that state complacently, in his report for 1847; but it must be confessed that New England in the preceding decades had not been taking so much care of the mind produced as it might.

Anyone who has had the illuminating experience of sitting on modern boards of education in small communities knows well how, when the question of spending money is fought to

---

[1] It is not necessary to do more than call attention to the smaller experiment in simple living mixed with metaphysics which Bronson Alcott tried at Fruitlands. *Vide* C. E. Sears, *Bronson Alcott's Fruitlands*, (Boston, 1915).

the last ditch, the ideal of "the little red schoolhouse" of old New England is trotted out as a reproach to the useless luxury of the present age. Let us take a look at not one but thousands of those little red schoolhouses as they existed in New England and New York in the period of this chapter. A description of those in the latter state may be quoted, for conditions were precisely similar in New England, as is amply testified by trustworthy evidence, though we have no such vigorous and brief description. In 1846 Miss Catherine Beecher, commenting on the report of the superintendent of schools in New York for 1844, said that "the nakedness and deformity of the schools, the comfortless and dilapidated buildings, the unhung doors, broken sashes, absent panes, stilted benches, yawning roofs, and muddy, mouldering floors, are faithfully portrayed; and many of the self-styled teachers, who lash and dogmatize in these miserable tenements of humanity, are shown to be low, vulgar, obscene, intemperate, and utterly incompetent to teach anything good. . . . [Of the schoolhouses] only one third of the whole number were found in good repair; another third in only comfortable circumstances; while 3319 were unfit for the reception of either man or beast. 7000 we found destitute of any playground, nearly 6000 destitute of convenient seats and desks, and nearly 8000 destitute of any proper facilities for ventilation; while 6000 were destitute of outdoor facilities for securing modesty and decency."[1] She stated that the ordinary schoolhouse had become "a pesthouse, fraught with the deadly malaria of both moral and physical disease." And it was in such places, she continued, deprived of wholesome air, with no proper facilities for study, "driven by dire necessity to violate the most common rules of decency and modesty, that upward of 600,000 children of this state are compelled to spend an average of eight months each year."

In Connecticut the report of the School Commissioners in 1841 stated that in more than seven eighths of all the schoolrooms visited in that state the amount of air per child was less

[1] C. E. Beecher, *The Evils Suffered by American Women and Children*, (New York, 1846), p. 4.

than one half that considered necessary for the prisoners in the state prison at Wethersfield or the county jails of Hartford, New Haven, and Norwich.[1] The report of 1848 drew a damning picture of conditions such as the lack of ventilation, improper heating and lighting, torturing seats, and "the fact, so outrageous to common decency, that most of the schoolhouses have no out-buildings whatever." That at Suffield, for example, located in the middle of the highway and in an exposed situation, had none of the facilities "required by modesty." Of the 1663 schoolhouses in the state, 873 had outhouses and 745 had none. "This fact," says the report from Vernon, "is, undoubtedly a burning shame and a deep disgrace to the State. It is unworthy of a civilized country, and indicates a state of things that ought to exist only among savages." [2]

In 1839, in a survey made in one county, of forty schoolhouses only one had any means of ventilation, yet the average size of these child-pens was eighteen and a half feet long, seven and a half wide and only seven feet high. Into each of them was crowded an average of thirty children.[3] No wonder that *The Common School Journal* spoke of "the slave-ship stowage of children," and contrasted the buildings for the youngsters with those which enterprising farmers were then erecting for their hogs, with "promenades." [4]

In New Hampshire, in 1847, "multitudes" of the schoolhouses were pronounced to be "absolutely dangerous to health and morals," and this in the most flourishing villages as well as in the rural districts.[5] In Rhode Island the first survey of the situation was made in 1843–44, and it was found that of the 405 schools supposed to be in existence under the laws, only 312 were actually so; that these were mostly in bad shape, and, as usual, "had no places of retirement for either sex." [6]

---

[1] *3rd Annual Report, Board of Commissioners of Common Schools, Connecticut,* (Hartford, 1841), p. 16.

[2] *3rd Annual Report of the Superintendent of Common Schools of Connecticut,* 1848, pp. 113 f., 118.

[3] *1st Annual Report, Board of Commissioners of Common Schools, Connecticut,* 1839, p. 64.   [4] Vol. IV, pp. 66, 69, [1842].

[5] *Report of the Commissioner of Common Schools, New Hampshire,* 1847, p. 13.

[6] *Report on the Condition and Improvement of the Public Schools of Rhode Island,* 1846, pp. 30, 32.

Massachusetts seems to have been somewhat better off, but the same complaints come from Maine and Vermont. Indeed, in the latter as late as 1857, 760 houses were reported as "bad," "miserable," or "unfit for use." [1]

Complaints of the ability and frequently of the character of the teachers were as numerous and apparently as well founded as those against the buildings. The one idea throughout New England seems to have been to spend as little as possible. In Massachusetts the average wages paid to a woman teacher were just on a level with those paid to the lowest in the mills and only about one half those paid to skilled female labor. The average wages, exclusive of board, paid to the women was $6.49 a month and to men $23.10. [2]

Even these poor facilities, however, were not offered to all the children, and it is not too much to say that only a moderate proportion had more than irregular schooling for a few weeks a year. No exact statistics are available, but there are plenty of indications of general conditions. In Massachusetts, for example, in 1839 it was stated by the Board of Education that of twenty-nine "rich and populous towns" which had failed the previous year to maintain a school as required by law, only two had complied in the current year, twenty-seven being still recalcitrant. [3] In Maine, some years later, the average length of time that all schools were open ran from eight weeks and five days to thirteen weeks and four days, for all counties. [4] In Vermont, of the 100,000 children of school age, less than 10,000 had as much as 70 days a year; 6500 attended for only 20–30 days, 5600 from 10–20, 4300 for less than 10 days, while 18,000 had no schooling at all. [5] The story was the same in Rhode Island. Of 30,000 children, 11,000 attended no school for any part of the year; 5000, or only one sixth of the whole, may have had a full year each, but the average attendance was

[1] *1st Report of the Board of Education of Maine*, 1847, p. 16; *1st Annual Report, Secretary Board of Education, Vermont*, 1857, p. 22.

[2] *Common School Journal*, vol. II, p. 28. Figures do not vary greatly for the other states, and may be found in the annual reports of the Boards or Commissioners.

[3] *2d Annual Report, Mass. Board of Education*, 1839.

[4] *1st Report of Board of Education*, 1847, p. 20.

[5] *2d Annual Report, Superintendent of Common Schools*, 1847, p. 22.

only 13,500.[1] In Connecticut, out of 70,000 children, 20,000 never went to school at all, with the exception of a moderate deduction to be made for those rich enough to attend private schools and academies.[2] Much of the nonattendance was in the factory villages and closely related to child labor, which will be discussed later. It must also be remembered that although Negroes were taxed, Negro children, as a rule, were not allowed in the schools.[3]

Public opinion, however, was rapidly being aroused to the conditions, and as may be noted from the citations in the notes above, all the states were establishing boards of education of one sort or another, in the reports of which facts were being presented year by year that could not fail to arouse resentment and a desire for betterment. Massachusetts, under the able leadership of Horace Mann, improved rapidly, and Mann's ideas and influence extended throughout the entire country. There was progress in this period also in the academies and colleges, but the notable advance was in the facilities afforded for the education of the children of the poorer classes, and the insistence of the more intelligent element in those classes upon their right, both as men and as citizens, to a fair chance to gain knowledge.

The chief characteristic, indeed, of the period is just this insistence upon the rights of man as man, and not as a member of a special class. Almost every movement of the times was prompted by a recognition of the rights of human nature to free expression and to as full a development as it might prove capable of. Democracy was coming into its own, and expressing itself rather in terms of the brotherhood of human beings than in those of abstract equality in political rights and obligations. Looked at from the standpoint of the broad humanitarianism of the 1830's and 1840's, the doctrinaire equality-philosophy of the Revolutionary period seems narrow and coldly intellectual. The "people," to whom so many appeals

[1] *Report on Condition, op. cit.*, pp. 35 *f.*
[2] *2d Annual Report, Board of Commissioners of Common Schools*, 1840, pp. 20 *ff.*
[3] *1st Annual Report, Board of Commissioners of Common Schools, Connecticut*, 1839, pp. 33 *f.*

had been made in the propaganda of 1776, was at that time but a select privileged class among the population, whose "rights" were based not on their character as men but on the fact that they happened to be property-holders. By the time of the period covered by this chapter not only had such political rights as the suffrage been so broadly extended as to include almost all adult males, — except in Rhode Island, — but the far more important rights to "life, liberty, and the pursuit of happiness," which had been so glibly promised a half-century before, were at last beginning to acquire a significance in practice. The right to the pursuit of happiness was no longer confined to those who had freehold estates of a certain value and to those who were strong enough in mind and body to win their own way. It was beginning to embrace the poor and unsuccessful, the debtors, those in prison, the blind, the insane, the weak of will. In the remainder of this chapter we shall consider briefly what was being done for the amelioration of the condition of such as these.

As has frequently been noticed in the course of our narrative, the rights which the Federalists considered paramount to all others were those of property. The rights which the people had been taught to expect in the war propaganda of '76 were those of man. It was the conflict between these two conceptions which slowly worked itself out in the continuation of the Revolution — a continuation no less real because peaceful.

Perhaps no other law which was theoretically equal for all men pressed more hardly on the poor as a class than that of imprisonment for debt. For one rich man who, overtaken by misfortune, found himself in a debtor's prison in America, there were constantly thousands of the poor. It was estimated in 1829 that there were 75,000 persons confined in jail for debt, and more than half of these were for sums of less than twenty dollars. The following year it was said that three thousand persons were annually imprisoned in Massachusetts, and a number proportionate to population in the other New England states. In Boston alone, in 1830, fourteen hundred persons, including one hundred women, were jailed, most of them for owing trifling amounts. Among cases which may be cited were those of a blind man with a dependent family, who was imprisoned for a debt of six dollars; a widow in Providence who was jailed for owing sixty-eight cents to a man in an attempt to save whose property her husband had lost his life; and of a man seventy-six years of age in Salem, a veteran of Bunker Hill, who was kept in jail for owing a few dollars.[1]

Reformers began to point out the absurdity as well as the injustice of locking up an honest laboring man whose only chance to pay his debts was his ability to work. As early as 1820 a small magazine was started in Boston, called *The Debtors' Journal*, devoted to the reform of this abuse.[2] Such papers as *The Manufacturers' and Farmers' Journal* of Providence complained that the law and practice were a "reproach on the sense and intelligence of the state."[3] Successive governors of Massachusetts denounced the practice in frequent messages; individual reformers and such bodies as the Prison Discipline Society of Boston condemned it; and the Workingmen's Party brought its whole strength to bear; but the laws were continued — due, it was said, to "a secret influence among us, which works behind the curtain, and controls our reason and interest."[4] Little by little the pressure of public opinion, and more particularly working-class opinion, made itself felt, and in the 1830's and 1840's the New England states were forced to modify the laws, so as virtually to abandon imprisonment except in cases of fraud, the fraud and not the debt being the crime.[5]

The condition of the jails, both for debtors and for criminals of all sorts, was extremely bad. Overcrowding was in itself a

---

[1] Commons, *Hist. of Labor*, vol. I, pp. 178 *f.*

[2] Of the prisoners in the Boston jail that December, thirty were for debt. *Debtors' Journal*, vol. I, p. 62.

[3] Issue of Aug. 31, 1829; *cf. The Liberator*, Feb. 5, 1831; *Christian Herald*, Jan. 15, 1831; *Boston Statesman*, Nov. 27, 1830.

[4] Commons, *op. cit.*, p. 329.

[5] *Vide Acts, Legislature*, Vermont, 1826, pp. 109 *ff.*; *Laws of New Hampshire*, 1922, vol. X, p. 1831; *Laws of New Hampshire, New Series*, 1840, c. DXLVII; *Public Acts*, Maine, Jan. Sess. 1831, c. DXX; *An Act for Relief of Insolvent Debtors*, Maine, 1840; *Public Laws of Rhode Island*, 1844, sec. VIII; *Laws of Massachusetts*, 1834, c. CLXVII; *Independent Chronicle*, Jan. 16, 1836; *Acts and Resolves*, Winter Sess., Mass., 1842, c. LVI; *Mass. House Doct. No. 24*, 1842; *Connecticut Courant*, July 20, 1835; *Public Statutes*, Conn., 1837, c. XCVII; *Public Acts of Conn.*, May Sess., 1842, c. XXIII; *Hartford Times*, May 31, 1845.

great evil in the consequences that ensued. In New Bedford, for example, sixteen debtors were at one time confined in a room less than twenty feet square.[1] This applied to the poorhouses — where there were such — as well as to the jails, the House of Industry, in Boston, crowding over seven persons on an average into each of its eighty-seven rooms, the children and adults being herded together indiscriminately.[2] It was the practice in many of the prisons to place all the prisoners in one large room for the night — with consequences which may easily be imagined. Probably the worst prison of all was that known as "the Old Prison" in Connecticut, where it was stated, in a report made in 1827, that "there probably has never been on earth a stronger emblem of the pit, than the sleeping rooms of that Prison, so filthy, so crowded, so inclined to evil, so unrestrained." The prisoners even used to volunteer to sleep "in the dungeons seventy feet below ground, because they were free to commit anything they wanted there."[3] Other reports of the moral conditions of this hell are indescribably shocking. Old and young, the most depraved criminals and little children incarcerated for petty offenses were all kept together.

About 1820 pamphlets and articles begin to appear calling attention to conditions, and two years later Josiah Quincy published a severe indictment of the whole system.[4] Largely under the leadership of the Prison Discipline Society, organized in 1825, a slow reform began.[5] Prisoners were segregated; were separated in cells at night; work was provided. The selling of the product of prison labor and the hiring of prisoners to contractors, however, aroused the opposition of free labor,

[1] Commons, *op. cit.*, p. 179.

[2] *Report of the Commissioners on the Pauper Surplus of Massachusetts, Mass. House Doct. No. 6*, 1833, p. 45. The custom of auctioning off the poor of towns to those who bid lowest for their support was still practised in many towns, and was evidently just beginning at this time to give way to newer and more humane methods. *Ibid.*, pp. 83 *ff*.

[3] *2d Report of the Prison Discipline Society*, (Boston, 1827), p. 17.

[4] *A Dialogue on the Penitentiary System*, Boston, 1820; *State Prisons and the Penitentiary System Vindicated*, Charlestown, 1821; *Remarks on Some of the Provisions of the Laws of Massachusetts Affecting Poverty, Vice and Crime*, (Cambridge, 1822). "Strangers," said Quincy, "who know nothing of our laws but in the statute books, will wonder and admire at the providence of our legislature. But citizens, who know facts and see effects, must feel something like contempt for such provisions." *Ibid.*, p. 18.

[5] *1st Annual Report of the Prison Discipline Society*, (Boston, 1826).

which complained of the unfair competition.[1] In line with
the general tendencies of the day, there was considerable agitation for the abolition of the death penalty and the substitution of imprisonment for life.[2]

It is to the feeling that, whatever the accidental circumstances might be in which a man was placed, he should nevertheless be treated as a man and given every possible opportunity, that we may trace the new attitude toward the blind, the
deaf and dumb, and the insane. In 1829 the first attempt
was made to ameliorate the condition of the blind by opening
new channels of enjoyment to them and training them to be
self-supporting. In that year the Perkins Institute for the
Education of the Blind was incorporated, although it was not
in operation until five years later. The inmates were instructed
in various trades and had the good fortune to be taught music
by Lowell Mason.[3]

In 1815 a group of men in Hartford, among whom were
Ward Woodbridge, Daniel Wadsworth, the Reverend Nathan
Strong, and others, agreed to establish a school for deaf-mutes,
and the Reverend Thomas H. Gallaudet was chosen to go to
Europe and study methods of instruction. To his surprise, he
found on arrival in England that for two generations teaching
deaf-mutes had been a monopoly in the hands of one family —
a monopoly so heartless that permission had always been refused to allow schools to be established in Ireland, "and so
grasping that at the moment of Gallaudet's visit to England a
member of the family, of doubtful reputation and unsteady
habits, was in America seeking to establish the monopoly in
the New World." [4] Unable to make any progress in Great
Britain, Gallaudet went to Paris, where he learned the method
of instruction in vogue there, and returning to Connecticut
in 1816, opened an institution for teaching in the following

---

[1] Commons, *op. cit.*, pp. 346 f.; cf. *Report of the Committee on the Connecticut State Prison to the General Assembly*, (New Haven, 1842).

[2] *Cf., e.g., Mass. House Doct. No. 15*, 1831; *ibid., No. 43*, 1837; and the discussions in the *Independent Chronicle* and other journals during 1836.

[3] *Address of the Trustees of the New England Institution for the Blind*, (Boston, 1833), *passim.*

[4] E. M. Gallaudet, *Life of Thomas H. Gallaudet*, (New York, 1888), p. 59.

year.[1] For a long time it remained the only one of its kind, all the other New England states assisting in its support with the exception of Rhode Island.[2]

Although the Massachusetts General Hospital, chartered in 1811, opened its first department in 1818 as the McLean Asylum for the Insane, no other place of refuge for persons of unsound mind was available until the opening of the State Asylum at Worcester in 1833.[3] Throughout the whole United States, and indeed the world, the treatment of these unfortunates had scarcely improved since the Middle Ages, when in 1841 Miss Dorothea Dix became interested in them and began her wonderful life-work for the improvement of their condition. After spending two years in a painstaking investigation into the care and treatment of such persons by the public authorities throughout the whole of Massachusetts, she addressed a long memorial to the legislature in 1843, stating what she had found as to "the present state of insane persons confined within this Commonwealth, in *cages, closets, cellars, stalls, pens; chained, naked, beaten with rods*, and *lashed* into obedience!"[4] The conditions revealed were so frightful and the carefully collected evidence so overwhelming that public opinion swept aside the attempts of the politicians to block any relief, and an Act was passed providing for the accommodation of two hundred more patients at the State Hospital under proper conditions. Miss Dix, who was one of the most remarkable women New England has produced, then proceeded to carry out similar work in Rhode Island, and eventually covered state after state of the Union and even several countries of Europe, in her self-appointed and marvelously successful work of benevolence.

Intemperance in the use of liquor had always been as rife in Puritan New England as elsewhere, and grew worse after the Revolution. The first serious effort to check it by organized action, however, did not occur until after the War of

[1] *Report of the Committee of the Connecticut Asylum for the Education and Instruction of Deaf and Dumb Persons*, (Hartford, 1817).
[2] *Christian Register*, July 25, 1829.
[3] F. B. Sanborn, *The Public Charities of Massachusetts*, (Boston, 1876), p. 39.
[4] Francis Tiffany, *Life of Dorothea L. Dix*, (Boston, 1890), pp. 76 ff.

1812.[1] There was an immense amount of drinking, not only among the laity but among the clergy; and in 1811, after his experience at two ordinations, where the room in which the assembled clergy met "looked and smelled like the bar of a very active grog-shop," Lyman Beecher became disgusted and made up his mind to attack the evil in his usual vigorous fashion.[2] Although the General Association of the Presbyterian Church was lukewarm on the subject, Beecher secured action by it the following year, and the campaign was on. In 1813 the Massachusetts Society for the Suppression of Intemperance, the parent of all subsequent organizations, was formed, and by 1820 was recommending legal action by the state to prevent drinking.[3] The evil was not materially lessened, and conditions were extremely bad.[4] It was, indeed, high time that a reform should be instituted, and the temperance movement shared in the general outburst of reform and humanitarianism from 1825 onward. The Medical Societies of both Massachusetts and New Hampshire passed resolutions favoring abstinence, and the movement spread even among the sailors in the navy, three hundred and twenty-six out of four hundred and eighty-six men becoming total abstainers on the frigate Brandywine![5] The fourth Report of the American Temperance Society, in 1830, stated that more than one hundred and fifty vessels had sailed from Boston with no liquor on board; and in the following year there were reported to be one hundred and forty temperance societies in Maine, ninety-six in New Hampshire, a hundred and thirty-two in Vermont, two hundred and nine in Massachusetts, twenty-one in Rhode Island, and two hundred and two in Connecticut.[6]

In 1838 a memorial signed by fifteen hundred persons was presented to the Massachusetts legislature, asking that the

[1] The first organized effort was that of Ephraim Kirby and thirty-four others of Litchfield County, Connecticut, who agreed to abstain from liquor and to make their employees do so, in 1787. This, however, was merely local and isolated. G. F. Clark, *History of Temperance Reform in Massachusetts*, (Boston, 1888), p. 5.

[2] *Autobiography*, vol. I, pp. 245 ff.; A. F. Fehlandt, *A Century of Drink Reform in the United States*, (Cincinnati, 1904), pp. 39 ff.   [3] *Ibid.*, pp. 8, 12.

[4] *The Reminiscences of Neal Dow*, (Portland, 1898), pp. 156 ff.

[5] *Permanent Temperance Documents*, (New York, 1852), vol. I, pp. 21, 35.

[6] *Ibid.*, p. 38.

sale of liquor be made a penal offence, and as result the so-called "Fifteen-Gallon Law" was passed, forbidding sale of less than fifteen gallons at a time except on medical prescription.[1]   Active war on the law was at once started, and a petition for its repeal was signed by seventeen hundred citizens, but petitions remonstrating against repeal were then presented with the signatures of thirty-two thousand men and thirty-four thousand women.   Meanwhile, many towns had taken local action, and by 1837 six counties out of fourteen in Massachusetts had gone dry.   The years from 1831 to 1837 have been called "the Golden Age of temperance literature," and the distribution of tracts was enormous.   Mrs. Halsey's *Who Slew All These?* sold by the hundred-thousand, and two million copies of the Reverend Eli Merrill's famous "ox sermon" are said to have been distributed in one year.[2]   John B. Gough, the most noted of the temperance speakers, began his public work in 1842, and was soon followed by Neal Dow.[3]   It was not until just after 1850, and so beyond our period, that the so-called Maine Law was widely adopted by practically all the New England states.

Scarcely any suggested reform failed, in this epoch, to become organized and loudly vocal, and many of them became intertwined in the same organizations and movements. William Lloyd Garrison, for example, although first and foremost the leader of the Abolitionists, undertook to advance among other causes those of woman's rights and of universal peace.   It was a sign of the general ferment of the times. The peace movement, like a number of the others, may be said to date from the War of 1812, but it was not until the decades covered by this chapter that it became widespread.   Several publications had appeared on the subject by the time that the New York, Massachusetts, Ohio, and London Peace Societies were organized, all independently of one another, in 1815 and 1816.[4]   The American Peace Society was founded in New

---

[1] Clark, *Temperance Reform*, pp. 40 f.   [2] Fehlandt, *op. cit.*, pp. 67 f.
[3] *Autobiography and Personal Recollections of John B. Gough*, (Springfield, 1869); *Reminiscences of Neal Dow, op. cit.*
[4] *American Advocate of Peace*, (Hartford), vol. I, pp. 5 ff.   Cf. *The Friend of Peace*, (n. p.), pp. 33 ff.

PROGRAMME OF THE
TEMPERANCE
CONVENTION,
MIDDLETOWN, Oct. 26, 27, 1841

Tuesday, 26th. The Connecticut Temperance Society will commence its Annual Meeting in the North Cong. Church, at 2 o'clock P. M. Hon. Chief Justice WILLIAMS, President. The Society will proceed immediately to the appointment of Committees, and as far as time will permit, will hear reports of the Delegates from County and local Societies.

Tuesday Evening.—ANNUAL REPORT of the State Society, and several Addresses, at the North Church.

Wednesday Morning.--A TEMPERANCE PROCESSION

will be formed on the South Green, under the direction of LINUS COE, Esq., Chief Marshal, aided by Messrs, Wm. S. Camp, John L. Smith, Edward Treadway, J. H. Merrow, Charles W. Newton, Geo. E. Taylor, and Norman Smith, Assistant Marshals.

ORDER OF PROCESSION.

Chief Marshal, and Aid, on Horseback.
Music.
Sabbath Schools, and other Children and Youths.
Connecticut Temperance Society and Visiting Strangers.
Washington Temperance Societies.
Faculty and Students of Wesleyan University.
Citizens.
Assistant Marshal on Horseback.

The Procession will form in the above order, at 10 o'clock A. M. and passing through William, Broad, Washington and Main streets, will return to the south Green.

Sabbath Schools and other children and youths, will repair to the South Congregational Church, and be addressed by Nathan Crosby, Esq. Secretary of the Mass. Temperance Union, and Commander in Chief of the Mass. Cold Water Army, and by several other Gentlemen.

All others will repair to the Methodist Church, and be addressed by Messrs Pollard and Wright of Baltimore, and other distinguished laborers in the cause.

Wednesday Afternoon, and also in the *Evening,* the Meetings of the State Society will be continued in the North Church, to hear addresses, and discuss important Resolutions.

The "Hurrah for bright Water," and other Temperance Music, to be sung, and the Temperance Hymn Books to be used in these meetings, may be obtained at the Bookstore of Luke C Lyman, opposite the Post office, where Delegates, and visiting strangers will record their names, and be directed to accommodations.

York in 1828, and after that similar associations became very numerous, particularly in the New England states, where not only state but county and other local societies were formed.[1] The movement does not seem to have taken deep root in public interest, and as one goes through the reports of the various societies one is impressed by the seeming fact that they were being carried along without support, and by a small group of enthusiasts.

The movement, however, brought forth one remarkable man, William Ladd, who was born in New Hampshire but later lived in Maine. Becoming intensely interested in the question of universal peace, he yet maintained a common-sense view of the difficulties, and had little use for the wilder extremists. To Garrison, when the latter was instrumental in forming the New England Non-Resistance Society, he wrote that "there is such a thing as going beyond the millenium. I am content to stop there."[2] Ladd's own sanity and remarkable grasp of the realities of international relations were shown in his *Essay on a Congress of Nations*, which he wrote in 1840.[3] The scheme of an international court, as outlined by him, was presented, unaltered, at the Peace Conferences held at Brussels in 1848, at Paris in 1849, at Frankfort in 1850, and at London in 1851. Eventually both his plans for a Congress of Powers to agree upon principles of international law and the erection of a court were carried out at The Hague, and followed very closely the lines laid down by this New Englander eighty years before. His name is probably unknown to all but a few specialists, and his fate is an example of that "conflict with oblivion" waged with death, which has so many strange results. Yet few men in the New England of his day have had a more lasting or a wider influence throughout the whole world, and none had a clearer or more far-seeing mind.

[1] The reports of many of these may be found scattered through the issues of *The Advocate of Peace* (Hartford, 1834–35), and *The Calumet*, 1831–34.
[2] John Hemmenway, *Memoir of William Ladd*, (Boston, 1872), p. 77.
[3] It was republished by the Carnegie Endowment for International Peace and edited by J. B. Scott, (New York, 1916).

WILLIAM LADD, PIONEER OF INTERNATIONAL PEACE

From a portrait in the possession of Dr. William E. Ladd of Boston

CHAPTER XVI

STRIFE

Maine Boundary Dispute — Dorr War in Rhode Island — Irish Immigration — Business Recovery — Large Profits of Manufacturers — Wages — Housing and Working Conditions of Labor — Changes in Factory Personnel — Discovery of Gold in California

WHILE William Ladd was organizing Peace Societies and planning an international court for the arbitration of controversies between sovereign Powers, a dispute between his own state and Great Britain, which had been smouldering for fifty years, was rapidly nearing a flaming-up into war. From the time of the signing of the Treaty of Peace after the Revolution, the question of the northern boundary of the present state of Maine had been a perpetual source of disagreement with England.[1] It is unnecessary to follow the complicated problem in detail until it reached an acute stage in the summer of 1838, at which time events occurred that threatened to plunge the United States into war with Great Britain.

Although a certain portion of northern Maine had been acknowledged by both parties to be of uncertain title, the valley of the Aroostook had long been considered as indubitably within the limits of the state. In June 1838, however, a New Brunswick official, known as the "warden of the disputed territory," complained to the surveyor-general of Maine, who was then engaged in carrying out his duties in the Aroostook Valley, that he was violating an agreement between the two governments, and called upon him to desist. On the other

[1] H. S. Burrage, *Maine in the Northeastern Boundary Controversy*, (Portland, 1919), chaps. I-XII.

hand, some Englishmen were trespassing on Maine territory and carrying off lumber to the value of a hundred thousand dollars.[1] On January 2, 1839, Governor Kent, on his retirement from office, sent a long message to the Maine legislature, reviewing the entire question of the boundary controversy, and the new Governor, John Fairfield, in his first message stated that the settlement of the matter could be delayed no longer, and that if Maine had to resort to arms alone, the Federal government could not fail to sustain her.[2]   In the same month, as a result of another message from the Governor, the legislature ordered a force of men, under command of the land agent, to proceed to the Aroostook and Fish Rivers and to break up the work of the trespassers, appropriating ten thousand dollars for the purpose.[3]   The company of about two hundred proceeded to carry out their orders, and had succeeded in capturing about twenty English when they were themselves surprised and the land agent and two citizens of Bangor were taken prisoners by the "enemy" and carried to jail in Fredericton. A message from the Governor of Maine to the legislature and a proclamation by the injudicious Lieutenant-Governor of New Brunswick followed quickly on these events.   The Maine legislature at once voted to send a military force to the border, and appropriated eight hundred thousand dollars for the expense of the expedition.[4]

Feeling throughout the state rose to a high pitch, and the papers of both that and the neighboring states are filled from then on with dispatches about the "Boundary War."   On February 16 the Governor called out a thousand men, and three days later the Adjutant-General issued orders to draft ten thousand more, although the number actually engaged in the subsequent movements did not exceed about thirty-three hundred.[5]   Such a situation called for immediate action by the Federal authorities, and if for many decades they had allowed

[1] H. S. Burrage, *Maine in the Northeastern Boundary Controversy*, (Portland, 1919), p. 258.
[2] Both messages are printed in the *Kennebec Journal*, Jan. 8, 1839.
[3] Burrage, *op. cit.*, pp. 258 *ff*.
[4] *Ibid.*, pp. 260 *ff*.; *Kennebec Journal*, Feb. 19, 1839.
[5] Burrage, *op. cit.*, pp. 263, 274.

the controversy to drag without taking the steps which they should have taken to end it, they now acted with promptness. General Winfield Scott was dispatched from Washington, to serve as peacemaker if possible, and as a result of his efforts the Aroostook country was left in sole possession of Maine, the British, in turn, retaining exclusive control of the Madawaska section, pending negotiations between Great Britain and the United States. The political situation in Maine was a complicated one, and both Democrats and Whigs seemed to be afraid lest the other should wrest some advantage out of the boundary struggle. Scott appears to have acquitted himself well as a political manœuverer and he also had the advantage of being a friend of the Lieutenant-Governor in New Brunswick. As a result of his successful negotiations, both the American and the British agreed to withdraw their troops, and this was accordingly done, although not without much protest on the part of many in Maine.[1]

Danger of immediate war was thus averted, but the matter continued to drag, and it was only three years later — in 1842 — that a treaty negotiated by Daniel Webster and Lord Ashburton was finally entered into, and the question disposed of in a way that met the wishes of Maine fairly.[2] Although the chief points were then settled, it may be noted that an absolutely final adjustment was not reached until 1910, over a century and a quarter from the time the dispute first started.

Another so-called "war" broke out in New England in the same period, which, while not threatening international complications, had far more significance as indicating the trend of thought of the times. In the preceding chapter we spoke of the chief characteristic of these years as being an insistence upon the rights of man as man, and not simply as a member of a special class in society. In politics this had taken the form of an extension of the franchise in almost every state of the Union. The conception of what constituted "the people" had steadily broadened to meet the growing demands of democracy. In Rhode Island alone had the wishes of the people —

[1] *Independent Chronicle*, March 30, 1839; *Kennebec Journal*, April 9, 1839.
[2] Burrage, *op. cit.*, pp. 328 *ff.*

understood as the free adult male population — been thwarted by the obstructionist tactics of an unusually arbitrary land-owning class. Efforts had repeatedly been made — from 1797 to 1834 — to force an extension of the suffrage, only to be met by the obstinate and even contemptuous resistance of those in control of the government.[1] We have already noted the manner in which the last of these demands, made under the leadership of Thomas Dorr, had been disdainfully thrown aside by the legislature, which refused to give any consideration to the merits of the question.[2]

The trend of the times, however, was too strongly toward democracy to make such opposition wise, and conditions in Rhode Island had so altered as to make the old system of suffrage and representation a dangerous anachronism. That the ownership of land does not confer brains or ability to govern was amply shown by the stupid resistance offered to the will of the people by the small farmers who constituted, in the main, the governing class. By 1841 Rhode Island was almost the only state that had not adopted an almost unrestricted manhood suffrage, and the stubbornness of the landowners in that state was to result in a mild civil war, averted from more disastrous consequences by last-minute concessions.

The state also occupied the anomalous position in the Union of being the only one which had not adopted a written constitution, and of being still governed by the old Royal Charter. This charter, liberal as its terms had been for the colonial system of the seventeenth century, had in fact created, not a republican form of government such as it was contemplated should be enjoyed by the several states under the Federal Constitution, but, on the contrary, a very close corporation. The original grantees had had the sole right to admit any others to a voice in the management of its affairs, and they had decreed that a landed estate of moderate size should be one of the essential qualifications for such admission, save in the case of the eldest

---

[1] Demands had been made in 1797, 1811, 1820, 1824, 1829, 1832, and 1834. *Burke's Report, U. S. House of Repres. Doct. No. 546, 28th Cong., 1st Sess.*, p. 14; *Might and Right, by a Rhode Islander*, (Providence, 1844), pp. 63 *f.*

[2] *Vide supra*, chap. XIV.

son of such a proprietor. In the simplicity of the early agricultural days this probably did not work any severe hardship, as almost any man of even the most modest means could secure a voice in what was, nevertheless, a close, self-perpetuating body of rulers. By the early nineteenth century the situation had altered with great rapidity.

The growth of manufacturing had created a large unenfranchised class which had become wholly divorced from the soil, and had developed large centres of population, which had brought about great inequality in representation. Furthermore, the new forms of investment available left large capitalists who did not happen also to be landowners no voice whatever in the affairs of government.[1] In 1840, of the total adult male citizens, numbering 22,674, exclusive of insane, aliens, paupers, and convicts, only 9590 were entitled to vote, over three fifths of the males who would have been so entitled in almost any other state being excluded. In Providence alone there were 421 persons who had no votes, but who were nevertheless taxed on property amounting to between one and two million dollars.[2]

Moreover, owing to the unchanging apportionment for representation, it had come about that a majority of the legislature was elected by nineteen towns, having only about 3500 voters, so that the state, with a total population of 108,000, was in the complete control of about 1800 persons. The question of freehold, however, was not merely one of the suffrage. No citizen who did not own real estate could bring a suit in any court of law for the recovery of debt or to obtain redress for personal injury, unless a freeholder endorsed his writ. The most upright citizen, who might have a million dollars in securities but no land, was thus debarred from claiming his rights unless the owner of a few acres somewhere would allow his name to be used in the case. As the state had no constitution, and as the charter provided no means by which the absolute will of the small body of freemen could be balked, the situation was one which was irritating in the extreme to the disfranchised elements.

[1] "The Recent Contest in Rhode Island," *North American Review*, April, 1844, p. 20.
[2] *Burke's Report*, pp. 11 f.

Thomas W. Dorr, who was to lead the revolt which almost brought on civil war, was no mere agitator. He was the son of a wealthy manufacturer and had been educated at Phillips Exeter Academy and Harvard College. He had been actively interested in the question of the extension of the suffrage since his first attempt to secure reform in 1834. In 1840 the Rhode Island Suffrage Association was formed, and in the same year the suffrage journal, *The New Age*, began publication. In the next January the suffragists asked the legislature to call a convention to draw up a constitution for the state, but that body, as before, refused to consider the issue seriously. Thereupon a popular meeting, at which over three thousand citizens were present, was held at Providence. In the procession which marched to the State House, banners were carried with such devices as "Worth makes the Man, but Sand and Gravel the Voter," and "Virtue, Patriotism and Intelligence versus $134 worth of Dirt." [1]

A meeting was also held at Newport in May, and a second at Providence in July, at which latter it was voted to hold a constitutional convention and to carry into effect by all necessary means such a constitution as might be adopted. The election of delegates to the convention was held in August, all male citizens over twenty-one years of age who had resided in the state for one year being declared eligible to vote. This convention of the suffragists, or People's Party as they were called, finished its work in November and offered a constitution remedying all the evils complained of. When it was submitted to the people, the vote disclosed that 13,955 ballots had been cast in favor of adopting it and only 46 against. Of those in favor, 4925 were qualified freemen, so that the constitution was favored not only by a majority of the male inhabitants over twenty-one but even by a majority of the legal voters of the state. [2]

All these proceedings, however, had no legal foundation. They had in no way been sanctioned by the existing government. That the government did not represent the will of a

---

[1] I. B. Richman, *Rhode Island*, (Boston, 1905), p. 292.
[2] *Burke's Report*, p. 18.

THE GREAT POLITICAL CAR AND LAST LOAD OF PATRIOTS.

DORR, JACKSON, SIMMONS AND ARNOLD!

"We stoop to Conquer."

"BETTER TO REIGN IN HELL THAN SERVE IN HEAVEN."

CARTOON OF THE DORR WAR

Library of Congress

majority even of its own electorate was clear from the vote on the "People's Constitution"; nevertheless, it persistently refused to comply with that will. Moreover, there was no provision in the charter for the calling of any legal convention to alter the mode of government. The constitutional question involved, therefore, was by no means a simple one. If an existing government, as long in operation as that of Rhode Island, refused to meet the will of the people, — understood either in its broadest sense or even merely as a majority of the freemen, — what course was open except revolution, peaceful or bloody? The defenders of the People's Party could bring a long array of eminent opinions to their support to prove that the people had at all times the right to alter their form of government with or without the consent of those temporarily in power.[1] It is difficult if not impossible to condemn the action taken by Dorr and his followers on any ground up to this point. Dorr himself was elected governor in an election held under the new Constitution.

Meanwhile, the legislature had at last been forced into action, and had itself called for a constitutional convention. That body, after some months, proposed to the people a constitution which embodied most — though not all — of the reforms in the People's Constitution. When submitted to practically the same body of voters as had passed on the other, it was defeated by the narrow margin of 676 votes in a total of 16,702. Unfortunately, the suffragists, owing to the bitterness of feeling which had been engendered by the long process of bullying and obstruction employed by the legislature, voted to a great extent against its constitution. Had they been willing to accept the genuine victory which they had won by forcing the landholders to submit a new instrument of government embodying practically all that had been contended for, Dorr and his party would have scored a great success. By continuing the fight they broke themselves and almost their cause against the rock of technical legality.

The Landholders' Constitution having been defeated, there remained the existing government under the old charter and

[1] *Burke's Report*, pp. 25 ff.

BY HIS EXCELLENCY,

SAMUEL WARD KING,

GOVERNOR, CAPTAIN-GENERAL, AND COMMANDER-IN-CHIEF OF THE STATE OF
RHODE-ISLAND AND PROVIDENCE PLANTATIONS.

A PROCLAMATION.

WHEREAS on the eighth day of June instant, I issued a Proclamation, offering a reward of one thousand dollars for the delivery of the fugitive Traitor, THOMAS WILSON DORR, to the proper civil authority: and whereas the said Thomas Wilson Dorr having returned to
this State and assumed the command of a numerous body of armed men,
in open rebellion against the Government thereof, has again *fled* the sum-
mary justice which awaited him; I do therefore, by virtue of authority in
me vested, and by advice of the Council, hereby offer an additional reward
of four thousand dollars for the apprehension and delivery of the said
Thomas Wilson Dorr to the Sheriff of the County of Newport or Providence, within three months from the date hereof.

GIVEN under my hand and the seal of said State, at the City of
Providence, this twenty-ninth day of June, in the year of our Lord
one thousand eight hundred and forty-two, and of the Independence of the United States of America the sixty-sixth.

L. S.

SAMUEL WARD KING.

BY HIS EXCELLENCY'S COMMAND:
HENRY BOWEN, Secretary of State.

BROADSIDE OF THE DORR WAR
Library of Congress

the new government headed by Dorr under the People's Constitution. In the course of the next few months both sides appealed to Washington. Dorr himself made a journey thither in a vain attempt to enlist Federal support, which, however, the President threw on the side of the Charter government. On his way back Dorr was fêted by Tammany in New York, and he believed he would receive military aid from that city. No genuine support for an armed revolution, however, appeared from any quarter, and although Dorr returned to Rhode Island and an abortive attempt was made under his leadership to seize the arsenal in Providence on May 17, it utterly failed. The other members of the People's Party government promptly resigned, and Dorr fled from the state.

The Charter government then, in turn, lost its head; and after the proclamation of martial law the legislature proceeded to pass the stringent Act known as the "Algerine Law," directed against all who had taken any active part, however humble, in the course pursued by the People's Party. Five thousand dollars was offered for the capture of Dorr, and many persons of minimum importance, whose rôle in the "revolution" had been trifling, were cast into prison, some of them under indictment for treason being threatened with the death penalty.[1] Dorr voluntarily returned to Providence, was seized by the authorities and illegally carried to Newport, where he was tried by a packed jury before a hostile judge and sentenced to life imprisonment at hard labor in solitary confinement.

Meanwhile, the legislature, realizing that with the new government crushed and with popular sentiment such as it was against the old, something had to be done, had again called a convention to draft a constitution. In due course this was submitted to the people, but the extent of disaffection is shown by the fact that only 7024 votes were cast in all on the question, as compared with 16,702 in the preceding year. Of these, however, 6973 were in favor of adoption, and the Constitution was declared in force, though less than a majority of the voters entitled to vote under it had approved it. The franchise was conferred upon all male citizens, without distinction of color,

[1] *Burke's Report*, pp. 65 ff.; *Might and Right*, p. 178.

who paid taxes of at least one dollar and who possessed certain other minor qualifications.[1]

The suffrage party thus won in the end and, in spite of the blunder of its leader at a critical moment, its course calls for far more commendation than that of the Charter party of constituted authority and conservative landowners, who changed from a policy of stupid obstruction merely to one of stupid cruelty, granting the demands of a majority of the citizens only after years of delay and when it was obvious that there was nothing else to do. Their "Algerine Law" and their treatment of Dorr aroused a storm of protest in the neighboring states among the more democratic elements and, of course, in the Democratic Party. The legislatures of Maine and New Hampshire passed resolutions strongly condemning the government of Rhode Island, but that of Connecticut, in turn, passed one condemning such resolutions as "impertinent and unjustifiable interference with the administration of justice."[2] Dorr was liberated in 1845 and restored to his civil rights six years later.

In the contest over the Constitution, the Landholders had sought to confuse the issue, as they had done ten years earlier, by stirring up race prejudice. "Up to May last," said a contemporary writer in 1842, "the suffrage party were hooted at for wishing to admit 'the *low Irish* and the *niggers*' to the polls."[3] In neither the People's nor the Landholders' proposed constitutions were the Negroes readmitted to the franchise; but this was done in the constitution finally accepted, it being said that the Landholders had been forced to admit their domestics to vote, in order to carry their measure with even the modicum of success which it achieved.[4]

In the 1840's the Irish immigration assumed enormous proportions, more particularly after the Irish famine in 1846. Whereas in the years 1820–30 only about fifty thousand came

[1] *Report of the Committee on the Action of the General Assembly on the Subject of the Constitution, 1842,* (Providence, 1859).

[2] *Maine Legis. Doct. No. 32,* 1843, *No. 21,* 1845; *Journal of House of Representatives, Connecticut,* 1845, p. 238.

[3] Wm. Goodell, *The Rights and Wrongs of Rhode Island,* (Whitesboro, 1842), p. 6.

[4] *Ibid.,* p. 6.

to America, in the decade 1840–50 over seven hundred and eighty thousand arrived.[1] Their poverty and clannishness, their religion, and to some extent their lawlessness all created a strong prejudice against them.[2]   Even in 1838, a Congressional Committee, reporting favorably on a report from "The Native American Association of the United States," claimed that the number of foreign immigrants was increasing so rapidly as to "jeopardize the peace and tranquillity of our citizens, if not the permanency of the civil, religious, and political institutions" of the country.[3]   It is impossible to estimate accurately the number who found their way into New England, but by 1845 the question had become a serious one politically.[4]   For the most part the Irish continued, as always, to remain in the seaboard cities and did not spread out into the country.   In Boston, in 1848, of the 10,162 children in the primary schools, 5154, or over one half, were of foreign parentage.[5]   In the preceding year, out of 2434 inmates of the Boston Almshouse, nearly 2000 were foreigners or children of foreign parents.[6] On the other hand, although the first Irish had come to Lowell in 1822, and a Catholic church had been built there eight years later, in 1842 the Merrimack Mills reported that of fifteen hundred hands only fifty were foreigners.[7]

Ignorant and extremely poor, the immigrants were put to work at the coarsest tasks only, and at wages far below American standards.   Contractors set them to manual labor at the rate of fifty cents for fifteen hours' work.[8]   A report to the Massachusetts Senate stated that foreigners could live on one third of what it cost a native citizen and be much better off

[1] *Tables Showing Arrivals of Alien Passengers*, U. S. Bureau of Statistics, 1889, p. 32.

[2] L. D. Scisco, *Political Nativism in New York State*, (Columbia Univ. Studies, 1901), p. 21.

[3] Report of a Select Committee . . . on Foreign Paupers, *House of Rep. Doct. No. 1040, 25th Cong., 2d Sess.*, 1838, pp. 1, 63 *ff*.

[4] *Mass. Senate Doct. No. 109*, 1847; E. E. Hale, *Letters on Irish Emigration*, (Boston, 1852), p. 27.

[5] *Life and Works of Horace Mann*, (Boston, 1891), vol. IV, p. 331.

[6] T. W. Page, "Some Economic Aspects of Immigration," *Journal of Political Economy*, vol. XX, p. 1913.

[7] F. W. Coburn, *History of Lowell*, (New York, 1920), p. 171; *Mass. House of Repres. Doct. No. 50*, p. 14.

[8] Darling, *Political Changes in Massachusetts*, p. 309.

than they had been in their native lands, adding that this unfair competition prevented the educated native from occupying
the position he had had heretofore.[1] Complaints might have
been better directed against the contractors who were exploiting the immigrant at fifty cents a day than against the poor
devils who received it; but petitions were presented asking that
American labor be protected against such competition, on the
same principle as capital was protected by the tariff.[2]

It is probable, however, that much of the agitation, though
cloaked as economic, was in reality political. The Irish from
the beginning had naturally gravitated toward the Democratic
Party and had become an important, though not a dominant,
factor in elections by 1843.[3] The Whigs by their political and
social attitudes had completely alienated the Irish when these
had first begun to arrive, and, when their numbers increased
so rapidly as to make them important as a voting element,
the Whigs cast about violently to retrieve their initial error
by the method of stopping the inflow. They expressed their
"deep indignation towards the priest-ridden Irishmen who
have been led like cattle to the polls," as one writer stated it
in 1845.[4] The hue and cry about the danger to American institutions and American labor very likely had its origin in
nothing less human than a desire to win on election day. The
short-lived "Native American Party" was formed, and Congress was flooded with petitions for a drastic revision of the
naturalization laws. With the exception of a few localities,
however, the American working classes do not seem to have
been so deeply troubled as the Whig politicians until toward
1850. They had other things to think about.

The country had been slow in recovering from the panic
of 1837, but by 1843 "big business" was once more in the saddle
and making enormous profits. The Democratic Party, as
representing the laboring and rural population, was, as always,
violent in its attacks on the corporations of the day. An
editorial, a sample of many, in the *Hartford Times*, has a very
modern ring. "We had supposed," it said, "that it was one

[1] *Mass. Senate Doct. No. 109*, p. 4.
[2] *Ibid.*, p. 5.
[3] Darling, *op. cit.*, p. 409.
[4] *Hartford Times*, Oct. 4, 1845.

of the great duties of a Legislature, whenever it deemed it proper to charter a railroad, to guard the public rights to every possible extent. But the charter of the N. Y. & Boston RR. Co. violates some of the dearest and most valuable rights of the people; it protects the corporation but not the individual. In its whole history it is one of the most discreditable pieces of law making we know of; and if our Legislatures are thus laying down sovereign power and public right at the feet of a gigantic corporation, we at least are determined to take a stand against a system of legislative oppression, which will subject the people to the worst of all despotisms, the narrow minded and heartless domination of stockjobbers and brokers." [1]

There was, indeed, not a little basis for the popular discontent with the corporations and the general attitude of capital. Labor had suffered very severely in the panic of 1837 and the years immediately following. When the recovery set in, about 1842 to 1843, it was as natural as it was just that labor should consider itself entitled to some share in the new prosperity. Instead, it found itself losing ground throughout the new decade, whereas capital reaped the entire benefit. In 1834 it was noted in the *Boston Post* that the textile mills were making large profits and that prices of their stocks were advancing rapidly, that of the Nashua Mills, for example, selling actively at over $480 a share. It also noted that the mills were in a favorable position to make large profits, as wages had been reduced forty per cent since 1840.[2] By 1845 the Nashua and Jackson corporations were paying twenty-four per cent dividends, and most of the mills were distributing large profits, in many cases on watered stock.[3]

A report to the Federal Government in the same year estimated that the manufacturers in Connecticut were earning forty per cent net per annum. The Massachusetts Mills in 1846 declared dividends of twenty per cent, although a labor paper claimed that only one half of the $1,200,000 capital had been actually invested, and that therefore the mill was paying forty per cent. In the same year another paper called atten-

[1] Issue of July 4, 1846. *Cf.* Aug. 8 and Oct. 10.   [2] Issue of Dec. 25, 1843.
[3] Ware, *Industrial Worker*, pp. 5 f.

tion to similar large earnings in other mills, whereas one of the largest in Lowell had just reduced wages twenty-five per cent.[1] In 1848 there were general wage-reductions, although mills had been making twenty-five to forty per cent profits for the past five or six years, and the wages of the operatives had not been raised at all since the cuts after the panic.[2]

Moreover, even when the actual money wages had not been reduced, they had been maintained by the workers only at the expense of greatly increased labor. In the 1830's the girl operatives in the cotton mills had tended two looms making from 216 to 324 picks per minute. By 1849 they were obliged to tend four looms making 480 picks a minute, involving much closer attention and greater effort and strain. Whereas wages remained practically stationary, the piece-cost was enormously reduced, the increased work being done by labor and the profit going to capital.[3]

There were various strikes during the decade against reduction in wages and the speeding-up process, but these almost invariably failed. A report to the Massachusetts legislature stated that there could be no legislation as to the hours of labor without affecting the question of wages. In that commonwealth, the report continued, "labor is on an equality with capital, and indeed controls it, and so it will ever be while free education and free constitutions exist." "Labor is intelligent enough to strike its own bargain." Admitting that the hours were too long, the legislators denied that the remedy lay with them, and asserted that it would have to be looked for "in the progressive improvement in art and science, in a higher appreciation of man's destiny, in a less love for money, and a more ardent love for social happiness and intellectual superiority."[4] As, so far, the only result of the improvement in art and science had been to make the operative work approximately twice as fast for the same wages, it was not encouraging to tell him, in the name of the state, that his plight could be remedied only by a less love for money.

There had been a considerable reduction in the hours of

[1] *Ibid.*, p. 8. [2] *Ibid.*, p. 115. [3] *Ibid.*, p. 122.
[4] *Mass. House of Repres. Doct. No. 50*, p. 16.

labor everywhere in the country except in New England before 1840, and this was, perhaps, the greatest abuse in the textile industry of that section.   Outside of those states, the ten-hour day had been achieved by almost all mechanics and other workers in the 1830's, whereas the New England mill-hands were still forced to work from twelve to fourteen hours of speeded-up labor.   From 1840 to 1850 the movement for the shortening of hours was best carried on in Massachusetts, but continually broke against the influence of the capitalists in the legislature.   The demand was mainly fostered by the workers themselves, a rather remarkable woman, Sarah Bagley, who organized the Lowell Female Reform Association in 1845, leading the fight for the women.

The desire for profits was, as in the cases of the earlier strikes we have described, cloaked under a Pharisaical care for morals. "The morals of the operatives," contended an opponent of shorter hours, "will necessarily suffer if longer absent from the wholesome discipline of factory life, and leaving them thus to their will and liberty, without a warrant that this spare time will be well employed.   No limits can be ascribed to the abuse of these privileges conferred, or time misspent, should the legislature see fit to accede." [1]   Considering that at this time the operatives came mainly from the best farming homes in New England, and that many of the girls alternated mill work with teaching, this care for their morals was a little far-fetched on the part of capitalists who were engaged in doubling the work and strain of their self-appointed wards without increasing their pay.   In spite of all the efforts of the workers and floods of petitions from them to the Massachusetts legislature in the period of this chapter, nothing was done by legislation to shorten their hours until far beyond the limits of this volume, in 1874.

In 1847 a ten-hour law was passed in New Hampshire, but apparently with little intention of making it effective.   The mill-owners, in anticipation of the passage of the law, had been busy getting signatures of their employees to contracts by which they bound themselves to work as many hours as the employers

[1] Quoted by Ware, *op. cit.*, p. 127.

should think proper; and although two thousand employees of the Nashua Mills held a meeting of protest, the power of capital was too strong for them to resist. Any employee who refused to sign was blacklisted and his name was sent not only to other mills in New Hampshire but to the great centre of Lowell and elsewhere. The employers banded together, and when an employee who had refused to work more than the legal number of hours went elsewhere to seek employment, he found that all doors were closed to him.[1]

This method of blacklisting was the favorite one used by the employers in their system of "moral police" which governed the lives of their employees. Much was made of the care for the moral welfare of the girls, but while good may occasionally have been done by getting obviously unfit persons out of the way and so saving the younger girls from contamination, the system was abused outrageously. Not only were girls discharged "on suspicion of criminal conduct, association with suspected persons, and general and light behavior and conversation," as one defender of the system stated, but it was made use of to keep down any agitation by the workers for improved conditions.[2] By the extensive combination of capitalists in more than one state, and the use of the blacklist, the position of a discharged employee was practically hopeless, and even merely subscribing to a labor paper is said to have been sufficient cause for discharge.

It is not easy to arrive at a fair estimate of the housing and other living conditions of the city factory-worker and the extremely poor at this time. On the one hand, we read in a report made to the American Medical Association on conditions in Boston and Lowell, by Dr. Josiah Curtis in 1849, that "the dwellings of the poor are mostly filthy, often from neglect on the part of the occupants, as often from neglect on the part of the landlords, who get large rents, and do not provide suitable drains, privies, yards, etc. The number of families in a house varies with the number of rooms. I have found from six to forty or more in one house of two stories, eleven and more in one room constantly, and eight in one bed (women and men)."

[1] *Ibid.*, p. 146.   [2] *Ibid.*, p. 109.

This was in a house owned by a Boston physician.[1] Similar conditions were found by Dr. Henry Clark, who made a report to the city of Boston. Among other places described were a cellar which served as a home for thirty-nine persons; another in which the tide flowed in, so that he had to reach his patient's bed across a plank while a dead child was floating about the room in its coffin; and conditions in other sections of the city, such as Half-Moon Place, he characterized as indescribably loathsome.[2]

In 1847 the *Lowell Courier* had an article advocating the appointment of a city health officer, and stating that "the faithful report of such an officer would astonish the public, for very few are aware of hundreds of places now inhabited by a horde in a horrid condition." In one house in a central location the writer had found a store and twenty-five families numbering one hundred and twenty persons. In one room he found a man, his wife, eight children, four of them over fifteen, and four boarders, all living together. Similar conditions were reported by other observers.[3]

On the other hand, if we take the pictures painted of the boarding-houses run by some of the mills for their girl operatives, we get an entirely different view. Before the coming of the foreigners, and while the operatives were mainly daughters of farmers who merely worked in the mills for a few years to broaden their experience or get extra money for one purpose or another, conditions were entirely unlike those which we associate with a factory population of the present day. There are almost idyllic pictures left us of the mill girls and their life, as painted by some of themselves and other observers of the time.[4] The conditions in Lowell were much better than elsewhere, the system of boarding-houses there introduced by Francis Cabot Lowell and his brother-in-law Patrick T. Jackson

---

[1] J. Curtis, *Brief Remarks on the Hygiene of Massachusetts . . . Being a Report to the American Medical Association*, (Philadelphia, 1849), p. 16.

[2] *City of Boston, Doct. No. 66*, quoted by Ware, *op. cit.*, p. 13.

[3] Curtis, *op. cit.*, pp. 36 ff.

[4] *E.g.*, Lucy Larcom, *A New England Girlhood*, (Boston, 1892), pp. 146 ff.; "Abby's Year in Lowell," *The Lowell Offering*, vol. I, pp. 1 ff.; Elisha Bartlett, *A Vindication of the Character and Condition of the Females Employed in the Lowell Mills*, (Lowell, 1841), *passim*; Edith Abbott, *Women in Industry*, (New York, 1909), pp. 109 ff.

accounting in part for the better quality of the operatives.[1] There was at that time almost no opening except the poorly paid work of a school-teacher for the woman who wished to earn her own living, and girls poured into Lowell from all the New England states.

The Lowell mills had originally been established by men who were sincerely desirous of maintaining a standard of morals and right living among their employees; but from about 1840 onward, as the stocks of the corporations became more widely distributed, the attitude changed from an individual paternalism to mere corporate greed for profits. Moreover, although the foreign element had not yet entered the factories to any great extent, the fact that many girls became enamored of the town life with its freedom or that they failed to save their money and for one reason or another were unable to return to their homes, tended to form a permanent factory population and labor supply. This gave the factory-owners an advantage in dealing with strikes and increased their power over the hands.

As the prosperity of the mills increased, they became more crowded with workers, and working conditions became worse. As stated in Curtis's medical report, the air in the rooms where the girls worked, "which ought to undergo an entire change hourly, remains day after day, and even month after month, with only the precarious change which open doors occasionally give! There being no ventilation at night, the imprisoned condition of many of the rooms in the morning is stifling and almost intolerable to unaccustomed lungs. After the day's work is ended, two hours' release is enjoyed, a part of which is frequently spent in a crowded lecture-room, and then they retire to dormitories scarcely better ventilated than the mills. From four to six and sometimes eight are confined during the night in a single room of moderate dimensions." He estimated that ten cubic feet of air per minute was required for each operative, and that if this were so the ordinary mill-room should have had 450,000 feet a day whereas they got by measurement

[1] H. H. Robinson, *Loom and Spindle*, (New York, 1896), p. 7; Rev. H. A. Niles, *Lowell As It Was and Is*, (Lowell, 1845), pp. 67 f.

only 60,000.[1] Yet the Lowell mills were generally acknowledged to be the best in New England.

Outside of that city and such mills as had adopted the "Waltham system" of paternalism and moral police, the method in vogue for dealing with operatives was the *laissez faire* one of England. The hands were considered as part of the mill machinery and not as human beings. The manager of the largest mill in Fall River said in 1855 that so long as the hands were able to work, he would get all that he could out of them, and when they gave out and could not work any longer he replaced them as he would worn-out parts of the machines. A manager at Holyoke who found the hands "languorous" in the morning conceived the brilliant idea that they might work better on an empty stomach, and by forbidding breakfast he succeeded in getting three thousand yards more of cloth a week for the same wage-bill.[2] What the life of the employees was outside of working hours was considered no concern of the owners, except that the hands were forced to trade at the company store to realize on such part of their wages as was paid in orders and not in cash. In a petition "of certain residents of Fall River to the Legislature" in 1842 it was pointed out that "the population of manufacturing places are now, in a great measure, dependent for the means of physical, intellectual and moral culture, upon the will of their employers," and that the latter were moved only by competition and desire for gain.[3]

The *laissez faire* system also involved, to a far greater extent than the Waltham, the use of child labor, as we have already noted. In 1831 it was estimated that there were 3472 children under the age of twelve at work in Rhode Island mills at wages of $1.50 a week, that state having the unenviable reputation of employing more young children than any other.[4] The hours of labor for these youngsters varied from ten to fourteen, but the manager of the mills at Franklin, where the children worked

[1] Curtis, *Brief Remarks*, p. 33.

[2] Ware, *op. cit.*, p. 77.

[3] *Mass. House of Repres. Doct. No. 4*, 1842.

[4] James Montgomery, *A Practical Detail of the Cotton Manufacture of the United States*, (Glasgow, 1840), p. 161.

twelve hours a day for six days a week, noted with much satis-
faction that they were allowed to go to school on Sundays.[1]
In 1840 the Rhode Island legislature passed an Act that no
child under twelve should work in a factory unless it had had
three months' schooling the preceding twelve months; and
two years later Massachusetts passed its only legislation with
reference to working-hours when it was enacted that no child
under twelve should work for more than ten hours in a day.[2]
In spite of a few such laws, approaching the subject from the
standpoint of education only, practically nothing was done for
the child worker in the whole period under review.[3]

Owing almost wholly to the rapacity of the factory-owners
and managers, the position of the native American worker
became steadily worse throughout the decade. The workers
who had gone into the mills at the beginning, particularly at
Lowell, had been splendid material. Factory work had seemed
to open a new career for the ambitions and self-respecting
daughters of farming folk, and it has been pointed out that
they trooped into the mills in much the same spirit that the
same type of girl now goes to college.[4] By 1850 this class had
been driven out in the hopeless struggle against the greed of
their employers. The enormous profits and high dividends
paid prove that this situation was not forced upon the owners
by competition or anything but the simple desire for greater
and greater profits.

In the effort to reduce wages and thus secure a larger share
of the social product for themselves the owners began to employ foreigners because they could be got cheaper. The Fall
River petition of 1842 stated that " in consequence of the influx
of foreign laborers, whose habits of cheap living enable them
to work at very low prices, the wages of the workmen, in many
of the departments of the manufacturing establishments, are
reduced so low, as to be wholly insufficient to enable them,

---

[1] S. M. Kingsbury, *Labor Laws and Their Enforcement*, (New York, 1911), p. 7.

[2] *Legal Provisions Respecting the Education and Employment of Children in Factories*,
(Hartford, 1842), p. 13.

[3] *Cf.* M. E. Loughran, *The Historical Development of Child-Labor Legislation in the
United States*, Catholic University of America, Dissertation, 1921, *passim*.

[4] Abbott, *Women in Industry*, p. 112.

with the exercise of the utmost frugality and prudence, to obtain for themselves and families the necessaries and conveniences of life, and to provide for their comfort and support in sickness and old age." [1]   The exodus of the American worker began first at Fall River and in Rhode Island, but even at Lowell the low wages and the abuses of the blacklist and moral-police system led to a complete change in personnel of the workers.   In 1836 rosy-cheeked girls had come cheerfully and hopefully from neighboring farming districts to have their share of life's experiences in company with their fellows, and to save their money to lift a mortgage or send a brother to college or provide for their own married homes.   Just a decade later we learn that "a long, low, black wagon, termed a 'slaver,' makes trips to the north of the state, cruising around in Vermont and New Hampshire, with a commander who is paid $1 a head for all [the girls] he brings to the market and more in proportion to the distance — if they bring them from a distance they cannot easily get back.   This is done by representing to the girls that they may tend more machinery than is possible and that the work is so very neat and wages such that they can dress in silks and spend half their time in reading." [2]

By 1850 the agitation for the ten-hour law, so long and so bitterly resisted by New England employers, began to get into politics, and this gave the employers an added reason for employing only foreigners who had no votes.   In Rhode Island, if a native American voted against his employer's expressed views he was told that his tenement, owned by the employer, was wanted, and the man with his family was turned into the street with no chance of employment elsewhere at accustomed work.   In Lowell, by 1851, so blatant had become the habit of dictating to the hands that a few days before election the Hamilton Company posted a notice at its gates that "whoever, employed by this corporation, votes the Ben Butler, Ten Hour ticket on Monday next will be discharged." [3]   The year before, the minority of the Ten Hour committee of the Massa-

---

[1] *Mass. House of Repres. Doct. No. 4*, 1842.
[2] Quoted by Ware, *op. cit.*, p. 151.   [3] *Ibid.*, pp. 101, 152.

chusetts legislature had pointed out in their report that "the infusion of foreigners among the operatives has been rapid and is going on at a constantly increasing rate. . . . It will be found that in a few years an entire modification and depression of the state of society in and about manufacturing places will be wrought by this cause."[1]

The owners had won. They controlled the lives of the operatives, the politics of the municipalities and the legislature of the state, and left no loophole of escape for the type of self-respecting American youth with decent standards of living who had so willingly offered themselves for employment in the industries of New England. The owners, with their ten to forty per cent profits had beaten down those who asked only a fair wage and decent hours of labor. The discovery of gold in California offered a way out for many of the most energetic of the men, who went West and took permanently from New England some of the best of her human material. In 1849 two hundred and fifty vessels sailed from Massachusetts alone, carrying out men by thousands to try their luck in the new El Dorado.[2]

In the decade from 1840 to 1850 the labor movement had been wholly defensive. Its aggressive phase belongs to a later period and different conditions. The former was mainly an effort to save a certain standard of living, outlook on life, and social status, for the man and the girl who offered themselves as workers in the new industrialism that was springing up and which no one as yet understood. Could the "rich, the wise, and the good," in the old Federalist phrase, have increased as rapidly in wisdom and goodness as they did in riches, the outcome might have been different. That was too much to expect; but the story of the industrial revolution in any country shows that it requires more than intelligence to govern and guide wisely, either in the economic or political spheres.

---

[1] *Ibid.*, p. 153.
[2] O. T. Howe, *The Argonauts of '49*, (Cambridge), 1923., p. 174. The author gives the number of vessels but not of men. Allowing only forty persons to a vessel, there would have been 10,000.

The labor movement in this period cannot be considered as a thing apart. It was an integral portion of the whole humanitarian movement of the times, which aimed to secure the widest and best development of man as man. The experiments such as Brook Farm, the various causes such as temperance, woman's rights, abolitionism, religious toleration, the franchise, land reform, anti-Sabbatarianism — all the "isms" with which the age was rife — were bound together by their fundamental idea. By 1850, however, they were all engulfed in the swelling tide of Antislavery, the rise of which will be briefly discussed in the next chapter.

CHAPTER XVII

THE BLACK CLOUD

Attitude toward Slavery Issue — Virginia Debate — Garrison and "The Liberator" — Northern Sentiment — Negro Education — Attacks on Schools — American Colonization Society — Antislavery Societies — Position of the Churches — The Garrison Mob — Lovejoy Murder — Latimer Case — Hoar and South Carolina — Changed Policy of Abolitionists — Texas and the Mexican War

In the last few chapters we have noted the extraordinary activity of thought regarding the freest development of man and of his individual personality. Reform was in the air, and reforms of every sort were discussed in every place, from the workman's tenement to the lady's boudoir. As has already been said, this was a phase of thought that was world-wide, but whereas in Europe discussion ranged over the whole of man's social life, in America there was an ominous exception — a door closed on one room of humanitarianism. There was one topic of vital importance to the race and nation which it was felt must not be mentioned. "The patriotism of all classes of citizens must be invoked to abstain from a discussion" of it, warned Edward Everett, the new Governor of Massachusetts, in his inaugural address to the legislature in 1837. His father-in-law, Peter C. Brooks, one of the richest men in Boston, who read the address in manuscript, wrote that he "could see nothing for a practical man to object to" in it.[1]

This fear to have upon one's lips what was in all men's anxious thoughts was one of the most curious phenomena in the

---

[1] P. R. Frothingham, *Edward Everett*, (Boston, 1925), pp. 132, 134.

history of the nation, and had a profound influence on the minds and characters of all Americans in the decades from 1830 to 1850.   Before 1830 the tabooed topic could be freely discussed. After 1850, when it had entered American politics as the leading question of the day, it did become freely discussed.   But in the intervening two decades a craven fear seized upon the American soul.   For the most part all the men of wealth, of learning, of leadership in society, business, and the churches, entered into a vast unspoken conspiracy, dictated by fear, to force the American people to abstain from mentioning what was, in reality, the most vital question of the day.

What was this topic which even the Governor of the state of Massachusetts warned American citizens that they must not discuss?   It was nothing less than the question whether, in the state of civilization which had then been reached and in view of the doctrines of the Christian religion, it was justifiable for one portion of the human race forcibly to submit another portion to the evils of slavery.   In 1833, after open discussion in Parliament and among the people, the Government of England abolished slavery throughout the entire Empire; but in free America wealth and religion banded together to adjure all men not even to mention the existence of the problem.

It is not often that any phase of national thought or emotion is so sharply delimited in time as was this disgraceful one in the United States.   Abolition of slavery had from time to time been openly considered, even in the South, but the enormous development of the growth of cotton had apparently riveted the chain on the slave more firmly than ever.   The year 1831 marks, both North and South, the beginning of a new era with regard to the question.   In that year and the first month of the following one a long debate was held in the legislature of Virginia on schemes to colonize free blacks and gradually emancipate the slaves.   In the course of it, Virginians referred to slavery as "the heaviest calamity which has ever befallen any portion of the human race," and as "a curse upon him who inflicts as upon him who suffers it." [1]   The proposed bill was defeated by the narrow margin of one vote in the State Senate,

---

[1] Quoted by Channing, *Hist. of U. S.*, vol. V, p. 143.

and from that fatal day onward there was never again free discussion of the topic anywhere in the South.

In that same year, in Boston, William Lloyd Garrison founded *The Liberator*, a journal devoted to immediate emancipation. Up to then there had been, perhaps, a more open mind as to the possibility of gradual emancipation in at least some of the Southern states than there had been in the North, but Garrison shattered forever the smug complacency of Northerners who were wholly satisfied with "things as they are." What Garrison intended and what his effect was likely to be can be best shown in his own words in the first issue of the new paper. "During my recent tour," he said, "for the purpose of exciting the minds of the people by a series of discourses on the subject of slavery, every place that I visited gave fresh evidence of the fact that a greater revolution in public sentiment was to be effected in the free states — *and particularly in New England* — than at the South. . . . I found contempt more bitter, opposition more active, detraction more relentless, prejudice more stubborn, and apathy more frozen, than among the slave owners themselves. . . . I determined at every hazard, to lift up the standard of emancipation in the eyes of the nation, *within the sight of Bunker Hill and in the birthplace of liberty*. That standard is now unfurled. . . . I shall strenuously contend for the immediate enfranchisement of our slave population. . . . I am aware that many object to the severity of my language; but is there not cause for severity? I *will be* as *harsh* as truth, and as uncompromising as justice. On this subject I do not wish to write, or speak, or think, with moderation. No! No! Tell a man whose house is on fire, to give a moderate alarm; tell him to moderately rescue his wife from the hands of the ravisher; tell the mother to gradually extricate her babe from the fire into which it has fallen; but urge me not to moderation in a cause like the present. I am in earnest — I will not equivocate — I will not excuse — I will not retreat a single inch — AND I WILL BE HEARD." [1]

---

[1] *The Liberator*, Jan. 7, 1831. For an account of the events leading to the establishment of the paper, *vide* W. P. and F. J. Garrison, *William Lloyd Garrison*, (New York, 1885), vol. I, pp. 219 *ff*.

And he was heard. But from that time forward, North and South, every effort that men could be induced to put forth by fear and anger and love of gain and every motive except truth and justice and humanity were put forth to stifle every voice raised to question the "sacred compromise" of the Constitution. In the North, the highest motive and the only one deserving any consideration was the fear lest an agitation of the slavery problem should result in a dissolution of the Union between the States. There were many who held that that Union was the highest good, and that any evil should be suffered to exist in the nation rather than imperil that. They believed, moreover, or professed to believe, that in the future slavery would somehow melt away of itself, although it was becoming more strongly entrenched economically every day. But there were also many, and probably many of these who cloaked their less worthy motives under professed love of Union, who felt that agitation would disrupt their particular political party or decrease their business profits. All through the next two decades there was a curious and increasing subserviency of Northern sentiment and manhood to the South. Northern cotton manufacturers were closely bound to the Southern producers of their raw material. "Cotton thread holds the Union together; write John C. Calhoun and Abbott Lawrence," said Emerson in his Journal.

There was only too much truth in this statement. If the rich cotton-planters of South Carolina and the other cotton states felt that their prosperity was dependent upon slavery, no less did the rich manufacturers and merchants of New England feel that their own prosperity was bound up with the South, and that nothing must be done to disturb Southern production and business relations. Social as well as business connections were in many cases close between the two sections, and cultivated Northern gentlemen felt it unbecoming to criticize their charming Southern friends for any peculiar institution they might cherish. Had not all that been settled when the Constitution was adopted? Why make things unpleasant now? The same men who gave as an excuse for not reducing the hours of labor of their own employees to ten a day, that to do so would give them so much leisure as to ruin their morals, could have no great compunction as to what Southern friends and business correspondents might or might not do with their slaves. As for the brutalities and atrocities talked about by the Abolition-ist "cranks," they were considered as either lies or grossly over-rated — as, indeed, to some extent they were. So ran the minds of cultivated, high-bred sons of the Puritans.

Nor among the plain men of New England did the Negro find any more sympathy than among the rich. About the only difference between the feeling on the subject in the cottage and the feeling in the mansion was that in the former the Negro was heartily disliked in a personal and racially antipathetic fashion, whereas in the latter the feeling on the subject was usually rooted in what we may call a social-economic-political complex, which caused any sympathy for the Abolition cause to be con-sidered extremely bad form. Every class in society instinc-tively protects itself against attacks from without and any too insistent self-questioning or criticism from within, by adopting certain ideas as right or wrong, good or bad form, without troubling to analyze them. In the higher ranks of New Eng-land society, in the case of the Negro, this assumed the shape of social ostracism of anyone who took his antislavery feelings too seriously. In the humbler ranks it assumed the shape of direct action.

The racial feeling against the Negro was strong in all classes. As we have seen, the blacks were disfranchised in Rhode Island until 1842, and in Connecticut, where the anti-Negro feeling seems to have been strongest, until a decade after the Civil War. They were segregated on the new railways, which provided "Jim Crow" cars as in the South. They were not allowed in the churches at all in some cases, and occasionally, as in the Baptist Church at Hartford, the Negro pews were boarded up, leaving only peepholes, so that the white Christians should not have their religious feelings disturbed by the sight of them.[1] It was probably partly as a result of the treatment which the Negroes received that they constituted an alarmingly large proportion of the criminal class, considering their relative

[1] A. H. Grimké, *William Lloyd Garrison*, (New York, 1891), p. 161.

numbers; and this, in turn, reacted upon the feeling against them. In Connecticut it was stated that although they formed only one twentieth part of the population they perpetrated one sixth of all the crimes.[1]

It was perhaps in the matter of education that the prejudice against them came out most strongly. The School Commissioners in Connecticut, in pointing out the above figures as to crimes, stated that there was no reluctance to include Negro children in the school enumeration, and asked why, therefore, facilities should not be provided for them, adding that for the cost of prosecuting and imprisoning Negro criminals the colored children of the whole state, between the ages of four and sixteen, might be educated.[2] Separate colored schools existed in some of the large cities, such as Hartford and Boston, but for the most part the Negroes were denied even the most rudimentary education.

This opposition was sometimes merely a dislike to the mingling of blacks and whites in the same schools, as was shown in the agitation in Boston in 1846.[3] This had been preceded two years previously by a clash in Salem, where the feeling had run very high and the colored school had been discontinued altogether.[4] Some years earlier the Noyes Academy at Canaan, New Hampshire, had admitted a few colored boys, with the result that a legal town-meeting resolved to pull the building from its foundations; and this was subsequently done by a mob of about three hundred citizens with a hundred yoke of oxen.[5]

Unfortunately, the opposition to Negro education also took the form of refusing to allow them to receive any at all, even in separate institutions. In 1831 it was proposed to found a manual-training school for them in New Haven. The mayor at once summoned a meeting of the citizens, and with only one dissenting voice it was resolved not only that they should resist the establishment of such an institution by every lawful means,

---

[1] *1st Annual Report, Board of Commissioners of Common Schools, Connecticut*, 1839, p. 34.

[2] *Ibid.*, p. 34.

[3] Channing, *Hist. of U. S.*, vol. V, p. 158.

[4] *Address of the Mayor of Salem*, March 25, 1844, (Salem, 1844), p. 10; *Salem Register*, March 7, 14, 21, July 31, Aug. 10, 1844.

[5] Henry Wilson, *Rise and Fall of the Slave Power in America*, (Boston, 1875), vol. I, pp. 239 f.

but that the education of colored people "was an unwarrantable and dangerous interference with the internal concerns of the state" and ought to be discouraged.[1]

The most notorious case of the sort was that of Prudence Crandall. Miss Crandall, who had been a teacher at Plainfield, Connecticut, opened a school of her own at Canterbury in the autumn of 1832. A young colored girl wishing to attend, Miss Crandall allowed her to do so, and some of the parents of the white girls objected. Miss Crandall then decided to take colored girls only, and a town meeting was called to protest against having a colored school in the village. Miss Crandall was denied any opportunity of a hearing through her counsel, although they were prepared to state for her that if the town would repay her for what the place she had taken had cost her, she would then retire to a more distant part of the community to carry on her project. Failing to secure a hearing, she resolved to persevere where she was. Although this was explained afterward, the leader of the opposition declared that it was their intention to prevent the setting-up of such a school anywhere in the state, and that the colored people were an inferior race who could not and ought not to be allowed to rise from their position.[2]

Various forms of disgraceful intimidation were used against her, such as filling her well with refuse, and threatened physical violence; but she declined to be swerved from her purpose. Her opponents then secured the passage of an Act in the legislature making it illegal for anyone to set up a school for colored people who were not inhabitants of the state, without the consent of the selectmen of the town in which the school should be located. Under this law Miss Crandall was arrested and placed in jail. Eminent counsel were retained to defend her, and the trial is noteworthy as involving the question of the citizenship of Negroes long before the Dred Scott case.[3]

[1] *Ibid.*, p. 238.
[2] S. J. May, *Some Recollections of the Anti-Slavery Conflict*, (Boston, 1869), p. 47.
[3] *Reports of Cases Argued and Determined in the Supreme Court of Errors of the State of Connecticut*, (New York, 1877), vol. X, pp. 339 ff.; J. C. Hurd, *The Law of Freedom and Bondage*, (Boston, 1862), vol. II, p. 46; *Report of the Arguments of Counsel in the Case of Prudence Crandall*, (Boston, 1834), p. 5.

Miss Crandall was released from jail, but her neighbors continued to persecute her while the trial was pending. It is said that physicians refused to attend the sick of her family, and that she was forbidden to enter the church.[1] Her house narrowly escaped being burned by incendiaries; it was attacked by night and partially wrecked, and she was finally forced to leave the town for safety. In the court proceedings the first trial resulted in a divided jury, but a new case was brought against her, and in spite of the argument that the law was unconstitutional — on the ground that Negroes were citizens and that it therefore infringed that clause of the constitution which gave citizens of one state all the privileges of those in another — the case was decided against the defendant. It was then appealed to the Supreme Court of the State, but that body dodged the real issue, although it reversed the decision of the lower court on the ground of insufficient information.

The work of the Abolitionists of this period has frequently been condemned, and it has even been said that they had nothing to do with the later freeing of the slaves and were merely fanatics who created bitter feeling without securing any practical results for their cause. It is difficult to agree with this opinion. That they were fanatics may be readily admitted. A man has to be a fanatic to carry through any reform against the almost solid opposition of all classes of society. When the gentle-souled Abolitionist, Samuel May, expostulated with Garrison regarding the extreme violence of his language, Garrison replied, "I have need to be *all on fire*, for I have mountains of ice about me to melt." It may also be admitted that the chief and characteristic work of the Abolitionists was accomplished by 1840, and that thereafter the Antislavery cause was mainly forwarded by other means. But in the years when they began their work neither North nor South wished even to discuss the question of slavery. Craven with fear of what might result to society, to their own business, to the Union, men did not want to listen to a word about it. Garrison had said he would be heard, and he was heard. The nation had become a nation of ostrich-like hypocrites, well-meaning perhaps,

[1] Wilson, *op. cit.*, vol. I, p. 244.

WILLIAM LLOYD GARRISON

From a mezzotint engraving by John Sartain (1836), after a painting by M. C. Torrey (1835)

human enough in their dislike of having an established order disturbed, but nevertheless hypocrites. Garrison and the others forced them, against their wills, to think and talk and act. The anger aroused was intense, but it was a sign of life and not the death of a pusillanimous silence. Can anyone claim that the nation, even the South, would be better off to-day if the slavery question had not been settled? It is pleasant to dream that the issue might in time have adjusted itself by the voluntary abandonment of the institution, but is there any reason to believe it? If it had to be determined by war, then the sooner it could come and pass, the better; and there is little doubt that the passions aroused in both sections, particularly the South, by the Abolitionists, hastened the coming of the conflict by so shaping events as to preclude any other method of settlement.

One of the noteworthy attempts to remedy the evil without striking at the roots was the American Colonization Society, which had been formed in 1816 for the purpose of colonizing free blacks in Africa and gradually emancipating the slaves.[1] Many philanthropists had joined in the movement and Garrison himself was deceived for a while. On investigation, however, he became convinced not only that the Society would never accomplish anything, but that its very existence had a pernicious influence. He at once began a violent attack upon it and showed the absurdity of sending the Negro back to his "native land," pointing out that Africa was no more the native land of those Negroes who had been born here, and possibly of generations of American-born, than England was the native land of the white members of the Society.[2] The Negroes in Boston held a meeting at which they themselves denounced the scheme of "dragging us to Africa — a country to us unknown except by geography."[3] Garrison then published his findings and conclusions in a pamphlet which created an enormous sensation. Among other counts against the Society, he claimed that it was

[1] E. L. Fox, *The American Colonization Society, 1817–1840*, (Baltimore, 1919), pp. 46 *ff*. This doctoral dissertation would seem to give rather too favorable a view of the Society.
[2] *The Liberator*, Jan. 8, 1831.
[3] *Ibid.*, March 12, 1831.

pledged not to oppose slavery as a system; that it recognized slaves as property; that it increased their value; that it denied the possibility of raising the position of Negroes in this country; and that it was misleading the nation.[1]

Allowing for motives of genuine philanthropy in many who believed in the colonization scheme, it must be admitted that the plan was utterly impractical as a solution of the slavery problem; that its main value was to the slaveholders in ridding them of the disturbing influence of free Negroes; and that it did divert the mind of the country from facing the problem squarely.[2] How little such a plan could ever have accomplished, aside from the injustice of deporting men who had never known any conditions other than those of American life to the wilds of Africa, is shown by the fact that after fifty years of effort and expenditure, the Society had succeeded in colonizing only six thousand Negroes, or about the natural annual increase in one slave state.[3]

In January 1832 the New England Antislavery Society was formed in Boston, with the object of the abolition of slavery and the immediate emancipation of the slaves. Arnold Buffum, who had long been identified with the cause of abolition, was made president, and Garrison corresponding secretary.[4] Gradually a group of distinguished men and women joined the ranks of the Abolitionists, among them Samuel J. May, whose saintliness and gentleness of character were praised by all who knew him; Wendell Phillips, who abandoned social position and the prospect of a lucrative legal career for the social ostracism which was meted out to any "friend of the niggers"; the poet Whittier; the merchant Francis Jackson; C. T. Follen of Harvard; Edmund Quincy; Lydia Maria Child, and others. Not only was every form of pressure which society and the Church could bring to bear against those who threatened to disturb the established order exerted against these men and women, but they were over and over again threatened with physical violence.

[1] Chapman, *Garrison*, p. 64.
[2] *Cf*. Wm. Jay, *An Enquiry into the Character and Tendency of the Colonization and American Anti-Slavery Societies*, (New York, 1835).
[3] Fox, *op. cit.*, p. 211.
[4] Garrison, *Garrison*, vol. I, pp. 279 *ff*.; Wilson, *op. cit.*, vol. I, pp. 223 *ff*.

Throughout the whole period covered by this chapter, it must be confessed that the churches, with few exceptions, were in favor of slavery, or at least opposed to any agitation of the question. There had been a steady decline in their humanitarian attitude in regard to the matter since the Revolution. The voices which should have been raised in favor of the moral issue were either silent or raised on the wrong side. Garrison complained that the clergy were far more dangerous opponents to the Antislavery cause than all its other enemies combined. "If the church and clergy had not utterly failed to perform their peculiar and appropriate duty of relieving the oppressed and pleading for the friendless, the fatherless, and the widow, antislavery societies would never have existed. They were literally called into existence by the delinquencies of the churches."[1] The Reverend Wilbur Fisk, leader of New England Methodism, came out openly in favor of slavery. The Reverend Dr. Wayland, a Baptist, and president of Brown University, published a book to prove that the question should not be agitated, and that it would be an act of bad faith for the government to abolish slavery even in the Federal District of Columbia. Professor Moses Stuart of Andover Seminary and President Lord of Dartmouth were strong defenders of slaveholding.[2] The pressure of congregations and the spirit of the times can be seen exemplified in the course of even such a man as William Ellery Channing.[3]

In 1845 it was pointed out that in the protest against slavery signed by some of the Unitarian clergy, the names of all the most distinguished leaders of the church were conspicuously absent.[4] Commenting on the attitude of the churches in 1849, Wendell Phillips asked, "Where is Hubbard Winslow? Teaching that a minister's rule of duty, as to what he should teach and preach, is 'what the brotherhood will allow and protect.' Where is the pulpit of the 'Old South'? Sustaining slavery as a Bible institution. Where is Park Street? Refusing to receive

[1] *Herald of Freedom*, Feb. 9, 1844.
[2] Martyn, *Phillips*, pp. 174 *ff.*
[3] Chapman, *Garrison*, pp. 26 *ff.*
[4] *The Liberator*, Oct. 31, 1845. *Cf.* May, *Anti-Slavery Conflict*, pp. 329 *ff.*

within its walls, for funeral services, the body of the only martyr the Orthodox Congregationalists of New England have had. . . . Where is Essex Street Church? Teaching that there are occasions when the Golden Rule is to be set aside. Where is Federal Street Church? Teaching that silence is the duty of the North with respect to slavery, and closing its doors to the funeral eulogy of the Abolitionist Follen. . . . And I might ask, where are the New South and Brattle Street? But *they are not.*" [1]

The Abolitionists confined their activities wholly to the written and spoken word. The acts of violence which became more and more frequent were all directed against them by the proslavery parties North and South. A possible exception might be made with regard to the "underground railroad," for assisting escaped slaves to remain in hiding or pass on to places of safety in the free states or Canada. The routes came to form a network all over the North, probably being first established in New England about 1830; but this was never an organized institution, and it came into existence only by the gradual linking up from point to point of individuals who were willing to assist in the escapes. [2]

The activities of the Antislavery Societies, however, and most of all, Garrison's fiery denunciations in the *Liberator*, aroused the country to a pitch of anger, North and South, that has never been equaled in our history. The genteel conspiracy of silence, the refusal to discuss a burning issue because it might burn, changed into a mad mood that brought even gentlemen in Boston and elsewhere down to the level of gutter ruffians. It makes little difference what section of the country we look at, the story is the same — that of an insane anger against those who dared, in the press and by public speech, to attack what the growing humanitarianism of the epoch was beginning to regard as the iniquity of slavery. The story of the Abolition movement in New England is, of course, linked at every step with the history of the country at large, and in one short chapter

[1] Quoted by Martyn, *Phillips*, p. 220.
[2] W. H. Siebert, *The Underground Railroad from Slavery to Freedom*, (New York, 1898), pp. 22, 56.

we can do nothing but glance briefly at certain episodes. The narrative in its entirety takes volumes, and has been told elsewhere.

By 1835 the South — and to some extent the North — was demanding legislation of the most drastic sort to curb the tongues and pens of the Abolitionists. In an effort to keep any Antislavery literature out of the South, a mob at Charleston, South Carolina, attacked the post office and robbed the mails. Postmasters undertook, without a shadow of legal right, to stop the mailing of any papers or pamphlets dealing with the question, and were upheld in this course by Amos Kendall, Postmaster-General and a Massachusetts man.[1] The South openly threatened the North with secession if slavery were touched, and warned the Northern states, particularly Massachusetts, that heavy retaliation would follow on Northern business men if they did not see to it that discussion of the slavery question should cease. In a word, they called on the North to suppress free speech.[2] But the Northern business men needed no such menacing, and were as angrily anxious to suppress the disturbers of their tranquillity as were the slave-owners themselves.

On August 21, 1835, a monster mass-meeting of fifteen hundred citizens of Boston, presided over by Mayor Lyman and such distinguished men as Harrison Gray Otis, was held in Faneuil Hall to placate Southern feeling, oppose the Abolitionists, and "vindicate the fair name" of Boston. Otis, who had become proslavery, made a memorable address in which he said that free speech was one thing and spreading disaffection and poisoning "the sweet fountains of domestic safety and comfort is a different thing."[3] It is unquestionable that the Negro was not considered as a man with the rights of man in the North any more than in the South, and when Otis spoke of the "sweet fountains of domestic safety" both he and his auditors had nothing in mind but the homes of the four hundred thousand slave-owners, giving no thought whatever to the millions of slaves.

[1] Wilson, *Slave Power*, vol. I, pp. 322 *ff*.
[2] Garrison, *Garrison*, vol. II, pp. 4 *f*.
[3] Morison, *Otis*, vol. II, p. 272. *Cf.* pp. 276 *ff*.

That was exactly the startling difference between the Abolitionists and the rest of the nation in all sections. That there
were innumerable kindly slave-owners and happy slaves was
unquestionably true. But where the rest of the country saw
only an economic system of labor, long accepted in law and
society, and regarded the slave as something less than human
and almost animal, the Abolitionists could see only human
beings, and the effects on both whites and blacks of the abuses
of the slave system. What Garrison and the others accomplished was to drive home the unwelcome truth, which no one
wanted to consider, that the Negroes were human; that they
were men and women, not chattels; and once this truth sank
deep it made the abuses of the system blaze up in a new and
lurid light, even though, to a far greater extent than the Abolitionists believed and preached, those abuses were limited and
not universal.

After the Faneuil Hall meeting, in accordance with the suggestion of Mayor Lyman, the Abolitionists were extremely dis-
creet in their public activities and suspended public meetings
of their own for a time. On October 21, however, a meeting of
about thirty women was held after being advertised. At that
time the English Antislavery advocate, George Thompson,
who had centred upon himself all the animosity felt for one who
was not only an Abolitionist but a foreigner, was in the city.
As it was thought that he would attend the meeting, a mob of
several thousand persons, including a large proportion of respectable elements and men who considered themselves gentlemen,
assembled for the purpose of capturing Thompson and tarring
and feathering him. Handbills had been circulated, offering
one hundred dollars to the person who should first lay hands on
him.[1] Although the Boston police consisted of only six men
on day duty, and Mayor Lyman had been anticipating trouble,
he took no measures to protect the meeting.[2]

Thompson could not be found, but the mob broke into the
meeting and howled and stormed at the defenseless women

---

[1] Theodore Lyman, 3d, *Papers Relating to the Garrison Mob*, (Cambridge, 1870),
p. 14. This pamphlet is a defense of Mayor Lyman.
[2] *Ibid.*, p. 53.

while they prayed.   Garrison had been in attendance, but had left, in order to protect the women from a scene of violence. He retreated to his own office in the same building, where the mob suspected his presence and some of them broke a panel in the door, disclosing Garrison within.   Meantime, Lyman had arrived and urged — or, as it was said, ordered — the women to leave, saying that he could not protect them if they would not do so.   They passed out from the building amid the howls and hisses of the mob, made up, as one of the women wrote, of men of wealth and respectability.   "We saw the faces of those we had, till now, thought friends," she wrote, "men whom we never met before without giving the hand in friendly salutation."   So far had passion swept away the veneer of manhood and courtesy, even in the North, that Boston gentlemen could thus treat thirty defenseless women of their own acquaintance.[1]   Garrison himself was saved only by being escorted by the Mayor to jail and lodged there for the night, and that not without imminent danger to his life.   Although not slave-owners, the upper classes in Boston had as truly thrown in their fortunes with slavery as had the Southerners, and, as has been said, the anger of the North was the anger of the man who sees his property attacked.[2]   Garrison was forced to leave the city and take temporary refuge in the country.

Little by little, however, the Abolition cause began to gain recruits among the men of social and business standing.   Although they may not have approved altogether of the tactics of the Abolitionists, they became disgusted with the unjust and physically violent methods of their adversaries.   The hearings before the so-called Lunt Committee, for example, gained some adherents in unexpected quarters.   The Southern legislatures had been urging Massachusetts to take action against the Abolitionists, and pliant Governor Everett, that "reed shaken by the wind," as John Quincy Adams called him, appointed a committee to consider the complaints and demands of the Southerners.   In the hearings, the Abolitionists were treated with such utter unfairness by the stupid chairman, George Lunt, that two such men as Gamaliel Bradford and

[1] Garrison, *Garrison*, vol. II, p. 16 *n*.   [2] Chapman, *Garrison*, p. 119.

George Bond, the latter one of the most prominent merchants in Boston, were moved to protest and speak in favor of Garrison and his followers.[1]

In Congress the aged ex-President, John Quincy Adams, continued to present petitions regarding slavery by the score and hundred from Northern states, in spite of the enraged opposition of Southern members. These petitions reached their full flood in 1836, but Adams stood for years almost alone, untouched by the most virulent abuse, insisting upon the right of petition against every effort of the South to suppress it. With the rising tide of anger, which attained its high point about the same year, it had indeed become a question not merely of slavery in the South but whether the maintenance of that institution was to involve the suppression of free speech and a free press, and abolish the guaranties of the Constitution throughout the whole land — free states as well as slave.

In 1837 came the murder, by a proslavery mob, of the editor and young Presbyterian minister, Elijah P. Lovejoy, in Alton, Illinois. The Boston Abolitionists at once asked for the use of Faneuil Hall for a meeting to defend the rights of free speech. It was refused; but when Dr. Channing joined in the demand and it was seen that public sentiment was strongly aroused, permission was reluctantly accorded. The meeting, however, was packed to a great extent with proslavery elements, and the Attorney-General of the state, James T. Austin, denounced Lovejoy instead of his murderers, and almost carried the meeting with him. He compared the leaders of the Alton mob with the Boston patriots in the Revolution, and claimed that Lovejoy, who was not an Abolitionist but who edited an Antislavery paper, had died "as the fool dieth." It was at this point that Wendell Phillips made his first appearance as an orator in the Antislavery ranks. Having come with no expectation of taking part in the discussion, he was so aroused by the denial of the right of free speech that he advanced to the platform and made an impassioned appeal to the turbulent meeting. Addressing the chairman in the course of it, and referring to the remark of the Attorney-General, he said: "When I heard the

[1] Wilson, *Slave Power*, vol. I, pp. 330 *ff.*

gentleman lay down principles which place the murderers of Alton side by side with Otis and Hancock, with Quincy and Adams, I thought those pictured lips [pointing to the portraits in the Hall] would have broken into voice to rebuke the recreant American — the slanderer of the dead." [1] From that time forward, the gifted young lawyer abandoned all his brilliant prospects to serve the cause of Abolition.

In 1842 Boston was again thrown into confusion by the case of George Latimer, a Negro who was seized without warrant by request of James Grey of Norfolk, Virginia, who claimed him as his slave. The city attorney and other officials involved in the case all showed great alacrity in forwarding it, and much indignation was aroused in the city by this attempt to recapture a slave who had sought refuge in a free state. A mass meeting of four thousand persons was held in Faneuil Hall and was addressed by Edmund Quincy, Phillips, and others. As usual, an effort was made to break up the meeting, and the disgraceful proceedings of the mob stirred general resentment. Finally, four hundred dollars was paid for the freedom of the Negro, and he remained in Massachusetts as a free man. [2]

A couple of years later, in 1844, the state was again aroused, this time by the treatment in South Carolina of an official agent sent there to procure a remedy of abuses. That state, as well as some others in the South, had passed laws from time to time forbidding the entry of free Negroes. This excluded all colored sailors on vessels touching at their ports, and although South Carolina had receded from her position when England had protested with regard to citizens of foreign countries, she refused to allow the same freedom to citizens of her sister states. From time to time, Negro sailors on vessels belonging to Massachusetts had been taken off their ships, fined, imprisoned, flogged, and otherwise maltreated. In 1844, Samuel Hoar was sent to represent Massachusetts at Charleston and to secure what protection he could for citizens. South Carolina declined either to desist from her treatment or to allow the dispute to be brought before the United States Supreme Court for adjudica-

---

[1] Martyn, *Phillips*, p. 96.
[2] Wilson, *Slave Power*, vol. I, pp. 479 f.

tion, and Hoar was not only unable to accomplish anything but, with much indignity, was expelled from the state.

This unwarranted action aroused the Massachusetts legislature, and the Senate passed resolutions denouncing South Carolina and alleging that for a quarter of a century she had persisted in executing laws which infringed the rights of her sister states and had refused to be judged by the Supreme Court; that she claimed the right to seize, maltreat, and sell into slavery citizens of other states who entered her territory on peaceful business; and that she expelled citizens going there for the sole purpose of securing legal redress of wrongs. As Congress had declared itself powerless to intervene, — the protest continued, — it had become evident that the citizens of the aggrieved states were thrown back wholly on their own ability to defend their rights by themselves. South Carolina claimed that Negroes were not citizens of the United States and therefore not entitled to protection, to which Massachusetts replied that they were citizens of Massachusetts, and that that was sufficient.[1] Although the South Carolina case attracted most attention, a similar one occurred when Henry Hubbard was sent to Louisiana to secure redress for the same grievances suffered from that state.[2]

Meanwhile, although Antislavery sentiment had made distinct gains in all New England, certain dissensions had become evident in the ranks of the movement. For one thing, the woman question had come up at more than one convention, both here and in England, in an acute form.[3] Women were among the most ardent as well as the most able advocates of the cause, but so great was the prejudice against any public activity on their part that their right to speak at meetings was bitterly opposed. In 1837 the General Association of the Massachusetts orthodox churches condemned the public work of the Grimké sisters on behalf of the slaves as unchristian and demoralizing. When, in answer to the challenge, the conven-

---

[1] *Mass. Senate Doct. No. 31*, 1845, pp. 13, 33; *Mass. House of Repres. Rept. No. 66*, 1845. *Cf. Journal of Senate of Connecticut*, 1845, p. 250, and of the *House*, pp. 233 *ff*.
[2] *Mass. House of Repres. Rept. No. 65*, 1845. *Cf.* also *Rept. No. 14*.
[3] May, *Anti-Slavery Conflict*, pp. 230 *ff*.

tion of the New England Antislavery Society voted that all members, regardless of sex, might participate in the proceedings, eight clergymen at once resigned, the clergy, apparently, forming the backbone of the opposition to the women. Indeed, the general body of the clergy had become inexplicably reactionary at this period. In the pastoral letter of the General Association just noted, not only was the right of women to speak in public attacked, but that of men as well, unless approved by the clergyman of the parish. "Deference and subordination are essential to the happiness of society," it said, "and peculiarly so in the relation of a people to their pastor. . . . The respect due to the pastoral office" was violated, in their opinion, when lecturers were encouraged to speak on topics of reform without having obtained the consent of the settled pastor! It seems as though we were in the Middle Ages instead of in Massachusetts in 1837, when we hear the voice of the churches proclaiming that "your minister is ordained of God to be your teacher," and that if he does not choose to present and preach on certain topics, "it is a violation of sacred and important rights to encourage a stranger to present them." [1]

Another question which began to create division among the Antislavery advocates was that of the ballot. There was more or less acrimonious discussion as to the advisability of entering politics and the possible advantages of a third party. The short-lived "Liberty Party" had been started in 1840, breaking up three years later, and it was felt by many that political action was unlikely as yet to secure results, whereas it might easily sow discord and dissension. [2] From about this same time the leadership of Garrison began to be questioned, and in fact, as we have said, his distinctive work had already been accomplished. His disunion views had also served to alienate many. He had early foreseen what was the truth — that the roots of slavery were so deep and the possibility of a peaceful settlement of the matter so slight, that the question of slavery was at bottom the question of the Union. It was not that slaves were held in the South and not in the North. Large classes in the

[1] *Ibid.*, p. 243.   [2] Garrison, *Garrison*, vol. II, pp. 310 *ff.*, 550 *ff.*

North were committed to the defense of slavery. The responsibility for its continuance lay as much upon them as upon the actual slave-owners, and if the Union continued, not only could that responsibility not be avoided but the influence of slavery would be forced more and more by the South on the Northern states. Believing this issue paramount to all others, Garrison finally came out in fiery denunciation of both the Union and the Constitution.

In January 1843 he secured the passage of a resolution at the annual meeting of the Massachusetts Antislavery Society, to the effect "that the compact which exists between the North and the South is 'a covenant with death and an agreement with hell' — involving both parties in atrocious criminality, and should be immediately annulled." [1] At the meeting of the New England Antislavery Society in the following June it was resolved that it was the first duty of every Abolitionist to agitate for the immediate dissolution of the Union, and that they could not consistently support the Constitution, even to the extent of voting for any candidate for Federal office. Garrison, Quincy, and Phillips supported the resolution, which was passed by 250 to 24. [2] From about 1845 to the passage of the Fugitive Slave Law in 1850, which marks the end of our period, the Antislavery agitators adopted a new policy and abjured political parties, churches, and other organizations, and indulged in a violent propaganda, mainly through the press and meetings of their own bodies. This new phase was due to the annexation of Texas and the Mexican War.

We need not go into the details of that long and tangled story in so far as they belong to national politics. [3] Texas had been a matter for debate for nearly a decade before it became the leading issue in the presidential campaign of 1844. The project had been justly regarded as an effort of the South to extend slavery through a territory as large as France and England combined, a suspicion which was considered amply confirmed at the time by the letter written by Calhoun in answer

[1] Garrison, *Garrison*, vol. III, p. 88.
[2] *The Liberator*, June 14, 1844.
[3] Justin H. Smith covers the ground in his *Annexation of Texas*, (New York, 1911).

to the expressed desire of England to abolish slavery throughout the world. The New England Antislavery elements were naturally bitterly opposed to the Texas project, and the opposition was loudly voiced in the legislatures of several of the states. That of Maine resolved that the annexation would increase slavery; that the government had no constitutional power to annex foreign territory; and that the plan, if persisted in, would "tend to drive the states into a dissolution of the Union." [1] Massachusetts went further, declaring that she would never consent to the admission of Texas or any other territory except on the basis of a free state, and, after the annexation, voted that the act was not legally binding on the states. [2]

Although the threats of nullification and of secession were not carried out, and the fact of annexation was finally granted as settling the question, the slavery issue had been pushed to the fore in New England to an extent it never had before. Multitudes who had been willing to leave it alone so long as it seemed to concern only the old South, now realized that slavery was not merely an ancient institution, not to be interfered with under its constitutional guaranties, but was a growing menace to the free states.

The feeling which had been liberated by the Texas question was intensified by the war with Mexico that followed. Such papers as *The Liberator* and the *Herald of Freedom* were naturally filled with scathing denunciations of what they regarded as an utterly unjust and uncalled for conflict. Nor did the legislature of Massachusetts stand alone in its constant succession of resolves demanding that Congress put an end to the struggle. "In the name of Jesus Christ," reads one of these numerous resolves, "in the name of the people of Massachusetts who are unwilling that innocent blood should defile their garments, we protest against the further perpetration of a great national crime." [3]

[1] *Maine Legis. Doct. No. 46*, 1844, p. 13.
[2] *An Appeal to the People of Massachusetts*, Boston, 1844; *Mass. House of Repres. Doct. No. 12*, 1845. *Cf. Journal of Vermont Senate*, Oct. Sess. 1844, pp. 123 *f.*; *Journal Vermont House of Repres.*, Oct. Sess. 1845; *Journal Connecticut House of Repres.*, 1845, pp. 223 *ff.* *Mass. Senate Doct. No. 27*, 1844, p. 17; *ibid., No. 104*, 1845.
[3] *Ibid., No. 16*, 1848, p. 7.

The slavery question had ceased to be one that must be hushed up. In the ten years that had passed since Governor Everett had called upon the people of Massachusetts to avoid discussion of it as a patriotic duty, it had been forced into the open. From 1850 onward, not only that question but the entire national life entered upon a new phase. The struggle which was to settle once for all the questions of slavery and Union was still a decade off, but the old era closed with the mid-year of the century; and the new one lies beyond the limits of this work. The years from 1850 onward belong with those which follow rather than with those which precede.

In the three volumes which form this series, we have now traced the story of New England, often only in brief outline, from the first explorations along its coast to the period which marked the final accomplishment of its most distinctive work in the life of the American nation. We saw in the first volume how the geographical nature of the section tended, under the conditions of the early days, to foster that isolation which had been desired by the earliest settlers. Throughout the whole colonial period, that isolation had been maintained until pressure of the common cause against England brought all thirteen colonies into partial unity of thought and action and a somewhat loose political bond. It was still many decades, however, before a genuine national sentiment could develop; and in the War of 1812 the old geographical influences were still at work to keep New England an isolated section. The lack of adequate land transportation, the poverty of soil, and the absence, as yet, of manufactures, made her commerce still her most important factor. The interests of that commerce were diverse from those of the rest of the nation, and the political leaders of New England were led to the brink of secession.

Following that struggle, we have seen how quickly new conditions came to alter the old. Foreign commerce was to a great extent replaced by domestic manufactures. Canals and railroads were the equivalents of a changed geographic environment. Distances and mountains, which had been effective barriers, were such no longer. In the change from commerce to manufactures the leaders of New England, who had hitherto looked only overseas, now looked to the South for their raw materials and to the West for markets for their finished products. Imperceptibly, but rapidly, New England became linked with the other sections. Geographic factors were still of influence, it is true, and the section has always maintained a certain aloofness from national interests and the national life, but from the middle of the nineteenth century onward its history becomes rather that of a mere section than of a distinct unit in the nation.

Both the national nature of the great contest upon which the country was entering and which was to absorb all its energies, and the growth and subsequent development of the great West, tended to diminish the extreme sectionalism as well as the comparative importance of the New England states. In spite, therefore, of the continuance even to-day of a New England type, of a New England point of view, and of distinct New England contributions to the national culture and outlook, we may be justified in bringing our narrative to a close with New England's sectional contribution to the slavery struggle. We thus end the story as we began, with the leaders of the New England people wrestling with a transcendent moral problem, willing to abandon the new political union with sister states as they had, two centuries and a half before, abandoned their homes and connections with the old mother state, when the first few immigrants landed on the shores of Massachusetts Bay.

The story has not been without its deep shadows. From the days of John Winthrop to those of William Lloyd Garrison, the leaders of New England, as well as its lesser characters, were human beings with all the mixture of motives which characterizes men. Perhaps, at times, in a reaction against the old point of view which regarded all Puritans and all Revolutionary soldiers and agitators as saints and patriots, we may have been tempted to stress the shadows rather than the lights. But it is well that all sides of the story be told, for our forbears were men like ourselves, and the work which they wrought can bear the truth.

INDEX

INDEX

ABOLITIONISTS, in New England, 401–405, 408–417, 419, 420.

Adams, John, and revolutionary naval forces, 15, 16; and choice of commander-in-chief, 22; quoted against leniency to Tories, 64; against the Cincinnati, 70; drafts new constitution for Mass., 60; quoted on difficulties of confederation, 109; and the peace treaty, 116; advocates establishment of a navy, 206; quoted on New England aristocracy, 217, 218; averts war with France, 227.

Adams (Abigail), Mrs. John, quoted, on enlistment and bounties, 18, 19; on cost of household supplies, 41; on rise of new men to leadership, 53; on cost of farm labor, 58; on comparative simplicity of dress in London, 59.

Adams, John Quincy, quoted on impressment of seamen, 246; on tendencies to disunion, 257, 259, 260; on New England's attitude during War of 1812, 300, 301; on Edward Everett, 415; presents petitions in Congress against slavery, 416.

Adams, Samuel, on probable length of the war, 5; on necessity of propaganda, 61; against the Cincinnati, 70; approves independence of Vermont, 96; takes conservative side during Shays's rebellion, 153, 154, 162, 163; opposes Federal Constitution, 171.

Agricultural conditions and problems. *See* Farmers.

Alcott, Bronson, 358, 362, 363 *n.*

Algerine pirates, 206.

Alien and Sedition Laws, 224.

Allen, Ethan, as an author, 75; opposes New York claim to Vermont, 94, 95, 100; involved in intrigue with British, 102–108, 181.

Allen, Ira, 101, 104, 106–108.

Allen, Levi, 101, 181, 182.

Ames, Fisher, as spokesman of conservatives in Mass., 147; his personal record, 148, 149; quoted on commercial basis of the Constitution, 174; quoted on feeling toward England and France, 211; Federalist leader, 212; his opinion of democracy, 213; on the

Democratic Clubs, 215, 216; on danger of Democratic influence in politics, 229.

Anti-Catholic demonstrations, 334, 335, 336, 337.

Anti-Federalists' grounds for objection, 171, 172, 175; broadening of their ground, 220.

Antislavery movement, 360, 401–422.

Appleton, Nathan, 306, 309.

Aristocracy in New England, 217, 218; protest against, 223; leadership of, 301; revolt against control by, 328, 329; workingmen *vs.*, 347; and Unitarianism, 355, 356.

Army officers, inadequate pay of, 68–70; press attacks on, 69, 70.

Arnold, Benedict, 13, 14.

Austin, James T., 416.

Authors, New England, 352, 353.

BACKUS, ISAAC, 76, 91.

Ballou, Rev. Adin, 360, 361.

Bancroft, George, 352, 362.

Banks, incorporation of, 202, 203; said to be under Federalist control, 232; and politics, 317; Jackson and, 348–350.

Baptists, 76, 91, 220, 221.

Beecher, Catherine, on country schools, 364.

Beecher, Lyman, on connection of churches with politics, 318, 319; on toleration measures, 321; attitude toward Catholics, 335; the Unitarian movement, 354; the temperance movement, 373.

Bennington, Vt., 10, 95.

Bentley, Rev. William, quoted, 78, 216.

Berlin Decree, 241, 247.

Beverly, Mass., privateers sent out from, 16, 54; decline of fisheries, 32, 37; fortunes made in Eastern trade, 202; changes after war, 304.

Bigelow, Timothy, 296.

Bishop, Abraham, on relations of Church and State, 223; against Federalists, 224.

Blind, training the, 371.

Blockade of American ports, 272.

Bond, George, 416.